Cheyenne

A Biography of the "Magic City"
of the Old West, 1867–1903

For Jim and Theresa,
With warmest personal regards —

Bill O'Neal

Bill O'Neal
9-9-06

EAKIN PRESS ✥ Austin, Texas

FIRST EDITION
Copyright © 2006
By Bill O'Neal
Published in the United States of America
By Eakin Press
A Division of Sunbelt Media, Inc.
P.O. Drawer 90159 ☎ Austin, Texas 78709-0159
email: sales@eakinpress.com
💻 website: www.eakinpress.com 💻
ALL RIGHTS RESERVED.
1   2   3   4   5   6   7   8   9
ISBN 978-1-57168-839-2
ISBN 1-57168-839-0
Library of Congress Control Number 2006928250

For my youngest daughter and fellow teacher,
Causby O'Neal Henderson.

Contents

Acknowledgments

I have long been fascinated by the history of towns and cities, particularly communities of the West. In every history class I teach at Panola College, I stress architectural history and what may be learned about the people of an era from their buildings. When writing a book I seize the opportunity to describe the development—or the decline—of related communities, and one of my favorite projects was a ghost town book.

In 2003 I was struck by an interview in the March issue of *American Heritage*. The subject of the interview was Dr. Donald L. Miller, author of *City of the Century, The Epic of Chicago and the Making of America*, which was the source for a superb PBS documentary. Dr. Miller explained his approach to writing "the biography of a city." He explained that "certain cities represent the character and spirit of their age," and said, "I thought I'd write about Chicago till it reached the point where almost everything that it would become would be seen." I became excited about applying Dr. Miller's approach to Cheyenne, a colorful and important example of the settlement of the last West. Dr. Miller's brilliant work on Chicago served as an inspiration and a model for my less gifted efforts.

My publisher, Virginia Messer of Eakin Press, was immediately captivated by the concept of a "biography" of Cheyenne, and she offered welcome encouragement and support at every stage of this project. Melissa Locke Roberts, my long-time editor, improved my work with her inspired sense of style and her staggering mastery of detail.

Once I decided to pursue this project, I enlisted the aid of Sherri Baker, a Panola College librarian whose duties include interlibrary loan. With the resourcefulness of a detective, Sherri located and obtained for me numerous obscure books and articles, as well as microfilm of daily Cheyenne newspapers for the period of 1867–1903. Her efforts on my behalf permitted me to conduct several months of research while remaining at home.

I have enjoyed numerous visits to Cheyenne through the years, but in the summer of 2004 my wife and I spent two weeks researching the Magic City on site. In Cheyenne I sought out William R. Dubois III, a fourth-generation Cheyenneite and a noted local historian. Bill's great-grandfather was Col. E. A.

Slack, founder of the Cheyenne *Sun,* and his grandfather, William Dubois, was a noted Cheyenne architect. Bill did graduate work at the University of Wyoming under Wyoming's preeminent historian T. A. Larson, and he has contributed to numerous books and other projects to preserve Cheyenne's rich history. He welcomed us to his city, responding to my many queries with information, insights, and helpful suggestions. Bill also graciously volunteered to pursue any research needs I might discover after returning to Texas, and he took time from his schedule to solve every problem I threw at him from long range. I am deeply grateful to Bill for his invaluable help.

Bill Dubois introduced me to another author-historian, Shirley Flynn. Shirley was a founding board member of the Old West Museum at the Frontier Days rodeo grounds, and among her books and articles about Cheyenne is a centennial history of the West's most famous rodeo. Like Bill Dubois, Shirley shared with me her encyclopedic knowledge of Cheyenne and generously offered to help with the project. Cheyenne is indeed fortunate to have two local historians with the ability and devotion of Shirley Flynn and Bill Dubois.

On our principal research trip to Cheyenne, my wife and I entered the spirit of the project by spending our first night in the magnificent Nagle-Warren Mansion. Our host, Jim Osterfoss, thoughtfully placed us in Francis E. Warren's bedroom, and I happily soaked up the spirit of Cheyenne's most noted founding father. Jim and his lovely assistant, Jane Branigan, revealed details of this historically significant home. Jim graciously offered to host a book signing at his splendid mansion, and Jane enthusiastically expressed her willingness to assist with research needs.

The State Archives in Cheyenne yielded a wealth of sources and photographs. Day after day Holly Geist, Cindy Brown, Carl Hallberg, and Lizzie Stroebel produced one item after another for us. The Cheyenne Public Library also contained a treasure trove of resources, and I am grateful for the able assistance of several staff members.

Kim Winters, reference librarian of the American Heritage Center at the University of Wyoming in Laramie, provided a number of important files. During a time of heightened security measures, Lt. Rachel Van Tine facilitated our visit to F. E. Warren Air Force Base, formerly Fort D. A. Russell, and to the excellent museum overlooking the parade ground.

For more than a year I called the Cheyenne Chamber of Commerce to ask for phone numbers, addresses, and other bits of information, and every request was answered with unfailing courtesy. At Cheyenne's First Presbyterian Church, I was conducted through historical displays by Rev. Robert L. Garrard, while church secretary Judy Bezak photocopied for me pages of the church history and other documents. At the First Baptist Church, Jan Baker generously provided a copy of the church history she had written. At the newly expanded offices of the Wyoming Stock Growers' Association, Dora McComas, longtime WSGA administrative assistant, escorted me into the boardroom so that I could view the wall photos and other displays which illustrate the rich history of the association. I offer cordial thanks to each of these individuals, as well as to a great many other citizens of Cheyenne whose countless small courtesies convinced me that frontier hospitality still thrives in the Magic City.

My wife, Karon, brought immeasurable contributions to this project. As we explored Cheyenne, she photographed scores of venerable structures and miscellaneous other sites, and she had the idea to shoot the author's photo beneath the Cheyenne sign at City Hall. During research sessions, Karon produced hundreds of photocopies. We attended a rehearsal of an old-time melodrama at the Atlas Theatre, visited Cheyenne's museums together, ate at the Victorian Whipple Mansion—and because she experienced Cheyenne so intimately, she was able to make discerning recommendations as the manuscript took shape. As always, Karon converted my handwritten manuscript to disk and hard copy. My debts to her are even greater than usual, and my appreciation of her is deep and heartfelt.

The
1860s

"Men, women, and children, with all their furniture, all the tools of a colonist, were arriving in covered wagons drawn by heavy oxen or long-eared mules."
—Louis Simonin

"Cheyenne was then a city of shanties and tents, camps and covered wagons."
—Francis E. Warren

"Houses were erected by day and by night. Sometimes for two or three days there was not a break in the sharp sound of hammers."
—Judge William Kuykendall

"Last evening right by us here there was a terrible shooting affray, and one poor wretch was shot through the jaw and another through the arm."
—Rev. Joseph W. Cook

"The above parties will leave this territory in twenty-four hours. By order of VIGILANCE COMMITTEE."

"Cheyenne Folks can keep pace with even those of Eastern cities in style and taste."
—Cheyenne *Daily Leader*, February 29, 1868

1

Birth of the Magic City

The wickedness is unimaginable and appalling," wrote Rev. Joseph W. Cook, who arrived at Cheyenne six months after its founding to organize an Episcopalian church. An educated Easterner, Rev. Cook was aghast at Hell on Wheels Cheyenne: "This is the great centre for gamblers of all shades, and roughs, and troops of lewd women, and bull-whackers. Almost every other house is a drinking saloon, gambling house, restaurant, dance hall or bawdy. In the east, as a general thing, vice is obliged in some measure to keep somewhat in the dark. . . . But here all is open and above board, and the eyes and ears are assailed at every turn."[1]

Reverend Cook arrived at the height of Cheyenne's end-of-track boomtown period, a boom so rapid that a ramshackle city arose from the empty plains as if by magic. It would be dubbed the "Magic City of the Plains." During these wild, explosive months, the thousands of men and 400 or so women who crowded into the raw railroad community drank and gambled and fought in saloons and dance halls and bordellos. But the drunken violence which erupted soon was confronted by a lethal vigilante movement, thus paving the way for more conventional law enforcement in Cheyenne. Although the turbulent debauchery so deplored by Reverend Cook created a lingering stain on the reputation of Cheyenne, the minister became part of an impressive force of urban pioneers who helped to civilize this wolf-howl community, building churches and schools, and pressing for cultural uplift.

Like every western territory and state, Wyoming tried to make itself attractive to women by legislative inducements. Only two years after its founding,

**Business and Finan-
cial Statistics of
The "Magic City,"
CHEYENNE!**

From its earliest days Cheyenne was referred to as the "Magic City." The nickname frequently was used in newspapers, as in this December 23, 1867, issue of the Leader.

Cheyenne hosted a legislative session which granted women the right to vote—the nation's first act of women's suffrage. From then on Cheyenne would boast female doctors and dentists, the first woman in the United States to be elected to a statewide office, and an exceptionally assertive set of wives and daughters.

Nothing exemplified the Wild West more than cattle, cowboys, and ranchers. Wyoming became a paradise for open-range ranching, and Cheyenne—home of the West's most powerful stockmen's association, as well as the most famous cattlemen's club—also became known as the "Holy City of the Cow." When the West's most famous range war broke out in Wyoming, Cheyenne was a focal point. And Cheyenne's Frontier Days, a celebration of cowboy culture, eventually became the most famous of all western rodeos.

Another western icon, the blue-clad trooper, inhabited a permanent base beside Cheyenne. Fort D.A. Russell, established at the same time the Magic City sprang up, was a major military installation that would have a great impact on the economy of Cheyenne, just as forts all over the West economically benefited adjacent communities. Other means of federal support were avidly sought by political leaders of underdeveloped frontier regions, and Cheyenne's leading citizen, Senator F. E. Warren, proved unexcelled at obtaining federal largesse for Wyoming and for the Magic City.

A notable trait of the West was innovation, the willingness to try something new in a frontier environment. Under the leadership of progressive businessmen and politicians, Cheyenne embraced the latest innovations of a remarkably inventive age. It was no coincidence, for example, that Cheyenne was the second city in the country to install electric lighting, and the Magic City readily adopted telephones, streetcars, the linotype, and the latest fashions.

As a capital city located astride a major transportation route, Cheyenne hosted a remarkable roster of notables. Presidents and generals visited Cheyenne, and so did internationally famous entertainers. A host of frontier celebrities added color: Wild Bill Hickok was married in Cheyenne, Calamity Jane drank in the city's saloons, and Tom Horn was tried and executed there.

Spectacular boomtown. Pioneer railroad center. Raucous Hell on Wheels. Vigilante battleground. Army town. Holy City of the Cow. Home of women's rights. Host city of a parade of distinguished and notorious celebrities. Throughout the era of the last West, from the end of the Civil War until the close of the frontier, Cheyenne embodied most of the conditions and developments that characterized one of the most memorable periods in American history. Indeed, Cheyenne experienced—and was even at the forefront of—so many major developments of this captivating period that it truly deserves its label as the "Magic City" of the final frontier. The story began in the summer of 1867.

⋙◉⋘

In 1867 America's most electrifying subject was the long-anticipated Pacific railroad. Since the discovery of gold in California, serious efforts had been made to launch a railroad to the Pacific. During the 1850s, the federal government surveyed four possible routes across the West. Selection of one above the others was stymied by the fact that southern congressmen insisted upon a southerly route, while northern politicians wanted a line that would connect with the railroad network in their section. Although government support of railroad construction, through federal loans and land grants, already had been utilized on eastern railroads, a western line could not be commenced until a route was determined. This impasse finally was solved by the outbreak of the Civil War.

Throughout the war northern congressmen, in the absence of their southern counterparts, were free to pass all manner of legislation that had been delayed by the bitter sectional conflict of the 1850s. In 1862 the Pacific Railroad Act was approved by Congress and signed by President Lincoln, an enthusiastic supporter of railroads. Two railroad companies were chartered, each incorporating the magic word "Pacific." The Union Pacific (UP) would lay track westward from Omaha, while the Central Pacific would struggle eastward from Sacramento across the Sierra Nevada Mountains. As the Civil War raged, these companies tried to raise capital, recruit workers, acquire materials and equipment, and prepare their respective roadways. Progress was discouragingly slow at first, but the end of the war would signal an explosion of construction.

Grenville Dodge was the railroad man who would determine the site of Cheyenne and provide key efforts on the city's behalf. Born in Massachusetts in 1851, Dodge was bright, energetic, and a natural leader. He trained to be a civil and military engineer, and while in college he became excited over the possibilities of building a Pacific railroad. Dodge pursued railroad work during the 1850s, surveying a western route later taken by the Union Pacific. During an 1859 conversation with Abraham Lincoln, Dodge made an invaluable acquaintance and was pumped for railroad information by the towering lawyer who was an expert in railroad law. When the Civil War erupted, the patriotic Dodge obtained a colonelcy and eventually was promoted to major general of volunteers. Wounded twice in combat, General Dodge also performed spectacularly in repairing southern railroads

Grenville M. Dodge, Civil War general, accomplished railroad engineer, and founder and early patron of Cheyenne. (Courtesy National Archives)

for General Sherman's invading army. In 1864 he was summoned to the White House to confer with President Lincoln, who remained "very anxious that the road should be built...."[2]

By the end of the Civil War, General Dodge was in command of Union forces west of the Mississippi, operating against the horse Indians who posed a deadly menace to railroad surveyors and construction crews. Returning from the Powder River campaign in September 1865, Dodge used the opportunity to search for a pass suitable for a railroad through the Black Hills (later renamed the Laramie Mountains), about twenty-five miles west of the future site of Cheyenne. While most of his men marched south at the base of the mountains, Dodge and a small squad rode southward "along the crest of the mountains to obtain a good view of the country." Encountering a war party at midday, Dodge and his six men "dismounted and started down the ridge, holding the Indians at bay ... with our Winchesters." The long descent to the safety of the main body revealed the pass that railroad explorers had sought "for over two years."[3]

Dodge resigned his commission in 1866 to become chief engineer of the Union Pacific, having earned "the cordial and active support" of the army's commander-in-chief, General Grant, and General Sherman, commander of the Military Division of the West. Sherman often visited the railroad and communicated regularly with Dodge (who named the crucial pass he had accidentally discovered "Sherman Pass"), and the army was instructed to provide every support to the railroad effort. Grant, Sherman, and other celebrated generals soon would be visitors to Cheyenne.[4]

As chief engineer, Dodge immediately led a detailed exploration and survey of Sherman Pass and its approaches. In November 1866 he convinced the company to direct the UP line from Omaha through Sherman Pass. As the track moved west from UP headquarters in Omaha, temporary bases, or "division points," would be established. The UP wintered in 1866–67 at North Platte,

Cheyenne and Cheyenneites

The Cheyennes encountered by Grenville Dodge and everyone else who helped name the new railroad town were nomadic plains Indians. The men were superb horsemen and fierce warriors. The Sioux called them "People of a Strange Tongue," a term adapted by French trappers as "Shaiena." For a time the final vowel was pronounced, but—as often happens with final vowels—the pronunciation eventually became "shyANN," and

the spelling was Americanized to "Cheyenne."

Inhabitants of the boomtown were variously called "Cheyenneites" and "Cheyenners" and "Cheyennese." Gauging from newspaper usage, the latter term was the least popular. As the years passed, Cheyenneite became the most common term for residents of Cheyenne.

Nebraska, a village which temporarily expanded to 5,000 and became the first "Hell on Wheels." But in 1867 most of North Platte's population moved to the next division point—and next Hell on Wheels—Julesburg, Colorado. The next division point, Cheyenne, would be established just east of the Black Hills range, with an army post nearby.

Dodge led a large expedition to the area in 1867. Gen. C. C. Augur, department commander, and his staff were present with instructions to establish a base where Dodge placed the division point town site. Following "a thorough examination of the country," related Dodge, "I located the division point on Crow Creek, where Cheyenne now stands, and named it Cheyenne."[5]

Dodge certainly was responsible for placement of the town site, and he may have suggested the name. But "Cheyenne" was settled upon at a Fourth of July celebration conducted at a lonely encampment set up by soldiers at Crow Creek. Dodge brought a party of Union Pacific engineers and directors from Omaha by rail to end-of-track Julesburg. Proceeding overland, the party reached the army camp on Wednesday evening, July 3, 1867. The next morning Dodge, characteristically, left camp with a party of surveyors (during his distinguished career Dodge surveyed 60,000 miles of proposed railroad track) while approximately 400 men remained in camp to celebrate the Fourth.

After the crowd assembled on the plains, General Rawlins delivered a patriotic speech. Col. Silas Seymour, a consulting engineer for the UP, was asked to read the Declaration of Independence: "When in the course of human events it becomes necessary for a community composed of military officers, with 350 rank and file, Government Directors, and civil Engineers of the Union Pacific Railroad...." Seymour had composed his own preamble, which stated that this group's purpose was "to establish this goodly city of Cheyenne." A committee had been formed to select a name for the new community, and they decided to honor "the very interesting Savages" who roamed the region. A toast was made to "The Embryo City of Cheyenne." A great many other toasts were made, enlivening the holiday. "I learn it was quite a good time," remarked Dodge when he returned to camp.[6]

Colonel Seymour said that "upon this memorable occasion that the name 'Cheyenne' was given to the future city ... there was not a house, nor a piece of lumber with which to construct one, to be found within fifty miles of the locality." He could have added that there was not a single settler yet. Before the tents were set up, the site featured only "a few bluffs, a bleak prairie, a small stream," according to a later newspaper description. "The view from Crow creek bluffs still suggested the abode of wild deer, and antelope, and wolf, that it had been for ages. No bush or bramble was to be seen in the landscape; no sound was heard save the rushing of the winds, or at night the howling of the wolves."[7]

But word had spread about a new railroad town and its general location, and pioneers who wanted to be first-comers already were moving toward the recently christened town site. James R. Whitehead, forty, and William L. Kuykendall, thirty-one, were partners in Colorado in freighting, cutting timber, and raising livestock. (They also had married sisters, but when Mrs. Whitehead died in 1866,

Mrs. Kuykendall took the four motherless Whitehead children to raise alongside her two sons.) After learning that a town would be established at the crossing of Crow Creek, Kuykendall reminisced, the partners moved wagons and workmen to the timbered mountains west of the rumored site in April 1867. There they cut railroad ties and hewed "house logs and other timbers." On July 4 Whitehead moved out with a wagon train of logs, finding the camp beside Crow Creek four days later. Almost immediately several other prospective residents arrived, including three men with their wives. By the next day, Tuesday, July 9, at least thirty men, women, and children had "pitched their tents on both sides of Crow creek," and more were on the way.[8]

Within a week Dodge began a town site survey, even though there had not yet been a general survey to determine if the town site was located on one of the alternate sections of federal land allotted to the railroad. Similar situations existed with "all the towns" along the fast-moving line. Town sites would be claimed by the company, then city lots were "leased" to occupants, with the UP "agreeing to deed it to them when we got a title."[9]

The Cheyenne town site measured two miles on each side, but the four-square-mile grid would not sit on a true north-south axis. Because the planned railroad tracks would angle through Cheyenne toward the southwest, streets would run parallel to the tracks and at right angles. The streets parallel to the tracks would be numbered, beginning with First Street at the bottom of the square; the next thoroughfare toward the north would be Second Street, and so on. The cross streets, angling toward the north, were named by Dodge after Union Pacific officials or army officers of his acquaintance: Ransom Avenue, Hill, O'Neill, Ferguson, Eddy, House, and, of course, Dodge Avenue. (In later years many of these streets were renamed with labels more appropriate to Cheyenne: Capitol, Central, Carey, Pioneer, and Warren avenues.) Few thoroughfares were actually established south of the projected tracks, but the surveyors laid out a network of streets and avenues north of the railroad right-of-way. The first parallel street north of the future tracks was Fifteenth.

One of the town site surveyors, John H. Collins, had brought his pregnant wife, and their baby "was the first white child born in Cheyenne." (Another claim to "the first white child" recognition was the baby daughter of Pvt. and Mrs. J. D. Manderville. Provision for the wives of enlisted men was not made at military posts, except as laundresses, but the pregnant Mrs. Manderville came to Cheyenne anyway, and the post surgeon attended the birth.) First deaths were also recorded. John Collins found the arrow-riddled body of another surveyor, L. L. Hills, who was killed by Arapahoes on July 18, 1867, six miles east of Cheyenne. Earlier, on July 5, two railroad employees were slain at a ravine of Crow Creek. "We buried the men and started the graveyard of the future city," recounted Dodge.[10]

A growing stream of settlers "were on the ground or encamped in the vicinity, waiting for such action as might enable them to secure title to ground for permanent occupancy." Dodge directed lot surveys in the blocks near the railroad, and he permitted lots to be sold by Glenn and Talpey, partners in a general mer-

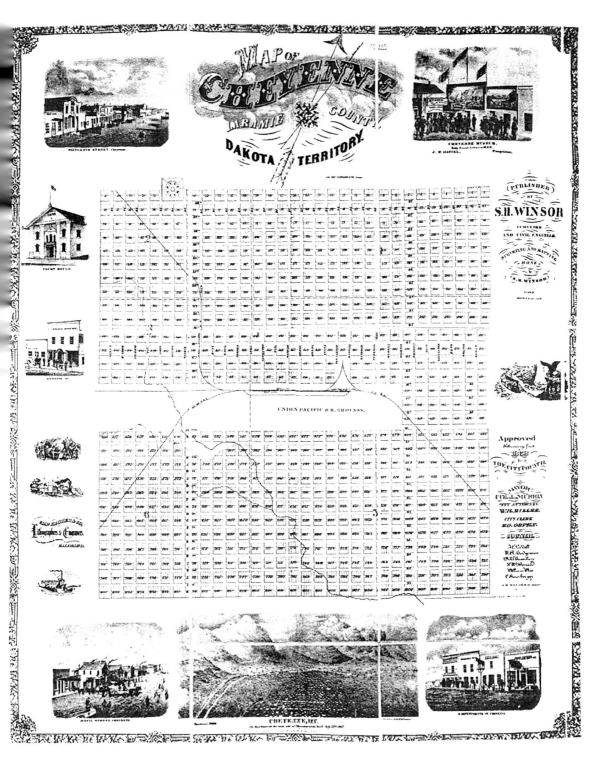

Cheyenne's early town plat was two miles on each side, but it was many years before the streets and "squares" south of the tracks were developed. (Author's collection)

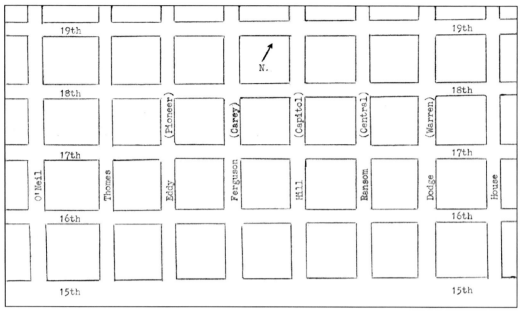

Cheyenne's original plat of "squares" and streets numbered the east-west thoroughfares. Grenville Dodge named the north-south streets after himself and other Union Pacific engineers and officials. Later some of the north-south streets were renamed: Carey, Capitol, Warren, etc. (Author's diagram)

chandise business. Lots were offered for sale, "the ruling price being $150, one-third cash." But within a month these same lots could be resold for $1,000.[11]

The first house inside the city limits "was a very rude log affair" built by future mayor Matthew Sloan. Sloan's cabin was just south of Crow Creek, but most structures were erected north of the projected railroad. William Kuykendall arrived at the head of a wagon train carrying logs, many of which were used in building the two-story "Whitehead Block" on Eddy Street. The open second floor of the big log structure would become Cheyenne's city hall. Less imposing were the shacks, adobes, tents, and dugouts in which many citizens lived and did business. Some people used wagon beds topped with canvas covers. Soon lumber was hauled in from Denver, and frame buildings were erected, along with a few masonry edifices. Within a month of the survey, the town site was dotted with 300 structures.[12]

In the uncertain hurly-burly of an unregulated boomtown, claim-jumpers disputed the lot titles of the earliest settlers. Hearing of this anarchy and "other depredations," Dodge "immediately wired General Stevenson, calling his attention to the condition of affairs and asking him to use his troops to bring about order and a recognition of authority." Stevenson, commander at Fort D. A. Russell (another tent city that was being converted to a permanent community) had served under General Dodge during the Civil War, and he understood the support of the railroad that was expected of the army. Dodge was pleased that even though Stevenson "had no legal right in the matter he turned out his troops as skirmishers and drove every citizen in the town to a mile or so south of the track and then held a parley with them." Stevenson made it clear that "the land belonged to the United States and the railway was occupying it under the Government's charter." With his troopers in formation behind him, Stevenson told the civilians that until they acknowledged the authority of the Union Pacific they could not return to their property. "This brought them immediately to terms and they immediately made peace, and were allowed to come back to town," reported Dodge. If Stevenson's use of his soldiers was arbitrary, there was no other authority in town, and during the wild months to come the army would restore order on other occasions.[13]

The businessmen who intended to prosper realized that Cheyenne needed a city government. However, Cheyenne was part of sprawling Dakota Territory, and authorization of any sort of city charter would have to come from the territorial capital, in faraway Yankton. Unwilling to wait on a process that could take months, James R. Whitehead and a few other leaders called a public meeting for Wednesday evening, August 7, at the store of A.C. Beckwith. Whitehead, who had practiced law elsewhere and who opened an office in Cheyenne, called the meeting to order. He was appointed chairman of the committee to draw up a city charter, and another meeting was scheduled for the next night. At the second meeting, Whitehead submitted Denver's city ordinances and the procedural rules of the Denver City Council, along with the code of laws of Colorado Territory, as the foundation of Cheyenne's new provisional government. His proposal was accepted by the assemblage, and a city election was announced for two days later, August 10. Within three weeks of Cheyenne's town site survey, the American instinct for self-government had manifested itself in the Magic City.[14]

During Cheyenne's first boom, the town site was dotted with tents and hastily built frame structures, many with canvas roofs. (Courtesy Wyoming State Archives)

On August 10 H. M. Hook, who had opened a livery stable, was elected first mayor of Cheyenne, and Whitehead was named city attorney. Members of the city council were R. E. Talpey, S. M. Preshaw, W. H. Harlow, G. B. Thompson, and J. G. Willis. The city clerk was Thomas T. McLeland and the city treasurer was H. N. Meldrum. Ed Melanger was elected city marshal, while the police magistrate was veteran frontiersman John N. Slaughter, who spent the rest of his long life in Cheyenne and always was addressed as "Judge." These men collected license fees from Cheyenne businesses and tried to impose order, with occasional reinforcement from Fort Russell. Although Cheyenne's provisional government and elected officials had no legal sanction from a higher authority, there was sufficient local consensus to provide needed organization to the expanding boomtown.[15]

On the day the first city election took place, August 10, the Cheyenne post office opened (the first post office in what would become Wyoming Territory). Many Cheyenne residents were nomadic frontiersmen, and for many years the post office periodically published in the newspaper long lists of names of those who had unclaimed mail. Cheyenne's first newspaper was printed on September 19, 1867, by twenty-four-year-old Nathan A. Baker, who became the foremost booster of the city.[16]

A native of New York, Baker was seventeen when his family moved in 1860 to Denver. Young Baker was an enthusiastic urban pioneer, opening one of the first schools in the gold boomtown, practicing law, working on newspapers, and joining the Masons. Married and the father of a baby boy, he was irresistibly drawn to the new boomtown 112 miles north of Denver. He hauled a press to Cheyenne, installing it and paper stock in a log building with a false front on the east side of Eddy Street. The first issue, and a number of subsequent issues, of the Cheyenne *Leader* was a folio of four pages, four columns to a page. While the first

License Fees

Cheyenne's provisional government established license fees for more than thirty categories of occupations or businesses. The licenses were good for three months and ranged from fifty dollars (for saloons and "each hack, wagon or dray") to five dollars (for tailors, shoemakers, barbers, blacksmiths, and "each brick or adobe manufacturer"). Doctors and lawyers paid ten dollars every three months, and so did bakers, brewers, gunsmiths, saddlers, insurance agents, peddlers, and hotels. Circuses and entertainment troupes paid the city twenty dollars each day they performed in Cheyenne. Also, the city clerk charged $2.50 for each license. Mayor Hook approved this ordinance on August 17, 1867, and the list was printed in the second issue of the Cheyenne *Leader*, on September 24, 1867.

issue was being printed, an excited crowd of 400 men "thronged the office and street in front, eagerly catching up, at a quarter each, the first copies as they came from the press." Within a couple of days first issues were being resold for one dollar. The sellout of the initial issue of the *Leader* allowed Baker to pay his employees and put out another issue five days later, on September 24. Baker then began publishing the *Leader*, "A Wide Awake Journal For the People," every Tuesday, Thursday, and Saturday, at fifteen cents per copy. When Baker's equipment arrived, the size of the sheets was expanded to eight columns. Soon the paper came out every evening except Sundays, and it was labeled the Cheyenne *Daily Leader*. Baker also published the Cheyenne *Weekly Leader*, which proved consistently popular as a journal that could be mailed to other communities in Wyoming and elsewhere.[17]

About a month after Baker introduced the *Leader*, he faced competition in the form of the Cheyenne *Daily Argus*, which first appeared on October 24, 1867. As Cheyenne exploded with growth, the *Rocky Mountain Star* was introduced to the boomtown on December 8, 1867. The *Daily Leader* became the newspaper that would publish official announcements, and on his masthead Baker proudly proclaimed his journal as "Official Paper of the City." The *Argus* and the *Star* both started as daily papers but soon could only justify weekly editions. The *Argus* and the *Star* were morning papers, and Baker often sniped at his competitors with his evening *Leader*. The *Argus* limped along for less than two years before shutting down in May 1869, while the *Star* went out of business the next month. Three other journalistic attempts, the *Commercial Record*, *Fast Life*, and *Northwestern Journal of Commerce*, came and went quickly in 1868.

During the late 1860s, therefore, the newspaper read by most residents was the *Daily Leader*. Every evening, except Sundays and holidays, 2,000 copies of the *Leader* circulated around Cheyenne and Fort Russell. With a telegraph connection to the East, Baker was able to fill his front page with stories from across the nation and Europe. Often a local story or two also reached the front page. The inside pages were filled with ads from Cheyenne establishments and professional men, along with a list of church meetings and civic and fraternal organizations. On the last page, amid other ads, Baker devoted a couple of columns to happenings around town, sometimes including events that had occurred shortly before press time. Fistfights, shootings, runaway horses, theatrical performances, arrests, court reports, business news—every evening such occurrences were described in the *Daily Leader*. In hotels and saloons, in boardinghouses and private residences, citizens of Cheyenne shared the communal experience of reading the same newspaper at about the same time.

N. A. Baker found better quarters for his newspaper, on the west side of O'Neill Street, between Seventeenth and Eighteenth. There were numerous other early businesses on O'Neill, one of Cheyenne's westernmost streets. The next three north-south streets toward the east, Thomes and Eddy and Ferguson, also sported numerous ramshackle commercial structures. Running east-west between these streets, Sixteenth and Seventeenth also boasted many business houses and offices.

Between Sixteenth and Seventeenth on Ferguson stood the two-story City Hospital. Cheyenne's first "hospital" was a tent purchased for $125 by the city and placed on Fifteenth Street. Dr. James Irwin, the first physician to practice in Cheyenne, entered a partnership with another early arrival, Dr. J. W. Graham. Irwin and Graham were paid $225.70 for five days' service at the tent in January 1868, along with $50 to Dr. L. L. Bedell and $20 for a coffin. When Irwin and Graham erected a two-story frame structure on Ferguson, the 24-by-30-foot building became known as the City Hospital. The city rented the second floor, while the doctors maintained offices on the ground floor. The City Hospital could accommodate forty patients, although Rev. Joseph Cook "was very much distressed to find two men each in several beds." Reverend Cook frequently visited the hospital, bringing newspapers and conducting services.[18]

Cheyenne Newspapers

The Cheyenne *Leader* published its first issue on September 19, 1867, and it long would remain the city's leading newspaper. From three issues per week, the Cheyenne *Daily Leader* soon was publishing every day except Sundays and holidays. From 1884 to 1887 there was a name change to *Democratic Leader*, then the familiar Cheyenne *Daily Leader* was resumed until 1895. That year the Leader merged with the Cheyenne *Daily Sun*, and the new name was the Cheyenne *Daily Sun-Leader*. In 1900 the publication again assumed the old name, Cheyenne *Daily Leader*, although there would be other name changes during the twentieth century, after the period covered by this book.

Late in 1867 the *Leader* faced two fledgling competitors, the Cheyenne *Daily Argus* and the *Rocky Mountain Star*; however, both of these newspapers went out of business in 1869. During the remainder of the nineteenth century, many journalists tried their luck in Cheyenne. Most of the following publications were weeklies, and many were short-lived.

Commercial Record, 1868
Fast Life, 1868
Northwestern Journal of Commerce, 1868
Wyoming Tribune, 1869–72
Cheyenne *Daily Sun*, 1870–71
Wyoming Railroad Advocate, 1870
Wyoming News, 1870–71
Wyoming Daily Morning News, 1871
Cheyenne *Daily News*, 1874–75
Cheyenne *Daily Sun*, 1876–95
The Spur, 1877
Cheyenne *Daily Gazette*, 1877–78
Daily Advertiser, 1878
Daily Hornet, 1878
Northwestern Livestock Journal, 1883–92
Cheyenne *Daily Tribune*, 1884–93
Mirror, 1886
Cheyenne *Board of Trade*, 1888
Cheyenne *Review*, 1889
Wyoming Commonwealth, 1890–92
Magic City Record, 1890–91
Cosmopolitan, 1893
Wyoming Bee, 1894
Big Horn Basin Savior, 1894–95
Wyoming Tribune, 1894–1921
Wyoming Industrial Journal, 1899–1911

—Source: Lola Homsher, *Guide to Wyoming Newspapers*, 1867–1967

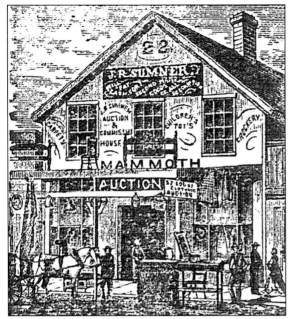

J. R. Summer's "Mammoth Auction and Commission House," at No. 22 Seventeenth Street (and at a second location, No. 50 Eddy Street), held sales at ten in the morning every Tuesday and Saturday. Summer handled a vast miscellany of goods, from furniture to marbles to "Hair Mattresses, all kinds." (From a Cheyenne Leader *ed, January 1869)*

In 1868 Dr. Irwin left the hospital to resume solitary practice, and the next year the building was acquired by the city council and city commissioners "for a city and county Hospital." The hospital remained in this location for more than a decade. Meanwhile, Dr. J. N. Douglas and Dr. George H. Russell opened practices in 1868. Less than a year after Cheyenne was founded, ten doctors advertised their services in the *Leader*. In 1869 a French physician, Dr. J. A. Rouseleaux, opened an office in Cheyenne, along with Dr. J. B. Wilson, "Surgeon, Dentist & Chiropodist." A dentist, Dr. F. A. Hall, advertised optimistically: "Teeth Extracted Without Pain."[19]

One of the largest buildings at Fort Russell was the well-equipped post hospital. The military facility was staffed by hospital stewards

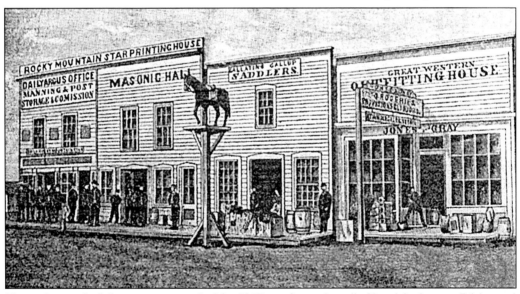

These frame buildings were erected in 1867 on Seventeenth Street between Eddy and Ferguson. The commission house of Manning & Post, at left, cost $6,000; upstairs were located two early newspapers, the Argus and the Rocky Mountain Star. Next door was a building of identical cost and size (22 by 60); Masons began meeting upstairs in February 1868. The 20 by 40 saddle shop cost $1,700, while the 20 by 40 Great Western Outfitting House cost $4,000. (Leader, December 24, 1867)

The small frame boot store of C.H. Edwards was built in 1867.
—Courtesy Wyoming State Archives

and by a civilian contract surgeon or a commissioned army physician, who some-times treated Cheyenne citizens. Railroad workers suffered a profusion of indus-trial accidents, and the Union Pacific employed a physician, Dr. H. Latham, re-placed in 1869 by Dr. G. W. Corry. In the spring of 1868 the UP erected a frame hospital on the corner of Seventeenth and Hill, complete with operating rooms, bathing rooms, and private rooms as well as wards. Years later the UP built a brick facility on East Seventeenth—which still stands—as a residence and office for the company doctor.[20]

Most of these doctors, like urban pioneers in other occupations, were adven-turous and restless and did not stay long in Cheyenne. But soon there were doc-tors who made their homes in the Magic City. Without the sophisticated equip-ment or advanced medication of modern times, physicians in those days relied on experience and heightened senses—sight, touch, hearing, smell, and even taste. They brought their medical bags and the hope inspired by their profession to the bedsides of their patients. The ones who stayed were revered, and became lead-ing citizens of Cheyenne.

Other early leading citizens included "men of stability" from Julesburg, "who knew that Cheyenne would be the railroad terminus during the following win-ter," related William Kuykendall. "Their number was greatly augmented by sev-eral hundred reliable, law abiding people from Colorado." Kuykendall soon would move his family to Cheyenne from Denver, joining other pioneers who

The Cheyenne Leader.

MISCELLANEOUS,

EXCELSIOR!

Is our motto. We

Defy Competition,

For quality. The best goods and the latest and neatest patterns of all imaginable kinds of

VARIETY GOODS,

Always on hand and always coming
THE LATEST PICTORIALS AND DAILIES ALWAYS ON OUR COUNTER.

The finest Tobaccos, and Cigars on our Shelves!

The most complete assortment of notions, stationery, paper, envelopes, ink and pens, fire arms and amunition, toilet articles, fancy soaps, brushes, etc., cutlery, blank books and slates, at our emporium,

Post Office Building.

nov2-3m   R. M. BEERS & CO.

GO TO THE

Leader Office

FOR

NEAT JOB PRINTING!

SPAID'S

Celebrated

FRESH OYSTERS!

RECEIVED daily, by express, at Chas. Mc Donald's, corner Twentieth and O'Neill streets, opposite Hook & Moore's Corral; for sale

By the Case or Can,

And Warranted as fresh as when shipped from the East.

C. A. Henry, General Agent for the Northwest.
nov5tf

BOOTS, SHOES, ETC.

C. H. EDWARDS & CO.,

Wholesale and Retail

DEALERS IN

BOOTS & SHOES,

South Side Sixteenth Street, Cheyenne, Dakota

CORRALS.

THE

GREAT WESTERN

CORRAL!

Hook & Moore, Proprietors,

COR. O NEILL AND 20th STREETS

CHEYENNE,   DAKOTA

Have just completed

The Most Convenient

AND

Largest Stable

IN the Western country. The Corral covers half a block, and is constantly supplied with an abundance of

HAY AND GRAIN,

and the

only Fairbanks' hay scales

IN THE COUNTRY.

In connection with the Corral, the proprietors will keep a first class

PILGRIM HOUSE,

For the accommodation of Travelers

[oct29-3m]

CHEYENNE

Livery, Feed & Sale Stable,

CORNER BENTON AND NINETEENTH STS.,

Cheyenne, Dakota.

Hartman, Van Wormer & Taggart, Proprietors.

HAVING located ourselves as above, we are prepared to accommodate the traveling public, and freighters and teamsters, with

---

OUTFITTING.

Glenn & Talpey,

GENERAL

OUTFITTING HOUSE,

Corner Sixteenth and Ferguson streets,

Cheyenne, - - - - - - - - Dakota.

Dealers in

GROCERIES, PROVISIONS,

LIQUORS,

TOBACCO AND CIGARS,

DRIED AND CANNED FRUITS

COFFEES AND TEAS,

RANCH PRODUCE,

ETC., ETC.,

HAVING just received an extensive and choice assortment of the above articles we solicit the patronage of wholesale and retail buyers. Our prices are as

LOW AS THE LOWEST.

sept24tf

John S. Andrews,

Grocer and Commission

MERCHANT,

Seventienth st., Cheyenne, D. T.,

AND Sole Manufacturer of ANDREWS & FARWELL'S celebrated

SELF RISING FLOUR.

sept19-3w

CHEYENNE BRANCH.

Cornforth Brothers,

Wholesale and Retail

GROCERS,

Forwarding & Commission

MERCHANTS,

Corner Eddy and Seventeenth streets, Cheyenne, and F st., below Blake, Denver.

HAVING opened a branch store in this place, we ask the patronage of our old friends and the public, and hope that by fair dealing we may deserve the patronage so liberally bestowed on us at our house in Denver.
sept19tf

Prominent businesses in early Cheyenne, as advertised in the Leader on November 28, 1867.

dared to try to create a home where recently there had only been a vacant prairie.[21]

The first wife to arrive in Cheyenne was fifty-year-old Elizabeth Whitebread, and the second was Julia Schweickert. Both women arrived in August 1867, and both made Cheyenne their home for the rest of their lives. Other wives settled in, and many brought children. Wives and children were civilizing forces, responsible for churches and schools, along with cultural activities.

Stephen Ambrose, in his history of the first transcontinental railroad, *Nothing Like It in the World*, emphasized that the Union Pacific and the Central Pacific set a precedent by building their lines "into a land without people." Certainly Cheyenne was a land without people — except for roaming Indians — before the UP declared the site a division point. "Instead of building a railroad that would connect one town or city with another, they had been building into a void. They were not striving to take over trade routes; instead they hoped to attract settlement."[22] Cheyenne was the embodiment of this policy, attracting settlers in spectacular numbers.

People arrived by the hundreds during Cheyenne's first few months. There were 3,000 residents by the time the railroad arrived. The first wave of UP workers, more than 2,000 strong, were graders who approached Cheyenne in the fall of 1867. "THE CARS ARE COMING," proclaimed the *Leader* on October 12, adding that the projected arrival of the first train was November 10. The vast grading crew, readying the railbed well ahead of the far more numerous tracklayers, followed the surveyors' stakes through Cheyenne, then continued westward toward the Black Hills. The grade they built bisected the town site, although most of the structures were north of the line. By November the tracklayers were within twenty miles of Cheyenne, putting down at least one or two miles of track every day.[23]

The massive construction effort was led by Gen. Jack Casement, a Union division commander during the war, and his brother, Dan. Although the Casement brothers were diminutive (Jack stood only five-foot-four and Dan was "five-foot-nothing"), they bristled with confidence and efficiency. General Casement operated his construction army like a military force. Indeed, a great many of his men were veterans from the Union army. With the end of the war an enormous number of discharged soldiers needed employment — and an immense amount of investment capital was freed up as well, along with such resources as iron and explosives. With a 10,000-man work force, the Union Pacific, along with the 10,000 men toiling for the Central Pacific, represented America's largest enterprise. Work force, financing, materials, equipment — all reached unprecedented scale. Dodge explained that "material for a mile of track required forty cars, besides the necessary cars for supplies and for the population that was along the side of the road." Logistical problems were enormous, but men who had dealt with vast logistical demands during the war were available. Former army officers handled railroad logistics and were in charge of other divisions, and former non-coms served as crew foremen.[24]

One of the UP work cars carried a large supply of Spencer repeating carbines, and when there was an Indian threat the veterans drew weapons and rapidly deployed. In the same manner, these men were easily drilled into laying track in a rapid, precision assembly line. "The whole organization of the force engaged in the construction of the road is, in fact, semi-military," observed surveyor William A. Bell. "Track-laying on the Union Pacific is a science," he stated, describing the process in detail.

"Less than thirty seconds to a rail for each gang, and so four rails go down to the minute! Quick work, you say, but the fellows on the U.P. are tremendously in earnest. The moment the car is empty it is tipped over on the side of the track to let the next loaded car pass it; and then it is a sight to see it go flying back for another load, propelled by a horse at full gallop ... ridden by a young Jehu, who drives furiously. Close behind the first gang come the gaugers, spikers, and bolters, and a lively time they made of it. It is a Grand Arrival Chorus that these sturdy sledges are playing across the plains. It is in triple time, three strokes to a spike. There are ten spikes to a rail, four hundred rails to a mile, eighteen hundred miles to San Francisco."[25]

NEW TO-DAY.

Union Pacific Railroad.

NOW OPEN, FROM

The Missouri to the Rocky Mountains!
Omaha to Cheyenne!

ON and after Monday, November 18th, 1867, Trains of the Union Pacific Railrord will leave Cheyenne for Omaha, daily, Sundays excepted, as follows:

7.00 A. M., *Express and Passenger.*
10.00 " *Freight and Accommodation.*
8.00 P. M., *Through Freight.*

Trains will arrive at Cheyenne daily, Sundays excepted, as follows:

3.15 A. M., *Freight and Accommodation.*
1.20 P. M., *Through Freight.*
7.00 " *Express and Passenger.*

The Express Passenger Trains

connect direct at Omaha,
With Trains of the

Chicago and Northwestern Railway,

TO AND FROM CHICAGO AND AND ALL EASTERN CITIES.

at

CHEYENNE
Trains make direct connections with

Wells, Fargo and Co.'s

Daily line of Overland Mail and Express coaches to and from

DENVER CENTRAL CITY, SALT LAKE, AND ALL POINTS IN COLORADO, UTAH, IDAHO, MONTANA, NEVADA AND CALIFORNIA.

Trains run by Omaha time, which is forty minutes faster than Cheyenne time.
For Through Tickets, Freight Rates, &c,, apply to   F. H. SNYDER,
nov19tf   Ag't at Cheyenne.

The first Union Pacific train schedule was published in the Cheyenne Leader *in November 1867.*

By November 1867 the people of Cheyenne were eager to see this process race through their town site. The advance of the tracks was rapid and inexorable. Although merely forty miles of track had been laid in 1865, 260 miles were built in 1866, and well over 200 more had been bolted down in 1867 as the line approached Cheyenne. On Wednesday, November 13, everyone in town turned out to view the spectacle. "Our citizens swarmed along the grade, and watched, with the most intense delight, the magic work of track-laying," reported the *Leader*. Everyone was strangely silent, "too deep and full for expression. There was no shouting and cheering, but one full tide of joy." A few shook hands and uttered subdued remarks:[26]

"No use of talking," breathed one.

"It beats the world," said another.

"Just ahead of the Atlantic cable," which had been completed in 1866.

"The English language needs revising."

On November 14 the *Leader* proudly announced that Cheyenne would "have daily mails after tomorrow," and on Monday, November 18, passenger service commenced over the UP to Chicago and other points east. The day after the tracks arrived in town, a meeting was held at city hall to plan a reception for "Gen. Casement and other gentlemen of the UPRR." The following evening a "jolly, up-roarious and jubilant crowd" gathered in front of city hall on Eddy Street. The street and the big log building were "splendidly illuminated," and a speaker's stand had been erected. Signs proclaimed, "Old Casement, we welcome you" and "Honor to whom honor is due." Judge W. H. Miller read three resolutions that had been drawn up ("WHEREAS, The completion of the Union Pacific Railroad to the city of Cheyenne has inaugurated a new era in our existence...."), and the crowd roared its approval. Casement, who also was the delegate-elect to Congress from Dakota Territory, was shouted for, "and his appearance was greeted with a storm of applause." But Casement was no speechmaker, and he quickly announced, "Gentlemen, good night." Then he "disappeared as nerv-ously and suddenly as if there was a night job on hand, of laying four or five miles of track." Numerous other "distinguished speakers" stepped up to fill the void.[27]

Jack Casement and his workers immediately proceeded through Cheyenne toward the Black Hills. By November 21, UP work trains had begun passing over Crow Creek bridge, west of town, "with 15 miles already graded" ahead. Accompanying the tracklayers "hour by hour, are the boarding cars and a con-struction train," described a Union Pacific progress report. "The boarding cars are each eighty feet long. Some are filled with berths: two are dining halls; one is a kitchen, store room and office." Twenty miles to the rear were "immense con-struction trains, loaded with ties and rails, and all things needed for the work. It is like the grand reserve of an army. Six miles back are other trains of like charac-ter." Cheyenne became accustomed to a constant parade of Union Pacific rolling stock—which continues in the twenty-first century.[28]

Ahead of the tracklayers, 1,500 "tie-getters and wood-choppers" readied 100,000 ties for the next year, their axes "resounding in the Black Hills, over Laramie Plains, and in the passes of the Rocky Mountains." The tracklayers reached "the summit of the Black Hills," then had to shut down for winter. The UP "wintered at Cheyenne," related Dodge, and spent the next few months stock-piling "all the material possible" in anticipation of launching a massive construc-tion effort in April 1868. The big boarding cars spent the winter on long sidings built at Cheyenne. The UP also constructed "immense warehouses" and a round-house, and many employees devoted the winter to equipment maintenance.

With thousands of railroad workers in town, Cheyenne's population soared. On January 20, 1868, the *Leader* estimated the total at 7,000. Curiously, four days later the *Leader* printed an estimate of 4,000, which seems far too low, unless railroad workers were not included. On February 21 the *Leader* guessed the population at more than 6,000, with "only 400 ladies," and William Kuykendall agreed that there were 6,000 "from nearly every country on earth." Dodge said that the population was "nearly 10,000."[29]

Freight trains now brought in large quantities of construction materials for houses and stores, as well as frame buildings. When the division point was established at Cheyenne, Julesburg was virtually abandoned. In November 1867 a freight train arrived in Cheyenne bearing frame houses, tents, and furniture from the former division point. "Gentlemen," announced a man on the train to onlookers, "here's Julesburg." One commercial building had originated in Omaha, later was shipped to Julesburg, then brought to Cheyenne. Another structure was erected in end-of-track North Platte, then shipped to the next end-of-track, Julesburg, and finally brought to Cheyenne, where for nearly a decade it was the shoe store of prominent merchant Stephen Bon. "Buildings were torn down in Denver, and other parts of Colorado, at Julesburg and North Platte, and the component" segments hauled to the Magic City. "Houses come by the hundreds from Chicago, ready made," recorded an astonished French tourist, Louis Laurent Simonin. "In Chicago they make houses to order, as in Paris they make clothes to order."[30]

"Houses were erected by day and night," commented William Kuykendall. "Sometimes for two or three days there was not a break in the sharp sound of hammers."[31]

Sixteenth Street late in 1867. The Rollins House, a three-story hotel, stands left of center. The Temple of Fashion catered to Cheyenne's ladies. At right is one of several city wells. Water also was drawn from Crow Creek or purchased from a water wagon. (Courtesy Wyoming State Archives)

"Everywhere I hear the noise of the saw and the hammer; everywhere wooden houses are going up; everywhere streets are being laid out," wrote Simonin, who also noted the movement of buildings within the boomtown. "Here are houses changing places, traveling down the street.... The dwellers have not left their home, and you can see the sheet-iron chimney smoking while the house moves along."[32]

Arriving in November 1867, Simonin sought lodging at the Dodge House, on the corner of O'Neill and Eighteenth. The "common sleeping-room" was upstairs. "There were no less than thirty beds there, most of them occupied by two sleepers at a time." Then the Frenchman visited "the common lounging-room, where everyone cleaned up [and] had to share the same brushes, the same combs, and even the same towel. I rolled the soiled linen, spotted with dingy stains, until I found a clean place, and then bravely rubbed my face."[33]

In addition to the Dodge House, there were several other hotels: the Wyoming House, Dickinson House, Talbot House, Meigs House, Sherman House. These and other early hotels practiced the dormitory-style "nocturnal fraternity" described by Simonin. The largely male population of Cheyenne lived in hotels and ate in restaurants—the restaurant of B. L. Ford on Sixteenth "leads them all," reported Simonin—or slept and ate in boardinghouses. The boardinghouse of Mrs. Karnes, on Thomes Street, charged sixteen dollars a week for room and board, twelve dollars for board without lodging, and seventy-five cents for a single meal. A meal at Ford's cost one dollar, and with 200–300 customers at each meal, revenue (counting the bar) was more than $1,000 per day. On November 12, 1867, construction began on the Rollins House, a three-story hotel that would measure 132 x 132 feet. There would be individual rooms sufficient for 200 guests. Two and a half months later, proprietor J. Q. A. Rollins opened his "new and com-

Bathing Resorts

With no running water in early Cheyenne, bathing was a luxury. The Rollins House and other sizeable hotels provided bathing rooms, but most men in Cheyenne lived in small boardinghouses and had to settle for a water pitcher and basin in their rooms. Private homes were similarly equipped.

Cleanliness would have to be sought in Cheyenne's bath houses. Young's Bath House at the corner of Ferguson and Sixteenth somewhat dubiously boasted, "Creek Water Bathing, hot and cold." The City Bath House, on Thomes Street, advertised itself as "the place to go to."

In June 1869 a unique facility was opened "on the bank of Crow Creek," a combination bath house and beer garden. This "splendid bath house" featured separate "apartments" for men and women, "a first-class restaurant," music during the afternoons, and a beer garden—"the great feature of this magnificent suburban resort."

—Source: Leader, March 12 and July 3, 1868; June 2, 1869

modious hotel" on the north side of Sixteenth. The Rollins House was advertised as the "Only First-class House in the City."[34]

"Already stores are everywhere, especially of ready-made clothes, restaurants, hotels," recorded Louis Simonin. "Already there are two printing shops, two newspapers, book shops, banks, stages, then the postoffice and the telegraph." A laborer named Jordan, who earned ninety dollars a month building barracks at Fort Russell, wrote his sister that Cheyenne was becoming "the Chicago of the West," and that, one week after the "Iron Horse" reached town, "lots are selling from $500 to $3,000 each."[35]

Simonin found most men in Cheyenne "rough and crude in appearance ..., with their long hair, their felt hats with the broad brims, their ill-kept beards, their clothing of nondescript color, their great leather boots in which their pantaloons are engulfed. But what virile characters, proud, fearless! What dignity, what patience! No one complains here." The Frenchman detected deep pride and "local patriotism" — Cheyenne "already had dreams of the title of capital. It does not wish to be annexed to Colorado, it wishes to annex Colorado."[36]

The thousands of "virile characters" in Cheyenne brought new meaning to the term "Hell on Wheels" during the winter of 1867–68. Grenville Dodge admitted that Cheyenne "was the greatest gambling place ever established on the plains, and it was full of desperate characters." William Kuykendall also recalled many "dangerous characters" in Cheyenne. "Gambling, dance houses and other resorts were run wide open," continued Kuykendall, who acted as a "special policeman" to help curb the unrestrained rowdyism. As previously mentioned, the Episcopalian missionary, Rev. Joseph W. Cook, was appalled by the wide-open vice and wickedness, the gambling and drinking, and the "troops of lewd women." Hubert Howe Bancroft, distinguished nineteenth-century historian, found that "all the scum of society" gravitated to Cheyenne, where "every manner of vice abounded."[37]

Although the city council passed an ordinance against carrying firearms in Cheyenne,[38] shootouts continued, and there were outright murders. Burglaries and other forms of theft added to an unstable and perilous environment. The first effective response to killings and robberies was led by 200 vigilantes, who were quick to resort to hanging when their warnings went unheeded.

Violence and crime subsided when thousands of railroad workers headed west in April 1868. Union Pacific construction crews forged westward, not halting during the next winter and laying 555 miles of track before linking up with the Central Pacific in Utah in 1869. Many gamblers, saloonkeepers, and prostitutes, as well as merchants and professional men, moved out of Cheyenne to follow the tracks — first to Laramie, sixty miles across the Black Hills, then to other new railroad boomtowns. Businesses and residences were advertised for sale in the newspapers, and business owners pressed for the payment of credit accounts. The stock of Glenn and Talpey's Outfitting House was sold at auction when the owners were "adjudged bankrupts." Boardinghouses reduced their rates; the Western House charged merely seven dollars per week for meals. With hotel business down, the big Rollins House remodeled, sold barroom fixtures, room furniture, mattresses and bedding, "and converted into stores, offices and rooms."[39]

Cheyenne's population plummeted. But not everyone left. In 1870 about 1,500 citizens remained in town, still a substantial population for a frontier community. The UP roundhouse, repair facilities, and warehouses assured a solid number of salaried railroad workers. A far larger source of wages was the federal government. A major quartermaster depot, Camp Carlin, was established between Cheyenne and Fort Russell. Hundreds of teamsters, along with blacksmiths and other civilian workers, were employed to deliver supplies from Camp Carlin to forts in the region and to troops in the field. Other civilians earned excellent wages constructing barracks, stables, and other buildings at Fort Russell and Camp Carlin. Of course, the soldiers stationed at both posts frequented the saloons, brothels, and stores in Cheyenne. Even though thousands of UP graders and tracklayers left Cheyenne to work their way west, a number of permanent jobs remained upon which to anchor the local economy.

Prospective developments were adding exciting promise to Cheyenne's future. A daily stagecoach ran between Cheyenne and Denver, along with a constant procession of freight wagons. But Denver's city fathers wanted a railroad connection to the transcontinental line, and "Colorado people" put up "$500,000 cash" to attract a "Denver Branch." In December 1867 Grenville Dodge announced that during 1868 a line would be built from Denver to Cheyenne. The "Denver Pacific" was surveyed, and in the spring of 1868 graders and tie cutters went to work. Ground was broken just outside Denver on May 18, with local belles manning the plows to the cheers of a crowd primed by lager beer and a brass band. With tracks building toward Cheyenne from the south, it was anticipated—correctly—that another line soon would extend to the north, making the Magic City a railroad crossroads.[40]

The *Colorado Herald*, published in Central City, proclaimed that Union Pacific officials "have made Cheyenne the great Central Depot of all the trade and resources of the great expanse of country on either side of it." The *Herald* predicted that "Cheyenne is to be the New Chicago, the great emporium of the wealth and traffic of the great West." Many who chose to remain in Cheyenne agreed.[41]

Another cause for optimism was the likelihood that Cheyenne would become the state capital. The path to governmental organization was rapid. The provisional city government, established in August 1867, had no legal sanction. Mayor H. M. Hook and City Attorney J. R. Whitehead soon worked to organize a provisional county government. At a "mass meeting" on September 27, "resolutions were adopted appointing an election for territorial and county offices." Although there also was no legal sanction for this proposed territory and county, 1,900 votes were cast on October 8, 1867. A full complement of officials was elected, including Gen. Jack Casement, "territorial" delegate to Congress; J. R. Whitehead, "county" representative to the Dakota legislature; W. L. Kuykendall, probate judge; D. L. Sweeney, sheriff; and Dr. James Irwin, county coroner. General Casement traveled to Washington, and even though he held no legal status in Congress, he employed the influence of the Union Pacific to lobby on behalf of territorial legislation that already was in progress. By the time Whitehead reached Yanktown, the territorial legislature had organized Laramie County and granted a charter to the city of Cheyenne. The *Leader* rejoiced that the Magic City was now "clothed with a legislative charter."[42]

On January 10, 1868, the *Leader* complained that even though the city charter had become law on December 25, no copy had yet reached Cheyenne. But one week later J. R. Whitehead arrived from Yanktown, bringing the city charter and copies of the bills creating Laramie County and a district court. The city charter was printed in its entirety on the front page of the *Leader*, while a municipal election was scheduled for Thursday, January 23. H. M. Hook, J. R. Whitehead, and most other members of the provisional government did not stand for reelection. (The next year Hook joined a party of prospectors on the Green River, but in June 1869 Cheyenne's first mayor and a companion were swept away and drowned.) City Marshal Ed Melanger ran for reelection; however, with vigilantes finding it necessary to impose order at the time of the election, he finished a distant fourth. The new marshal was D. J. Sweeney, who had been elected sheriff of the provisional county government in October.[43]

Luke Murrin was elected mayor over three opponents, collecting 593 votes out of 1,002 cast. "He is a man of sterling worth and capacity," proclaimed the *Leader*. Murrin was an Irish immigrant who arrived in the United States in 1855. Intelligent and ambitious, he attended college in Ohio, studying business and law. Murrin enlisted as a lieutenant in an Ohio infantry regiment in 1861. Twice wounded in combat, he later served on the staff of Gen. Rutherford B. Hayes before earning promotion to colonel and commanding a regiment in the Shenandoah Valley in 1865. Single and restless after the war, Murrin gravitated to the West. In Cheyenne he would become a successful liquor merchant, described by the *Leader* as "one of our most reliable and successful business men." A ranking combat veteran, well-educated and gregarious, the stoutly built Murrin effortlessly generated respect and popularity. He would provide strong leadership to young Cheyenne and remain as a prominent citizen for many years to come.[44]

Reorganizing under a new mayor and other city officials, Cheyenne also was the seat of newly formed Laramie County. Simultaneously, legislation was being advanced in Congress to create the territory that would be named Wyoming. As the largest community in the new territory, Cheyenne could expect to become territorial capital, and, at some point in the future, state capital. And as a county seat and territorial capital, Cheyenne would be the home of numerous important offices and of salaried officials.

Indeed, it proved possible to hope for even more. The growth of the West caused widespread speculation that the national capital should be moved from Washington, D.C., to a more central location. On October 4, 1869, N. A. Baker published a long editorial in the *Leader* promoting Cheyenne as "the Future National Capital." Baker pointed out that Cheyenne was near the center of the United States, commanded a prominent location on the recently completed transcontinental railroad, and enjoyed a "salubrious and equitable" climate that was "less liable to extreme heat and cold" (as though frequent sub-zero winter temperatures were not extreme). "The cost of grading streets and avenues would be infinitely less than in any other location that could be selected," Baker said, and he stressed other pragmatic advantages, such as the difficulty "an invading army" would have in marching to Cheyenne. "No more central, more healthful or more beautiful location for the future Capital can be found in America. Cheyenne is herself the fairy-like creation of a great national conviction," he assessed.

If the population of Cheyenne had plummeted from its early boom, N. A. Baker was not the only community leader who harbored unyielding faith in the future destiny of the Magic City.

2

Fort Russell and Camp Carlin

he decision to place a major military installation near Cheyenne was crucial to the future of the Magic City. As the first settlers arrived and set up tents, the army took steps to establish their newest frontier base. At this time five companies of the Thirteenth Infantry, commanded by Col. John D. Stevenson, were operating against hostile raiders from an encampment in western Nebraska. On July 15, 1867, Colonel Stevenson was ordered to set up a camp near the Crow Creek crossing. Companies, B, G, and K arrived on July 21 and established the Camp at Crow Creek crossing, about half a mile north of the tent boomtown. (Another of Stevenson's companies stayed behind to break down the Nebraska camp, while his fifth troop was detached to guard railroad workers.)[1]

Ten days later, on July 31, 1867, Department of the Platte General Order No. 23 officially designated the name and location of the post: Fort D. A. Russell, christened after a brigadier general killed during the Civil War, would "be established on Crow Creek, D.T., at its intersection by the Union Pacific Railroad." An army surveying team located the boundaries of a military reservation three miles northwest of Cheyenne. Measuring three miles wide (east to west) by two miles in length, the reservation encompassed 3,840 acres, although additions soon were made on the southeast to accommodate the supply depot. While the company tents were moved to this site, Colonel Stevenson and his staff formulated designs for a regimental post. A large and unusual diamond-shaped parade ground stretched 1,040 feet north to south and 800 feet east to west. Customarily the parade ground was rectangular, but the diamond shape allowed a greater number of buildings to front the parade. The commanding officers' quarters would be at the northern tip of the diamond, flanked by seven story-and-a-half officers' quarters to each side. Eleven company barracks, 80 feet by 30 feet, were planned, with separate mess halls attached. Six infantry barracks would be on the southwest side of the parade, with the infantry officers quartered on the northwest side. Cavalry officers' quarters and five company barracks were on the eastern sides of the diamond, with stables below the barracks near Crow Creek. A forty-eight-bed hospital and quartermaster and commissary warehouses were east of the parade ground, while quarters for laundresses were west of the infantry barracks. Various other buildings were placed outside the parade under the master plan.[2]

While Cheyenne sprang up as a sprawling collection of tents and ramshackle frame structures, three miles to the northwest Fort Russell would become a large, orderly military community. All of the nearly 100 buildings would be frame, so sawmills were brought in, with soldiers providing most of the labor. At a new frontier post, soldiers always became construction workers, usually with a great deal of grumbling ("we are obliged to perform all kinds of labor, such as all the operations of building quarters, stables, storehouses, bridges, roads, and telegraph lines; involving logging, lumbering, quarrying, adobe and brick making, lime-burning, mason-work, plastering, carpentering, painting, & c."). In later years, as Fort Russell was improved and expanded, there would be frequent employment for Cheyenne carpenters, bricklayers, and contractors. But during the first formative months of Fort Russell, civilian contractors and artisans were not present, and soldiers worked hard on quarters and barracks. No one wanted to

Gen. David A. Russell

New Yorker David A. Russell graduated from West Point in 1845, and as a young officer he distinguished himself during the war with Mexico. By the outbreak of the Civil War, Russell was a captain in the Fourth Infantry.

Rapidly advancing in rank as the army expanded, Russell became a brigadier general of volunteers in November 1862. General Russell campaigned actively with the Army of the Potomac, leading an assault during the fight at Chancellorsville and spearheading the attack at Rappahhannock Station, where he was wounded. The injured hero was given the honor of taking eight captured battle flags to Washington.

General Russell commanded a division under Phil Sheridan during the campaign against Jubal Early in the Shenandoah Valley. At Winchester on September 19, 1864, he shrugged off a chest wound to retain command on the battlefield, but an exploding shell sent a piece of shrapnel into his heart, instantly killing the forty-four-year-old general. Russell was posthumously breveted to major general, and three years later he was further honored by having a western outpost named after him.

be in tents when winter struck. Until the railroad reached Cheyenne, building supplies had to be brought in to the fort from end-of-track by wagon trains. In November 1867 the tracks reached Cheyenne, and the next month a spur line was built to the Quartermaster Depot. With construction materials now available by rail, progress on the post buildings accelerated.[3]

Barracks were the first priority, and by January 1868 most of the men were quartered indoors. By this time seven companies of the Thirtieth Infantry had arrived at Fort Russell, along with four troops of the Second Cavalry. A band also was assigned to the post, bringing Fort Russell's complement to more than 900 men, along with twenty-three officers. A number of officers' wives also were present, although the officers' quarters were not completed until February. Even while still in their tents, officers offered the best at their disposal to friends passing through Cheyenne. "The most cordial hospitality awaited us here," recorded a French visitor, Louis Simonin, who was rescued from the primitive accommodations of Cheyenne in November 1867. "General Stevenson [the colonel had been a general of volunteers during the Civil War], who commands the fort, the major, the quartermaster, the officers, all have received us as friends. We have set at their mess, we have toasted one another, and drunk the sacramental glass of

Fort D.A. Russell was built around a diamond-shaped parade ground. Company quarters are at right; infantry barracks are just beyond the laundress quarters in the foreground; cavalry barracks are on the opposite side of the parade. Officers' quarters are at left, with the big commanding officer's quarters at the top of the parade, at left. The large building above the COQ is the hospital. Four sets of stables are on the plain at right beside Crow Creek, winding its way southeastward toward Cheyenne in the distance. Camp Carlin is visible at upper right. (Courtesy Wyoming State Archives)

whiskey without which no good acquaintance is made in the United States. A sentinel watches our tent."[4]

Military hospitality would become a hallmark of the relationship between Fort Russell and Cheyenne. Colonel Stevenson invited citizens of Cheyenne to the post on February 22, 1868, to view a dress parade in honor of George Washington's birthday. A few nights later Cheyenne's leading citizens, at the invitation of Colonel Stevenson, attended a reception at the two-story commanding officer's quarters. The newly completed house was beautifully decorated, the post band provided music, and fine wines and refreshments were served. Fifty men, both officers and civilians, were present, along with twenty-five of their wives. The following week "the popular commander" hosted a larger event in a hall that would be used variously as a chapel, school, and reception area. Two lieutenants "had decked the walls and ceiling with handsome flags and other insignia; while the band played some choice, operatic airs from a raised platform at the end of the building." Colonel Stevenson opened the dancing with the wife of Cheyenne merchant F.E. Addoms, and as the evening progressed everyone was able "to enjoy cotillion, waltz or gallopade." At eleven o'clock the guests sat down "to a well laid table of choice provisions, and something from France to settle the same."[5]

The future would bring a succession of balls and receptions to the fort, with prominent Cheyenne citizens always in attendance. Civilians were welcome when the post band gave a concert or when there was a dress parade. Cheyenne newspapers would announce such events, and large numbers of citizens would drive or ride out to the fort to enjoy the martial entertainments. As the big post took shape, many citizens essayed pleasure rides in their carriages through Fort Russell. For visitors to Cheyenne, a ride to the fort was virtually a required event. Officers hosted friends from Cheyenne at private dinner parties. In return, officers were welcomed guests at social events in town. A great many officers and their wives were from the East, like most of the leaders of Cheyenne, many of whom had served in the Civil War. With much in common, the leadership class of the fort and of the city readily gravitated toward each other. Many junior officers were bachelors, and through the years a number of young ladies from Cheyenne became army brides. The military band always played at public events and was engaged for dances in town. From the beginning there were close ties between Fort Russell and Cheyenne, and the interaction and cordial relations would continue as both communities matured.

Concurrently with the development of Fort D. A. Russell, the "Quartermaster Depot at Cheyenne" also was erected. In August 1867, just weeks after the site for Fort Russell was determined, it was decided to locate "Cheyenne Depot" on Crow Creek between the fort and Cheyenne. As soon as Union Pacific tracks reached Cheyenne in November 1867, a spur was built northwest toward the Quartermaster Depot. Inside Cheyenne Depot were two parallel sets of tracks running east and west. Eight large warehouses faced the north set of tracks, while another eight faced the south set. Other structures went up: a company barracks, commander's quarters, guard house, quarters for quartermaster and commissary personnel, a mess hall, bunkhouses for civilian employees and laundresses, a bakery, offices, and shops for blacksmiths, carpenters, wheelwrights, and harness and saddle makers. More than three dozen buildings made up the Cheyenne Depot complex, along with stables, wagon sheds, corrals, and a lumber yard.[6]

The Quartermaster Depot at Cheyenne was built by the first commander, Capt. Elias B. Carling of the Quartermaster Corps. Brevetted a lieutenant colonel during the Civil War, he was generally called "Colonel Carling," and the depot he commanded began to be referred to as "Camp Carling" and "Camp Carlin." Captain Carling was transferred in 1869 (he committed suicide at Fort Sanders in 1875), but the Quartermaster Depot he commanded for two years would be popularly known as Camp Carlin for two more decades.[7]

Camp Carlin became the nation's second largest quartermaster depot, supplying fourteen forts in Wyoming, Nebraska, Colorado, Idaho, and Utah. Camp Carlin also supplied encampments in the region and large bodies of troops in the field, while also providing food and clothing for the Red Cloud and Spotted Tail Indian agencies. Equipment, ordnance, and uniforms were shipped by rail from the East, but great quantities of other items were purchased in and around Cheyenne: horses, cattle, hay, grain, vegetables, wood, and coal. Area ranchers and farmers (many from northern Colorado), as well as Cheyenne businessmen, enjoyed a voracious military market. (In 1868, for example, 450,000 pounds of vegetables were purchased.) Wagons and pack mules were regularly loaded in

The Commanding Officer's Quarters at Fort Russell. As soon as the COQ was completed early in 1868, Col. John Stevenson entertained leading citizens of Cheyenne. (Courtesy Wyoming State Archives)

Officers' quarters, completed in 1868 and used for three decades. These frame structures were duplexes, designed to house two officers and their families. (Courtesy Wyoming State Archives)

Camp Carlin, then sent out to deliver supplies to forts or agencies or troops in camp. Wagons usually were ox-drawn—Indians were more inclined to steal mules or, of course, horses—while mule trains could reach troops in the field. The pack train division was directed by Thomas Moore, who was named chief packer in 1870, when he was thirty-eight. Moore led pack trains into the field in most campaigns of the Indian Wars during the 1870s and 1880s. "Colonel Moore," as he came to be called, was transported to Arizona or Utah or Dakota Territory, or wherever else his services were needed. With his wife and daughter, Moore made his home in a cabin at Camp Carlin, where he became an institution.[8]

In addition to large numbers of teamsters, hundreds of civilian employees included blacksmiths, carpenters, stock tenders, harness makers, and cooks for the bunk houses. Although numerous civilians bunked at Camp Carlin, many others roomed in Cheyenne. Civilian employees sometimes numbered up to 1,000, outnumbering the soldiers posted at Fort Russell. For years a cavalry or infantry company was stationed at Camp Carlin to provide military escorts for supply trains.[9]

The pay of soldiers and civilian employees funneled significant cash infusions into Cheyenne. The soldiers were visited by a traveling paymaster, ideally every two months, but more commonly at three- or four-month intervals. When the paymaster reached Fort Russell, the anticipated event was proclaimed in Cheyenne newspapers. Announcements of the military payday were regularly printed for decades, into the twentieth century. These announcements were particularly welcomed by Cheyenne's saloonkeepers, gamblers, and prostitutes. Merchants received a smaller share of the soldiers' business, but Cheyenne always teemed with uniformed men after payday.

Everywhere that a frontier outpost was established, just outside the military reservation a "hog ranch" materialized to satisfy recreational needs of the soldiers. A dive or two dispensed hard liquor and coarse women (young, pretty prostitutes were in New Orleans or St. Louis—certainly not at a hog ranch servicing underpaid troopers), and gamblers haunted hog ranch saloons. But a short distance outside Fort Russell, and a shorter distance from Camp Carlin, was the capital city of Wyoming Territory. Cheyenne's lowest dives were maintained near the military reservation, forming the notorious west end of the Magic City. While Cheyenne's better saloons and classier bordellos were downtown, most off-duty soldiers rarely made it past the west end, or "Chicago," as it came to be called.

Drunken brawls were frequent occurrences in the west end, and Cheyenne peace officers remained on the alert for outbursts of trouble in "Chicago." In February 1869, for example, soldiers and policemen clashed with drawn revolvers at the Keystone dance hall. Although off-duty soldiers were not supposed to carry firearms into town, four Second Cavalry troopers supposedly were told by their captain to go into the west end, armed with service revolvers. Their mission was to locate and arrest a stock thief known as Dick Douglass. Douglass had stolen eleven mules from the pack train during a recent expedition, and on Thursday night, February 11, word reached Fort Russell that the mule thief was in the west end. About ten o'clock the four troopers found Douglass at the Keystone, and "after talking with him a few moments drew their pistols and fired at him." At the sound of gunshots, Cheyenne policemen raced to the scene and confronted the soldiers. "Revolvers were drawn and heads hammered with them," reported the *Leader*, "but finally the soldiers were arrested." During the fracas one of the dance hall girls "sung out at the top of her voice 'go in you ----- -----s, that's music in my ears!'"[10]

When Chief of Police George Hardin learned the nature of the trouble, he arrested Douglass and marched the stock thief to city hall. Incredibly, a policeman who was a friend of Douglass drew his revolver on Chief Hardin and tried to force his pal's release. The foolhardy policeman was promptly arrested, and Douglass was sent to Fort Russell for military justice. (Unfortunately for Douglass, military custody proved lax, and he was seized and lynched, as described in the next chapter.)

Despite Chief Hardin's assistance regarding Douglass, the clash with Cheyenne policemen triggered resentment among enlisted men. Payday at Fort Russell was a week later, and that evening, after a drunken trooper was arrested, nearly a score of his comrades armed themselves with carbines and marched into town. The post commander, Maj. James Van Voast, soon learned of the incident, and he dispatched an officer and six cavalrymen to bring the armed soldiers back to the fort. Major Van Voast simultaneously sent a note to City Marshal Hardin:

Dear Sir: I have just been informed that several men have left this fort, without permission, and have taken their arms with them. These men have just been paid, and I fear they, probably being intoxicated, may create trouble. I therefore send Lieut. Bartlett with a squad of men to arrest these persons. Please give Him such assistance as he may require.

Very Respectfully,

J. Van Voast

Major 18th Infantry, Commanding

The armed soldiers surrounded the jail, and when City Marshal Hardin hurried onto the scene he was confronted by loaded carbines. Coolly, Hardin informed the soldiers that keys to the little jail were downtown at city hall. "Three of the riotous cavalrymen accompanied him with carbines leveled on his person," stated the *Leader*. Shortly after Hardin left the jail, Lieutenant Bartlett and his mounted squad arrived. Bartlett sent "the riotous cavalrymen" back to the fort under the supervision of his squad, while he remained behind to have the prisoners released into his custody.

On the outskirts of town a few drunken soldiers "recklessly fired at nothing or nobody in particular." Hearing gunfire in the direction of the fort, Lieutenant Bartlett galloped toward the sound of trouble. Two troopers actually fired wildly at the officer, who continued on to Fort Russell. Major Van Voast promptly sent 150 men into town to arrest "the rioters," rounding up all of them that night and the next morning.[11]

A couple of months later, soldiers and civilians clashed in a west end dive, trading five pistol shots at four in the morning. No one was hit, and the antagonists fled before policemen could arrive. The officers followed the road toward the fort, and on the prairie outside town arrested a soldier and a civilian who were engaged in a fist fight.[12]

Such incidents were taken in stride by the citi-

Gen. U. S. Grant, Civil War hero and commander of the U.S. Army, first visited Fort Russell and Cheyenne in July 1868. The most prominent visitor to early Cheyenne, he would return several times after assuming the presidency. (Courtesy National Archives)

zens of Cheyenne. West enders, of course, shrugged off drunken brawls by their customers as part of business life, and soldiers provided their largest customer base. The political and business leaders of Cheyenne enjoyed amicable relations with the officers of Fort D. A. Russell. They understood better than anyone the crucial economic role played by the fort and Camp Carlin in the life of the Magic City. "One of the most important adjuncts to the prosperity of Cheyenne is Fort D. A. Russell," emphatically declared the *Leader* only a year after the fort and city were established. The *Leader* also pointed out that Camp Carlin "employs a great number of men and teams, and annually expends millions of dollars, all of which operates in favor of this city."[13] Cheyenne was inextricably linked with Fort Russell and Camp Carlin. From time to time good relations between the civilian and military communities were strained by drunken scrapes in the west end, or by occasional theft. But these unpleasantries may be compared to the periodic spats of a strongly devoted married couple.

The marriage between Cheyenne and its adjoining military base would prove to be long and fruitful.

3

Vigilantes and Peace Officers

Lawlessness abounded in each Hell on Wheels boomtown along the Union Pacific construction line. The first Hell on Wheels was North Platte, Nebraska, where the Union Pacific encamped during the winter of 1866–67. Five thousand men and a few women spent that winter among the tents and shanties of North Platte. Most of the men were railroad workers, and virtually all of the women were prostitutes. Gamblers and saloonkeepers came too, as did a few merchants. Throughout the winter North Platte throbbed with drinking and gambling and carousing, along with frequent brawls and shootings. In the spring, when construction resumed, Hell on Wheels shifted eighty miles to the west to Julesburg, where the UP established the next supply depot. Located in the northeast corner of Colorado, Julesburg was even wilder than North Platte, which shriveled into a quiet village after the tracks moved west.[1]

The next division point would be Cheyenne, which grew rapidly in anticipation of a Hell on Wheels period. By the time the tracks arrived in November 1867, the gamblers, saloon men, and soiled doves had moved over from Julesburg. "Saloons were opened in the open air," recalled an oldtimer. These one-man operations were stocked "with a gallon keg or jug filled with whiskey, and a glass or two to deal it out in."[2] A saloonkeeper named Cunningham built a 16 by 24-foot frame structure for $175 and went into business.[3] Saloons, dance halls, and brothels soon were housed in more substantial structures.

Cheyenne's first few weeks were raucous and unruly. When a provisional city government was established in early August 1867, J. R. Whitehead submitted a resolution of gratitude to General Stevenson and the officers of Fort Russell for the police measures they had "inaugurated and maintained in our embryo city."

36

Whitehead agreed to serve as city attorney, and Edward Melanger was elected city marshal, at a salary of $120 per month. Two city policemen were "confirmed," Jake Overlander and Joshua Felter. At this point Cheyenne's population was 600, but within a few months it would explode at least tenfold. Accordingly, by 1868 the police force swelled to twelve officers, along with the city marshal and a constable for each of Cheyenne's three precincts.[4]

When the municipality was organized, in August 1867, there was no jail in the month-old boomtown. Officers were instructed that anyone who required confinement should "be placed in irons and guarded in some building or tent." At the same time, provisions were made "for the erection of a jail 20 x 20 feet." Cheyenne's first jail was built on Sixteenth Street by Tom Rutledge at a cost of $2,606. Two heating stoves, costing twenty-five dollars apiece, were provided for this "comfortable calaboose." Marshal Melanger lived nearby, although he was defeated by Dennis Sweeney in the city's first legal election, conducted in January 1868. Melanger soon was hired by businessmen as one of two "special policemen" who patrolled the commercial district. Plenty of work was available for men willing to serve as officers.[5]

"The police court does a vast amount of business each week," reported the *Leader* only a few months after the court and the police force were established. The first issue of the *Leader*, published on September 19, 1867, included articles about a robbery attempt at a gun shop, a citizen being beaten and robbed, and the theft of guns and blankets from wagons and tents. As an irate sergeant dragged a drunken soldier back to Fort Russell, he pistol-whipped the trooper—

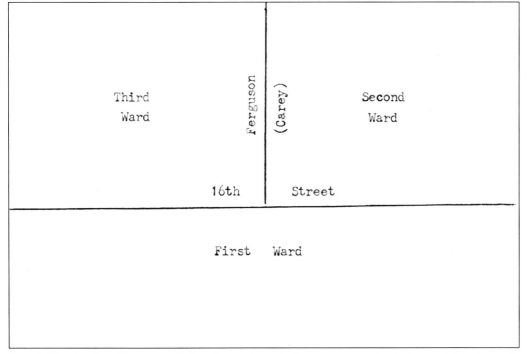

In addition to the Cheyenne Police Department, there was an elected constable in each of the three city wards, or voting precincts. (Author's diagram)

fracturing the man's skull and wounding himself when the revolver discharged accidentally.[6]

The next issue of the *Leader*, five days later, contained reports of more fights. One miscreant "who fired a shot at a member of the police force" was hauled off to Fort Russell to toil on a chain gang. Subsequent newspapers described brawls in bawdy houses, street fights, and conflicts between soldiers and civilians. "Quite a few occurred at the Tremont House, last evening," reported the *Leader* in December 1867, adding that when policemen showed up they joined the fray. In January 1868 a railroad worker was fired "for imagining a saloon a livery stable, and riding his horse inside." A few days later a city officer was thrown in jail for drunkenly brandishing his revolver, and fellow prisoners eagerly "gave Mr. Policeman a terrible beating" until the jailer intervened.[7]

On the night of October 4, 1867, a wild shootout at "a house of ill fame" resulted in the death of a man called "Limber Jim" and of popular saloonkeeper Pat Mallally, who was blasted in the chest with a shotgun. Lead Beader, the woman who ran the bawdyhouse, had feuded with Mallally and was wounded in the wrist. The shooting attracted hundreds of people, and the "crowd resolved itself into a mob." Lead Beader's bawdyhouse was burned to the ground, and "the raging multitude of excited men" marched uncontrolled through the streets. Arrests did nothing to halt the rampaging horde, so Mayor Hook made a desperate appeal to Fort Russell. In the middle of the night three infantry companies marched into Cheyenne at the double quick, followed by three troops of cavalry. The mere appearance of this imposing military force sent the riotous mob scurrying into the darkness.[8]

The interior of one of the fabricated saloons that were brought to Cheyenne on flatcars from Julesburg, the previous Hell-on-Wheels. (From Frank Leslie's Weekly, *1877)*

A little later in the month a teamster was shot ten miles outside of town and fell dead, clutching his whip. In December 1867 a man known as Shorty Burns opened fire on three men in a dugout inside the city limits. Two of the men were killed, while the third man, wounded in the chest, "rushed into the Police Court, bootless, hatless and breathless." Burns escaped into the countryside. A jail escapee, horse thief John Cavanaugh, was shot to death by William Keane while running away from Cheyenne's lockup. About this same time a "brutal and fiendish" crime was discovered. A widow with two small boys had married Jack Williams, but "the inhuman step-father" abused the boys, causing the death of one and severely injuring the other. Williams was taken under arrest to Fort Russell to avoid a lynch mob.[9]

Lynching and vigilantism were extralegal activities that had been commonplace since the 1760s, when violence was directed against British authority in the years leading up to the American Revolution. While the Revolution still raged, in 1780, a prominent Virginian, Col. Charles Lynch, presided over a court designed to combat outlawry in Bedford County. Illegal trials were held regularly, with flogging as the common punishment. The court thus dispersed "Lynch Law," and in time the term came to mean a far more lethal form of justice than flogging.[10]

During the eighteenth, nineteenth, and early twentieth centuries, more than 6,000 men—and a few women—were executed by vigilante activities. Vigilantism flourished on the frontiers of the nineteenth century, when the westward movement repeatedly outraced the establishment of courts, law officers, and even jails. Indeed, vigilante action was quicker and cheaper than any system of courts, judges, juries, attorneys, trials, appeals, and institutional punishment. When the westward movement leaped across half a continent to the California gold fields, vigilance committees were organized in one community after another. San Francisco's Committee of Vigilance was formed in 1851 to control a soaring crime rate, and was revived on a larger scale, with 6,000 members, in 1856. In Montana in 1864, a vicious outlaw gang led by Sheriff Henry Plummer committed thievery and more than a hundred murders in the gold fields around Bannack and Virginia City. Citizens finally banded together as vigilantes and hanged Plummer, along with more than a score of his gang members.

Three years later, in Cheyenne, businessmen and other concerned citizens felt driven to take similar action against violence, thievery, and open prostitution in the Magic City. By December 1867 about seventy-five men, including such leading citizens as William Kuykendall, had formed an armed band of "Special Police," with a chief, captains of "several squads," a headquarters, and a "regular signal." Soon the special policemen evolved into a much larger force. At a night meeting of the special police at city hall, a vigilance committee was organized, according to Kuykendall. Within two weeks these vigilantes acted against three men who had been arrested for stealing $900. The thieves were released under bond on the same day they were arrested, January 10, 1868. But late that night they were seized, along with more than half of their ill-gotten gains, and bound together by two hundred vigilantes. Just before dawn the trio was found walking on Eddy Street with "a large canvas attached to them" which read ominously:

> $900 stole/ Thieves. / 500 Recovered.
> F. St. Claire,   E. De Bronville
> W. Crier
> City authorities please not interfere
> *Until 10 o'clock A.M.*
> Next *case* goes up a *tree*
> *Beware of Vigilance Committee*

About eight o'clock Deputy U.S. Marshal Goff, who had arrested the three men, removed the placard and cut the cords that bound them. In the next issue of the *Leader*, N. A. Baker editorialized against "the existence of a Vigilance Committee, two hundred strong, in our midst." While allowing that "the law's delays and the dilatoriness of Courts" had galvanized vigilantes in such places as California and Montana, Baker insisted that the legal system in Cheyenne by and large had been effective. Pointing out that "this self-constituted body had commenced proceedings in a rash manner," Baker warned the vigilantes to "beware of yourselves!"[12]

The vigilantes were undeterred. A few evenings later a shootout erupted at the New Idea Saloon, then carried over to the Champion Saloon. The following night two hundred vigilantes donned masks and marched through the streets at midnight, searching for the gunmen. Everywhere the vigilantes looked "they behaved civilly," but their prey prudently had left town. On the same day (January 18) that the midnight march of the vigilance committee was described, the *Leader* also reported another "row and shooting scrape," at the Iowa House. "We fear that the people of Laramie County will yet be driven to desperate measures."[13]

The *Leader*'s prediction was fulfilled within two days. Shorty Burns, who recently had killed two men in a dugout at Cheyenne, and two other ruffians fired their revolvers into Tim Dyer's saloon and a bawdyhouse during an evening rampage. The trio of desperadoes fled by train to Dale City, a rowdy construction site thirty-five miles west on the UP line. They "then went on a drunk" in Dale City. Back in Cheyenne, the vigilantes met before midnight and apparently arranged for a train. Late at night on Monday, January 20, 1868, "the Vigilantes visited Dale City." Sleeping off their drunk, the three miscreants were awakened by a roomful of masked men and taken outside to a tree. "All three were hung, and died game, making no disclosures," related the *Leader*. "This showed pluck, that's all!" The *Leader* seemed to concur that the execution of this trio was good riddance, and concluded the story in bold letters: "Too Bad!"[14]

Determined to use the triple hanging as an intimidation device, the vigilantes immediately published a list of undesirables to be banished from Cheyenne. The list of nine men included "Slippery Bill" and two of the $900 thieves, Frank St. Clair and Eugene De Boniville (the third thief, W. Crier, apparently had been

In 1867 James Whitehead erected a two-story log building, seen here in later years. Two structures to the left were incorporated into the "Whitehead Block." The building on the right was used as the first city hall. The second floor was an open hall where two police courts were conducted, and where the Vigilance Committee was organized. (Courtesy Wyoming State Archives)

smart enough to leave town), and a woman was listed as well—an especially objectionable member of Cheyenne's demimonde, Nell Murphy. The posted notice ended pointedly: "The above parties will leave the territory in twenty-four hours. By order of VIGILANCE COMMITTEE."[15]

Just over a week later, on Thursday afternoon, January 30, 1868, the city officials who had been chosen in Cheyenne's first election were inaugurated at the new city hall. Mayor Luke Murrin "made a neat address," during which he "declared himself hostile to the existence of any vigilance committees in our midst, and that means would be taken to suppress them, if they did not disperse." The *Leader* reported: "This last sentiment met the hearty approval of the throng."[16]

The city council met on Saturday, February 8, 1868, acting to strengthen the police force and provide a legal alternative to vigilantes. Several applications for police positions were considered, "and the special policeman employed by several business men on Eddy and Sixteenth Sts., was given permission to act with the same authority as a regular policeman, in making arrests, etc."[17]

But the roughest element of Cheyenne's underworld shrugged off any threat posed by policemen or vigilantes. Two days after the city council beefed up the police force, "a drunken quarrel" in Martin's Exchange Saloon resulted in a fatal shooting. Angrily cursing each other over a prize fight, Sam Reed and John Brennan scuffled, then Reed produced a derringer and shot his antagonist in the stomach.[18]

Three days later, on Thursday, February 13, two former partners, Charlie Martin and Andy Harris, walked together down Sixteenth Street and entered Harris's place of business. A quarrel broke out, then Harris called Martin "a little dirty bastard" and pulled a pistol. But Martin was a dangerous shootist who had badly wounded the city marshal of Julesburg, Capt. N. J. O'Brien. When Harris shifted his attention away for a moment, Martin whipped out a revolver and shot Harris twice. Harris died the next day. While awaiting trial in district court, Martin was permitted "the freedom of the city," although an officer was assigned to accompany him as he "goes about from saloon to dance house, and dance house to saloon." Similar treatment was afforded "the notorious Cyprian, Nell Leadbetter, who shot her man at the prize fight, at Dale City, on Saturday last" (February 22). The *Leader* reported that the public was "commenting quite strongly" about "this kind consideration for homicides."[19]

The *Leader* also issued an editorial complaint against dance halls "and the disgusting bawds who flaunt themselves ... so conspicuously." The *Leader* insisted that most of Cheyenne's shootings occurred or originated in "these modern institutions of crime and pleasure," and expressed concern that new dance halls were opening in the business section:

> Between bad whiskey and the wiles of the wantons, the sophisticated and unsophisticated are fleeced with unerring regularity and system. Extraordinary inducements one thrust forth to inveigle men with their money into these plundering dens, where the vile of both sexes ... congregate, and the luckless wight [person] who escapes therefrom without being cut, shot or beaten up, and minus his money is fortunate.... The jades who coy with intoxicated teamsters, or miners or laborers, and clean them out of every cent in their pockets, and then have their dupes set upon and maltreated by the pet roughs whom they subsist, are a terrible reproach and infliction on any community.[20]

On Tuesday night, February 25, 1868, seven prisoners broke out of Cheyenne's jail *"during the absence of the jailor,"* pointed out a disgusted *Leader* reporter. Apparently aided from the outside, the escapees sawed through a log and

Cheyenne's first courthouse, from a contemporary drawing of S. H. Winsor. (Annals of Wyoming, April 1943, cover)

disappeared. The next week the *Leader* editorialized against "the bedizened, bedaubed and disgusting bawds" who brazenly displayed "their hideous 'mugs' and flying plumage" in downtown Cheyenne. By March 13 a petition was circulating against "those vile retreats," dance houses: "The vicious and depraved, the vile and villainous of both sexes, frequent these nocturnal haunts." The following day the *Leader* called on city officials to remove the dance halls and bawdyhouses: "Close up those haunts of bad men and worse women."[21]

Although the vigilance committee had received criticism, the unrelenting misdeeds "of bad men and worse women" persuaded many committee members that their work was unfinished. During the second week in March, "rumors circulated about town that our vigilantes" had ventured into the countryside to seize and hang five evildoers. These rumors proved to be false. But on Saturday morning, March 21, "rumors of Vigilante doings were in circulation at an early hour"—and within a short time there was graphic proof that these rumors were true. Jim Chisholm, a new arrival in Cheyenne, accurately observed a local mood: "'It is a sign of good times,' they say here, 'when people begin to do a little hanging.'"[22]

Charles Martin recently had been acquitted of the February 13 murder of Andy Harris by a jury trial in district court. On Friday night, March 20, 1868, Martin celebrated his acquittal in the Keystone Dance Hall, arrogantly boasting "that he would soon furnish another man for breakfast, for the citizens of Cheyenne." But there were citizens of Cheyenne who decided that Martin would do no more killing. The next man Cheyenne had for breakfast would be Martin himself.[23]

An hour after midnight, Martin was swaggering around the dance floor in the Keystone when he was called to the door by a message "that a friend wished to see him." Once outside he was seized and hustled away, while those who might have wanted to help him were halted "by a display of several revolvers. The last that was seen of Martin, he was making some desperate struggles," which were subdued by several applications of a gun barrel to his head. He was dragged to the west end of Eighteenth Street. There were no trees at the edge of town, but three poles were lashed together to form "a rude gallows," and Martin was hanged.[24]

Earlier that night vigilantes had intercepted a mule thief named Charles Morgan. Morgan had been taken into custody on the road to Denver, and W. G. Smith, one of the owners of the stolen mules, brought him to Cheyenne to place him in official custody. Instead, upon reaching Crow Creek around nine o'clock, they encountered about a dozen vigilantes, who took Morgan from Smith. The vigilantes brought Morgan to the Elephant Corral at the east end of Sixteenth Street, erected another makeshift gallows with three poles, and hanged the mule thief.

The next morning two policemen found Martin's corpse and cut him down, and about the same time Morgan was discovered at the rear of the Elephant Corral. "The spectacle of a human being suspended in the air, with blue, swollen features, tongue and eyes protruding in a horrible manner, and fists clinched in the last convulsive struggle, is not a pleasing object to encounter in your morning ramble," related Jim Chisholm. "Such was the ghastly sight presented to the Cheyennese at sunrise this morning." By eight o'clock Saturday the two bodies had been brought in a wagon to the office of the county coroner, Dr. F. W. Johnson. Dr. Johnson assembled a six-man coroner's jury to handle both cases. With nooses still in place around the necks of the deceased, it was ruled that Martin and Morgan had met death by hanging: "Perpetrators Unknown."[25]

Incredibly, the boldest of Cheyenne's wild crowd remained heedless of the latest vigilante action. "Hardly have the bodies of Martin and Morgan become rigid in the arms of death," lamented the *Leader*, "before we are called upon to chronicle another shooting." On Sunday evening, March 22, a quarrel broke out in Ford's Restaurant. A bullet was fired into the throat of H. W. Dodge, striking his spinal cord and killing him instantly. The *Leader* gloomily announced that Cheyenne was acquiring "the worst name for its tragic scenes of blood and riot."[26]

Cheyenne's notorious reputation was intensified two weeks later. On Sunday night, April 5, 1868, Theo Landgreber, a German brewer, was murdered by a band of night riders. Landgreber's home was near his brewery, half a mile west of town. Landgreber's partner, Theo Winchell, and his wife slept in a bedroom adjacent to the brewery. Winchell had just gone to sleep when there was a knock at the door and a loud demand, "We want to get some beer."[27]

"You can't get no beer tonight," shouted Winchell.

But a dozen men forced their way into the room. "Don't you owe Pat Dyer some money?" Winchell was asked.

"Yes," came the lame reply.

"What is the reason you don't pay it?"

"We couldn't pay it. We tried to get the money of the bankers and we couldn't," explained Winchell. "Offered them ten per cent a month, but there was none to get."

"You've got a pair of grey horses belonging to Dyer, and we want them." Indeed, Pat Dyer would later be identified as a member—presumably the instigating member—of this troublemaking group.

"You have no right to take them now," said an intimidated Winchell, who grasped at a way to lure the intruders from his bedroom. "Ask my partner, and if he is willing, I don't care."

Dyer and his backers then went to Landgreber's house and beat on his door. While Landgreber found a pistol, his wife shouted that he was not home. The mob continued to call him out, and unwisely he opened the door. A shot rang out, and Landgreber collapsed in a spreading pool of blood. One of his children ran next door for help.

The community was outraged "by the foul murder of one of its best, most orderly and inoffensive citizens." On Monday, the day after the killing, Dr. F. W. Johnson assembled a coroner's jury at the murder site, and arrests were made. Mayor Luke Murrin called for a public meeting at city hall that afternoon. At three o'clock such "a vast body of citizens" had gathered that only one-fourth could crowd inside, so the mayor moved the meeting outdoors. Murrin, "in a few forcible remarks, ... appealed to the citizens to aid him in the enforcement of the laws." Several more civic leaders spoke, including "Dr. Johnson, who made a telling speech of some length." Resolutions were passed "expressing the sentiments of the meeting," and the *Leader* endorsed the criticisms of "the reign of ruffianism and terror." Declaring "that the reign of the 'vigies' is over," the *Leader* emphasized that Cheyenne's citizenry was ready to "stand up manfully" against the lawless element: "We have fought you, the people will fight you, and God will damn you."[28]

Vigilante executions and the explosive mood of the public finally served to moderate the worst depredations of Cheyenne's underworld. Furthermore, in 1868 the Union Pacific laid track at a record pace, and by August the end of the track was more than 200 miles west of Cheyenne. Many gamblers, saloonkeepers, and prostitutes left Cheyenne to follow the railroad, and there was a general population decline. A substantial core remained in the Magic City, however, including "a number of low doggery proprietors of hellish rum holes," complained the *Leader*. Such men still would "entice a customer within their dens, by the aid of an accomplice ... and serve out a glass of drugged liquor ... shove him into a convenient place ... and rob him at their leisure." Indeed, one month later, on the night of September 9, a citizen named Peter Mason was robbed of $500. And the next month the *Leader* issued another complaint: "Pistols are as numerous as men."[29]

Most criminal activities, however, were becoming small-scale. The city council had enacted ordinances against dance halls, bawdyhouses, and carrying firearms. On September 10, 1868, the *Leader* proudly announced that forty disreputable women had been fined five dollars and costs in the police court. On December 15 the *Leader* was pleased to report that the police had encountered no ordinance violations for several days. With a more subdued atmosphere enveloping Cheyenne, the police force was cut, and cut again, and the vigilantes had been inactive since the double lynching the previous March. Public opinion opposed further vigilante action, but the swift justice meted out by large numbers of vigilantes—and the possibility of future lynchings—surely served as a deterrent to many violent ruffians.[30]

Yet the lull in criminal—and vigilante—violence proved temporary. On December 19, 1868, Harry Powers was shot in the head by John Walters, alias "Blinkey Jack." Powers lingered for two weeks, but when he died his killer was confined at Fort Russell's guard house, as a safeguard against summary justice.[31]

Military custody proved no guarantee for safety for Dick Douglass, a notorious troublemaker who was arrested on February 11, 1869, for stealing eleven pack mules from the army. Although placed in the Fort Russell guard house, Douglass was deeply resented by the civilian employees at Camp Carlin, where the stolen mules had been stabled. On Monday, February 15, Douglass was taken to Camp Carlin for a lengthy interrogation. That evening he was on his way back to Fort Russell, accompanied only by two of Camp Carlin's civilian employees, when confronted "by about twenty-five disgruntled men" who brandished drawn revolvers. Douglass was spirited away into the darkness and then hanged from a telegraph pole with a rope like those "used for mule lariats." The next day a coroner's jury concluded that the hanging was committed "by parties un-known."[32]

It generally was recognized that the two dozen or so men who lynched Douglass were civilian employees at Camp Carlin. While they were not part of Cheyenne's earlier vigilante movement, they surely had been emboldened by the lynchings that already had taken place. By now vigilantes in Cheyenne had stepped aside in favor of authorized law officers and courts. Although the number of lynchings and victims would be exaggerated in future retellings, the vigilante movement reduced to dormancy in Cheyenne. But if the cessation of lynching and the general decline of lawlessness spread the impression that extralegal executions were occurrences of a rowdier past, a vicious double murder in 1883 would rekindle a spontaneous surge of vigilantism.

Meanwhile, Cheyenne's police force imposed order among the roisterers and criminals in the Magic City during 1869. On the night of March 16, for example, the "floor manager and a female artist of one of the dance halls" quarreled and shouted "pet names" at each other, but were arrested before the difficulty could escalate. Later the same evening a man named West tried to leave a saloon without paying his bill. When the bartender insisted that he pay up, West "drew a pistol, and cocking it said, here it is you --- of a -----." When West backed out the door, he was arrested by two alert policemen "who took him in irons to the calaboose," where he joined the foul-mouthed couple from the dance hall.[33]

On May 13, 1869, a drunken soldier, William Nelligan, tried to seize a pistol from behind a bar. Michael Cribbins struggled to retrieve a gun, but an accidental discharge killed Nelligan. The legal system proceeded promptly, and Cribbins soon was acquitted. Less than a month later, Emma Cleveland, "one of the fallen angels, who keeps a house of ill fame," strolled down Sixteenth Street after noon alongside another prostitute. They were followed at a distance by James McFatter, a sporting man who had clashed with Emma. Suddenly, she whirled around and triggered a pistol shot at McFatter. Missing McFatter and several bystanders, Emma retreated into a drug store and fired another wild round. McFatter came after her with a stool, but at this point they were arrested and hauled off to police court.[34]

In September a *Leader* editorial entitled "IMMORALITY IN CHEYENNE" railed against "the existence of harlotry and crime" and against "the unblushing and brazen displays of a demi monde" on the city streets. But peace officers remained alert and determined. Less than a week later, a soldier tried to rob a store but was immediately apprehended by a policeman and Ed Melanger, a "private night watchman" who had been Cheyenne's first city marshal. On the first night in October, at "a house of disreputable character on Ferguson Street," a drunken customer emptied his revolver. Although the only thing he hit was his own hand, the *Leader* was disgusted at yet another shooting fray. "If the police cannot suppress them ..., we think the vigilantes should call a meeting and 'spot' two or three of the worst characters that infest our city, and give them notice to leave town in half an hour or stretch a rope. When officials are too cowardly, or too cor-

Thomas Jefferson Carr, Wyoming's greatest nineteenth-century peace officer, established his family home in Cheyenne. (Courtesy Wyoming State Archives)

rupt, to suppress the crime order loving citizens must protect themselves and their families as best they can."[35]

This astonishing call for vigilantes, only a few months after the *Leader* editorialized against them, included a classic justification of extralegal justice. But there was no response from potential vigilantes for more than two months. On December 13, 1869, the *Leader* reported "a regular 'Schutzenfest'" downtown the previous night. "Pistols were discharged rapidly and some fifteen or twenty shots fired." The newspaper again suggested vigilante action, and notices were posted around town, "signed by the Vigilance or some other committee," ordering three troublemakers "to make themselves scarce in this locality." A week later a bold thief drove off with a wagon and team that had been parked in front of a place of business. A quick pursuit and arrest followed, but the *Leader* warned hopefully: "Such proceedings are very risky in a community where telegraph poles are so ready of access."[36]

The threat of vigilantes, however, was becoming empty. On New Year's Eve the notorious Keystone Dance Hall was the scene of a drunken shootout in which both adversaries were wounded. There was no vigilante response, and the *Leader* could only call for an end to carrying firearms in Cheyenne: "This practice encourages a false notion of honor, and discourages patience and moderation."[37] This sound advice would be largely ignored for years to come in Cheyenne.

The Magic City was relatively tame for the next several months. Not until November 1870, when there were three shootouts in two weeks, was there a reprise of Cheyenne's wild beginning. By that time, though, a singularly rugged lawman had pinned on a badge in Cheyenne. A big man sporting an auburn beard, Jeff Carr had come from the Colorado gold fields in October 1867. Born in 1842 in Pennsylvania, Thomas Jefferson Carr was a graduate of Iron Mountain College in Pittsburgh. Carr's degree in accounting and bookkeeping did not suit his restless, adventurous nature. Pneumonia cut short his Civil War service with the Quartermaster Department, and he was in Colorado looking for gold by 1864. One of the early settlers of Cheyenne, he went to work in S. F. Nuckolls's store on Seventeenth Street, then moved to Kountze Bros. Bank as a bookkeeper. During an 1868–69 sojourn as a bookkeeper at Fort Fetterman, Carr sent a drunken killer fleeing on horseback. Back in Cheyenne he was elected to the territorial legislature, then accepted a legislative appointment as sheriff of Laramie County. When a challenge was mounted based on the governor's power to appoint, Carr ran for sheriff in the fall of 1870. He won and immediately pinned on his first badge. Jeff Carr would serve three terms as sheriff, as well as stints as city marshal of Cheyenne, deputy U.S. marshal, U.S. marshal, superintendent of the Rocky Mountain Detective Agency, warden of the Territorial Penitentiary, and chief detective for the Union Pacific Railroad. Carr married and had three children, and for much of his career he made his home in Cheyenne. Tough and resourceful, Jeff Carr became a legendary Wyoming peace officer.[38]

Sheriff Carr was within earshot when gunfire broke out inside a "Chinese house of ill fame on Eddy Street" on the afternoon of November 10, 1870. Several soldiers were drinking and carousing when William Taylor shot a fellow member of the Ninth Infantry with his service revolver. Taylor fled on foot, but he was "overhauled by Sheriff Carr, and placed in irons." Sheriff Carr, who never hesitated to assume the role of city policeman, delivered Taylor to the guard house at Fort Russell. Carr was not near enough to help control two shootings a couple of weeks later. There were no fatalities, although an officer was shot in the leg while trying to wrestle a pistol away from a shootist.[39]

Sheriff Carr was on hand to supervise the first legal execution in Wyoming. On October 27, 1870, twenty-six-year-old John Boyer shot and killed two men at a dive near Fort Laramie. Tried and convicted of murder, Boyer was sentenced to hang in Cheyenne on April 21, 1871. There already had been executions by hanging in Cheyenne and elsewhere in Wyoming Territory, but none were legal. Rather than hold the hanging outdoors before a vast crowd, Sheriff Carr selected an adobe building near the jail as the execution site. There was room inside for only a dozen or so witnesses: the sheriff chose six, and Boyer picked six. Special policemen were hired to help other officers control the expected crowd outside. Because the ceiling of the adobe would not accommodate a standard gallows, a low scaffold was erected above a trap door leading into the cellar.[40]

On Friday, April 21, a large crowd gathered outside the adobe, "and at times became very noisy and boisterous." One unruly onlooker was walloped over the head by a special policeman with the barrel of his revolver. About fifteen minutes after noon, newspaperman and Rev. J. D. Davis were ushered to Boyer's cell. The condemned man, half Indian, stated that he was going to the "happy hunting ground" and was eager to meet his father and brothers there. "Tell my mother I died brave, without a whimper."

At half past twelve Boyer, clad in a fresh white shirt, was taken from the jail to the execution building. Everyone jostled for a look at the prisoner before he dis-

Jeff Carr—Great American

By 1876 Thomas Jefferson Carr had served as a peace officer for more than a quarter of a century, and he was a legend in Cheyenne. He had worked variously as city marshal, Laramie County sheriff, U.S. marshal, Union Pacific detective, and in other law enforcement positions. The formidable lawman was widely known for rough treatment of troublemakers, and his volatility with criminals gained him the nickname "Red Cloud."

Around Cheyenne it was agreed that Jeff Carr was Wyoming's most effective law officer, and even children understood the general respect accorded the rugged symbol of authority. On Friday, February 21, 1896, the *Leader* reported that the day before, in one of Cheyenne's elementary schools, a teacher asked a little girl to name three great men besides George Washington. The young student listed General Grant, Abraham Lincoln—and T. Jeff Carr—and "the pupil was ordered to take her place at the head of the class."

appeared inside. With his arms bound, Boyer was seated "in perfect composure" on the scaffold. Sheriff Carr read the death sentence, then asked Boyer to speak. The condemned man stated his love for the Great Spirit and reiterated his lack of fear. "Look at me," said Boyer. "I no cry; I no woman; I man; I die brave."

Reverend Davis "offered a fervent prayer" before the rope was placed around Boyer's neck and a black cap dropped over his head. A moment later Boyer plunged into the cellar. His neck was broken, and within three minutes he was cut free and placed in a coffin, to be buried in the City Cemetery. Sheriff Carr was praised for the "excellent" arrangements. Three years later he would conduct another legal hanging in Cheyenne with equal skill.

During the first year or so of its existence, Cheyenne became notorious for a wild nightlife centered around brothels and saloons and punctuated by frequent shootings and harsh vigilante justice. Gradually, shootings became far less frequent, often nothing more than the harmless discharge of a pistol late at night, and vigilante hangings soon gave way to prison terms or legal executions as peace officers and courts were afforded growing public support. But once acquired, Cheyenne's reputation for unrestrained drinking-gambling-whoring-gunplay became a standard image that proved almost impossible to reverse.

4

Urban Pioneers

ountain men, gold prospectors, farmers in covered wagons, and cowboys riding an open range were not the only pioneers in the West.
Indeed, the settlement of each successive frontier was concluded by
urban pioneers who created towns in a wilderness. Like fur trappers, prospectors,
and land-hungry farmers and ranchers, urban pioneers sought opportunity in an
undeveloped West while relishing the adventure of a new land.

"The attitudes of urban pioneers differed from those of eastern city dwellers,"
stated frontier historian Ray Allen Billington. "Most were restless seekers after
wealth who . . . deliberately selected a promising frontier community as the site of
their next experiment in fortune making. There they built a mill, opened a general
store, set up a portable printing press, or hung out a shingle as a lawyer
or . . . teacher, confident that the town's rapid growth would bring them affluence
and social prominence. When they guessed right and the village did evolve into
a city they usually stayed on as prosperous businessmen or community leaders. . . . Their mobility and restlessness distinguished them from the more stable
souls who filled the eastern cities."[1]

Of course, Cheyenne was never a village. The Magic City of the Plains became
a bustling, raucous frontier city almost overnight. The urban pioneers who tried
their luck in Cheyenne would not have to move on to a more promising western
community. The risk-taking entrepreneurs who established a variety of businesses in Cheyenne—along with lawyers, doctors, editors, teachers, preachers,
and their wives, who shaped the culture of the Magic City—would enjoy prosperity and local prominence. The ablest of Cheyenne's urban pioneers would achieve
great wealth and national importance.

Leading businessmen and professionals of Cheyenne were friends who worked closely together to improve their community. They understood that by contributing time and effort to grow their city, they were likely to increase their personal positions and fortunes. Serving together on boards and commissions, they built schools and churches, public utilities, and a first-class opera house. They organized public events and fraternal groups, while their wives formed clubs and conducted fairs in support of churches and other causes. They socialized together, at weddings and at masquerade balls, and, attired in full evening dress, at opera house performances. This close-knit group also produced political leaders: mayors, city councilmen, legislators, territorial delegates to Congress. Territorial governors were outsiders appointed by the president, but eventually the governorship went to a notable member of Cheyenne's leadership clique. And when Wyoming attained statehood, Cheyenne's two most prominent leaders became the new state's first U.S. senators.

Most of the future leaders who arrived during Cheyenne's first year or two were young, frequently in their mid-twenties. Indeed, most frontiersmen, including urban pioneers, were young, filled with energy, ambition, and optimism. Cheyenne's urban pioneers were progressive and confident in the future of their city. Most were from northeastern states, and many were Union veterans of the Civil War.

W. W. Corlett, for example, was a twenty-five-year-old Union veteran when he arrived in Cheyenne on August 20, 1867. Born in Concord, Ohio, he grew up working on his family's farm, attending rural schools during the winters. At the age of seventeen he began teaching in Concord, simultaneously taking courses at the Collegiate Institute of Willoughby, Ohio. During the Civil War, Corlett volunteered for service with Ohio infantry and artillery units. Although he became a Confederate prisoner of war following a general surrender at Harpers Ferry, Corlett returned to uniform after being paroled. After the war he enrolled in the school of law at the University of Michigan in Ann Arbor, then graduated in July 1866 from the Ohio Union Law College of Cleveland.[2]

A year later, restless and ambitious for the opportunities available in the West, Corlett ventured to Denver. There he learned about the railroad boomtown to the north, and within weeks of its founding he arrived in the ramshackle Magic City. Corlett and charter citizen J. R. Whitehead were mutually impressed and formed the legal firm of Whitehead & Corlett. A Republican, the able Corlett was regularly tapped for public service: as Cheyenne postmaster, as Laramie County prosecuting attorney, as a member of the legislature, and, from 1877 to 1879, as Wyoming's delegate to Congress. Meanwhile, on the first day of 1873 he married an Iowa girl. Minerva Corlett would become an active member of Cheyenne society. Corlett was a Mason and a member of the G.A.R., he helped found Cheyenne's Knights of Pythias lodge, and he and his family (a son, Willie, was born in 1855) belonged to St. Mark's Episcopal Church. Between his public and social responsibilities, Corlett made time for his law practice with unrelenting work habits that caused his countless friends to worry about his health.

"R. S. Van Tassell was about the youngest man in business in Cheyenne,"

W. W. Corlett, Union veteran and hard-working attorney, settled in Cheyenne in 1867 and immediately became a community leader. (Courtesy Wyoming State Archives)

reminisced George Lemmon, who came to Cheyenne as a twelve-year-old boy with his family late in 1867. Lemmon also noted Van Tassell's swift black horse. A superb horseman, Van Tassell rode the streets of Cheyenne for more than half a century astride a succession of black saddle horses named Crystal. He cut a fine figure in the saddle, and on foot he had the erect bearing of a skillful rider. Born in New York State of Dutch heritage, Renessalaer Schuyler Van Tassell restlessly went west as a teenager. By 1866 the young adventurer had penetrated Wyoming, on more than one occasion trading shots with war parties. Van Tassell and two other hardy frontiersmen established a wilderness camp west of the future town site of Cheyenne, cutting ties for the projected route of the Union Pacific. Twenty-two when Cheyenne was founded, Van Tassell promptly cast his lot with the raw boomtown. He operated a small livery stable, engaged in freighting, and secured a contract to carry mail. Soon Van Tassell began freighting for James A. Moore, a connection which would vault him to wealth and prominence.[3]

During 1860–61 Moore was one of the daring young men who captured the country's imagination as a Pony Express rider. He once covered 280 miles in twenty-two hours, an epic ride which earned him a gold watch and a certificate of commendation. In early Cheyenne he became a partner in the Great Western Corral, which dominated the northwestern edge of town. With space for 200 wagons and 250 horses and mules, the Great Western served as a terminal for freighters and stagecoaches and as a sale barn for horses and other livestock. Moore also became one of Wyoming's first big ranchers, with herds totaling 9,000 head of cattle. He lived with his wife and two children in a substantial home he built on Ferguson Street.[4] In 1873 Moore died from injuries sustained in a fall, and R. S. Van Tassell soon won the affections—and property— of the widowed Mary Moore. Van Tassell adroitly multiplied his wealth, expanding his ranching operations, owning and running Cheyenne's stockyards, and eventually investing in a great many of the Magic City's businesses. After Mary Moore Van Tassell died of tuberculosis in 1883, her widower twice more ventured

R.S. Van Tassell made his home in Cheyenne as a young man, then stayed to earn a fortune in the livestock business. A superb horseman, he was a familiar sight on the streets of Cheyenne for decades. (Courtesy Wyoming State Archives)

into marriage, each time to younger and younger brides. In addition to enlivening Cheyenne's social scene, Van Tassell would buttress the business community throughout a long and colorful lifetime.

Lawrence R. Bresnahan, a seventeen-year-old Irish immigrant, established a meat market in Cheyenne in November 1867 and went on to serve five terms as mayor. At the age of seven, Lawrence had been brought by his widowed mother to the United States, settling in Phelps, New York. When he was sixteen, Lawrence and a friend adventurously followed the "Pacific Railroad" to the west. At Julesburg, Lawrence found a job in a meat market. When the owners realized that Julesburg would wane as the tracks moved westward, they sold out to their young employee. Bresnahan soon took his business to Hell on Wheels Cheyenne, and later built up a ranch near town to provide his own beef. Now referred to as "L. R.," Bresnahan was first elected mayor in 1876, when he was just twenty-six and Cheyenne was entering a major boom period. Mayor Bresnahan expanded the boundaries of his growing city, provided waterworks and other infrastructure, and was instrumental in building the capitol. Another teenaged Irish immigrant, nineteen-year-old Tim Dyer, also went into business in 1867. He bought a little restaurant on Pioneer Avenue, then built the Dyer Hotel on the property. For the rest of his long life Dyer was a prosperous Cheyenne businessman, raising a large family, serving four terms as a county commissioner, and actively participating in the Masonic Lodge.[5]

At the opposite end of the age spectrum from these teenagers was John Slaughter, fifty-eight when he moved to Cheyenne from Colorado in 1867. Shortly after his arrival he was appointed justice of the peace, and until his death at the age of ninety-four he would be known as Judge Slaughter. He served as territorial librarian and as state librarian and, by virtue of these positions, as ex-officio superintendent of public instruction. Gen. Joseph W. Fisher was fifty-six when he arrived at Cheyenne in 1871 as a justice of the territorial court. A native of Pennsylvania, Fisher became a lawyer and member of the state legislature, and during the Civil War he won promotions from captain to brigadier general in the Union army. Within a matter of months of arriving in Wyoming, Judge Fisher was promoted to chief justice, a position he held for eight years. Later he spent nine years as United States commissioner in Cheyenne, while practicing as one of the city's most prominent attorneys. Judge and Mrs. Fisher were mainstays of Cheyenne society for three decades.[6]

Also conspicuous in society circles were Mr. and Mrs. Henry G. Hay. Hay moved to Cheyenne in 1869 as a surveyor. He entered ranching, helped to found and served as president of the Stock Growers National Bank, and signed the Wyoming State Constitution. Erasmus Nagle was a native of Ohio who operated a lumber business in the Colorado gold fields until 1868, when he saw opportunity in Cheyenne. Prospering in business, Nagle was dubbed the "Merchant King of Wyoming."[7]

Another successful merchant was Amasa R. Converse, who reached Cheyenne in 1867 at the age of twenty-five. As his mercantile business grew, Converse engaged in ranching on a large scale, eventually registering twenty-eight brands. He became president of the First National Bank, which he helped organize. Indeed, for the 1886 city directory Mrs. Converse proudly identified herself as "Capitalist." A.R. Converse twice was appointed territorial treasurer, and Converse County was named in his honor.[8]

Urban pioneer Erasmus Nagle, who formed the Union Mercantile Company and made a fortune in the wholesale grocery business. Nagle erected one of Cheyenne's first fine brick homes, on Seventeenth, then built an even grander residence beside it. (Courtesy Wyoming State Archives)

After a few months in Cheyenne, the young merchant decided that he needed help to turn the corner to prosperity. Converse contacted a lifelong friend from his hometown, Hinsdale, Massachusetts. Although Francis E. Warren was two years his junior, Converse was impressed with his ability and character. Throughout Warren's life people who met him were impressed with his ability and character—a character that had been shaped on his father's hardscrabble farm. Joseph Warren worked his son so relentlessly that neighbors worried aloud about the boy's health. "Better die rather than to be no account," came the stern reply.

Francis was sent to school at three so that his mother could concentrate on younger children. When he was eight, because he was not paid anything for his farm chores, his mother urged the boy "to do something for himself." When he earned thirteen cents—at a penny a day—picking up nails at the construction site of the Baptist Church, Cynthia Warren told her son to "put up" the tiny sum. The barefoot boy (his wardrobe consisted of "a little pair of blue trousers, a little calico jacket upon which the trousers were buttoned and upon his head a little five-cent chip hat") spent his spare time working for neighbors: he drove a flock of sheep twenty miles for six cents; he cleaned out cellars for ten cents; cleaned a well for fifteen cents; dug potatoes one fall and earned $3.66.

Soon after his mother died, when he was twelve, Francis said to his father, "Let me go and earn a living for myself."[9] An unsentimental Joseph Warren warily consented. "Here is your home; come any time, but don't attempt to eat the apple and give me the core. If you are sick or wanting, come; but be prepared to work if you come strong."[10]

The smart, industrious lad hired on at a dairy farm, and by the time he was seventeen he was manager. But when the Civil War erupted, he enlisted in the 49th Massachusetts Infantry. When he was nearly fifty, speaking in the third person, Warren reflected on his introduction to combat: "In the first engagement he could not tell one hand from the other. He could not tell his name. His first impulse was to run to the rear, but he said he could not run away from himself and he would not be a coward."[11]

The young soldier conquered his fear. On May 27, 1863, by then a tested veteran, Warren volunteered to help prepare the ground for an assault against Port Hudson. Many members of the party were killed, and Corporal Warren suffered a scalp wound. Three decades later he received a Congressional Medal of Honor for his heroism. Mustered out of his unit, Warren became captain of a militia company in Massachusetts by war's end. Saving his pay, he accumulated $450 during the war.[12]

Warren again was hired as a farm manager, but like many young veterans he was restless and sensed opportunity in the West. Warren found work as foreman of a construction crew on the Rock Island Railroad, laying track out of Des Moines, Iowa. Soon, however, a letter reached him from A. R. Converse, and Warren left the Rock Island for Cheyenne in May 1868.

"Cheyenne was then a city of shanties and tents, camps and covered wagons," he reminisced nearly half a century later. "The people were migratory. The railroad having built further on ..., the prevailing idea seemed to be, that in six

Francis Emroy Warren, ambitious and hard-working, came to Cheyenne in 1868 and wrote to his future bride that he was staying because he was "doing well"—a massive understatement. (Courtesy Wyoming State Archives)

months hardly a stake would be left to mark the location of Cheyenne." Optimistic and progressive by nature, Warren did not share the general discouragement, but his new home was undeniably raw.[13]

"There was then not a graded street, ditch, sewer or crossing in the town— nothing but a lot of tents and shanties, dropped down or thrown together on the bare prairie, covering space enough, perhaps, to make a large city," he said.[14]

Warren had an impressive physique that radiated energy and strength. His face was open and handsome, with a sweeping moustache and neatly combed hair. Always well dressed, he was polite and well-spoken. The customers he encountered were impressed. Indeed, the young clerk spent almost all of his time in the Converse furniture store. In addition to the long hours that the firm conducted business, Warren slept in the store, fashioning a bunk that slipped beneath a counter. With typical frugality, he washed his own socks and underwear, saving the twenty-five cents per garment charged by laundresses.

By 1871 Warren had accumulated enough capital to buy half of the business, which became Converse & Warren. Six years later, Warren bought out Converse, naming his firm F. E. Warren & Company. Warren's formidable commercial gifts produced great wealth, and he expanded his enterprises in many directions. He acquired real estate and built numerous business structures, including his "Emporium," one of the most impressive and innovative commercial buildings in the West. Soon he was collecting $30,000 annually in rents alone. And he built a ranching empire: the Warren Livestock Company held property across much of Wyoming, as well as in Colorado and Nebraska. On his ranches Warren ran cattle, horses, and vast numbers of sheep (he was called "the greatest shepherd since Abraham"). It was widely speculated that during tax assessment periods in Wyoming he moved most of his livestock onto Colorado lands, then brought them back to Wyoming when Colorado assessors came around.

Warren's peers demanded his leadership talents for public office, and he readily acquiesced. He was confident that he could accomplish considerable improvements for Cheyenne and Wyoming, while also benefiting his own interests. A staunch Republican who organized and financially supported the party in

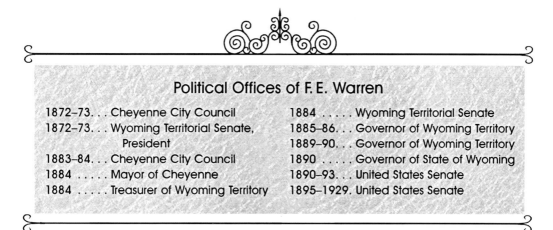

Political Offices of F. E. Warren

1872–73. . . Cheyenne City Council	1884 . . . . . Wyoming Territorial Senate
1872–73. . . Wyoming Territorial Senate, President	1885–86. . . Governor of Wyoming Territory
	1889–90. . . Governor of Wyoming Territory
1883–84. . . Cheyenne City Council	1890 . . . . . Governor of State of Wyoming
1884 . . . . . Mayor of Cheyenne	1890–93. . . United States Senate
1884 . . . . . Treasurer of Wyoming Territory	1895–1929. United States Senate

Wyoming, Warren served at various times as city alderman, mayor, treasurer of Wyoming Territory, president of the Territory's upper house, territorial governor (twice), first governor of the state of Wyoming, and United States senator — for thirty-seven years. His political gifts proved as great as his commercial talents, and he provided a constant flow of public improvements and benefits from his succession of positions. Furthermore, he was a generous benefactor for Cheyenne, providing funds and leadership for a series of institutions in the Magic City.[15]

At the age of twenty-eight, following a long courtship by correspondence, Warren returned to Massachusetts to marry Helen Maria Smith, who was one year his junior. Gracious, refined, and widely loved, she was as effective a social leader as her husband was in business and politics. First Lady of Wyoming and of Cheyenne, Helen Warren proved just as comfortable in Washington circles — an asset and ally to her prominent husband.[16]

Francis and Helen did not have children for nearly a decade after their marriage, but there was always a lot of family around. His spinster sister and Helen's widowed father shared their Cheyenne home, and her brother and his brother worked for the Warren Livestock Company. In 1880 Helen Frances was born, and Frederick Emroy came along four years later. "Frankie" and "Fred" enjoyed every material and educational advantage, from Shetland ponies to Wellesley and Harvard.

Francis E. Warren had arrived at Cheyenne when it was a boomtown in decline. But he made the frontier community his home, and for the next six decades Warren would do more than any single individual to develop and modernize Wyoming's capital. He found in Cheyenne an ideal arena for his multiple talents, and in the Magic City he would attain wealth and prominence, domestic happiness, and high position. Cheyenne found in Warren a business and civic leader of exceptional ability, a politician who would use his position to funnel a stream of federal largesse into Wyoming and its capital. Cheyenne and F. E. Warren would complement each other in a mutual rise to prosperity and prominence. With his diverse contributions and longevity of service, Warren would stand foremost among a remarkable group of urban pioneers who would advance their fortunes and those of their adopted city.

Close behind Warren in business, civic, and political accomplishment was Joseph M. Carey. A year younger than Warren, Carey was born in 1845 in Delaware and moved to Wyoming Territory one year later than Warren. After attending Union College in Schenectady, New York, he enrolled in the University of Pennsylvania law school, simultaneously reading law in the office of Philadelphia attorneys. Carey began speaking for Republican candidates before he could vote, and in 1869 President Grant appointed him the first United States attorney in newly created Wyoming Territory. Arriving in May, the young lawyer opened an office in Cheyenne for private practice, and in 1872, at the age of twenty-seven, he was appointed by President Grant an associate justice of Wyoming's Supreme Court. Although he held an assortment of high offices in future years, Carey always would be referred to as "Judge."

Young Joseph M. Carey arrived in Cheyenne in 1869 as Wyoming Territory's first U.S. attorney. Appointees from the East were generally resented in Wyoming as opportunistic "carpetbaggers" or "interlopers." But Carey stayed to become one of the most distinguished citizens of Cheyenne and Wyoming. (Courtesy Wyoming State Archives)

In 1876, with Cheyenne booming, Judge Carey resigned and closed his law office in order to take full advantage of business opportunities. He already had begun a large ranching enterprise, and was a founding member of the Wyoming Stock Growers' Association. Actively engaging in real estate, he built a series of commercial "blocks" in downtown Cheyenne and was one of three founders of the Stock Growers National Bank. As his wealth grew, he attracted his brothers, R. Davis Carey and Dr. John F. Carey, into business with him, and Dr. Carey moved to Cheyenne and opened a medical practice.[17]

In 1877 Joseph Carey married twenty-one-year-old Louisa "Lulu" David, whose father had moved the family to Cheyenne from Iowa after his appointment as Wyoming's territorial surveyor. A pretty, charming brunette, Louisa was an engaging conversationalist and a firm believer in women's suffrage. She eagerly embraced the role of hostess as the wife of a man of affairs. The Carey mansion — a three-story brick Victorian that stood on a street eventually renamed Carey Avenue — became a social center of Cheyenne, and would be used by its owner as the governor's mansion. The mansion also was home to two boys, the oldest of whom would follow his father as governor and senator.[18]

Carey was elected to the first of three consecutive terms as mayor in 1880, and from 1883 to 1887 he served as president of the politically powerful Wyoming Stock Growers' Association. In 1884 he won election to the first of three straight terms as territorial delegate to Congress. As congressional delegate, Carey wrote the bill which provided Wyoming's admission to statehood, and he was instrumental in persuading his colleagues to pass the bill. Then Carey was elected as the first senator from Wyoming, and years later he capped an impressive political career by winning a four-year term as governor. For two decades, until a personal rift with Wyoming's most skilled and influential politician cost him his Senate seat, Carey worked so closely with F. E. Warren that the powerful duo was referred to as "Me and F. E."

Certainly "Me and F. E.," along with their other Cheyenne friends and associates — and their wives — provided the major impetus and direction for the growing frontier community. As N. A. Baker observed in the *Leader* after meeting newly arrived Joseph Carey for the first time: "He is apparently one of those enterprising young men who almost invariably prove the most valuable citizens of new communities like this, where they advance with the same rapidity as invariably attends the progress of the Western Territories."[19] Baker's assessment was on target for Carey and Cheyenne. It would have applied just as accurately to F. E. Warren, R. S. Van Tassell, A. R. Converse, Henry G. Hay, M. E. Post, Erasmus Nagle, and the other "enterprising young men" who would form the leadership corps of the Magic City. These ambitious and capable urban pioneers came to Cheyenne when it was a raw frontier town, put down deep roots, then fashioned a truly Magic City on the widespread plains of Wyoming.

5

After the Boom

Cheyenne's urban pioneers quickly began establishing schools and churches and civic organizations. Even though the population of Cheyenne declined after the winter of 1867–68, these institutions grew in size and number.

"I see children in every street and alley," declared N. A. Baker in the *Leader*, calling for a public school when Cheyenne was only three months old. Although Cheyenne's population was predominantly male, with several thousand people in the boomtown, even the small minority of women and children added up to enough pupils for a school. With the *Leader* calling for a school, in part to take Cheyenne's children away from the streets and alleys, the provisional city government quickly responded. A three-man School Committee was appointed, including J. R. Whitehead and R. E. Talpey. By mid-November a site had been selected on Nineteenth Street and plans drawn for a frame school measuring 24 by 40 feet, with a twelve-foot ceiling. Public-spirited citizens contributed more than $1,300 toward the cost of the school.[1]

As with every other building in town, construction was rapid. On Sunday evening, January 5, 1868, a large crowd braved temperatures which dropped to 23 degrees below zero to attend the dedication of Wyoming's first school. Dr. D. W. Scott opened with a prayer, Dr. George H. Russell and W. W. Corlett offered addresses, and Rev. G. S. Allen provided a benediction. The following day, at the hearing of Jack Williams, charged with murdering his stepson, the crowd was so large that proceedings were moved to the new school. The "mass of congregated humanity" buckled the floor, and although "no bones were broken," repairs had to be made. The school would not yet be opened to students.

Construction costs had totaled $2,235, while only $1,335 was raised by contributions. The builders held a lien on the school and would not allow it to be used "until it is cleared." When Cheyenne's city charter went into effect at the end of January 1868, the duly elected officials issued $900 in bonds (bearing five percent interest per month) to pay off the school indebtedness.[2]

The new school board hired as principal and teacher M. A. Arnold, whose wife helped with teaching, but after several weeks the couple resigned. J. H. "Doc" Hayford, editor of the *Rocky Mountain Star*, agreed to take over the school. Hayford was buried under an avalanche of "112 scholars," however, and quit within a few days. Aware that the facility was bursting at the seams, in March 1868 the school board decided to erect "a large addition" onto their new building. S. J. Scriber replaced Hayford as principal, and later a Miss Glenn was engaged as "assistant teacher." Students had to pay $1.50 to offset expenses.[3]

With the new public school scrambling to accommodate well over one hundred pupils, there was room for private schools. On Monday, January 13, 1868, a "Select School" taught by Miss Joanna Kelley opened at her parents' residence on O'Neill Street. Arriving that same month to establish an Episcopalian church, Rev. Joseph W. Cook quickly recognized the need for a parish school. There were reports that some parents were "dissatisfied" with the overcrowded public school, "and there are some families who do not send their children at all." Reverend Cook was assured that he could start a church-affiliated school "at once with 25 or 30 scholars." Although Cook had no building even for worship services or Sunday school, a parochial school remained a primary goal. Soon after completing his sanctuary, Reverend Cook wrote to his bishop, on September 7, 1868: "today I started my parish school, on faith." He rented a building for twenty dollars a month and engaged a young woman as teacher. The school opened with nineteen students, and by the end of the year the number had doubled.[4]

At the same time that schools were being established in Cheyenne, progressive citizens were also organizing churches. The first sermon in Cheyenne was preached by an itinerant Baptist minister on Sunday, September 22, 1867, but a decade would pass before a Baptist congregation was formed. One week after the Baptist sermon, a traveling Methodist preacher, Rev. W. W. Baldwin, conducted a service at the city hall. Following the service, Dr. D. W. Scott, a Cheyenne physician and Methodist lay preacher, organized Wyoming's first congregation and Sunday school. There were only nine charter members of the Methodist church, but the congregation swelled rapidly. Dr. Scott, aided by another lay preacher, Rev. G. S. Allen, conducted weekly worship services at seven in the evening; Sunday school began at two in the afternoon. In January 1868 the Methodists held a weeklong revival, then soon transferred their Sunday activities from city hall to the new school building. Scott and his wife moved on after a year, and Allen left Cheyenne after another year, late in 1869. Dr. Scott was replaced by Rev. Andrew J. Cather, who secured the donation of two lots, at the northeastern corner of Eighteenth and Ransom, from the Union Pacific. On a trip back East, Reverend Cather raised another $1,110 toward the construction of a sanctuary. Although Cather soon departed Cheyenne for good, fundraising efforts continued, including church fairs. These fairs, which were utilized by every congregation in Cheyenne, as well as by many other organizations, became a feature of the local social scene for decades. Lasting from one to several days and conducted by ladies of the congregation, the fairs offered for sale food and items sewn and otherwise made by hand. The Methodist ladies raised hundreds of dollars, and their church was completed in September 1870. The frame structure seated 200 and featured a tall steeple.[5]

Although the Methodists organized Cheyenne's first congregation, four other denominations put up church buildings before the Methodist sanctuary was dedicated. Father William Kelly organized Catholics in Cheyenne late in 1867. Father Kelly ministered to Union Pacific (UP) construction crews during the week, then conducted services in Cheyenne on Sundays. By June 1868 Catholics were meeting in their own chapel, which had been partially prefabricated in Omaha and shipped on the UP. St. Mary's first building was Cheyenne's northernmost structure, at the northwest corner of Twenty-first and O'Neill.[6]

The second church erected was Episcopalian, engineered by Rev. Joseph W. Cook. The thirty-one-year-old missionary arrived in January 1868, at the height of

Charming Winter Days

During Cheyenne's first winter, a large number of citizens ignored the sub-zero temperatures to attend dedication festivities for the new school. Cheyenne inhabitants adapted quickly to the challenging weather of a city built on a wind-swept plain beside a towering mountain range.

"The air was quite cold, but I found that I did not suffer from it in the least, but that on the contrary it was delightful." These remarks were written a few days after the school dedication by one of Cheyenne's most determined urban pioneers, Rev. Joseph W. Cook. Two days later, on January 17, 1868, Reverend Cook again wrote enthusiastically in his diary about the weather, despite snow and ice: "One of the most charming winter days I ever experienced." Repeatedly Cook wrote about the "charming" days. "The climate is magnificent," he stated, even though at times "the wind made it unpleasant to be out." Indeed, he conceded that the "very terrible winds" some-

times reduced the crowds at his services. Within a few months he learned that summer weather in Cheyenne, while brief, could be withering. "Almost sick from the heat," he recorded on July 1, 1868. (Cook, *Diary and Letters*, 8, 13, 14, 15, 37, 40, 49, 77)

On October 10, 1867, the *Leader* reported about three days of hard winds, which "increased almost to a hurricane." Three weeks later, when Frenchman Louis Simonin arrived in boomtown Cheyenne, "we encountered a regular cyclone, as though in mid-ocean." The wind "blew with frightful violence, lifting the gritty sand in thick clouds from the prairie." A snowstorm "filled the calaboose with snow," reported the *Leader* on February 13, 1868. Prisoners had to be moved to city hall, and trains bound for Cheyenne were stalled until hundreds of workmen could clear the tracks. Turbulent weather promised to be a sometimes unwelcome factor in the life of the Magic City.

Cheyenne's Hell on Wheels excitement. Even though the recently ordained minister was horrified at the wide-open depravity, he recognized a spiritual opportunity: "If there ever was a place which needed a standard lifted up against the enemy, it is here."

Cook worked diligently at his calling, visiting the sick and grief-stricken, conducting funerals and weddings, organizing religious services for Cheyenne's African-Americans in a private home, and constantly working to develop his congregation and erect a church. Unable to find suitable quarters in the crowded boomtown, Reverend Cook stayed at the fort, boarding with various officers and, for a time, the post chaplain and his wife. Post Chaplain E. B. Tuttle from Illinois was an Episcopalian, like Cook, and he often prevailed upon his civilian counterpart to substitute for him. Tuttle preached to as many as 200 worshipers in the assembly hall at the fort, although he was not an accomplished speaker. "The sermon, alas!" critiqued Cook. "Rambled all over creation, and I failed utterly to see the point he was driving at." When Tuttle returned with his wife to Illinois, Cook temporarily assumed his duties, a role that Cheyenne ministers would share whenever a post chaplain was not on duty.

Reverend Cook conducted his first services in town on Sunday, January 19, 1868, only a few days after his arrival. "There were about 75 persons present yesterday, and they entered heartily into the services," he reported to his bishop. "The singing I conducted myself," he said, and the thirty prayer books he had brought were not enough. Since the Methodists had reserved the school for Sunday afternoon and evening, Episcopalians worshiped there in the morning. A week later a meeting of interested congregants elected a seven-man vestry, subscribed money toward a building and Cook's salary, and officially named their parish St. Mark's Church, after St. Mark's in Philadelphia, which had pledged $1,000 to their sister church on the frontier. The UP donated two lots at Nineteenth and Dodge, but this location was on the outskirts of town, and Cook persuaded UP officials to change the donation to "Eighteenth and Ferguson, one square from postoffice." Attendance rapidly grew, and in April Cook organized a choir and a Sunday school. Within a few months the "scholars" in his Sunday school increased from eighteen to seventy-five. Cook raised more than $5,500, allowing the congregation to pay nearly $4,000 in construction costs and still remain free of debt. Reverend Cook and several members held down expenses by donating their labor, and a carpenter crafted a handsome pair of alms basins as a contribution.[7]

The first St. Mark's was dedicated on Sunday, August 23, 1868, with a crowd of 300 squeezing into a frame building designed to seat 200. There was a portable pipe organ, and a 600-pound bell had been sent by St. Mark's in Philadelphia. The next year Cook supervised the construction of a rectory, assigning some of the rooms to the parish school.

Having led St. Mark's to a strong start, Reverend Cook resigned in January 1870 to become a missionary among the Sioux in Dakota Territory, where he would spend the rest of his life. By the time he left, there were two other churches in Cheyenne. On Saturday evening, June 12, 1869, the Congregational Church was organized by thirteen members, led by Rev. J. D. Davis. Davis, who had arrived only a week earlier, had served as a Union colonel during the Civil War. Following his recent graduation from the Chicago Theological Seminary, Reverend Davis requested a post in the "toughest town west of the Mississippi." Sent to Cheyenne, the former combat officer soon decided "it needed more courage to plant the Gospel here than it did to hold up the old flag in battle." The Reverend Colonel Davis persevered, raising $1,500 toward a sanctuary within a month. He traveled to Chicago, returning in September with lumber, paint, an organ, Sunday school literature—and a bride. The Union Pacific made their customary donation of two lots, on the northwest corner of Nineteenth and Hill. Construction took only three months, at a cost of $1,409.50, and dedication services were held on Sunday, December 19, 1869. Next, Rev. and Mrs. Davis built a parsonage on church property, providing virtually all of the labor themselves, then started a Sunday school with forty-five participants.[8]

The Presbyterian church developed simultaneously with the Congregationalists. In May 1869 Rev. John L. Gage arrived in Cheyenne as a Presbyterian missionary, spending three months organizing a congregation. The first permanent pastor was Rev. W. G. Kephart, who launched a building program with substantial support from Rutgers Church of New York City. A frame church on the northwestern corner of Eighteenth and Eddy, and across the street from the Episcopalian church, was dedicated on Sunday, July 17, 1870.[9]

"Another new church is going up in our city," reported the *Leader*, as the Presbyterians began their sanctuary. "Once our dance-houses outnumbered our churches, but now, the former have all disappeared and we are building churches." The sporting girls certainly had not disappeared from Cheyenne, but the presence of five churches undeniably produced a calming effect, especially on Sundays. "To the surprise of myself and many others the city was remarkably quiet yesterday," reported Rev. Joseph Cook to his bishop on January 20, 1868, when Cheyenne was at the height of its Hell on Wheels turbulence. "Many of the shops were closed, and numbers of persons were to be seen on the streets who had seemingly made an effort to recall some of the associations of Sunday and civilization by changing their clothes and tidying up, and trying to enjoy a little rest from the turmoil and excitement of the week." The minister also was pleased that "the band which by day and night calls multitudes of poor simple souls to the great gambling 'Hall' opposite paid respects to the Lord's Day also."[10]

Another bold sound also took an unaccustomed break during the Sabbath. "The hurdy-gurdy at the 'Museum' ceased its daily and nightly groaning and grinding, to the great relief of the nerves of many," wrote Reverend Cook.[11] The Museum was a remarkable establishment created by James McDaniel, who labeled himself the "Barnum of the West" and "Professor McDaniel." The entertainment complex created by McDaniel provided a radically different menu of activities than those offered by Cheyenne's five churches.

Despite his small stature, McDaniel pulsated with energy and high spirits. The *Leader* often called him "the irrepressible Mac." Mac laughed easily and met everyone with a hearty greeting and an "athletic handshake." After establishing

The imaginative James McDaniel erected the most successful saloon and variety theater in early Cheyenne. His free museum was a unique attraction, and McDaniel constantly added to the display exhibits. (From early town plat, author's collection)

the Olympic Theatre in bustling Denver, he soon recognized opportunity in the new railroad town to the north. Leaving a manager in charge of the Olympic, McDaniel moved to Cheyenne in 1867 and acquired lots on Eddy between Sixteenth and Seventeenth. By the end of October McDaniel opened one of Cheyenne's first variety theaters, a combination saloon and performance hall and museum. The innovative impresario created McDaniel's Museum to distinguish his amusement hall from other variety theaters. As "Professor McDaniel," he advertised "1,001 Marvels," with admission free to any man who patronized one of his two bars.[12]

Emulating the spectacular example of the promoter-showman he so greatly admired, the "Barnum of the West" found wide-open Cheyenne an inviting arena for his flamboyant efforts. He constantly changed and upgraded the curiosities in his museum, including animals from "all parts of the world," such as anacondas and monkeys and a massive grizzly bear. In October 1869 the grizzly broke loose, although somehow the beast was corralled within an hour. And in January 1869 a patron walked out of McDaniel's with one of the monkeys under his coat, but was arrested when he tried to sell the animal for five dollars at the Magnolia Saloon.[13]

Also in January 1869, McDaniel returned from a trip to the East with "the world renowned Circassian girl who is . . . a beauty of the rarest description." Other treasures he brought back included exotic additions to his menagerie and "a life-like statue of the Fegee [Fiji] mermaid." The next month he brought to Cheyenne Gen. William O'Brien, "the wonderful American dwarf," who stood thirty-three inches and weighed fifty pounds. Both General O'Brien and the Circassian beauty were introduced to the public at a series of "levees" held at the Museum. In July the celebrated Tom Thumb, along with his wife, arrived by train and greeted Cheyenne citizens at an evening levee. Another July visitor was dime novelist Ned Buntline (a.k.a. "Colonel" E.Z.C. Judson), who presented lectures on "Mormonism" and "The Curse of Chinese Immigration" at McDaniel's new Concert Hall.[14]

For several months in 1869 McDaniel featured on his stage William Kelly, "a musical genius" on the violin, banjo, and cello. Appearing with Kelly was "the extraordinary Indian boy, Master Willie," who performed "marvelous gymnastic and terpsichorean feats." McDaniel engaged an acting troupe, led by J. W. Carter, "an artiste of surpassing skill," and his lovely wife Carrie, who became a special favorite of the men of Cheyenne. The Carters starred in *Othello*, *Lady of the Lyons*, *Lucrezia Borgia*, *Honey Moon*, and other standards during their stay. In November 1869 McDaniel brought in the Brignoli Opera Company, starring Brignoli, along with "two lady singers and five gentlemen." At the other end of the entertainment spectrum from opera and Shakespeare, McDaniel occasionally staged animal combats, such as a battle between a dog and "a wild cat"—on a Sunday in May 1869—and, three months later, "a terrific fight" between "two savage dogs."[15]

McDaniel was an expert mixologist who often worked behind one of his bars. In November 1867 he mixed 215 Tom and Jerries in forty-five minutes, a bartending feat he happily proclaimed to be a record. (A Tom and Jerry is a hot drink, named after characters in an English novel, made of liquor, beaten eggs, sugar, and water or milk.) Because his customers freely imbibed Tom and Jerries (a Tom and Jerry bowl was kept on the bar) and other drinks, "fights were frequent." McDaniel always tried to act as peacemaker, but sometimes he was forced into the role of bouncer. As a bouncer "he was occasionally caressed with a chair or slapped with the butt of a six shooter and several times shot at." Even though on occasion "the lights were shot out and the house riddled with bullets," recalled the *Leader*, "such things were expected there." But "Mac banished thugs from his place so rapidly as they were found out and did his best to protect his patrons." He was especially protective of his free museum. "Take your wives and children to the Museum," exhorted the *Leader*, stressing that "we know of no better place of entertainment for families." Despite his popularity, McDaniel failed to win election to the city council in 1869. But for years to come he would expand his operation and provide imaginative, entertaining recreation for people of the Magic City, while earning a great deal of money.[16]

While James McDaniel clearly was Cheyenne's most successful merchant of entertainment, many other men—and women—worked for their share of the lusty recreation business. During the Hell on Wheels period, as many as seventy establishments dispensed liquor: saloons, hotel bars, dance halls, variety theaters, and bawdyhouses. One of McDaniel's earliest competitors was the Melodeon Theater, on Seventeenth near O'Neill. In December 1867 owner A. J. Britton presented "M'lle Forrestelle in a rope-untying performance," and within a couple of weeks the flimsy building was "being remodeled and re-fitted." The Greenback Rooms, advertised as "the largest saloon in the West" (110 by 112 feet), boasted two bars, "the celebrated mixologist, D. M. Russell," a house orchestra, and a cigar stand. The gambling saloon rented for $2,000 a month in 1868. The Theater Comique on Sixteenth opened on Monday night, April 20, 1868. A full house enjoyed songs, dances, sketches, and a contortionist. That same night the Arcade, billed as "The Largest Billiard Hall and Saloon west of Chicago," opened with a brass band in the balcony playing waltzes and "popular airs." Also in April, the Big Tent was erected in Cheyenne as a saloon and gambling hall. Shipped from one Hell on Wheels to the next, the walled tent measured 40 by 100 feet. There was a plank floor and a long mahogany bar, and a brass band stood near the entrance, playing military music to appeal to the great number of Civil War veterans.[17]

Cheyenne's saloon crowd also enjoyed prizefighting. The *Leader* reported a prizefight in October 1867, and another one the following February. These bare-knuckle brawls were in official disfavor, even in Cheyenne, so both matches were staged out of town, "somewhere in this vicinity." A prizefight in September 1869 was held just outside town at the racetrack. The Cheyenne Race Course, complete with judges' stand, had been fashioned "at great expense" the previous July, and three days of races were planned for August 22–24, 1869. There would be trotting, pacing, and running events, and "celebrated" horses were brought in from Denver, Omaha, and Laramie, in addition to racing horses from Cheyenne and Fort Russell. "Purses will be given in all races," announced the *Leader*, and $1,000 was raised for the trotting purse above.[18]

Horseracing would remain popular in Cheyenne for the rest of the century, but the attraction of a new sport would last even longer. Baseball became America's first team sport, played by thousands of soldiers at hundreds of army camps during the war. After the war these young veterans brought the sport home to a multitude of towns and country villages. Baseball could be played on any vacant lot or open field, and the game exploded in popularity across the land. There were a great many veterans in Cheyenne who knew baseball, and of course the sport was played at Fort Russell. In April 1869 a practice game was called for the open area behind the post office: "An opportunity will be given to all who come." At least two "Base Ball" clubs were formed, the "Wyomings" and the "Bolivars." They played each other, and in May the Wyomings lost at Fort Russell's grounds to a military nine, 35–11. At a rematch in September the Wyomings won, 38–21. Also in September the first professional team, the Cincinnati Red Stockings, passed through Cheyenne en route to San Francisco but declined a challenge from the Wyomings. This rebuff from the pros failed to dull interest in the game; every spring and summer bats and balls—and later gloves and catcher's masks—would be in demand all over Cheyenne.[19]

Prizefights, horseraces, and baseball games generated considerable betting from Cheyenne's gambling fraternity. The gamblers were able to leave their smoky saloons for a little outdoor action, and sporting opportunities expanded through the years. A harbinger of the level of interest in Cheyenne sporting events was provided by a billiard match in January 1868 at the Metropolitan Saloon between a sharpshooter from Colorado and an "export" from Montana. The announced stake was $500, but there were "a great number of small bets." The Metropolitan "was filled to overflowing with a large crowd of our citizens," and the *Leader* took almost an entire page to print a detailed account of the match by turns: "... No. 58. Kessler plays with care and confidence, makes two good shots and scores 17. No. 59. Smith drives his ball around the table, and misses everything but the cushions."[20]

Special entertainment was enjoyed by Cheyenneites each Fourth of July. Throughout the nineteenth century, Americans held jubilant celebrations on the Fourth. On July 4, 1867, for example, 400 men camped on an isolated plain in southwestern Dakota Territory celebrated the holiday and declared the birth of an important frontier town. One year later, Cheyenne's citizens observed their first Fourth with a parade "through the principal streets" led by the Fort Russell band and including "nearly the whole body" of the population. Starting and ending at the new courthouse on Sixteenth, the citizens then heard introductory remarks by Mayor Murrin, a reading of the Declaration of Independence, and orations by J.R. Whitehead, W.W. Corlett, Judge G.W. Ford, and "other distinguished citizens." On July 4, 1869, a six-car excursion train hauled 200 celebrants, along with the Fort Russell band "and commissary supplies," to scenic Dale Creek. Following a prayer, the Declaration of Independence was read, and orators included Wyoming's first territorial governor, John A. Campbell. A picnic lunch was next, followed by "hunting and fishing, gathering flowers," and other afternoon amusements.[21]

Governor Campbell's Fourth of July speech was one of his first significant appearances since arriving in Cheyenne two months earlier. During the Civil War, he was promoted from second lieutenant to brevet brigadier general, and after the war he served for nearly a year as assistant secretary of war. Then the thirty-three-year-old bachelor was designated governor of newly organized Wyoming Territory by Ulysses S. Grant in April 1869, one month after Grant's inauguration as president. Governor Campbell was appointed to a four-year term.[22]

President Grant made a number of other appointments for Wyoming Territory: for secretary, Edward M. Lee, who, like Campbell, had reached the rank of brigadier general during the Civil War; United States marshal, Chuck Howe, another Union general; United States attorney, Joseph M. Carey; chief justice of the territorial court, John M. Howe; associate justices, W.S. Jones (like Carey, still in his twenties) and J.W. Kingman; surveyor general, Silas Reed; and receiver of public means, Frank Wolcott, former Union major and future U.S.

John A. Campbell, a Civil War general, came to Wyoming in 1869 as the first territorial governor. (Courtesy Wyoming State Archives)

marshal of Wyoming. All of these appointments were submitted to the U.S. Senate in April 1869, and readily won approval.[23]

All the appointed officials were Easterners, from such states as Ohio, Pennsylvania, Illinois, Kentucky, and Missouri. At this time Reconstruction was being imposed on the South by occupation troops and appointed politicians from the North. Many of these opportunistic political appointees came to the South with their few belongings packed into the cheapest valise of the day, and they were derisively called "carpetbaggers." Although circumstances were different in the West, the derogatory term for outside appointees was adopted by Wyoming and other frontier territories.

"From the very first the issue was one of Home Rule against carpet-bagism," recalled Judge William Kuykendall. Elaborating on this theme, Judge Kuykendall complained that the Republican administration of President Grant, "unmindful of the fact that its party had abundant material of able men, actual residents of the Territory well qualified for the offices, ... sent us men from the East who came early in 1869 with a commission in one hand and a carpet-bag in the other. Hence they were called carpet baggers and interlopers, resulting in more or less immediate friction." Resentment of these appointees from the East continued through the territorial years, even though "their personal standing morally and socially in most cases was good."[24] A few of these "interlopers" remained in Wyoming and became prominent citizens, most notably Joseph W. Carey and, to a lesser degree, Frank Wolcott.

Governor Campbell and Secretary Edward Lee, who was two years younger than Campbell and also a bachelor, came to Cheyenne together, arriving on May 7, 1869. The next day they boarded another westbound train to attend the completion of the transcontinental railroad, which was headlined in Cheyenne's newspapers—as well as virtually every other journal in America. Soon back in Wyoming, Governor Campbell named Cheyenne as temporary capital. Lee practiced law in Cheyenne, when his secretarial duties permitted, and worked with Campbell to help organize a Presbyterian church. Chief Justice Howe began operating a district court in Cheyenne in May, while two associate justices opened district courts the next month in Laramie and South Pass City. In June Marshal Howe and "16 deputies" began taking Wyoming's first census. The deputies were reluctant to venture into many of the territory's rural areas because of the mortal danger posed by hostile warriors, which meant that the census would be somewhat incomplete. But a total of 8,014 individuals were counted, including 2,665 in Laramie County, most of whom resided in Cheyenne. Little more than a year earlier, Cheyenne's boomtown population had numbered three or four times the 1869 census total.[25]

Designation as the territorial capital lent prestige and significance to the Magic City, as the first meeting of the legislature would prove. After acrimonious campaigning by Democratic and Republican candidates, which included enthusiastic party rallies in Cheyenne, an election was held on Thursday, September 2, 1869, to determine the congressional delegate and legislative members. More than 5,200 citizens, which constituted nearly two-thirds of the recorded census population, went to the polls. A small percentage of the population was composed of women and children, who could not vote, making the turnout of eligible voters even more impressive. Aroused by the hardnosed competition between candidates and parties, the men of Wyoming turned out in imposing numbers to exercise their franchise.

Democrat S. J. Nuckolls, a Cheyenne merchant, decisively defeated the Republican candidate, Cheyenne attorney W. W. Corlett, for the privilege of representing Wyoming Territory in Congress. Democrats also won all nine seats in the Legislative Council, as well as all thirteen seats in the House of Representatives.

The Wyoming Territorial Assembly was first convened at noon on Tuesday, October 12, 1869. Although just seven members of each house showed up, others soon reported for duty. Because there was no capitol, the two houses met in rented rooms: the Council on the second floor of Thomas McLeland's building on the south side of Seventeenth, and the House a block and a half away at the

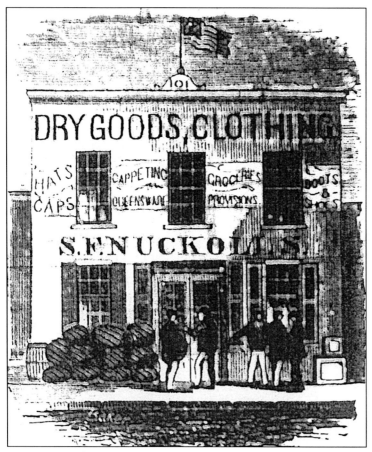

Arcade on the south side of Sixteenth. "Two or three inches of sawdust served as a carpet," observed Judge William Kuykendall. Nearby was the liquor establishment of Mayor Luke Murrin, where Assembly members often convened informally. Legislators worked diligently on the business of Wyoming Territory, and nearly all issues of the *Leader* featured a "Legislative Summary." Although Governor Campbell, a Republican, vetoed several bills from his Democratic assemblymen, they usually mustered the two-thirds majority necessary to override his veto.[26]

In 1867 merchant S. F. Nuckolls established a dry goods store in a two-story stone building on the south side of Seventeenth Street. According to the ad he ran regularly in the Leader *in 1869, Nuckolls sold clothing, carpeting, glass, coal oil lamps, Seth Thomas clocks, groceries, liquors, tobacco, and cigars.*

The most notable legislation of the First

Assembly was "the Female Suffrage Bill." For two decades suffragists had worked to gain the vote in the United States, and in 1868 both houses of Congress considered constitutional amendments for women's suffrage, although it would be another half century before the Nineteenth Amendment became law. In January 1869 the Dakota Territorial Legislature had failed to adopt women's suffrage by only a single vote, and other western territories were considering such a measure. With no established traditions, western territories were habitually innovative, willing to try something new, and women's suffrage was expected to attract female settlers. Legislators were keenly aware of the need to bring more women to Wyoming; invaluable publicity would be generated if the first female suffrage law in the United States were to be enacted by the newest territory. Female suffrage "would be an advertisement for the Territory," pointed out Judge Kuykendall. Two leading suffragist lecturers made timely appearances in Cheyenne: Anna Dickinson, on September 24, 1869, with Governor Campbell in the audience; and Redelia Bates, who was offered the hall rented by the House of Representatives on November 5. A bill to give women the right to vote and to hold office was developed late in November, passed both houses with amendments, and was presented to Governor Campbell on Monday, December 6. Although there was speculation that he would veto the bill, the governor signed it into law on the last day of the session, Friday, December 10, 1869.[27]

"We now expect at once quite an immigration of ladies to Wyoming," the *Leader* announced happily. "We say to them all, come on."[28]

On Friday evening, December 10, an "impromptu" ball was given for Governor Campbell and members of the First Assembly. Through the efforts of Judge Kuykendall and a few others, invitations went out on Friday afternoon, and about sixty couples arrived that evening for dinner at the Ford House. Although some of the men in attendance revealed a lack of propriety "by *smoking cigars* in the presence of ladies," everyone "enjoyed the dancing until a late hour."[29] Cheyenne would become noted for staging dinner dances, impromptu or carefully planned, in honor of special events or visiting celebrities, or simply to enrich the social calendar.

Women who attended the ball at the Ford House might have had their hair dressed by "the French Hair Dresser, Madam Croze," on Seventeenth, or by George Thomas, "late of Denver," who would leave the barber shop at the Rollins House to "wait upon ladies in any part of the city, at short notice."

Cheyenne women could select evening wear at Mrs. E. F. Stearns' New Temple of Fashion on Sixteenth Street, "at the Lowest Eastern Prices." Other wardrobe selections could be worn on Sundays to one of Cheyenne's five churches, each strongly supported by the women of the congregation. Cheyenne women also supported local schools, while nurturing their children and husbands. But in addition to these traditional female activities, the women of Cheyenne—unlike most American women—could vote. Wyoming women voted, and they began to hold minor offices and serve on juries. They also became more assertive and independent. These changes were occurring "whether man desires it or not," mused Judge Kuykendall. "Perhaps our women always have and always will influence and control affairs while making us men believe that we do."[30]

Kuykendall's reflections were strongly shaped by his redoubtable wife. Eliza Montgomery Kuykendall from Missouri had been married for nine years and had two little boys when, in 1866, she journeyed by wagon across Kansas to join her husband in Denver. "She brought a few cows and other cattle with her," related Kuykendall. After assuming responsibility for the four children of her deceased sister, Eliza took her squad of boys and girls and her cattle to Cheyenne late in 1867, again rejoining her husband in a new western town. For the next quarter of a century Eliza was a busy, respected citizen of Cheyenne. She bore two more sons, but during another long absence from Kuykendall, she maintained their home, raised their children, endured a stunning tragedy, and managed her property.[31] This diligent, stalwart citizen and her female friends made vital contributions to Cheyenne. These women voted as a natural part of life in Cheyenne, and the fact that they were among a tiny minority of American females who could vote added to their growing sense of worldly self-assurance.

When Eliza Kuykendall reached Cheyenne in December 1867, her husband established a small ranch a couple of miles east of town for her cattle. Her brand was the first one recorded in the county clerk's office in Cheyenne. But soon others brought cattle to the open grasslands around Cheyenne, largely to supply the town's meat markets. One of these men was John Wesley Iliff, who was building a cattle kingdom in Colorado that would earn him the appellation "Cattle King of

Sixteenth Street, looking west in 1868. The Theatre Comique, a popular variety hall, is at left. At right is the three-story Rollins House, which has expanded to the right. The Rollins House boasted a bar, billiard room, bath house, barber shop, and accommodations for 200 guests. (Courtesy Wyoming State Archives)

the Plains." Iliff opened a meat market in Cheyenne, and placed a herd on nearby ranges. Indeed, by February 1868 it was observed that cattle were "all over the hills around Cheyenne." A year and a half later, a short article in the *Leader* opened: "There's money in it—raising beef cattle on the rich grasses of Wyoming and selling it at retail for from eighteen to twenty-five cents a pound." The birth of the most important and colorful industry of nineteenth-century Wyoming—an industry that would bring fame to Cheyenne as "The Holy City of the Cow"—was proceeding rapidly.[32]

Judge William Kuykendall joined the new Odd Fellows Lodge in 1868. (The IOOF female counterpart, Eliza Rebekah Lodge, was later named after its most devoted and industrious member, Eliza Kuykendall.) The Masonic Lodge also was organized during the early months of Cheyenne's existence, and each lodge was referred to as "Cheyenne Number One." Kuykendall also joined the Masons and the Knights of Pythias. He attained high office in each lodge, and late in life he proudly related his long service to each of these fraternal orders. For example, he chaired the Odd Fellows building committee when they "erected the second two-story brick business house in Cheyenne on the corner of Eddy and Seventeenth Streets." These and two other fraternal orders would build substantial structures in Cheyenne, while taking the lead "in aiding humanity, in character building and in practicing the teachings for the welfare of mankind" in their community. Fraternal organizations exerted powerful appeal upon men in the nineteenth century, and through their lodges they accomplished positive achievements in their communities.[33]

Virtually all of Cheyenne's political officeholders were active in one or more of these lodges. Other organizations formed during Cheyenne's first couple of years included a Chess Club, the Cheyenne Drama Club, a Literary Association, and a YMCA, precursors of a host of clubs and civic groups that would enliven evenings in the Magic City. Few organizations, however, were as popular in any American city as hook and ladder clubs, which comprised volunteer fire departments.[34]

Fires frequently broke out among the ramshackle structures of boomtown Cheyenne. In September 1867 the provisional city government, under Mayor H. M. Hook, authorized the organization of a fire company and appointed S. M. Preshaw as fire marshal. Fire Marshal Preshaw, who was paid $75 the first month and $50 monthly thereafter, took his duties seriously. He "visited all houses," directing the owners to construct chimneys, flumes, and stovepipes according to the standards proclaimed in newly adapted regulations.[35]

Fires were not limited to Cheyenne's buildings. In October 1867 a prairie fire north of town was whipped by winds which "increased almost to a hurricane." As black smoke billowed into Cheyenne, "an army of our citizens" marched to battle the flames with gunny sacks. When they were driven back, the town was threatened with a general conflagration, "but the gunny bag outfit came off victorious, and deserve the thanks of all." Several months later, Cheyenne again was threatened by a blaze that consumed $7,500 worth of hay just outside town. During that same month, April 1868, a large stable at Fort Russell burned so rapidly that sixty-five horses "were roasted to death," and seventy cavalry saddles were destroyed; only four horses could be saved.[36]

The military established a fire department, "The Phil Sheridan Company," which battled conflagrations both at the fort and in town. Recognizing the desperate need for a fire department in Cheyenne, N. A. Baker called for the organization of a company in the second edition of his newspaper, and periodically he continued this plea. He pointed out that the city could equip a company "at a small cost, with truck, hooks, grappling irons, axes, rope and buckets. The loss of an ordinary building would be more than the expense of outfitting a squad of firemen." The Pioneer Hook and Ladder Company "was enthusiastically organized" on the evening of April 1, 1868. Judge Kuykendall, a founding force, was elected foreman; seven years later he became captain. He held company meetings in his office, and when someone walked off with a company ladder, Kuykendall ran an ad requesting its return. The Durant Steam Fire Engine Company was formed early in 1869, after Union Pacific executive T. C. Durant "donated $500 worth of lumber" to build an engine house. Cheyenne businessmen subscribed to purchase a fire engine, which arrived in January 1869, accompanied by a "machinist" in charge of assembly. "It has two reels of rubber hose of five hundred feet each, and about twenty feet of suction hose," to run into water wells. The firemen met regularly, trained with the equipment they had accumulated, socialized together, and developed the camaraderie of firefighters everywhere.[37] Soon Cheyenne's firemen and their equipment would face a conflagration that would test the limits of their training, equipment, and courage.

Hell's Half Acre

For years nearly all of Cheyenne's development took place north of the railroad. Four or five families, however, squatted on railroad land south of the depot. Because "of periodical riots among the families, when tents would be torn down and shanties overturned," this disreputable district became known as "Hell's Half Acre." The females often participated "in these shameful escapades," related Judge William Kuykendall (*Frontier Days*, 160). Following these brawls, continued Kuykendall, "there always appeared before me battered men and disheveled women, each seeking justice, which it was a pleasure for me to hand out to them in large or small doses."

The
1870s

"[Cheyenne in 1874] was a busy burg. There the cowman, the railroad man,
the politician met, and altogether it was an interesting place. I tarried
in the old Depot Hotel, a wooden erection long since burned down,
and the evenings were spent at a free and easy theatre.
The name describes it exactly."
—John Clay

"Cheyenne in those days was an amusing but unattractive frontier town;
... cows, pigs and saloons seemed to be a feature of the place."
—Martha Summerhayes (1874)
Bride of Lt. John W. Summerhayes of Fort Russell

"Cheyenne has more beautiful young ladies in proportion to population
than any other city in the west."
—Cheyenne *Daily Leader*, April 8, 1877

"We used to call this the west. You are no longer in the west, boys;
you are in the middle."
—Gen. William T. Sherman

"Every building in the city is full, and every room
which money will hire is occupied."
—Cheyenne *Daily Leader*, April 17, 1877

The roundhouse at Cheyenne is filled every night,
With loafers and bummers of most every plight;
On their backs there's no clothes, in their pockets no bills,
Each day they keep starting for the dreary Black Hills.
—Traditional song of the 1870s

6

Fires, Storms, and Other Disasters

The 1870s began with the most destructive fire in the brief history of the ramshackle Magic City. "THE GREAT DISASTER" erupted half an hour before noon on Tuesday, January 11, 1870. Fire broke out in a defective flue in T.A. Kent's liquor store near the corner of Sixteenth and Eddy. A brisk wind was blowing in a southeasterly direction, and the flames rapidly spread to adjoining buildings.[1]

Excited citizens sounded the alarm, and within minutes the Durant steam engine was wheeled to the scene of the growing conflagration. Members of the fire company had to build up steam in the boiler, however, and afterwards the engine quickly sucked the nearest well dry. Unchecked flames reached the Eagle Saloon and Lyons Barber Shop, and the Ford House hotel was next in line.

Hundreds of citizens were in the streets, and many began helping occupants of endangered buildings carry furniture and goods outside. Many merchants lived in quarters behind or above their places of business, and they scurried to save personal belongings. "Delicate women were seen staggering under heavy loads," reported the *Leader*. Bedding and other items were thrown out of the windows of the Ford House on the opposite side of the flames, but the wooden hotel was consumed so rapidly that the mattresses, sheets, and blankets were burned on the ground.

N. A. Baker and his employees, aided by the staff of the rival *Tribune*, tried to save the *Leader* office, "which was one of the most complete and extensive in the West." Some of the heavy equipment was carried outside, only to be destroyed moments later by the inferno. Willing hands emptied the Temple of Fashion of Mrs. Stearns, and empty wagons were brought up to help empty other buildings. Two heavy billiard tables were lugged out of the Germania House and set alongside piles of furniture and goods on the Fifteenth Street side of the block (or "square," the preferred term of the period). Like Baker's printing equipment, the billiard tables and other goods soon were consumed by the wind-blown flames.

The next square to the east lay across Ferguson, "and a tornado of flames swept across the street with resistless fury." The blaze now attacked another square of "dry, wooden structures," bounded by Ferguson, Sixteenth, Fifteenth, and Hill. A short distance southeast of Hill and Fifteenth stood the Union Pacific depot, and just beyond was the two-story Railroad Hotel. These frame structures "were believed to be beyond hope," but the wind suddenly abated.

Aside from the two squares that had been turned to smoldering ruin by the fire, the fronts of businesses across the street had been damaged. "The Gold Room and the Rollins House were badly scorched," related the *Leader*, "and the entire row of buildings on that side of 16th Street were more or less injured."

U.S. Marshal Church House, Judge William Kuykendall, Rev. Joseph W. Cook, former mayor Luke Murrin, James McDaniel, I. C. Whipple, and other community leaders played prominent roles in battling to save property. In the afternoon, as the smoldering fires cooled, Mayor Martin convened the City Council. As a precaution the saloons were ordered closed that night. Mayor Martin called

Cheyenne's depot in 1869. The Union Pacific also built the two-story Railroad Hotel. *(Courtesy Wyoming State Archives)*

upon Marshal Howe for aid, and a troop of cavalry was sent from Fort Russell to patrol the streets throughout the night.

The building which served as the U.S. Courthouse was gone, and so were the Star Brewery and the Ford House. The brewery was valued at $10,000 and the hotel at $30,000, and neither building was insured. N. A. Baker estimated his losses at $10,000, with no insurance. The Dyer House was destroyed, and Tim Dyer had suffered a loss of $15,000—with no insurance. Bootmaker Stephen Bon lost his shop and merchandise, at an uninsured value of $3,500. Mrs. E. F. Stearns lost $500 when her Temple of Fashion burned, and R. S. Van Tassell lost his livery stable valued at $3,000, uninsured. The Wells, Fargo building burned, at a cost of $2,000 with no insurance. The Germania House was gone, at a loss of $15,000— including the two billiard tables—and the damage to the Rollins House was $500. Neither sum was insured. Altogether more than seventy properties were destroyed or damaged, and only a very few carried insurance. Indeed, one of the reforms to emerge from this disastrous fire would be widespread insurance coverage in Cheyenne.

Rebuilding began immediately. The Bear & Miller Meat Market on Ferguson near Fifteenth was a total loss at $1,200, but the owners promptly began a new structure. "They have raised their frame, the first building on that square," it was reported. Stephen Bon rented a vacant building across the street from his old place of business while he constructed a new boot and shoe store on his old lot. Because of the recent drop in population, there were numerous vacant structures. Although many were "but poor makeshifts at any price," they would suffice as temporary quarters during rebuilding projects. Future mayor Tim Dyer and his brother bought two of these buildings and moved them to Fifteenth as a temporary Dyer House. The Eagle Brewery and Star Brewery began rebuilding on their original sites. "The majority of the sufferers by the late fire have already made arrangements either to build or to purchase buildings to replace those destroyed," reported the *Leader* just four days after the downtown disaster. N. A. Baker traveled to Chicago to re-equip the *Leader*, and on March 7 ground was broken for a new Ford House, which would stand 72 feet by 132 feet and cost $24,000. The urban pioneers who had stuck with Cheyenne despite the drastic population reduction would not be run off by fire.[2]

An upbeat ad was run by a jewelry store that escaped the fire: "The Fire King sent his crimson darts to the right and left, with merciless ferocity, until he reached the store of JOSLIN & PARKS, where he doubtless was too much dazzled by the magnificent display of Jewelry, to continue his depredations. Certainly, no reasonable Fire Fiend could have the heart to lay his destroying hand upon the beautiful Native Chains and rich Moss Agate Sets, which distinguish this establishment."[3]

Another ad was grateful—and politely chiding: "Mrs. E. F. Stearns, of the Temple of Fashion, returns her sincere thanks to her friends who kindly lent their assistance during the fire, and would thank any honest parties, who may have any of her goods in their possession, to return the same." Unreturned from her shop and living quarters were clothing, hats, feathers, flowers, trimmings, an overcoat and gloves, books and a few pictures, "and a box containing under clothes, sheets and pillow cases."[4]

Despite high winds and winter temperatures, carpenters and other workmen toiled relentlessly on new construction. "Building, moving and repairing goes vigorously forward," related the *Leader* just over a week after the fire. Buildings are appearing like magic.... Everyone is cheerful, hopeful and energetic. Cheyenne contains the most enterprising and indomitable population outside of Chicago." (Chicago, of course, would endure its own devastating fire the next year; an inferno would destroy much of the city, killing 300 and rendering 90,000 homeless.) James McDaniel offered the use of his theater "to put on an entertainment for the benefit of the sufferers."[5]

Three months after the fire, a "Bird's Eye View of Cheyenne" was produced by lithographic artist Augustus Koch. Bird's Eye Views were extremely popular in nineteenth-century America. Between 1825 and 1900, well over 2,000 urban views were drawn, printed, and sold. An artist would sketch the structures in a town, then put together an overhead view as a bird might see the town or city. Koch presented his 1870 view of Cheyenne from the southeast looking across the town toward the northwest, with Camp Carlin and Fort Russell in the background. With the Cheyenne project completed and selling for four dollars apiece, Koch went west to Salt Lake City. After finishing his 1870 view of the Mormon capital, he ventured farther west and began drawing California cities.[6]

The 1870 Koch view of Cheyenne encompasses the entire town. The color lithograph provides an image of all streets and buildings of Cheyenne, less than three years old and with a population of 1,500. The lots where the fire began, bounded

Prairie Dog Arnold

Warren Richardson, a prominent Cheyenne citizen of the early twentieth century, was fond of remembering the colorful 1870s of his boyhood. One enterprising Cheyenneite was called "Prairie Dog" Arnold. Arnold would haul a water barrel in a wagon out to one of the many prairie dog towns near Cheyenne. Flooding the prairie dog holes, Arnold would seize the little creatures by the nape of the neck when they came up for air. "I have a scar on my thumb now which I received learning the trick," recalled Richardson. (The author carries a similar scar from a prairie dog fang.)

Arnold sold the prairie dogs in "little wooden cages to people who stopped off for meals at the depot eating house." The prairie dog peddler used a sliding scale based on appearance. Arnold asked $1.50 of someone who was "poorly dressed," but he went up to $2.50 if a person was "well dressed," and if "a woman wore a fur coat, the price was $3.50."

With such entrepreneurial spirit, it is not surprising that Arnold later became a banker. (From Richardson's recollections of Cheyenne in Chamblin, ed., *The Historical Encyclopedia of Wyoming*, Vol. 1:59.)

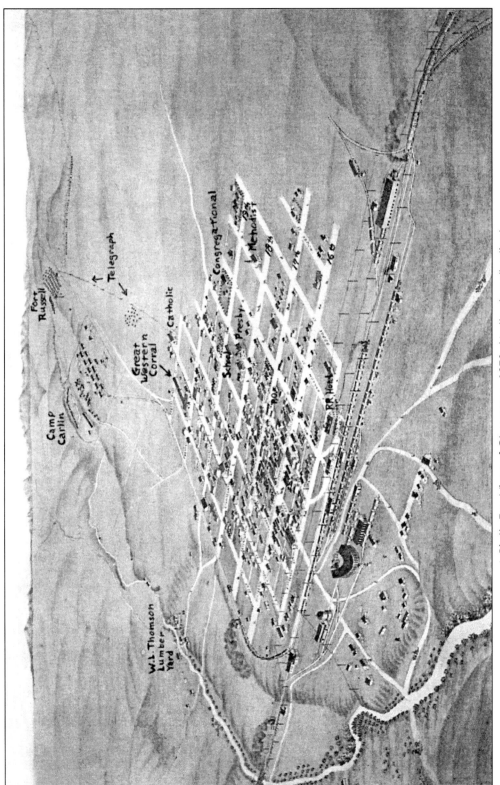

A Bird's Eye View of Cheyenne, 1870. (Author's collection)

by Eddy and Sixteenth, are vacant. But the remaining three-quarters of the block, as well as the adjoining block to the east, were shown to be covered with buildings erected since the fire.

On Saturday morning, May 7, 1870, the town was roused by fire alarm—first the city fire bell, then the steam whistle in the Union Pacific yard. A defective stovepipe had started a blaze in a hardware store on Sixteenth. A north wind was gusting, but the fire companies arrived quickly and extinguished the flames before another conflagration could spread.[7] This scene was typical for Cheyenne during this era. In a dry climate with high winds, a town built primarily of wood was a perpetual fire hazard, and the fire companies often were hard-pressed to control the latest blaze.

"During that time more than forty fires, great and small, occurred which the company had for nearly two years to fight alone," recalled Judge William Kuykendall, a founding member of the Pioneer Hook and Ladder Company. Kuykendall donated twenty-five dollars toward the purchase of the Durant steamer, and other volunteer firemen also made contributions. Indeed, "for nearly five years we had to go down into our pockets and resort to subscriptions and balls to pay for repairs and purchase of material," added Kuykendall. "Finally a city council was elected favorable to improving conditions." Kuykendall was asked to draw up plans for the new city hall, "with special instructions to provide for a meeting room and space for the steamer and carts."[8]

In November 1870 the Durant Engine Company gave a dinner and ball to raise money. One hundred people sat down to dinner, forty couples danced, and the Durants collected $300 in ticket money. But the fire engine still was not paid off, and an agent of the manufacturer was sent to Cheyenne to collect the remaining balance or the engine. A community meeting was held at McDaniel's Theater "to

DURANT FIRE COMPANY.

In the wake of Cheyenne's devastating 1870 blaze, four fire companies were organized, one of which was the Durant Fire Company. Two more are shown on page 90. The fourth company was the Pioneer Hook and Ladder Company. (From master's thesis of William R. Dubois III)

arrange payment."[9] The overdue bill was paid by the city, and the engine would continue to be needed in Cheyenne.

On Tuesday evening, December 12, 1871, smoke was seen billowing from the second floor of the Railroad Hotel, just above the kitchen. The alarm was sounded, and the fire companies hurried to the hotel with the Durant engine. Fort Russell's Phil Sheridan Company also soon arrived with "the government fire engine." But because of "a next to utter absence of water," the firefighters could do little to halt the flames. A large crowd dashed in and out of the hotel, removing furniture and personal belongings of forty guests. "Chairs, bedsteads, mirrors, fine vases, glassware, etc., were handled with commendable haste, but with a supreme disregard of their fragile nature," so that there was considerable breakage. More than two hours passed before the hotel was consumed. The Union Pacific depot, just east of the hotel, was threatened by sparks, but for once there was no wind and the building was saved. The Railroad Hotel had been built in the summer of 1868 for $23,000, and the UP held no insurance. George M. Jones, manager of the hotel, owned the hotel's furniture and fittings. His insurance totaled $4,000, "but in companies crippled by Chicago losses," so he expected little recompense. Nevertheless, Jones, who enjoyed an "excellent reputation as a caterer" among railroad travelers, announced that he would "at once make preparations for re-establishing" the railroad restaurant. The UP promptly sent men and building materials from Omaha to erect "a temporary eating house," and soon the railroad contracted to build a new hotel for $25,000.[10]

Cheyenne lost another hostelry to fire in May 1873. The Eagle House, on Seventeenth between Eddy and Thomes, was burned to the ground, but owner A. Simmons immediately secured the nearby Karns House. Mrs. Karns was one of Cheyenne's earliest urban pioneers. She had owned a popular restaurant and then moved into a two-story building to operate a boardinghouse, but the Karns House fell victim to Cheyenne's population plunge and was available when the Eagle House burned. Just over a week after the fire, Simmons opened the new Eagle House with a "Grand Ball" and supper. Recreation Hall was the site of the ball, with Simmons collecting two dollars per couple, and supper was served at the Eagle House, at one dollar per person.[11]

On Thursday evening, July 3, 1874, a lamp was overturned in a Chinese laundry on Eddy Street. The fire spread to a stack of ironed clothes, and within a few minutes the little frame building "was a sheet of flames." The alarm bell brought firemen, the Durant engine, and a crowd willing to help. "Never did men work harder to save property than on last evening," and every effort was needed. A strong wind blew burning embers to nearby buildings, destroying seven structures before the blaze finally was contained. "The city had a very narrow escape," breathed the *Leader*.[12]

A few months later, at midmorning on December 23, 1874, another fire broke out in another Chinese laundry. The wind was "blowing violently from the west," which quickly spread the blaze to other buildings. From Camp Carlin and Fort Russell came their "new Babcock Fire Extinguisher" and the Phil Sheridan engine. The Cheyenne and military fire companies halted a fire, then extinguished "the smoldering remains" of four buildings.[13]

The Fort Russell fire equipment was dispatched to Cheyenne fires, and Magic City firemen returned the courtesy. In February 1872, for example, Cheyenne firemen drove the Durant engine to Camp Carlin to help extinguish a blaze. While fighting the fire, the Durant hose was damaged. The depot quartermaster at Camp Carlin soon sent "a considerable quantity of hose" as a replacement, "and also as an acknowledgment of the services rendered on that and previous occasions" by Cheyenne firefighters. But before dawn on Monday, January 4, 1875, fire broke out in a lieutenant's residence at Fort Russell and quickly consumed six sets of officers' quarters on the west side of the parade ground. For once Cheyenne firemen did not respond to a fire on the military reservation, and the next day the fire department was chided in print by the *Leader*. The firemen explained that many men were in the bed and did not hear the alarm bell, and by the time that teams could be hitched to the Durant engine, it could be seen in the distance that the blaze was subsiding.[14]

The military held no grudges, and army firefighters aided greatly in halting a Cheyenne conflagration on the Fourth of July in 1875. During the afternoon of Cheyenne's eighth birthday, and the nation's ninety-ninth, shouts of "Fire!" came from Eddy Street. Smoke swirled out of the second-story windows of McDaniel's Theater, "and soon the flames burst forth and enveloped the whole structure, spreading rapidly to the adjoining buildings." Within moments the Cheyenne fire companies were in action, and a short time later they "were nobly assisted by Col. [J. J.] Reynolds's fire-corps from Fort Russell and the Babcock extinguisher" from Camp Carlin. Despite efforts of the firefighters, the blaze raged out of control in McDaniel's buildings and nearby stores, including Luke Murrin's liquor wareroom and David Miller's jewelry shop. The merchants managed to remove most of their merchandise before their buildings were consumed, but McDaniel "lost almost everything." Mayor I. C. Whipple directed the firefighters from a rooftop, but he was caught in the movement of a hose which sent him tumbling ten feet to the ground, dislocating his left arm. Wind-swept flames set fire to the frame front of the Dyer House across the street and cracked windows at Marks & Myers Dry Goods and other stores near the hotel. But the firefighters managed to extinguish this blaze, and within a few days Tim Dyer rebuilt the front of the Dyer House. Suffering the heaviest loss was James McDaniel, whose damages were estimated at $35,000. However, when he opened his safe "in the presence of a large assemblage," he found the contents undamaged. The redoubtable showman immediately leased another variety hall and resumed performances before large crowds who wanted "to prove by their presence that they are ready to back McDaniel in his efforts to make up for his losses." Soon McDaniel bought the old Planter's House and moved the frame hotel to the southwest corner of Sixteenth and Eddy, where it was renovated as a variety theater. Then he bought the old Gold Room on Sixteenth, and following another renovation the "Barnum of the West" opened McDaniel's New Dramatic Theater, with a dozen private boxes and seating for 800—double the capacity of any other theater in Cheyenne. For good measure

McDaniel opened a skating rink, operated by his wife. McDaniel's reaction to de-struction by fire was to multiply his entertainment empire.[15]

A recurring problem during Cheyenne fires drew public criticism from the *Leader* following a blaze on December 9, 1877. The Sunday evening fire destroyed a frame and adobe house at the corner of Eddy and Twentieth. The Pioneer Hook and Ladder Company and the Durant Engine Company were on the scene, but the foreman of the Hooks fell from the wall and broke his leg, and there was con-fusion from an all-too-common source: "Every man who rushes to a fire expects to manage the work from the moment he arrives, and if he chances to have a strong pair of lungs he will succeed to his efforts, but always by interference with the work of the fire department." The broken leg of the Hooks foreman was caused "through a hasty order from one of those officious idiots who are on hand at every fire, while two or three other firemen had hair-breadth escapes from dan-gerous injury, through the premature giving of orders by the same entry." The *Leader* called for official safeguards against "the very dangerous meddling of the fellows who, while they will not join the companies and work, are always on hand to give orders."[16]

By the late 1870s the "Hooks" and the "Durants" had been reinforced by the organization of two additional companies, the J. T. Clark Hose Company, formed by the Union Pacific to serve the growing population south of the UP tracks, and the Alert Hose Company, established in 1877 in the northern part of town. These volunteer companies provided their own buildings, equipment, and uniforms by staging balls and fairs and other fundraisers. In 1873 the Pioneer Hook and Ladder Company left its original building, a house on Sixteenth so decrepit that "one could throw a dog through the cracks." The new building on Seventeenth was erected "at the joint cost of the city and the company, which contributed nearly $500." During the next decade and a half, the Hooks purchased "an $875 truck" and $2,300 in uniforms and furnishings. "Individual members went down deep in their pockets many times," acknowledged the *Leader*. In 1878 the Durants ordered forty-two new uniforms from New York City: hats, shirts, and belts, dec-

How to Bankrupt a Museum

During the 1870s, Cheyenne's "Barnum of the West," James McDaniel, suffered the loss of buildings by fire and the collapse of a theater roof. And, ac-cording to the reminiscence of longtime Cheyenne jeweler Dave Miller, McDaniel's popular museum was once "pretty nearly bankrupted" by a boa constrictor he bought from a stranded sideshow. "The big snake was hungry one day and swal-lowed all the curiosities, including a mon-key, a lot of birds, two manufactured mer-maids, an antelope, a black-tailed deer and a scared cow," said Miller, who then shifted his tongue to his other cheek and told a tale on himself.

orated with the labels "C.F.D." and "Durant Fire Co." A few weeks after their uniforms arrived, the Durants secured the Fifth Cavalry band and staged a hop at their new fire house to raise money. Attired in red uniforms, the fire companies were featured at every parade, and they often represented Cheyenne in parades and contests in other cities.

With four companies in town, Cheyenne citizens often were treated to competitions in their streets. For example, on Tuesday evening, April 23, 1878, the Durants and Alerts each ran 700 feet, then laid 200 feet of hose. "Both companies made splendid time," reported the *Leader*: thirty-seven seconds for the Durants and thirty-nine seconds for the Alerts. The installation of a city water system in 1877 greatly improved the performance of the firefighters. Although in future years an occasional fire would blaze out of control, Cheyenne's most constant fire hazards ended in the 1870s.[17]

But there were other threats to property and safety. High winds periodically ripped off roofing and overturned privies and other outbuildings. A wild storm in July 1875 caused widespread hail damage around town. Two horses were killed by lightning near the UP roundhouse, and water ran in torrents through the streets, "a rather novel sight for the people of a dry country." Three years later, on the afternoon of August 13, 1878, a sudden storm brought hail stones, according to an old-timer, that "ranged from the size of an egg to the size of his head." A wagon driver was knocked unconscious. Windows were broken out at the Inter Ocean Hotel and several commercial buildings. Hundreds of shingle roofs were badly damaged, and the tin roof that covered the residence of Luke

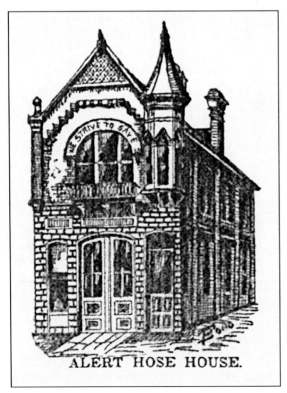

ALERT HOSE HOUSE.

Two more fire companies organized after the 1870 blaze. (See page 86.)

CLARK HOSE HOUSE.

Murrin "was filled full of holes" before being blown off the house. In April 1876, the roof of James McDaniel's New Dramatic Theater suddenly collapsed. There was no loss of life, but this unexpected event presaged a far more destructive collapse before the decade ended.[18]

Tragedy struck in downtown Cheyenne on Friday night, September 5, 1879. A few minutes before ten o'clock, "a thundering crash resounded through the streets ..., spreading terror everywhere." The loud, terrifying rumble brought people into the streets, and someone began ringing the fire bell. Citizens "ran wildly to and fro" before word spread "that the scene of horror" was on the south side of Sixteenth Street, just west of Hill.[19] The pale moonlight revealed a pile of brick and timber and dust. Two adjacent two-story buildings, housing L. R. Bresnahan's Washington Meat Market and F. E. Warren's Music Store, had collapsed without warning. Mayor Bresnahan and his nephew had darted outside as debris began to fall on their heads. Mr. and Mrs. Gaylord Bell, who managed the Music Store, and several young customers also dashed into the street as the building fell around them. Fifteen people went down with the rubble, many plunging all the way into the basement.

The Music Store building had been erected as the Delmonico Hotel, and the upper story now was run by Mrs. V. Bell as a boardinghouse. Mrs. Bell already had tucked her two little boys into bed, and several roomers also were asleep upstairs in both buildings. They were startled awake by what was thought to be "an earthquake" or "a whirlwind" or "a hailstorm." A few survivors quickly struggled out of the chaos of brick rubble, splintered boards, and fallen plaster, but cries for help indicated that many still were trapped.

The fire bell quickly brought the fire companies to the scene. Indeed, a blaze broke out, probably ignited by a lantern, in the depths of the rubble, but it was quickly extinguished by the firemen. At McDaniel's Theater the performance was halted, and men in the audience hurried to the rescue. Unstable portions of the walls still stood, threatening rescue workers. Timbers quickly were set up to brace some walls, while the hook and ladder companies pulled other teetering walls down into the street. Doctors Crook, Corey, and Graham soon appeared to provide medical assistance. Manager Caswell of the Inter Ocean and his son, Charlie, offered the facilities of their hotel for those pulled from the wreckage.

As debris hastily was removed, onlookers broke out in cheers when a young woman was rescued. Peter McKay and his wife, who lived above the meat market, had dropped in their bed to the basement. But McKay came to his senses, saw an opening cleared away above him, and climbed out, carrying his wife. The McKays were taken across the street to the Inter Ocean, where Peter, wearing only a nightshirt, borrowed a pair of trousers and a belt from Caswell and went out to join the rescuers.

A dozen survivors were brought from the debris. However, G.J.F. Van de Sande, an attorney and a Union colonel during the Civil War, was found dead, "crushed and entirely covered with the dust of plaster and bricks." By one o'clock everyone had been accounted for except Mrs. V. Bell's sons, six-year-old Gussie and four-year-old Frankie. It took two more hours to find the boys—dead in each other's arms. The stricken mother wailed that when she put her boys to bed she had failed to kiss them.

Workmen were contracted to clear away the rubble. While most personal property was lost, two gold watches were found, along with Mrs. Gaylord Bell's pet mockingbird: "although the cage was demolished the bird was saved." The day after the crash a pet dog, belonging to the bereaved Mrs. V. Bell, crawled out of the debris.

It was determined that no insurance applied to any of the losses. F. E. Warren suffered the greatest monetary loss, although it was thought that some of the pianos from the Music Store might be repaired.

A coroner's jury was formed to investigate the three deaths, and testimony was taken not only from those who had survived the crash but also from carpenters and other builders. During the ensuing days it became clear that the two structures, which had been erected during the boom of 1875, had been constructed with defective bricks and mortar. "The brick was very soft," testified one witness. "I think the most of them were about half burned brick, and the mortar did not have sufficient lime in it to make a good cement." L. R. Bresnahan, who had built the meat market at a cost of $7,000, spoke of complaining to a contractor about concerns he noticed during construction. "I told Mr. Bresnahan that the building would fall down," testified a carpenter who had noticed the poor materials and a problem with the joists. The coroner's jury concluded the builders "are deserving of severe censure." The *Leader* campaigned for a building inspector: "No city in the east of any pretensions is without its building inspector."[20]

Almost immediately, construction began on new and better buildings. When the Railroad Hotel burned in 1871, George Jones ignored several thousand dollars in losses and promptly began efforts to reestablish his business. The *Leader* credited him with "the true pluck characterizing western men."[21] Such "true pluck" characterized most of the citizens of Cheyenne during the 1870s. Frequent disasters, large and small, were taken in stride by Cheyenne's urban pioneers, who repeatedly rebounded with resilience and determination.

7

Cheyenne and the Black Hills Gold Rush

The commercial slowdown which pervaded Cheyenne during the first half of the 1870s was swept away by one of the West's most spectacular gold rushes. For years rumors had persisted that there was gold in the Black Hills, about two hundred miles north of Cheyenne. Although these forested mountains stood within a vast region that was granted to the Sioux by treaty in 1868, late in 1869 the Black Hills and Big Horn Association was organized in Cheyenne.

Judge William Kuykendall and two other adventurous Cheyenne citizens conceived of an expedition to the Black Hills while visiting in his office on a December evening in 1869. After announcing an organizational meeting at McDaniel's Theater, Kuykendall, acting as chairman, called a full house to order. An association was formed, and an ad was placed in the *Daily Leader* inviting interested parties to apply "at Judge Kuykendall's office." Kuykendall recalled that letters "began immediately to pour in, resulting in the booking of two thousand who agreed to join the expedition." Honoring the 1868 treaty, President Grant prohibited the expedition from entering the Black Hills. But Kuykendall and other diehards could not let go of their dreams of gold. At Fort Russell, Kuykendall signed an agreement that his expedition would "go no further than the South Pass country." On May 20, 1870, Kuykendall marched out of Fort Russell leading 130 men, "armed with the best repeating guns and revolvers," along with a six-pounder for additional protection. Soon the countryside swarmed with mounted warriors, and near the future townsite of Lander three prospectors were killed and mutilated. The expedition reluctantly returned to Cheyenne, but Kuykendall and many others remained susceptible to Black Hills fever.[1]

The desire for quick riches in the West was intensified by the Panic of 1873, and there was a widespread conviction that the next El Dorado lay within the Black Hills. In 1874 Lt. Col. George Armstrong Custer of the Seventh Cavalry was assigned to lead a large expedition that would penetrate the unexplored Black Hills. The primary objective of the Black Hills Expedition was to find a site for a new fort, but the party also searched for gold. Departing from Fort Abraham Lincoln on July 2, 1874, the Black Hills Expedition returned nearly two months later with tantalizing gold samples.

For years the *Leader* had predicted hopefully that gold would be discovered in the Black Hills or some other mountain range in the region. Now *Leader* owner Herman Glafcke could proclaim with confidence that gold was within reach of Cheyenne. In back-to-back issues in October 1874, for example, the *Leader* recounted numerous eyewitness accounts that established the Black Hills "as a region rich in gold." Although the army ordered seekers not to enter the Black Hills, prospectors could not be restrained, and small parties began to infiltrate the Sioux sanctuary. "The number of miners in the Black Hills is estimated at about 300," reported the *Leader* on January 23, 1875. In August 1875 six hundred prospectors were discovered by the army. After being escorted out of the Black Hills, most of these men defiantly slipped back to their diggings.[2]

Cheyenne was an obvious gateway to the Black Hills. Yankton, the capital of Dakota Territory, offered a long overland approach from the East. Easterners also might prefer Sidney, Nebraska, which was on the Union Pacific about one hundred miles east of Cheyenne. But Sidney was a town of only five hundred, while Cheyenne was an established retail center that could outfit large parties of prospectors. Also, the overland trek faced a difficult crossing of the North Platte about forty miles north of Sidney. For experienced prospectors from the West, moreover, Cheyenne had no competition as a point of departure. Early in 1875 Maj. Herman Glafcke, new owner-editor of the *Leader*, announced to readers that "letters of inquiry ... reach this office daily."[3]

Glafcke and other Cheyenne leaders intended to capitalize on a Black Hills gold rush. A committee was formed late in 1874 to answer queries from prospective immigrants, often by forwarding copies of the *Leader*. In April 1875 Glafcke printed 50,000 copies of a special Black Hills edition of the *Leader* for national distribution, boasting to potential prospectors that "Cheyenne resembles ancient Rome—all roads lead to it." Throughout 1875 the *Leader* printed letters and other reports from those who had entered the Black Hills. On January 19, 1875, for example, a Wyoming pioneer named Raimond, who had served as a guide for the 1874 exploratory expedition, assured his interviewer that "he is ready to drop everything when an opportunity presents itself and start for the Black Hills."[4]

Many other men who shared Raimond's eagerness to become "Black Hillers" began to congregate in Cheyenne. "There are quite a large number of persons in town waiting for the first opportunity to go direct to the Black Hills," reported the *Leader* on February 20, 1875. As more prospectors arrived in Cheyenne, the *Leader* called upon the government to make "an agreement with the Sioux Nation.... We believe it is impossible to successfully prevent the whites from going in there." When Col. W. R. Steele, Wyoming's delegate to Congress, telegraphed that the federal government "has determined to bring a delegation of Sioux here immediately to treat for the cession of the Black Hills ...," the *Leader* exulted about "GLORIOUS NEWS FROM WASHINGTON!" Steele soon sent Glafcke a letter for publication, emphasizing that "every effort would be made immediately to open up Wyoming and the Black Hills.... In the meantime, every power of the government will be exerted to prevent parties entering the Black Hills."[5]

But no power of government could prevent gold seekers from entering the region. Right beside Steele's instructions that nothing should be done "which will arouse the animosities of the Indians," a letter was reprinted from an illegal prospector to his wife: "I have been prospecting to-day, have found coarse gold." And on the same page was an announcement that "California Joe," or Moses Milner, who had scouted with Custer's 1874 expedition, had arrived in Cheyenne "at the head of a party of Coloradians" who were bound "for the Black Hills."[6]

The following day the *Leader* ran a lengthy article proclaiming the Black Hills "THE FINEST TIMBER REGION IN THE COUNTRY!" and describing "Its Agricultural and Pastoral Advantages," in addition to its mineral resources. Two routes from Cheyenne to the Black Hills were described. The shortest was "by way of Fort Laramie ... Raw Hide Buttes, Old Woman's Fork and Beaver Creek is 182 miles." The first ninety-eight miles of the journey was a well-traveled road to Fort Laramie. Cheyenne livery stable owner J.C. Abney ran a stage line to the fort, carrying the U.S. mail and passengers. "This line will be extended to the Black Hills right away, if the government permits it to be done." Indeed, the government soon improved this route by allocating funds for an iron bridge across the North Platte just south of Fort Laramie.[7]

Individual prospectors and compa-

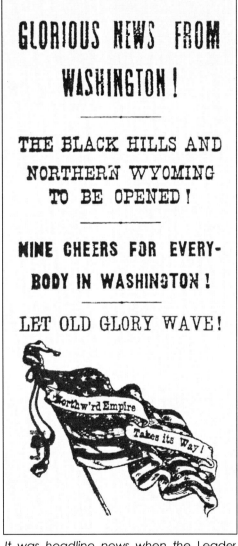

It was headline news when the Leader *learned that the government intended to treat with Sioux to open the Black Hills to prospectors. (Cheyenne* Leader, *March 18, 1875)*

HOSHIER & CINNAMOND,
(Successors to Todd Randall.)

Spotted Tail Mail and Express Line

from

CHEYENNE

to

SPOTTED TAIL AGENCY.

The Stage leaves Cheyenne on Monday and Thursday at two o'clock p m.;

Returning, It leaves Spotted Tail on Tuesday and Saturday.

Passengers and Express to and from the Agency.

Office at Great Western Corrall, Cheyenne.

H. S. TRACY, Ag't.

-mar9-d&wtf-

The first stagecoach to the Black Hills left Cheyenne with three passengers on Monday, March 8, 1875. On that day this ad was placed on the front page of the Leader.

nies of gold seekers came to Cheyenne in rapidly increasing numbers. In May a "Col. Carpenter" gathered several hundred men in the Magic City. Most of these adventurers purchased equipment and provisions in Cheyenne. They stayed in Cheyenne's hotels and boardinghouses, although Carpenter's large company erected a camp on the edge of town. "All branches of business have materially improved in Cheyenne within the past ten days," observed the *Leader* on March 30, 1875. Ads aimed at prospectors proliferated in the *Leader*: "All kinds of miners' tools and hardware at F. Schweickhert's, Sixteenth street," and "Black Hillers can now select a team of good horses at H. Glafcke's yard, on Seventeenth Street," and even "All aboard for the Black Hills! But before you start go to Hardin's Barber Shop, on Eddy

Looking east on Sixteenth Street, congested with freight traffic during the Black Hills Rush. Note the water wagon at right, just beneath the corner office of Dr. F. L. Warner, Dentist. (Courtesy Wyoming State Archives)

Street, and get your hair cut." Converse & Warren erected "an elegant two story, fire proof brick store," and many other brick commercial structures and homes began to go up. On the Fourth of July fire broke out in McDaniel's Theater, then spread to seven neighboring businesses on Eddy Street before "the almost super-human efforts of the firemen prevailed." The victimized businessmen did not hesitate: carpenters and painters immediately were engaged to repair and rebuild the damaged structures.[8]

News early in July revealed that a party from the Black Hills arrived at Fort Laramie bringing "plenty of gold and also fine specimens of quartz." A couple of hundred prospectors had gathered at Fort Laramie, hoping to be permitted access to the Black Hills. "There was wild excitement among them" when they saw what their bolder counterparts had found, and that night they all headed toward the Hills. Another prospector reported there were "at least 1500 men now in the hills and all are doing well." But he pointed out that a "want of provisions is a great drawback."[9]

Accordingly, several Cheyenne merchants began planning to establish "branch stores in the Black Hills." Converse & Warren soon would lead the way, followed by other firms, and in 1876 Stebbins, Post & Co. would open a branch of their banking firm in booming Deadwood. James McDaniel, Cheyenne's entertainment ringmaster, opened a variety theater in Deadwood. Businessmen as well

Ferguson Street following a snowfall in the 1870s. Note the Chinese laundry at left, and Whipple and Hay, Wholesale Grocers, at right. (Courtesy Wyoming State Archives)

as prospectors were encouraged by the announcement of U.S. Attorney General Edwards Pierrepont that "it is no offense against the law to invade the Hills." When the Sioux delegation demanded compensation which seemed excessive, the Grant Administration opened the Black Hills to encourage anyone willing to risk attack. Following the devastating defeat of Custer and the Seventh Cavalry at the Little Big Horn on June 25, 1876, the government took the Black Hills from the Sioux, although the military had yet to make this declaration a fact. Now thousands of prospectors swarmed into the new mining district, centered upon Custer City. That winter there were fresh discoveries in Deadwood Gulch, and during the spring of 1876 fortune-seekers crowded into a new boomtown, Deadwood, as well as other mining camps throughout the Hills.[10]

One of the first Cheyenne citizens to visit the Hills in person was, predictably, Judge William Kuykendall. He could not resist an opportunity to help open new country. If there was danger from Indian attack, there also would be high adventure and the chance to make a fortune. On Friday, Christmas Eve, 1875, the *Leader* reported that "Judge Kuykendall and twenty others are making preparations to start for the Black Hills Monday next." Reaching Custer City after the army stopped expelling white men, Kuykendall stayed for a few weeks and became impressed with "the great possibilities of the country." He wrote a friend in Cheyenne with typical enthusiasm, describing the Black Hills as "a perfect paradise" and expressing his intention to move his family and settle permanently. Eluding Sioux warriors, he returned to Cheyenne. Although he was unable to persuade his wife to bring their children into a raw wilderness, Kuykendall loaded a wagon "with a large stock of goods" and "a huge quantity of mail." Early in March he headed north again, struggling through a raging blizzard to become an early and prominent citizen of Deadwood. He bought commercial property, traveled to the Centennial Exposition in Philadelphia to promote the Black Hills, and worked to open a shorter route to Cheyenne.[11]

Not long after Judge Kuykendall first departed for the Black Hills, M. V. Boughton, former mayor of Cheyenne, dismantled his sawmill and transported it

A Cargo of Cats

Watson Parker, in *Gold in the Black Hills* (113), tracked down the persistent and irresistible story of "Phatty Thomas's famous load of cats." Thomas bought cats in Cheyenne for twenty-five cents apiece, then loaded them in crates onto his wagon. When Phatty's wagon tipped over on the trail, some of the cats escaped.

Prospectors helped Phatty round up most of the cats and resume his journey.

In Deadwood, according to one account, he sold his cargo to merchants for $1 per pound. But another version suggests that the felines were bought as pets by prostitutes—perhaps coining the term "Cat House."

aboard six ox-teams to Custer City. At this same time, Dr. James Lehane left "with a stock of medicines, dental and surgical instruments, proposing to engage in the practice of his profession among the miners."[12]

But for most men, business was too good to leave Cheyenne. "Cheyenne is the liveliest town west of the Mississippi to-day," reported the *Leader* in January 1876. "Her streets are crowded, her merchants are doing an immense business, her hotels are full to overflowing, magnificent new buildings of all descriptions are going up in all directions, and the 'Magic City' is making long and rapid strides in the path of prosperity." Following a hectic Saturday, the *Leader* observed: "Business was unusually lively yesterday, and merchants and employers were alike worn out by the labors of the day." As the weather improved, Cheyenne became even more packed: "The city is crowded with Black-Hillers, and elbow-room on the sidewalks is at a premium." By the onset of summer, business conditions were even better: "Crowded streets, weary businessmen and abundance of money tend to show that times are good in Cheyenne."[13]

A survey of "the Merchant Princes of Cheyenne" in 1875 revealed rising sales, as well as impressive revenue totals for fiscal year 1874, when boom conditions began. Pioneer grocer Erasmus Nagle enjoyed $150,000 worth of business during 1874, and he spent $5,000 of his profits erecting a brick residence on Seventeenth. Another pioneer grocer, Mayor I. C. Whipple, totaled $100,000 in sales in 1874, and so did the seven-year-old grocery firm of Pease & Taylor. B. Hellman Dry

Beef sides and hogs hang ready for customer selection. Notice the theatrical ads posted on the wall adjacent to the meat market. (Courtesy Wyoming State Archives)

Goods sold $60,000 worth of clothing in 1874, and the proprietor was in New York City selecting his spring stock. At the big furniture store of Converse & Warren, Amasa Converse allowed that business was good, totaling $75,000 in 1874. But the ambitious F. E. Warren added, "I wish it was a good deal livelier." Warren soon made it a good deal livelier when he bought out his partner and began expanding in multiple directions. Meanwhile Converse went into banking and continued to prosper, although he and his wife were staggered in September 1875 by the death of their only child. Predictably, two wholesale liquor dealers also did well in 1874: T. A. Kent, another future banker, $45,000 in sales; and former mayor Luke Murrin, $30,000, with rising sales in 1875.[14]

The malaise of the early 1870s had witnessed the reduction in size of Cheyenne's premier newspaper. But the *Leader* announced its expansion in March 1876: "the large addition to the number of our business houses, increase of population and the gratifying progress of our city and territory, have caused a large increase in our patronage." The growing population soon reached 3,000, the largest total since the original boom of the Magic City, and by the end of the summer there were no vacant dwellings in town. Commercial buildings continued to go up as rapidly as they could be built. "Large brick business blocks, magnificent fronts, immense plate-glass windows are becoming the rule," admired the *Leader*. One of the largest additions to downtown Cheyenne during 1876 was the Carey Block, while sidewalks were being laid out "in all directions."[15]

Beginning in January 1876, the dead of winter in mountain country, the *Leader* regularly detailed "the constant departure of large numbers of citizens and strangers, who are daily outfitting here and embarking in the alluring business of gold hunting." Before the month ended, hotels were so crowded that "at the Inter-Ocean beds were made on the parlor floor, all the rooms being filled." In

Lady Heavyweights

In November 1876 the *Leader* displayed a marked lack of gallantry in describing two local women who were somewhat oversized. "We have had a 'shower of flesh' in Cheyenne," reported the *Leader* on Tuesday, November 14. "A three hundred pound woman made a misstep on the stairs in Carey's block and spread herself all over the sidewalk." Clearly enjoying himself, the reporter found a similar story for the next day's paper.

"A woman weighing 250 pounds was arraigned in Justice's Fisher's court yester-day." (Although neither woman was named, their unique size probably revealed their identities around Cheyenne, which still had a relatively small female population in 1876.) "In answer to the usual question as to whether she was guilty or not guilty, she replied: 'Guilty, and I will throw myself on the court.' Fisher dodged, and begged her to go slow, saying he was not heavy enough to receive that mass of flesh. She threw herself into the calaboose."

March the *Leader* announced: "A special emigrant train will arrive here this evening at nine o'clock, having on board two hundred emigrants." Also in March, the 250 members of the "Chicago Black Hills Expedition" conducted "a harmonious and enthusiastic meeting at the Eagle house" shortly before departing for the Hills. A month later the "Pittsburgh Black Hills Expedition," more than eighty strong, spent a week in Cheyenne outfitting themselves before heading for gold country.[16]

The stream of smaller parties and in-

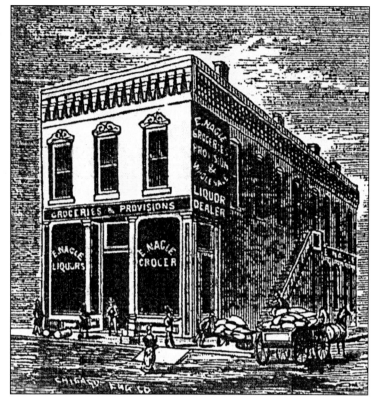

With a prominent location at the corner of Seventeenth and Ferguson, Nagle Groceries and Provisions outfitted large numbers of the "Black Hillers" during the gold rush of 1876. (From an ad that ran in the Leader during April 1876)

dividuals was constant. On one Saturday in March, for example, "E. Nagle outfitted 20 Black Hillers, Pease & Taylor supplied 10 gold hunters, Whipple & Hay a dozen," while "Draper & Hammond sold hardware to 15" and "six four-mule teams with 26,000 pounds of freight and six passengers were started for the Hills by A. H. Reed." The *Leader* printed news items from the Hills under such headings as "BLACK HILLS ITEMS," "BLACK HILLS BUDGET," "BLACK HILLS BUBBLES," "BLACK HILLS ORE," and "NORTHLAND NUGGETS."[17]

At seven o'clock on Thursday morning, February 3, 1876, the first stagecoach bound for the Black Hills left from in front of the Inter Ocean Hotel. F. D. Yates already made regular trips to Fort Laramie, but now he proposed to establish a route from Cheyenne to Custer City. Stagecoaches of "The Cheyenne and Black Hills Stage, Mail and Express Line" were scheduled to leave each Monday and Thursday morning for a five-day trip.[18]

Other experienced stagecoach men were investigating the possibilities of establishing stage lines from Cheyenne to the Black Hills. Only days after launching a run to Custer City, Yates sold out to a partnership that included H. E. Brown, who would manage the line. But on February 21, 1876, Brown was shot from ambush, perhaps by a war party or perhaps by a disgruntled employee.

Brown's death five days later, along with Sioux raids on relay stations and company stock, interrupted operations of the line.[19]

Veteran stagecoach operator Luke Voorhees was placed in charge. The new proprietors acquired "ten Concord overland coaches and sufficient harness.... Eating stations between here and Fort Laramie are already established, and from the Fort to Custer City are now being built, and will be ready to commence operations in about two weeks." Simultaneously the firm was arranging "for wagon trains for the transportation of freight, miners' outfits, supplies, and second and third class passengers." (First-class passengers traveled aboard the company's stagecoaches, while second- and third-class voyagers rode or walked alongside the freight wagons.) The first Cheyenne firm to haul freight to customers in the Black Hills was Whipple & Hay, late in 1875. By 1878 a score of firms, utilizing 400 freight wagons, operated out of Cheyenne.[20]

In April 1876 the six-horse Concord stagecoaches began leaving Cheyenne every other day. During the next six months there were seventy-two trips to the Black Hills. The company delivered 556 passengers to Deadwood, along with another 344 who took the shorter journey from Cheyenne to Fort Laramie. Over the next decade thousands of passengers rode the "Cheyenne stage," and the Cheyenne and Black Hills Stage Company became one of the West's most famous stagecoach lines.[21]

By 1877 road agents, including Texas badman Sam Bass, were practicing their own version of prospecting in the Black Hills. On the night of March 25, 1877, Bass and four other outlaws tried to stop a Cheyenne and Black Hills stage as it approached Deadwood. The stagecoach carried $15,000 in currency intended for the

Savvy Cheyenne merchants began to run eye-catching newspaper ads. (These ads were run daily in the Leader *in January 1878.)*

Cheyenne's principal hotel, the Inter Ocean, opened in 1875 at the northwest corner of Sixteenth and Hill streets. The frame building at the left was replaced in 1882 by F.E. Warren's Phoenix Block, which still dominates the corner. (Woodcut, Leslie's Illustrated News, 1877)

branch bank of Cheyenne's Stebbins, Post & Co., and the driver was Johnny Slaughter, son of city marshal John Slaughter. When ordered to halt, Slaughter courageously whipped up his team, but he was killed by a shotgun blast. Judge Kuykendall, from nearby Deadwood, lamented the brutal murder "of a fine young man whom I had known as a small boy in Cheyenne," and pointed out that following Slaughter's death "all" drivers stopped when commanded to stand and deliver.[22]

For gold shipments the Cheyenne and Black Hills Stage Company outfitted "an iron clad coach with an iron safe bolted down inside for treasure and valuables," according to the de-

The Cheyenne and Black Hills Stage Company began operating in 1876 and became one of the West's most famous stagecoach lines. (Cheyenne Leader ad)

A sale depot and lunchroom in 1872, located on the west side of Hill (later Capitol) near the UP tracks. (Courtesy Wyoming State Archives)

Freight wagons constantly plied the streets of Cheyenne, as in this busy scene on Ferguson. (Courtesy Wyoming State Archives)

scription of Judge Kuykendall. Three "treasure coaches" were built: "Old Ironsides," "Monitor," and "Salamander." Armed guards were provided, and only once was a treasure coach successfully attacked.[23]

The stagecoaches also carried mail, but more rapid communications became possible late in 1876. W. H. Hibbard, from Cheyenne, superintended the construction of a telegraph line from Fort Laramie to Deadwood (a line already existed from Cheyenne to the fort). On December 1 the first telegram from Deadwood arrived in Cheyenne:

> Amid salvos of artillery and shouts of joy, Deadwood unchains the lightning and flashes her greetings to Cheyenne on the completion of the telegraph line.... Many thanks for formerly your but now our Hibbard.

The mayor of Cheyenne, L. R. Bresnahan, promptly sent a telegram of congratulations. Acknowledging the contributions of W. H. Hibbard, Bresnahan added: "Having executed a contract for shortening the road from Cheyenne to Deadwood some 60 miles or 70 miles (which will be completed in a short time), we shall expect you to again recognize the efforts of our enterprising people."[24]

The new telegraph line out of Deadwood could have let the world know that more than $1 million worth of gold had been produced in 1876. The amount doubled in 1877, then increased steadily during the next few years.

In 1879 fire raged through Deadwood Gulch, destroying most of the ramshackle town. Deadwood rebuilt rapidly, with brick structures now dominating the narrow business section. Boom conditions gave way to hardrock mining companies, and gold production remained strong for years. Cheyenne would continue to enjoy solid profits and steady growth. A railroad from the east reached the Black Hills in 1886, and the Cheyenne and Black Hills Stage Line, which had been sold to Russell Thorpe in 1882, ceased to operate early in 1887.[25]

Can You Spell That Name Again?

When the Cheyenne and Black Hills Telegraph Line broke down after a few months of operation, wags claimed that the problem was caused because of a news story about a Russian general named Blovitskinourskiroquorobinskinasky. As related by Watson Parker in *Gold in the Black Hills* (122), this indigestible word ruptured the line and hurled lineman Pat Keeley off a telegraph pole.

8

Gamblers and Gunfighters

long with thousands of prospectors bound for the Black Hills, a great many sporting men and women also stepped off the trains in Cheyenne. "A fresh invoice of Denver gamblers and sneaks arrived yesterday," grumped the *Leader* early in 1876.[1] As long as the Black Hills remained officially closed, most of the sporting crowd, like most prospectors, congregated in Cheyenne. "The gold excitement has brought to our city many dangerous characters," the *Leader* complained in 1875, "who, while the Black Hills country remains a forbidden territory, make their headquarters in this city and vicinity."[2] When the Black Hills were opened, many of the gamblers, pimps, prostitutes, and thieves left for the wide-open mining camps, but a significant number elected to ply their trades in the more comfortable frontier urbanity of Cheyenne. The saloons and gambling halls and variety theaters of the Magic City pulsated with renewed vigor.

Still, there would be no return to the Hell on Wheels days of 1867. Although Cheyenne always had offered drinking and gambling and prostitution, the underworld was kept within limits in the Magic City. Businessmen required an atmosphere of order, and commerce was too profitable in Cheyenne to permit an excess of criminality. Drinking and a good time were available every night, and brawls and gunfire sometimes broke out, but civic leaders employed a substantial police force that was expected to keep a lid on the revelry. The county sheriff, of course, headquartered in Cheyenne; there were three city constables; and Cheyenne maintained a five-man police force—a city marshal and four policemen—who worked twelve-hour shifts, ten in the morning until ten at night, then another couple of officers until ten the next morning (in the 1870s the eight-hour shift and forty-hour work week were merely gleams in the eyes of a few labor organizers). Herman Glafcke did not hesitate to use the *Leader* to apply pressure in public. "Horse thieves and highway robbers are becoming too numerous in this vicinity," warned the *Leader* in August 1875. Several horses had been stolen, and on a recent Saturday evening two citizens were robbed just outside of town on the road to nearby Camp Carlin. Outlaws and policemen alike were put on notice: "if the officers do not put a stop to this practice, a people's committee will take the matter from their hands. A little hemp could be used to good advantage."[3]

Only eight years had passed since vigilantes had gone after the worst elements of the Cheyenne underworld, and the outlaws of 1875 could not assume that mention of "a people's committee" was an idle threat. But vigilantism proved unnecessary. Law officers went to work, as the *Leader* reported with satisfaction early in 1876: "A large number of cappers [shills], loafers and pimps have been ordered by the authorities to leave the city, on pain of imprisonment and heavy fine." A band of burglars continued to operate in and around Cheyenne for the next several weeks. As the burglaries became epidemic, Sheriff Nick O'Brien relentlessly searched for clues, "hardly taking time to eat or sleep for a whole week." On Tuesday, April 25, 1876, O'Brien arrested two suspects at the Crow Creek bridge. Later in the day the sheriff and a deputy captured five other gang members in town, and much of the stolen merchandise was quickly

A crowded variety theater in Cheyenne during the boom triggered by the Black Hills gold rush. (From Frank Leslie's Weekly, *1877)*

found. Incarcerated in the county jail, the seven prisoners included two female accomplices—the "paramour" of gang leader Jack Williams and the wife of one of the burglars.[4]

Two months later, a tragic murder horrified Cheyenne. At about eight o'clock on Saturday, June 3, 1876, three girls were walking hand-in-hand on Seventeenth Street. Suddenly, a young man ran up, shot fifteen-year-old Jennie Martin in the head, then fled into the darkness. Jennie fell dead, and the identity of her murderer was never determined. There was no apparent motive, and the crime seems to have been a random aberration, rather than a vicious incident in a lawless community crowded with gunfighters.[5]

Indeed, the occasional outbreak of violence demonstrated a decided lack of expertise with guns. On Sunday night, December 17, 1876, a "lively row" erupted in the northwestern section of Cheyenne "at Hattie Turner's bagnio ... between a party of colored men and some soldiers." Someone counted sixteen gunshots, but no one was hit. The only casualty was a soldier who "was struck on the head with a pistol, receiving an ugly gash." More characteristic of the orderly community was the holiday deportment described by the *Leader* a week later: "The celebration of Christmas in the Magic City was marked by an absence of brawls, boisterous drunkenness or disturbance."[6]

It is a further testimonial to the lawmen of Cheyenne and to the force of public opinion that a number of elite western gunmen came to town without resorting to gunplay. The most notable gunfighter to sojourn in Cheyenne during the lively era of the 1870s was the "Prince of Pistoleers," Wild Bill Hickok. Even as a youngster in Illinois, James Butler Hickok was an exceptional marksman, and by the time he reached Cheyenne he was a notorious mankiller. He had engaged in Civil War combat and gunfights in Nebraska, Missouri, Colorado, and in Hays City and Abilene, Kansas, and on the frontier Hickok had ridden as an army scout and had worn badges as a county sheriff, city marshal, and deputy U.S. marshal. By 1871 Wild Bill had slain at least seven men in confrontations that ranged from

A Rope and a Horse Thief

In the Old West, when men with a rope caught a horse thief, the result often was a lynching. But in September 1876 the scenario turned out differently. James Smith, a Texas cowboy who rode for rancher J. W. Collins, discovered that his horse had been stolen. Smith apparently suspected a culprit and kept a lookout.

Less than a week later, Smith spotted the thief riding his missing horse. Although Smith was unarmed, boldly the cowboy spurred his mount and built a loop with his lariat. Smith rode down the thief, roped him off the stolen horse, then "towed him to town, where he now languisheth in our jail." (From the Cheyenne *Leader*, September 30, 1876)

Wild Bill Hickok was in and out of Cheyenne during the 1870s, and he married in the Magic City in 1876. A natty dresser, his outfit in this picture featured checkered pants and a cape with a plaid lining. (Courtesy Kansas State Historical Society, Topeka)

a street duel to desperate saloon brawls. A tall man with long hair and a flamboyant taste in clothing, Wild Bill Hickok commanded attention—and respect—in any crowd.[7]

Restless and adventurous, Hickok led a nomadic lifestyle. He became a familiar figure in Cheyenne in 1874, when he was thirty-seven. Arriving by train late in July, Hickok was employed as a scout for a hunting party of wealthy Englishmen. "Mr. William Haycock, more familiarly 'Wild Bill,' is in town," announced the *Leader* on July 22 (Wild Bill's real name was James Butler Hickok). After a brief stay, Hickok took a southbound train to link up with the hunters in Denver.[8] He was back in Cheyenne by September 1874 and would remain in the Magic City for the next several months. Hickok occupied himself as a gambler, relying upon his reputation to attract play. He held forth at the Gold Room, a saloon-theater-dance hall which also boasted gaming tables. The Gold Room was near the railroad and attracted a respectable clientele which featured cattle ranchers.

Hickok found a room downtown above Dave Miller's jewelry store. Troubled with an eye problem, he visited the military surgeon posted at nearby Camp Carlin. He engaged in no altercations while in Cheyenne; as an experienced city marshal, he recognized and respected the order imposed by Cheyenne peace officers. In fact, after accidentally killing Deputy Mike Williams during an 1871 shootout in Abilene, Hickok was not known ever to have fired another shot at a man.

In Cheyenne Hickok was convivial, regaling listeners with tall tales about his frontier exploits. His favorite was a version of a hoary yarn reported by a mountain man. Hickok liked to tell of being attacked by a war party. When his gun was empty he faced overwhelming numbers with only a knife. "What could I do?" he would ask rhetorically, and someone would ask what he did do. "By God," he guffawed, "they killed me, boys!" The famous shootist fit comfortably into the masculine society of Cheyenne. "Wild Bill is still in the city," the Cheyenne *Daily News* happily reported on December 3, 1874. "He is a noble specimen of Western manhood."

On June 17, 1875, however, a warrant for Hickok's arrest was issued on a charge of vagrancy. Perhaps there had been some trouble over cards or liquor and the vagrancy charge was intended to remove Hickok from town. But Cheyenne's city marshal, John Slaughter, found it imprudent to try to serve a warrant on Wild Bill. A $200 bail bond was ordered, but by November, when the case was scheduled for court, Hickok had left Cheyenne.

Wild Bill soon was back, though, and there was no apparent effort to arrest him. Early in 1876 he was joined by Agnes Lake Thatcher, former proprietress of the Lake Hippo Olympiad and Mammoth Circus, which had played Cheyenne but had been sold off during the Panic of 1873. Agnes was a widow who had become infatuated with Marshal Hickok when her circus played in Abilene in 1871. On the road again, she corresponded with the handsome lawman, who was more than a decade her junior. When Hickok played New York City with Buffalo Bill Cody's stage production, *Scouts of the Prairie,* Agnes may have visited the fledgling actor.

Now, in March 1876, she was visiting in the Cheyenne home of friends, Mr. and Mrs. S. L. Moyer. Agnes and Wild Bill were reunited, and Hickok decided to marry. A bachelor and inveterate ladies' man, Hickok apparently felt the need for a measure of stability. He was nearly thirty-nine, his eyesight was failing, and he had no property or other assets. On Sunday, March 5, 1876, the Methodist minister, Rev. W. F. Warren, married Hickok and Agnes in the Moyer home. "Mrs. Lake came to Cheyenne ostensibly for recreation, but really to take advantage of the privileges which leap year gives to ladies," astutely observed the Omaha *Daily Bee* on March 31. "Hickok has always been considered as wild and woolly and hard to curry, but the proprietress of the best circus on the continent wanted a husband of renown, and she laid siege to the not over susceptible heart of the man who had killed his dozens of whites and Indians."

Mr. and Mrs. Hickok left Cheyenne for her home in Cincinnati, but Wild Bill soon would return. Quickly tiring of the East, he related a scheme to his wife that would place him back on the frontier. He returned to Cheyenne by March 23, moving into the Miner's Home boardinghouse, and began organizing an expedition to the Black Hills. He intended to assemble interested participants at St. Louis, travel by train to Cheyenne, then depart overland for Deadwood. In Cheyenne he found time to hold forth in saloons, "stuffing newcomers and tenderfeet of all descriptions with tales of his prowess, his wonderful discoveries of diamond caves, etc...."[9] Perhaps he was trying to drum up business for his expedition.

Hickok boarded an eastbound train in mid-April, journeying to St. Louis to promote his Black Hills expedition. He had circulars printed, listing outfit needs and announcing contracts with outfitters and train fares (St. Louis to Cheyenne would cost twenty-five dollars). Hickok sent copies of the circular to the Cheyenne newspapers, and the *Leader* ran a story on May 3, 1876, concluding "that Wild Bill proposes to lead the expedition to points where plenty of gold can be found." Although Hickok was back in Cheyenne by June 8,[10] the expedition of one hundred men or more seems not to have materialized. He stayed in town for a couple of weeks before leaving late in June with a small party of men.

After riding for about two weeks, Hickok reached Deadwood. At the rowdy boomtown Wild Bill spent most of his time gambling, and on August 2 he was murdered in Saloon No. 10 by Jack McCall. The day before he was shot, Hickok wrote Agnes of a premonition of death, and afterward the Cheyenne *Leader* published "WILD BILL'S PRESENTIMENT: A week before Wild Bill's death he was heard to remark to a friend, 'I feel that my days are numbered; my sun is sinking fast; I know I shall never leave these hills alive; somebody is going to kill me.'"[11]

But *Leader* editor Herman Glafcke exhibited scant sympathy over Hickok's death. The legendary shootist who spent most of his time in Cheyenne saloons seemed to Glafcke the kind of frontier riffraff that retarded the march of civilization in the Magic City. Two weeks after Hickok's murder, Glafcke editorialized:

> ... if we could believe half of what was written concerning his daring deeds, he must certainly have been one of the bravest and most scrupulous charac-

ters of those lawless times. Contact with the man however dispelled all these illusions, and of late years Wild Bill seems to have become a very tame and worthless loafer and bummer. Our city marshal ordered him out of town by virtue of the provision of the vagrant act, but Bill cordially invited the officer to go to a much warmer clime than this and expressed the intention of staying here as long as he pleased. Bill delighted in joining a crowd of "tenderfeet" at the bar and soaking himself with whiskey at their expense, while he stuffed them in return with Munchausenish tales of his thrilling adventures and hairbreadth escape from red fiends and white desperados. In such moments he was the personification of happiness.

Artist's depiction of a faro game in a Cheyenne saloon. "Bucking the Tiger" was a favorite of western gamblers. (From Frank Leslie's Illustrated Newspaper, *1877)*

Following another paragraph about Hickok's "astounding yarns," Glafcke concluded his harsh eulogy: "Years ago, before wine and women had ruined his constitution and impaired his faculties, he was worthy of the fame which he attained on the border."[12]

Hickok's murderer, Jack McCall, was tried in Deadwood by a miners' court presided over by Judge William Kuykendall. Known as a municipal judge in Cheyenne, Kuykendall agreed to supervise McCall's trial, including the orderly selection of a jury and the appointment of "able lawyers" as defense and prosecuting attorneys. The miners' court was held in the Langrishes Theater, which "was packed with men." Adhering as closely as possible to "the proper formalities," Judge Kuykendall heard a plea of not guilty from McCall. Testimony seemed to prove oth-

Gambler-gunfighter Bat Masterson rode a five-week winning streak in Cheyenne in 1876. (Courtesy Kansas State Historical Society, Topeka)

erwise, and at sundown the judge charged the jury, then helped select a pine tree with "a limb just right for hanging." Because the theater was in use that night, the court reconvened in the saloon where Hickok was slain. Astoundingly, McCall was declared not guilty, and he promptly left town.[13]

But these proceedings carried absolutely no weight, because the Black Hills were part of an Indian reservation and whites had no right to be there. Following his "acquittal," Jack McCall left Deadwood for Cheyenne, before proceeding on to Laramie City. There he was arrested on August 29, and two days later McCall was scheduled to appear in Cheyenne for a preliminary hearing. A large crowd gathered to meet the train from Laramie, but the onlookers were disappointed. At the last minute it was decided not to move McCall, and at his examination in Laramie City he confessed his guilt. His trial was held in Yankton, Dakota Territory, and he was executed on March 1, 1877.

Cheyenne was a significant location in the final period in the life of the Prince of the Pistoleers. But Wild Bill Hickok was not the only well-known gunman attracted to Cheyenne during the boom which accompanied the Black Hills gold rush. Not long after Hickok left Cheyenne for Deadwood, Bat Masterson arrived by train from Dodge City. Although only twenty-two, Masterson already boasted

John H. "Doc" Holliday spent several months in 1876 as a house dealer at Cheyenne's Bella Union Variety Theater. (Courtesy Kansas State Historical Society, Topeka)

a formidable reputation as a fighting man. As a young buffalo hunter in 1874, Masterson was one of the handful of defenders who fought off several hundred warriors at the Battle of Adobe Walls in the Texas Panhandle. And at nearby Mobeetie, on January 24, 1876, he killed an adversary during a wild saloon fight. Still limping from a wound received in this shootout, Bat found Cheyenne's gaming tables more to his taste than a prospector's pan in Deadwood. Riding a winning streak, he stayed in Cheyenne for five weeks before returning to Dodge City.[14]

Another gambler-gunfighter who matriculated to Cheyenne during this period was Doc Holliday. The Georgia native contracted tuberculosis about the time he completed training as a dentist. In 1873 he headed west, seeking a climate which might prolong his life. He practiced dentistry in Dallas and elsewhere but increasingly engaged in gambling. "Holliday had a mean disposition and an ungovernable temper, and under the influence of liquor was a most dangerous man," stated Bat Masterson. "He was hot-headed and impetuous and very much given to both drinking and quarrelling, and among men who did not fear him, he was very much disliked."[15]

But Holliday had a peaceful stay in Cheyenne. Although he had traded shots with a Dallas saloonkeeper on the first day of 1875, most of his gunplay came a few years later. He arrived in Cheyenne from Denver in January 1876, working as a house dealer for Tom Miller at the Bella Union Variety Theater. In the fall Miller moved his operation to Deadwood, where Holliday soon joined him. In the spring of 1877 Doc traveled back to Cheyenne on a Cheyenne and Black Hills stagecoach. Then he took a train to Denver and to points eastward for a visit with relatives. During his time in Cheyenne, Holliday did not yet have the dangerous reputation of Hickok and Masterson, and like Wild Bill and Bat, Doc did not exchange shots with anyone while in the Magic City.[16]

Two other gamblers, however, shot it out during this lively period. On Friday evening, March 16, 1877, Charlie Harrison and Jim Levy were drinking together at the new saloon of Shingle & Locke, on Sixteenth Street. The two gamblers began quarreling and, according to the *Leader*, "Harrison added fuel to the flames by repeated abuse." Bat Masterson, who no longer was in Cheyenne, knew Harrison well: "He was of an impetuous temperament, quick of action, of unquestioned courage and the most expert man I ever saw with a pistol." Harrison frequently practiced his gunhandling skills in front of others. But Levy, who twice had killed men in gunfights, became so provoked that he palmed a revolver. Although Harrison was not wearing a gun, he challenged Levy to allow him to arm himself and continue the dispute. The two antagonists walked out to the snowy street, while onlookers scrambled to lay bets, with Harrison the heavy favorite.[17]

The two men marched side by side up Sixteenth, then Harrison entered the Senate Saloon. He soon emerged, gripping a revolver, and walked north on Eddy Street toward Dyer's Hotel, where he was staying with his wife and daughter. Suddenly Harrison stopped and snapped off a shot at Levy, who stood across the street. Harrison missed, but Levy's return shot struck his adversary in the left side of the chest. Although the wound proved not to be serious, Harrison sagged into the snow. Levy continued to fire without effect, and Harrison triggered another wild shot. As the *Leader* described the fight, Levy "then ran across the street" and fired his last round into his fallen foe. The bullet entered through Harrison's lower abdomen, and he was carried to his hotel room. Two physicians were summoned, and by "midnight he was sleeping quietly in the arms of morphine."

Wyatt Earp in Cheyenne?

As an old man Wyatt Earp, influenced by western movie star William S. Hart, endeavored to turn his life story into a book and a film. Working with author hopefuls John Flood and, later, Stuart Lake, the old lawman indulged in the western practice of tall tales.

Among other embroidery, Wyatt placed himself in Deadwood during the boom days of 1876–77. When he decided to take the "Cheyenne stage" to the Magic City, he was asked by Wells, Fargo officials to act as shotgun guard for a $200,000 bullion shipment. After safely escorting the bullion past road agents, Wyatt arrived in Cheyenne in time to witness the gunfight between gamblers Jim Levy and Charlie Harrison. "Cheyenne didn't know much about Levy—he had just come down from Deadwood—but I had seen him in action and knew him as a topnotch gunwielder." Then he offered a description of the shootout which bore scant resemblance to the real fight. (Lake, *Frontier Marshal*, 158-164)

"While idling in Cheyenne," recounted Lake (164), Wyatt received a telegram from Jim Kelley, newly elected mayor of Dodge City, urging him to return to the cowboy capital to resume his job as marshal "at an increase of one hundred dollars a month in wages over his pay of the proceeding summer." But the preceding summer Wyatt was a member of the police force, not city marshal, and in 1877 he returned to Dodge as a policeman. When he rejoined Dodge's police force in 1879, he was paid seventy-five dollars per month. Wyatt was not marshal of Dodge, he was not in the Black Hills, he did not guard the Cheyenne stage, and he certainly did not see Cheyenne's Levy-Harrison shootout.

Levy was taken into custody. Because Harrison had fired the first shot, Levy, who acted in self-defense, was freed on bail. Although it was thought that Harrison would recover, he died in his hotel room before dawn on Thursday, March 29. The funeral cortege departed from Dyer's for the cemetery at four that afternoon. About forty carriages followed the horse-drawn hearse, carrying "probably about 125 occupants, embracing a majority of the sporting fraternity, with their wives and other females. Mrs. Harrison is, we believe, left in very destitute circumstances."

Herman Glafcke, no friend of gunfighting gamblers, headlined his account the morning after the shooting: "THEY DIDN'T KILL EACH OTHER, But the People Would Have Been Better Satisfied if They Had." Gamblers already disliked Glafcke because, through the *Leader*, he had waged an unsuccessful battle against the territorial law licensing gambling. Following Glafcke's unflattering account of the duel between gamblers, "three sporting men" immediately canceled their subscriptions, while "a delegation of leading gamblers" talked about "calling upon the editor." But Glafcke did not back down, upbraiding them in print.[18]

Nothing further came of this clash. Order was enforced in Cheyenne not only by the police force, but also by Sheriff T. Jeff Carr, a redoubtable lawman. On one occasion Carr was braced on Sixteenth Street by an enemy who, without warning, jammed a revolver against his chest and pulled the trigger. But the gun misfired, and Carr overwhelmed his adversary. Another close call came in December 1877, when Carr was jumped by four prisoners in the cellblock. The sheriff was wrestled to the floor and his pistol was pulled from a hip pocket. When two of the prisoners tried to bolt, Carr threw off the other two men. Then another prisoner, who worked in the kitchen, ran in and handed a small revolver to Carr. The sheriff fired two shots, and the riot ended as suddenly as it began.[19]

Other random violence in Cheyenne involved soldiers, usually after payday. One of the worst incidents occurred on Sunday night, January 20, 1878, when "a terrible melee" erupted in the Wine Parlor, a dive on Ferguson Street. The ringleader was Phillip A. George, known as "Long George." Long George pulled a pistol, but officers Ingalls and Howard arrived and arrested seven of the troublemakers. The next day Long George paid a fine and returned to the Wine Parlor. That night a Fifth Cavalry trooper emerged from the Wine Parlor with a sporting woman on his arm. They were followed outside by Long George "and a party of roughs," who assaulted the soldier.[20]

Hearing his cries, Sgt. John Moore bolted out of the Wine Parlor. But Moore also was pummeled, and one ruffian ran off with his hat. When Sergeant Moore gave chase, Long George suddenly turned and fired four rounds from his revolver. Moore, who managed to pull his pistol, collapsed with a bullet in his abdomen, and the hoodlums fled. Other soldiers carried Moore to a doctor's office, while police quickly arrived. Learning that the gunman was Long George, officer Bob Ingalls hurried to the stable where the criminal kept his horse. Finding him saddling up, Ingalls made the arrest, and Long George was incarcerated as "enraged soldiers" talked of hanging him. The agonized Moore was transported to the hospital at Fort Russell, where he died a week later. Charged with murder in the first degree, George was tried in Cheyenne and found guilty of the lesser charge of manslaughter. Sentenced to eight years in prison, he was pardoned by Governor John Hoyt after serving only three and a half years. The soldiers who had wanted to lynch George "immediately" after the shooting could not have been pleased at his early release.[21]

A well-known frontier ruffian gravitated to Cheyenne during the Black Hills boom and twice became the subject of arrest. Calamity Jane (born Martha Jane Cannary in 1844) was a sporting lady who decided that men had a better life. She chopped off her hair and adorned her husky figure in solid buckskins, topped with a slouch hat. Calamity loved to belly up to the bar with the boys, although she sometimes returned to her former profession. She chewed tobacco, swore like a teamster and drank to excess, and when she was drunk she committed rash acts. In Cheyenne in 1876 Calamity was charged with grand larceny, but in June a jury declared her not guilty.[22]

The alcoholic ruffian known in the West as "Calamity Jane" was twice arrested in Cheyenne in 1876. Although she was in and out of Cheyenne for years, Calamity caused no further trouble in the Magic City. (Author's collection)

Calamity began celebrating her release at a saloon. After a couple of days of celebration, she rented a horse and buggy from James Abney's stable, stating her intention to drive out to Fort Russell. "By the time she reached the Fort, however," reported the *Leader*, "indulgence in frequent and liberal potations completely befogged her not very clear brain," and Calamity drove merrily past Fort Russell and headed northward. "Continuing to imbibe bug-juice at close intervals and in large quantities," Calamity journeyed all the way to Fort Laramie. "She turned her horse out to grass, ran the buggy into a corral, and began enjoying life in camp after her usual fashion." When lawman Joe Rankin, who later would be appointed U.S. marshal, arrived in Fort Laramie, Calamity "begged him not to arrest her." Rankin had no warrant for her, but he saw that the horse and rig were returned to Cheyenne. Although Calamity was indicted for larceny, the prosecution chose not to prosecute the case.[23]

Calamity made her way to Deadwood, but she came back to Cheyenne in July 1877. She tried to hire a rig at Terry and Hunter's Livery Stable, but Frank Hunter, aware of what had happened to Abney's rig, declined her business. Then perhaps aware of how she had been described in the *Leader*, she went to the newspaper office. The city editor looked up to see a scowling woman, "clad in a cavalry uniform, with a bull-whip in her hand, a leer in her eye and gin in her breath."

"I want to see the fighting editor," she announced, cracking her whip at a fly on the ceiling. "I am Calamity Jane. I'm just in from the Black Hills. Be you the fighting editor?"

Denying his identity, the editor departed to find the "fighting editor." The *Leader* offered a tongue-in-cheek description of the incident which ended: "There is a vacant chair in our sanctum. The city editor has gone to Borneo." Soon drifting on, Calamity Jane is not known to have caused any further trouble in Cheyenne.[24]

Indeed, there was not a lot of trouble caused by anyone. Cheyenne was a small city with numerous saloons, gambling halls and bordellos, so inevitably there were drunken fistfights and an occasional exuberant gunshot. But only rarely was there a shootout. Cheyenne peace officers, strongly backed by the city fathers, maintained order. They controlled drunks and dealt with such nuisances as boyish troublemakers. (Most boys quit school after a few grades, and groups of idle teenagers pestered old men or broke windows in empty buildings or created other mischief. The *Leader* called on policemen "to teach the young hoodlums how to behave."[25]) Despite its early—and persistent—reputation as a wicked city, and despite the presence of gamblers and formidable gunfighters, Cheyenne weathered a second boom period with a minimum of street violence. Although Cheyenne was little more than a decade old, residents enjoyed an orderly business environment and a safe existence.

The Laramie County Courthouse was built on Eighteenth Street in 1872. The smaller adjoining structure to the rear was the jail, and the adjoining two-story building is the sheriff's residence. In 1903 Tom Horn was hanged in the jail yard. (Courtesy Wyoming State Archives)

9

Life in Cheyenne during the Seventies

President Ulysses S. Grant and his traveling party ate breakfast in Cheyenne on Saturday, October 2, 1875. As a four-star general, Grant had visited Cheyenne and Fort Russell in 1868. His first presidential visit was a thirty-minute handshaking stop at the Railroad House in April 1873, and he would make other appearances in the Magic City.

Presidents, generals, cabinet members, noted entertainers, and other celebrities of the late nineteenth century were in and out of Cheyenne. Famous individuals were simply names in a newspaper for most Westerners; but life in the Magic City frequently was spiced by the presence of noted visitors. And the people of Cheyenne eagerly offered exceptional hospitality, often on short notice.

Notified of a presidential trip along the transcontinental railroad to Salt Lake City, Cheyenne leaders arranged a reception and noon meal for Grant's midday stopover in October 1875. The host would be B. L. Ford, an African American from Chicago who recently had opened Cheyenne's premier hotel, the three-story Inter Ocean. But the westbound presidential special made better time than planned. Warned of the early arrival by telegram, Ford and the reception committee scrambled. The president's train pulled into the Union Pacific depot before eight in the morning, and waiting carriages brought the travelers a block and a half to the Inter Ocean. At "the handsome parlors of the hotel," President Grant and his entourage "spent a few minutes in conversation with some of our leading citizens" before Ford managed to present an elegant breakfast. "The table was loaded with all the dainties, not only of the season, but of what art could add;

119

everything in exceeding plenty and exquisitely prepared," the *Leader* reported. Following breakfast, President Grant was driven through the city to the depot. Four days later, on Tuesday afternoon, the presidential train halted for forty minutes on the return journey east.[1]

As a private citizen—a very famous private citizen—Grant returned to Cheyenne in 1879 and 1880. In 1879 he was hosted by Governor John Hoyt, a former college professor who would be chosen in 1887 as first president of the University of Wyoming. (Dr. Hoyt's wife, Elizabeth, also was a teacher who later earned a Ph.D. and became a faculty member at the University of Wyoming.) In October 1879 Governor Hoyt moved from rooms he had rented in 1878 to a handsome residence, and his wife came to Cheyenne from Chicago with their young son. While she was en route, and Governor Hoyt was in northern Wyoming, he learned that the former president was scheduled to stop off in Cheyenne on the last day of October. With a flurry of telegrams Governor Hoyt invited Grant to his home and informed his wife that she was about to be hostess for a former president and first lady. The Hoyts reunited in Cheyenne and scurried to make arrangements. But in the "carpetbagger" style so resented by gubernatorial appointees, Hoyt failed to enlist help from Cheyenne's leadership class. Consumed with last-minute preparations, he sent carriages to the depot, but inexcusably did not go himself. Although a large crowd cheered Grant's arrival, there was no one to offer an official greeting, and Grant expressed displeasure at the absence of his host. The Grant party eventually dined at the Hoyt residence, but the old soldier's demeanor "spoke volumes of displeasure." The next day the *Leader*, in a very long editorial, apologized to the nation for the "lamentable failure" of Governor Hoyt.[2]

Governor John W. Hoyt (1878–82) incurred the displeasure of U.S. Grant and many citizens during the former president's 1879 visit. (Courtesy Wyoming State Archives)

The next year Cheyenne made amends. In August 1880 General Grant and his wife were in Denver when they suddenly found it necessary to return home to Galena, Illinois. On Monday morning, August 24, word reached the *Leader* that during the afternoon the Grants would be changing in Cheyenne from the Denver Pacific to a UP private car. Maj. Herman Glafcke, who had purchased the *Leader* from N. A. Baker in 1872, "immediately drove to Fort D. A. Russell and notified Gen. A. G. Brackett." When the train arrived at three, the Third Cavalry band was playing and all of the officers "and other ladies" from the fort and Camp Carlin were waiting. "A number of leading citizens and officers" entered the car where the Grants were sitting, while outside a large crowd cheered lustily. The Grants were escorted to the dining room of the Railroad Hotel, and during their meal "distinguished citizens" filed in and out. After dining, Grant walked up to the hotel balcony and briefly addressed the assembled crowd. Three cheers went up, and while the band played the cheering continued. A "fine basket of flowers" was presented to Mrs. Grant, and there was more cheering as the Grants were escorted to their private car.[3]

Throughout most of the 1870s Fort Russell and Camp Carlin were adjacent beehives of military activity as the army campaigned against Sioux and Cheyenne tribes. The *Leader* began a "Military Items" column, listing the comings and goings of various officers and troop arrivals and departures. In February 1874, for example, Fort Russell's accommodations overflowed and tents went up: "the plain already begins to look like a small army was encamped upon it." Capt. Arthur MacArthur, who had earned a Medal of Honor at Missionary Ridge when he was eighteen, brought his Thirteenth Infantry company into this camp. (MacArthur was a brilliant officer who, in the future, would be lieutenant general—and the father of Douglas.) In addition to the constant economic benefits thus bestowed upon

Gen. Phil Sheridan, who visited Cheyenne in 1874 and on other occasions, was extremely popular with the large numbers of Union veterans in the Magic City. (Courtesy National Archives)

Wesley Merritt, a distinguished combat leader during the Civil War, took command of Fort Russell in November 1876 as colonel of the Fifth Cavalry. During the next few years, Colonel Merritt led the Fifth into the field against hostiles, leaving a skeleton garrison at the fort. When at the fort, Colonel and Mrs. Merritt were active socially. The Fifth was transferred to Fort Laramie in 1880. Merritt later was promoted to brigadier general, then major general. (Courtesy National Archives)

Cheyenne merchants and saloonkeepers, the Magic City had an increased opportunity to host high-profile army officers. The most prominent were Generals Sherman and Sheridan, who both had visited Cheyenne during the 1860s, and Crook, who stayed in town at the Railroad Hotel. Gen. Grenville Dodge returned to Cheyenne in 1879, in company with railroad financier Jay Gould, who had visited the city in his private car four years earlier. Such men were praised in Cheyenne newspapers and hosted by important citizens.[4]

In August 1878 Postmaster General D. M. Kay and a large party were welcomed to Cheyenne with a military band and decorative flags and a dinner. A year later Gen. Carl Schurz, secretary of the Interior, was greeted by Governor Hoyt, Gen. Wesley Merritt of Fort Russell, F. E. Warren, W. W. Corlett, and a dozen other officers and Cheyenne leaders. Secretary Schurz was driven to the fort, where General Merritt, "assisted by a staff of brilliant ladies" and the post band, hosted a reception. Back in town, a dinner was held at the Inter Ocean, followed by an "informal levee" in the hotel parlors.[5]

Cheyenne was primed for another presidential visit, and early in 1879 President Rutherford B. Hayes planned a sixty-day trip through the "Pacific and mountain states and territories." The press of events postponed this sweeping voyage, but by August 1880 the itinerary of President Hayes was made public. Cheyenne had just conducted an impromptu reception for Ulysses Grant, and the Magic City ardently issued an invitation to President Hayes. Although the proposed program "embraced a grand banquet," that event was declined because the presidential train included a dining car.

Mayor F. E. Addoms called a community meeting, and a committee of eighteen citizens was placed in charge of arrangements and finance. Mayor Addoms and A. R. Converse served as liaison with Fort Russell. On Saturday, September 4, a train left Cheyenne bearing Governor Hoyt, Mayor Addoms, and another two dozen prominent men and women. The train met the presidential special outside of town, so that local dignitaries could accompany President Hayes into Cheyenne. A crowd estimated at one thousand waited around the depot. The city was decorated with flags and bunting, and a pair of twelve-pounders from the fort fired a salute as the Third Cavalry band struck up "Hail to the Chief." A dais had been erected and decorated with flags, and President Hayes and his party took the platform. Governor Hoyt welcomed Cheyenne's distinguished guests, and Mayor Addoms introduced President Hayes. At that time in the final year of his presidency, Hayes delivered a brief, polished address that drew enthusiastic applause.[6]

There were cries from the audience for General Sherman, but President Hayes introduced Secretary of War Alexander Ramsey, who made a few remarks before stepping aside for the renowned army commander. General Sherman's speech was frequently interrupted by applause and laughter. "I say you are doing the work of your country and your God," he asserted to the assembled pioneers. "We used to call this the west. You are no longer in the west, boys; you are in the middle." Following "loud and prolonged cheering" and more band music, Mrs. Hayes was introduced, along with General Sherman's daughter, Rachel. The presidential party was paraded in carriages to a reception at Fort Russell, then returned to Cheyenne and another reception attended by "hundreds of ladies and gentlemen." (General Sherman insisted on riding back to town in an army ambulance drawn by four mules—the transportation he had been given

Rutherford B. Hayes was the second president to visit Cheyenne. (From Harper's Weekly, July 1876)

during his 1869 visit.) The westbound train finally pulled out after one o'clock, with President and Mrs. Hayes waving from the rear platform.[7]

Another private train brought the entertainment troupe of famed New York producer Tony Pastor. "It is by far the largest and best theatrical troupe that ever did Cheyenne the honor to pay it a visit," enthused the *Leader*. Pastor put together a western tour during the summer of 1878 and was booked by the resourceful James McDaniel for his New Theatre, built the previous year. After renovating the facility that had suffered a roof collapse in 1876, McDaniel's New Theatre seated 800 and featured a "dozen elegantly fitted private boxes, and four commodious parlors." A year before his Tony Pastor coup, McDaniel booked Tom Thumb, who created a sensation in Cheyenne. But no booking gave the "Barnum of the West" more gratification than bringing his namesake, the famed showman P. T. Barnum, to Cheyenne in 1870.[8]

A circus always drew a good crowd in Cheyenne during the 1870s. (From the *Leader*, July 2, 1874)

Buffalo Bill Cody, although not yet an international superstar, was mentioned by the *Leader* when he arrived from Denver with his family in 1877. After eating, the Codys entrained for North Platte, where he had a ranch. As his fame grew, his visits to Cheyenne always aroused attention. In 1879 "The Buffalo Bill Combination" brought "'May Cody' to a very large audience in Recreation Hall." The *Leader* provided a long account of "May Cody," which featured "scalp lifting and rifle shooting by Buffalo Bill, the hero of the play." The next night, in "Knight of the Plains," Cody astounded the audience with a shooting exhibition, then inserted a line about Cheyenne's famous gun shop: "This Freund Bros.' improved Sharps is a perfect terror, isn't it?" Cody's star was rising, and he would return to the Magic City with an outdoor show that would transform the public image of the Wild West.[9]

An equine celebrity spent the night in Cheyenne in 1872. Orrin Hickok, "the veteran reinsman," brought two trotting horses from the East for races in California. During a stopover in Cheyenne, Hickok left Lucy and famed champion Goldsmith Maid under guard in their railroad car. "Every man, woman and child who could possibly manage to do so turned out to see the Maid," and this memorable appearance was still recalled twenty years later.[10]

An American celebrity of the future, Rev. Josiah Strong arrived in Cheyenne in 1871 to become the second pastor of the Congregational Church. Tall, handsome, and personable, at the age of twenty-four Strong was a graduate of Western Reserve College in Ohio and the Lane Seminary in Cincinnati. Reverend Strong married only days before traveling west to enter his profession in Cheyenne, where he was ordained on September 8, 1871. Inheriting a congregation of fifteen members, he presided over the first wedding in the church the next year and held the first prayer meeting. The membership had risen to twenty-one in 1873, when he accepted a position at Western Reserve College. (It should be mentioned that Strong was not immediately replaced in Cheyenne, and the Congregational Church closed for two years. When Rev. C. M. Sanders was called in 1875, Cheyenne was booming and the church expanded to 200 members by 1878.) Strong's first book, *Our Country*, created a sensation when it was published in 1885. *Our Country* was translated into foreign languages and reissued in revised

Duplex officers' quarters at Fort Russell in 1875. Each company had a captain and two lieutenants. Sometimes a captain lived on one side, and both lieutenants on the other, although the presence of any wives and children altered these arrangements. (Courtesy National Archives)

editions in America. Now a national figure, Strong spent the rest of his life as a prominent lecturer and as the author of a dozen books, as well as published sermons and addresses. And his distinguished forty-five-year career began in frontier Cheyenne.[11]

Aside from the occasional appearance of famous or important Americans in Cheyenne, citizens of the Magic City regularly anticipated the Fourth of July and New Year's Day. Throughout the 1870s, Fourth of July celebrations featured cannon fire from Fort Russell, "pyrotechnic displays," parades led by the military band and Cheyenne firemen, horseraces, speeches, and baseball games (in 1871 the Fort Russell nine beat the local team "by about 25 points"). On July 4, 1876, the nation's centennial and Cheyenne's ninth birthday, a touch of rodeo was added to the customary horseracing: "A number of Bronchos have been entered." A Fireman's Tournament was staged in 1878, bringing volunteer companies in from Colorado and Nebraska to compete with the Cheyenne and Camp Carlin companies. There was a grand parade, along with the usual popular activities of the Fourth, and "hops" that night. Weeks of planning by local committees brought 3,000 visitors to the Fourth gala, "the largest ever held between the Missouri river and the Pacific coast." Cheyenne leaders would remember the possibilities and rewards of staging a major community event, but within two decades such efforts would switch from the Fourth to a rodeo extravaganza.[12]

New Year's always had been celebrated in Cheyenne by a "Grand Ball" or "Masquerade Ball" or some other type of ball, along with heavy drinking in the saloons. "The elite of the city" were present at the New Year's Eve ball in 1869,

Order of Parade, July 4, 1878

Fifth Cavalry Band
Carriage: Gov. John Hoyt, Gen. J. M.
   Thayer, Col. W. R. Steele—Orators
Carriage: Judge W. H. Miller—reader of
   the Declaration and others
Carriage: Central City Council
Carriage: Denver City Council
Carriage: Georgetown City Council
Carriage: Greeley City Council
Carriage: Black Hawk City Council
Carriage: Fort Collins City Council
Carriage: Laramie City Council
Carriage: Cheyenne City Council
Visiting Firemen from: Central City
Visiting Firemen from: Boulder
Visiting Firemen from: Denver
Visiting Firemen from: Omaha

Visiting Firemen from: Laramie City
Visiting Firemen from: Council Bluffs
Visiting Firemen from: Georgetown
Gillis Hose Company, Camp Carlin
Babcock Hose Company, Camp Carlin
J. T. Clark Hose Company, Cheyenne
Alert Hose Company, Cheyenne
Pioneer Hook and Ladder Company,
   Cheyenne
Knights of Pythias from Colorado
Knights of Pythias, Cheyenne
Visiting City Officials
Cheyenne City Officers
Juvenile Fire Department
Cheyenne Public School Children
Citizens on foot and horseback

and the same "elite of the city" attended the New Year's Masquerade Ball on the last evening of 1873. At a Grand Ball held on December 31, 1876, the Railroad Hotel "fairly swarmed with fair ladies and gallant gentlemen."[13]

By the late 1870s Cheyenne's "elite" were adopting a New Year's custom practiced at Fort Russell. Army officers and their wives long had spent New Year's Day calling on their commander and other ranking officers with wives, and at Fort Russell prominent Cheyenne citizens were invited to join officer friends in making their rounds of calls. This custom appealed to high society in Cheyenne, and to Governor John Hoyt. January 1, 1879, was Governor Hoyt's first New Year's Day in Cheyenne, and although his wife and son had not yet joined

Tantalizingly detailed ad for an act at Recreation Hall in 1879. (From an ad in the Leader *that ran in January 1879)*

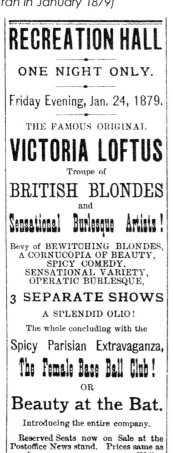

Baseball was popular from the earliest years of Cheyenne, and this nattily uniformed nine was one of several fine teams that represented the Magic City late in the nineteenth century. (Courtesy Wyoming State Archives)

him in Wyoming, he held an afternoon reception in the parlors of the Inter Ocean Hotel. Almost all of the territorial and city officials "dropped in during the afternoon to wish him 'a Happy New Year,'" along with army officers and friends of Hoyt. The *Leader* approvingly remarked that Governor Hoyt's New Year reception, "being the first ever given by a Wyoming executive, was a new departure." Following the governor's lead, fourteen homes were opened in Cheyenne to New Year's callers, along with various officers' residences at Fort Russell. The wife of cattle baron Alexander Swan, assisted by sixteen of her female friends, opened the "handsome" Swan home on Seventeenth Street to "a host of callers." Mrs. J. M. Carey, Mrs. F. E. Addoms, Mrs. E. A. Slack, and Judge Slaughter with his wife and daughter were among those who received callers. Mrs. Addoms was "assisted by Mrs. F. E. Warren," and the hostess of each reception was helped by at least one female friend or relative. Maj. J. W. Wham, army paymaster, had established his family home on Eighteenth Street, and his wife held a reception, assisted by her sister. Carriages, including almost all that could be rented at livery stables, traveled from house to house throughout the day. "The fashion of making New Year's Day calls may now be considered one of the institutions of Cheyenne."[14]

This *Leader* pronouncement proved accurate. By the next year Governor and Mrs. Hoyt had established a home on fashionable Ferguson Street. New Year's callers were received in their "fine, spacious parlors," where Mrs. Hoyt was assisted by two other scions of Cheyenne society, Mrs. F. E. Warren and Mrs. F. E. Addoms. (In addition to the receptions, the *Leader* reported on less polite celebrations: "There was a little random shooting on the streets New Year's night. There was some more also that was not quite so random.") One year later the *Leader* listed the

FOURTH INFANTRY TEAM.
200 YARDS.

Names.	1	2	3	4	5	6	7	Total.
Maj. S. P. Ferris	2	3	0	5	3	3	3	19
Capt. J. W. Bubb	4	4	3	0	2	4	3	20
Segt. W. S. Hanley	4	4	5	0	5	3	5	26
Cor. L. P. Lowe	4	3	5	4	4	4	4	28
Private P. H. Dice	4	4	3	3	3	3	3	23
Total,								116

WYOMING TEAM.
200 YARDS.

Names.	1	2	3	4	5	6	7	Total.
Maj. J. Talbot	3	3	3	5	4	4	3	25
A. Jackson	3	3	3	4	3	4	5	25
Geo. Bescherer	4	3	4	3	4	3	4	25
Geo. Freund	3	5	3	0	4	3	4	22
F. W. Freund	5	2	3	2	3	2	2	19
Total,								116

FOURTH INFANTRY TEAM.
500 YARDS.

Names.	1	2	3	4	5	6	7	Total.
Maj. S. P. Ferris	3	3	4	0	0	5	5	20
Capt. J. W. Bubb	2	3	4	3	3	4	5	24
Sgt. W. H. Hanley	3	0	2	0	2	3	3	13
Cor. L. P. Lowe	4	4	3	4	3	3	2	23
Private P. H. Dice	4	0	4	0	4	3	3	18
Total,								98

WYOMING TEAM.
500 YARDS.

Names	1	2	3	4	5	6	7	Total.
Maj. Talbot	4	4	4	4	4	5	5	30
A. Jackson	5	4	5	2	4	5	5	30
Geo. Bescherer	0	0	2	2	0	2	0	6
Geo. Freund	3	3	4	2	2	3	3	20
F. W. Freund	3	3	5	2	3	4	3	23
Total,								109

GRAND TOTALS.

Wyoming Team,	225
Fourth Infantry Team,	214
Wyoming wins by	11

When shooting matches became popular in Cheyenne during the late 1870s, the Leader ran detailed accounts with box scores, such as this graphic which accompanied a lengthy story of a match between the Wyoming Gun Club and a picked team from the Fourth Infantry at Fort Russell. (Leader, May 16, 1879) "Gun clubs have practically destroyed the interest in base ball," observed the Leader on May 4, 1879.

callers received at "Mrs. Secretary Morgan's" (Territorial Secretary E.S.N. Morgan, receiving in place of the governor), Mrs. A. H. Swan's, Mrs. R. S. Van Tassell's, and Mrs. W. W. Corlett's. "There was more calling done than anticipated," related the *Leader*, and many of the callers visited each reception. Among the listed officers were men of high rank—and a number of bachelor lieutenants.[15]

As the first lady of Wyoming Territory, Mrs. Hoyt was "at home" to callers every Tuesday afternoon and evening, and she held numerous public receptions. When criticized for conducting a reception for "mere teachers," Mrs. Hoyt—a former and future teacher—retorted that she esteemed the teaching profession as second only to the ministry. Governor and Mrs. Hoyt organized a literary and art association and hosted regular meetings in their home.[16]

Eagerly opening her "elegant residence" to "the elite of the city," Mrs. W. W. Corlett for years hosted popular musical gatherings. "The best musical talent of the city will be present," remarked the *Leader* about an 1877 "*soiree musicale.*" Never one to overlook a business opportunity, F. E. Warren opened a Temple of Music on Sixteenth opposite his big furniture store. To showcase the pianos and other instruments on display, Warren began staging regular musical entertainments in his Temple in 1879. Many of the men and women who participated in these musical evenings put together *The Streets of Cheyenne*, a play written, produced, and performed by local talent. There was a full house in Recreation Hall on April 4, 1878, to enjoy the "innocent but side-splitting hits at well-known citizens." Part of the humor derived from Cheyenne's early reputation for violence: "everybody gets killed except the doorkeeper and prompter."[17]

The first silver wedding anniversary ever commemorated in Wyoming featured a dinner and dance at the Railroad House. The twenty-fifth anniversary of Mr. and Mrs. J. G. Stearns was celebrated in July 1871 by "many leading citizens." During the 1870s weddings became major social events in Cheyenne. In December 1876, for example, Rodolph Glover, junior partner of Addoms & Glover, wed Anna Hurlburt, "sister of the popular Hurlburt Brothers." Both firms were successful wholesale and retail drug houses, and "the elite of the city" crowded into St. Mark's Episcopal Church, then enjoyed "a most elegant wedding breakfast" before escorting the newlyweds to the UP depot for their honeymoon trip. The *Leader* described the proceedings, then published a long list of wedding gifts—and givers.[18]

Two years later, St. Mark's was the scene of an even grander wedding. Walter Hurlburt, druggist, married Arabelle Whitehead, daughter of Judge Whitehead. Governor Hoyt led the "notable company of ladies and gentlemen, elegantly attired," who gathered at the church. The bridal gown was "one of the handsomest ever seen in Cheyenne," and after the wedding there was "an elegant repast" at the twelve-room Whitehead home on Seventeenth. The bride and groom departed for Chicago on the afternoon train, and the now-customary gift list ("strawberry and cream set, Mr. and Mrs. F. E. Warren") appeared the next day in the newspaper.[19]

Arabelle's bridesmaid was her seventeen-year-old sister Ella, who wrote a charming account of her girlhood. She fondly recalled social events at Fort

Russell, with the officers handsome in "army blue and gold." Ella was one of a party of six who piled into Governor F. E. Warren's sleigh for a drive through the snow to a dance at the fort. "We were completely covered with the buffalo robes, the temperature at twenty-eight degrees below zero," she described. The dance lasted most of the night, but Governor Warren waited until dawn, so that "the road would be broken by army wagons." Ella recalled a lovely sleigh ride back to town as "the snow sparkled like diamonds." She also enjoyed riding to the fort for band concerts with A. R. Converse, who drove his team "like the wind." She pointed out that it was easy to be well-dressed: "Cheyenne had good modistes and stores with fine materials." Ella later married in St. Mark's with four brides-maids.[20]

Another wedding of importance took place at the bride's home in Indiana, but Henry G. Hay brought her back to Cheyenne. Hay had arrived at Cheyenne in 1870 as a twenty-two-year-old deputy U.S. surveyor. The ambitious young man soon began ranching and entered a mercantile partnership with I. C. Whipple. Late in 1874 he returned to his native state to marry, but Henry and Ella Hay made their home in Cheyenne, where they had a son and daughter and became mainstays of society.[21]

The men who escorted their wives through Cheyenne's busy social scene spent their days working to create wealth. With the boom that began in the mid-1870s, business opportunities multiplied, and Cheyenne entrepreneurs simultaneously found profitable possibilities in cattle ranching. The Magic City reflected growth and prosperity with a profusion of impressive new commercial buildings and residences, along with the latest infrastructure of an inventive age.

In 1871 the *Leader* called for street improvements, because when it rained it was a "great annoyance to have many of our streets so flooded with water that they are almost impassable." When the Black Hills boom began a few years later,

Payment Overdue

Since its inception in 1867, the Cheyenne *Daily Leader* regularly printed appeals for the payment of overdue subscriptions or advertising bills. Occasionally the editor used a bit of imagination. On April 20, 1870, for example, N. A. Baker began a paragraph describing the magnificent weather and the beautifully attired ladies who were around town shopping. Then he mentioned that the most elaborately dressed lady "is the wife of a man that has owed this office a small sum for nearly three years. He always says he can't raise the money. No wonder."

Seven years later, Maj. Herman Glafcke, who had purchased the *Leader* from Baker, tried his hand at a clever turn on a familiar verse. "Lives there a man with soul so dead, who never himself has said, I'll pay before I go to bed, the debt I owe the printer? Yes, there are some we know full well, who never such a tale could tell, but they, I fear, will go to — well, the place where there's no winter."

the streets were graded and guttered. A city ordinance "for the erection of side-walks" was enacted in 1874, and two years later plank crosswalks were "ordered put down" at numerous intersections. In 1877 citizens voted to spend "$30,000 for supplying the city with water for fire and other purposes." Wells and an irrigation ditch from Crow Creek had provided Cheyenne's water, although the UP had erected a pump house to supply locomotive boilers. In the fall of 1877 excavations were made all over town, and water mains and several carloads of lead pipe went underground. (In 1883 the system was greatly improved by utilizing lakes to the north and above Cheyenne as a reservoir, and the network of mains and pipe was expanded.)[22]

A sewer system was begun late in 1878. Also in 1878, exactly two years after Alexander Graham Bell and Thomas Watson made their telephone workable, this revolutionary invention reached Cheyenne. Telephone wires were strung between two stores, and the newfangled instruments were installed on February 13, 1878. Western Union already was peddling a telegraph connection from homes or businesses to the police station to summon a messenger, but the company obtained a telephone franchise for Cheyenne. The *Leader* realized that people who installed a telephone "can speak to their physician if the baby is sick, summon a policeman should burglars be about, or tell their butchers what kind of meat to bring them for breakfast." Within days Charles F. Annett, manager of Western Union in Cheyenne and "agent of the Bell telephone," traveled to Laramie and, using the "No. 2 wire of the telegraph line" as a connecting link, made a series of experimental telephone calls back to the Magic City. Soon Henry G. Hay ordered a telephone, and Dr. W. W. Crook set up a phone connection between his office and the residence of Charles Annett. Late in 1879 Annett, banker M. E. Post, and another investor incorporated the Cheyenne Telephone Exchange Company. The *Leader* enthused that "there is scarcely an end to the conveniences of the telephone exchange," and telephone poles and wires began to go up all over Cheyenne. "The instruments are becoming plentiful as sewing machines," the newspaper soon remarked, and by 1882 the Cheyenne phone exchange listed 135 names.[23]

Cheyenne was on the cutting edge of another sweeping technological development, provided by America's most famous inventor. Thirty-one-year-old Thomas Edison, exhausted from traveling around the country promoting his phonograph (many Cheyenne homes soon would boast "the machine that talked"), took a rare vacation in the summer of 1878. He was invited to join a group of scientists who traveled to Wyoming in July 1878 to view an eclipse from Rawlins. Conversations with the scientists during this trip stimulated Edison to try to invent a workable electric light to replace kerosene lamps and gaslights used in homes and businesses. Back in his research laboratory at Menlo Park, New Jersey, Edison and his staff systematically worked for more than a year before developing a reliable incandescent lamp in October 1879. Lighting systems developed across America, and in August 1882 the Electric Light Company was incorporated in Cheyenne. Capitalized at $100,000, the company's trustees were F. E. Warren, Joseph M. Carey, banker M. E. Post, and ranchers William C. Irvine and Thomas Sturgis. Later in the year, electric wires were strung through the streets of Cheyenne, and one of the first commercial lighting plants in the West was erected on West Twenty-first Street near the railroad siding to Camp Carlin. A brick building housed two large steam engines, one of forty horsepower and the other of sixty, and two dynamos powered by these engines. An iron smoke-stack, towering seventy-five feet high, stood beside the building. Trustee W.C. Irvine ordered the first light connection for his residence, and the second for the cattlemen's clubhouse on Seventeenth. During the early months of 1883, experiments resulted in flickering lights or complete blackouts; however, electricians made adjustments, and soon Irvine and others enjoyed illumination far superior to that provided by Cheyenne's gasworks. City councilmen felt that funding the water system took priority over streetlights, but in 1884 eighteen arc lights were installed at key intersections. "Will it be cheap?" citizens had asked about electricity in December 1882. "Will it be dangerous? Can it be turned on and off? Will it flicker? Will it, in a word, be a success?" As these questions received answers, progress in the Magic City once again triumphed.[24]

By 1875 B. L. Ford was erecting his three-story Inter Ocean Hotel, Joseph W. Carey and his two brothers were building a large commercial "block," and "a dozen comfortable residences" went up in the northeastern part of town. Several two-story frame structures from the late 1860s were torn down to make way for M. E. Post's "elegant" bank and other new brick buildings. "Large brick business blocks, magnificent fronts, immense plate-glass windows are becoming the rule rather than the exception with us," observed the *Leader* the next year. The *Leader* went on to describe in detail the Wyoming Armory, the splendid new home of Freund & Bro's gun store on Ferguson Street. The Freund brothers were expert, innovative gunsmiths who had established a national reputation for their Cheyenne operation.[25]

"A large number of fine brick structures will be erected in Cheyenne this year," reported the *Leader* as the boom accelerated in 1877. A month later the *Leader* called for local capitalists to build houses: "Every building in the city is full, and every room which money will hire is occupied." A large Masonic Temple, "the finest building of its kind in the city," was erected on Sixteenth in 1878, while James McDaniel built a "block" on Eddy Street containing three ground-floor stores "with French plate fronts" and full basements, several offices, and a sec-ond-floor hall which became a "popular resort for select parties and dances."[26]

Shoppers bustled into the new stores downtown during the Christmas season of 1877. "The aspect of our streets yesterday, all day, was decidedly metropolitan," the *Leader* announced. "The sidewalks about the leading merchants' stores were crowded, and elbowing and jostling were frequent occurrences, especially in front of the attractive show windows." Winter shoppers traveled on vehicles with metal or wood runners instead of wheels. "The streets yesterday were lively with runners of all kinds and merry sleigh bells jingled in all directions. There were sleigh runners, hotel runners, runners keeping themselves warm, runners from mercantile houses with purchases, boys with runners sledding down the streets."[27]

Cheyenne was a busy place by 1878, in great part because the population had more than doubled in eight years, from 1,475 in 1870 to 3,078 in October 1878. The city's youth population was rising, with 981 children under the age of seventeen (452 girls and 529 boys) including 479 under six. Magic City schools expanded accordingly, and in June 1878 Frankie Logan and Ella Hamma became Cheyenne's first two high school graduates. Commencement exercises would be held in Recreation Hall on Saturday evening, June 29, 1878. "Cheyenne's best musical talent will be pressed into service," reported the *Leader*. Selected pupils "will favor the assemblage with exercises of a literary character," and Governor John Hoyt would address the crowd. Future commencements would be even more elaborate. High school graduation became a major event on the Cheyenne calendar.[28]

Frank and George Freund, master gunsmiths, opened their Wyoming Armory in Cheyenne in 1867. The brothers moved back to Denver, although they kept the Wyoming Armory open. Frank returned in 1875 during the Black Hills excitement. This 1877 scene shows the Armory on Ferguson between Sixteenth and Seventeenth, the third of four Cheyenne locations. Frank patented gunsight innovations, but his wife Klotilda never liked Cheyenne, although she gave birth to four of their eight children in the Magic City. Frank sold out in 1885 and moved his family to New Jersey. (Courtesy Wyoming State Archives)

The first American high school opened in Boston in 1821. Elementary schools were everywhere, in the smallest villages and in the rural countryside, but by 1860 there still were only 311 public high schools. Although elementary schools long had received tax support, there was opposition to using tax money for high schools. The problem was solved by the Kalamazoo case in 1874, when the Michigan Supreme Court decided that local governments *could* use tax money to support secondary schools. After this decision secondary education proliferated, with 2,500 public schools by 1890, 6,000 by 1900, and 14,000 by 1910. (Despite the expansion, a high school education long remained a rarity: the Census of 1890, for example, indicated that fewer than seven percent of Americans between the ages of fourteen and seventeen were attending the nation's 2,500 high schools.) The upwardly mobile men and women of Cheyenne, especially those who were parents, would make certain that the Magic City played a progressive role in America's educational movement.

At the start of the 1870s, as many as fifty students, on a good day, crowded into the frame schoolhouse in the northern part of town. In April 1871 the *Leader* pointed out the need for a new school, and the next month there was a large audience at the annual school meeting. Following "considerable discussion," it was voted to erect a new school and to raise taxes to pay for it. A site was secured northeast of the frame school, a full block "on the highest plat of land within the limits of our city." A large brick building was contracted, at a cost of $7,681, and school furniture was ordered from Cincinnati, Ohio. When completed early in 1872, "Central School" was the most prominent building in town.[29]

With a new school came a new principal, "Professor" N. E. Stark, who would

Central School opened in 1872, and there was a major addition in 1876. (Courtesy Wyoming State Archives)

propel Cheyenne's educational system into rapid expansion. Within a year, average daily attendance at Central School had exploded to 122, and by 1876 a major addition (costing $9,432.09) was built onto Central School. A year later, "210 female and 250 male scholars" were enrolled. Stark instituted a secondary program in 1875, the year after the Kalamazoo case, and within three years Cheyenne High School produced its first two graduates. One of those grads, Ella Hamma, was promptly hired as an elementary teacher; her classroom was one floor beneath the high school rooms she had attended only a few months earlier. She greeted 44 students in September 1878. The other elementary teachers were assigned 81, 71, 68, and 53 pupils — totals which would stagger modern educators, even if absenteeism usually ran about one-third. Professor Stark and Assistant Principal C.L. Wells split 74 high school students. Stark was paid $1,660 for the year; Wells, $1,230; and elementary teachers, $685 each. Female teachers, who were expected to remain single, were paid less than males, who needed more to support their families — and simply because they were males.[30]

The high attendance in Cheyenne schools was stimulated by a compulsory attendance education law passed by the Territorial Legislature, but the *Leader* frequently complained of truants: "How about the compulsory education law? We see urchins upon the streets at all hours of the day." The *Leader* often praised teachers, however, who "are doing a noble work for the youths of Cheyenne." A visiting clergyman also was impressed by what he saw at Central School in December 1877. "Seven teachers compose the faculty, but the presiding genius, Professor Stark, is the mainspring of the whole working of the institution, and his plans are seen from the lowest primary department up to his own room."[31]

City Salaries

In the last municipal election of the 1870s, on Tuesday, January 14, 1879, L. R. Bresnahan, who had spearheaded numerous civic improvements, was elected to another term as mayor. A week later Mayor Bresnahan convened the first meeting of the new city council. Meals had to be brought in, and the meeting lasted until nearly three in the morning. Among other business was the setting of salaries for city officials:

Mayor, per year	$500
City Clerk, per year	500
Marshal, per month, plus fees	65
Policemen, per year	900
Chief Engineer, Fire Dept., per year	250
Engineer, Durant fire engine per month	75
Supt. of Ditches, per month	50
City Treasurer, per year	700

By 1879 Cheyenne was so orderly that the number of policemen was reduced from three to two. Cheyenne maintained a city team and wagon, driven by the city teamster. And while the mayor and fire department engineer had other employment, they were paid more than token salaries. (From Cheyenne *Daily Leader*, January 15 and 22, 1879)

Stark was instrumental in organizing the Teachers' Institute of Wyoming, an annual event which began in 1874. Wyoming's teachers met for one week each August to discuss textbooks, methods of instruction and mutual problems, and to listen to lectures on geography, mathematics, reading, history, and other subjects. Stark and other Cheyenne teachers were prominent in presenting programs. There were sessions each morning, afternoon, and evening. This pedagogic grind provided needed training, especially for teachers like Ella Hamma, who went into the classroom with no college courses. For several years Cheyenne hosted the Institute, although later the event was rotated to other Wyoming communities.[32]

Ed Hurlburt, a product of Cheyenne schools and a member of the family of local druggists, won appointment to West Point in 1876. Cheyenne was enormously proud of Cadet Hurlbut, the first young man from Wyoming appointed to either of the service academies. Six months later the *Leader* curtly announced that Hurlbut "has thrown up his appointment and returned home to stay." Hurlbut married and became a Cheyenne businessman, and in time other young men from Wyoming would graduate from West Point or Annapolis.[33]

Cheyenne's public schools were supplemented by private schools. Occasionally an itinerant teacher would open a private school, but these efforts always proved short-lived. Rev. Joseph W. Cook began an Episcopalian school in 1868, and St. Mark's maintained the school for a few more years. Cheyenne's best and largest private school was St. Mary's, which would be opened by Catholic nuns in 1884.

The Catholics of Cheyenne lost their spiritual shepherd in 1877, when Father John McGoldrick died in October following a long illness. Father McGoldrick "loved and was beloved by all," and St. Mary's was jammed for his funeral. Father McGoldrick's body would be shipped by rail to his home for burial, and "the longest funeral procession ever seen in Cheyenne filed away from the church and followed the remains to the depot. There were eighty-two vehicles in the funeral train, containing nearly four hundred men, women and children." Undeterred by their loss and responding to the growth of the Magic City, the Catholics launched a building program. The new St. Mary's would be Cheyenne's first brick church, with ninety-two pews seating more than 500 worshipers.[34]

In 1875 the African Methodist Episcopal congregation built a brick church on West Eighteenth and Thomes, on a lot donated by Mrs. Lucy Phillips. Two years later another new church, Cheyenne's seventh, was organized by prominent citizens. Although a traveling Baptist preacher delivered Cheyenne's first sermon in 1867, there were not enough Baptists in residence to form a congregation. For a decade Cheyenne's Baptists attended other churches, some singing in the Presbyterian, Episcopalian, and Congregational choirs. Cheyenne's boom during the 1870s brought more Baptists to town, and an organizational meeting was held in September 1877. The driving force behind the First Baptist Church was wealthy businessman I. C. Whipple. Whipple persuaded Governor John Thayer, whose executive office suite was on the second floor of the Whipple Block, to attend the initial meeting. Mr. and Mrs. F. E. Warren also attended the organizational meeting, and so did the wives of Drs. J. J. and W. W. Crook. (Dr. J. J. Crook opened a practice in Cheyenne and became county physician, then persuaded his younger brother to join him. Although J.J. soon moved to Colorado, W.W. spent the rest of his career tending health needs in Cheyenne.) Governor Thayer and F.E. Warren became charter members of the First Baptist Church Board of Trustees, while I.C. Whipple served the church as lifelong deacon and benefactor. Women form the heart of any church, and Mrs. Warren, Mrs. Whipple, and Mrs. W.W. Crook devoted their formidable talents and efforts as much to First Baptist as to Cheyenne society. The First Baptist congregation met in the courthouse until 1881, when a brick church was erected at Eighteenth and Ferguson.[35]

Eighteenth and Ferguson became known as "Church Corner" during the 1880s, because Baptist, Episcopalian, and Presbyterian churches stood at this intersection. But just east of this spiritual center of Cheyenne—and at the opposite end of the morality spectrum—ranged a line of structures along the south side of Eighteenth called "The Row." The Row housed an array of sporting women who operated within the shadows of these churches. One of the establishments was called "The Double Decker," while the largest and most elegant house on The Row belonged to Ida Hamilton. A plump, shrewd businesswoman, in 1878 she built a "fine brick mansion" on Eighteenth boasting "two fine parlors," six upstairs bedrooms, gas lighting, and a heating furnace. The building cost $8,000 and the furniture was valued at $6,000. Ida's grand opening was a ribald party which immediately assumed legendary status in Cheyenne's history of vice.[36]

Dr. W.W. Crook, longtime Cheyenne physician. In March 1880 Dr. Crook lost two of his three children to scarlet fever. (Courtesy Wyoming State Archives)

John M. Thayer had served as a Union brigadier general and as a U.S. senator from Nebraska where he was appointed territorial governor of Wyoming (1875-78) by his friend, President Grant. Thayer later was governor of Nebraska. (Courtesy Wyoming State Archives)

Sporting women twice squared off during December 1878. Following a Saturday night of revelry, two of the girls engaged in combat. "For a short time the genuine hair, false hair, ribbons and snide jewelry filled the air around the combatants," observed the *Leader*. A few nights later, about two hours into Christmas, two girls battled in one of the variety theaters, scattering false hair, ribbons, and false teeth. "No lives lost," was the report. The *Leader* frequently campaigned against variety theaters and other dives. "The 'Concert Hall' and 'Wine Parlor' should be blotted out of existence," and within a couple of days success was announced. Another target: "The disreputable Concert Hall has been closed up. The late proprietor is in jail." The *Leader* also derided a "bagnio kept by some colored women in the old Rollins house building," which had been moved to the disreputable red light district in northwestern Cheyenne. Drunken disturbances were "of nightly occurrence," but the bartender soon was arrested and fined. Another temptation was Cheyenne's Chinese opium dens, and a list of the patrons "would startle the community." There never was a shortage of vice in nineteenth-century Cheyenne.[37]

The *Leader* dutifully pointed out to the public other disagreeable, if less wicked, problems around town. "There are 7,000 dogs in Cheyenne. Shoot 'em," demanded the *Leader* in 1877. Early in the decade a city ordinance was passed authorizing the shooting of stray dogs, and in March 1872 a city policeman was paid seventeen dollars for killing seventeen dogs. "Let the work go bravely on," urged the *Leader*. Five years later, though, stray dogs still roamed the streets, along with cows and "wandering swine." Furthermore, "alleys in all parts of the city are fairly reeking with filth, and full of old rubbish," the *Leader* complained in July 1877. "Hot weather is upon us, and the health of the city should be looked after." Although dogs and pigs and dirty alleys were common in western towns during the 1870s, this contrast with Cheyenne's modern improvements was especially irritating in a city with rapidly rising expectations. In 1876 a visitor who had not seen Cheyenne in six years stepped off the train from Denver: "I took a good look

Working for Their Keep

For years crews of jail inmates, under the supervision of a guard and often burdened with a ball and chain, worked to maintain Cheyenne's graded streets. City prisoners also cleaned alleys and performed other tasks around town. Prisoners with tools in their hands became a familiar sight in Cheyenne, and there was general approval that they were earning their keep.

Females often were arrested in the west end. While women were not forced to work with the street crews, sometimes "gender-appropriate" chores were found. For example, the *Leader* reported on September 12, 1878, that three female prisoners were busy scrubbing "the window casings and doors at City Hall."

at the town and was indeed astonished to see the substantial improvements made in it since I was there last. The town is at least four times as large as in 1870."[38]

The growth and development of Cheyenne during the 1870s was spearheaded by enterprising, ambitious men who grew their fortunes and positions along with the city. Most of these progressive citizens would lead Cheyenne into the 1880s, although James McDaniel moved his operations to booming Leadville. The popular showman had made a great deal of money and had accumulated a complex of buildings, but during the 1870s he was hit hard by fire, and he and his wife lost one of their three children. Perhaps the mining boomtown in Colorado exerted the same adventurous pull on McDaniel that the railroad boomtown of Cheyenne had in 1867. After providing fun and excitement to the Magic City for a dozen years, McDaniel sold out and started over in Leadville.

F. E. Warren stayed, as did Joseph Carey and Amasa Converse, Henry Hay and R. S. Van Tassell, I. C. Whipple and Erasmus Nagle, Luke Murrin and T. A. Kent. The army and, of course, the Union Pacific stayed too, continuing to exert a steady, powerful impact on life in Cheyenne. A leading newcomer during the decade was Col. E. A. Slack, who founded the Cheyenne *Daily Sun* in 1876, later purchased the *Leader*, and during the rest of his long life became one of Cheyenne's most important citizens. Although the Black Hills rush leveled off by the end of the 1870s, a boom in cattle ranching was bringing even greater wealth and growth to Cheyenne. Most of Cheyenne's prominent businessmen invested in stock raising, helping to identify their expanding city with America's most colorful industry.

I. C. Whipple, wealthy merchant who served a term as mayor during the 1870s, was a major force in organizing and sustaining the First Baptist Church. (Courtesy Wyoming State Archives)

The
1880s

"There are very wealthy people living in this town
but they all look to me like Cowboys."
Easterner John Feick

"In our business we are often compelled to do certain things, which,
to the inexperienced, seem a little crooked."
Cheyenne cattle baron A. H. Swan

"No wonder they like the club at Cheyenne. It's the pearl of the prairies."
Owen Wister

"I concluded long since, that while natural location has much to do with the success of a town, the right kind of men have much more to do with it."
Governor F. E. Warren

"Travelers say that the Cheyenne electric light is the best they have ever seen.
It is steady, bright, and sizzles but little."
Cheyenne *Daily Leader*, May 15, 1883

"One stormy day when a blizzard was sweeping across Wyoming and howling
through the streets of Cheyenne, the boys who liked their noon dram
leaned up against [Luke Murrin's] bar. Their faces very long and disconsolate,
backed up by low mutterings of loss on the range and visions of unpaid notes
in the fall, the witty but rather disreputable saloon keeper said:
'Cheer up boys, whatever happens the books won't freeze.'"
John Clay

10

The Holy City of the Cow

The cattle frontier marked an indelible brand on American history. The public imagination was captivated by cowboys galloping across the range while wearing big hats, boots, spurs, bandanas, and leather chaps. The cowboy culture included such colorful elements as longhorns and mustangs, roundups and trail drives, lariats and branding irons, stampedes and bronco busting. In an age of wealthy Eastern capitalists who commanded industrial empires, the western equivalent was the cattle king ruling over vast ranches. More cattle kings made their homes in Cheyenne than in any other city, more than in Fort Worth or San Antonio, Denver or Dodge City, Kansas City or Miles City. The most powerful stock growers' association in the West headquartered in Cheyenne, and the most glamorous cattlemen's club was erected in the city. Hundreds of carloads of cattle were shipped to the East every year from Cheyenne's stockyards. Soon Cheyenne was called "The Holy City of the Cow," and as ranching spread across the grasslands of Wyoming, this enormous cattle kingdom would earn permanent identity as "The Cowboy State."

Three decades before Cheyenne was founded, a parade of wagon trains crossed Wyoming along the Oregon Trail. At road ranches along the way, proprietors traded with immigrants for broken-down oxen. These animals thrived on Wyoming grasses, a harbinger of the post-Civil War "Beef Bonanza." In 1866 Nelson Story and a large crew of heavily armed cowboys braved a host of horseback warriors to drive a herd of Texas longhorns through Wyoming to a rich market in Montana. The year of Story's drive marked the beginning of the great trail drives north out of Texas, and a successful, timely drive could bring enormous profits. Ranches were organized across the open ranges of Texas, many of them financed by Eastern or British investors. As cattle ranching spread to ranges throughout the West, Wyoming's vacant grasslands beckoned.

Some of Cheyenne's earliest settlers brought a few head of cattle, and the animals multiplied rapidly on open ranges near town. By February 1868 the *Leader* remarked upon the large numbers of "the 'cattle upon a thousand hills' round about Cheyenne." In that same month, early cattle king J. W. Iliff placed longhorns on the grasslands around Cheyenne. A native of Ohio, John Wesley Iliff was named after the founder of Methodism, and he attended Ohio Wesleyan University. In his twenties he sought fortune in the West, first in Kansas, then, during Colorado's 1859 gold rush, in the boomtown that became Denver. By 1861 Iliff was buying Texas cattle and fattening them on nearby open ranges. He sold cattle to mining camps and Denver butcher shops and aggressively pursued beef contracts with army posts, Union Pacific construction crews, and Indian reservations. Eventually he grazed as many as 60,000 cattle on a range extending more than 100 miles westward along the South Platte from Colorado's eastern border and sixty miles northward into Wyoming. Iliff opened a meat market in Cheyenne and often visited the Magic City, staying in the Railroad Hotel. A devoted family man, he made his home in Denver, investing heavily in real estate. But "the cattle king of the plains" traveled tirelessly, making deals and checking his herds while incessantly smoking a chain of cigars. Early in 1878 Iliff, exposed too long to winter weather, fell ill and died. He was only forty-six. His widow erected a thirty-two-foot monument at his grave and continued to run the Iliff empire.[1]

In Cheyenne the death of Iliff "cast a pall over the city," and a large contingent of friends and fellow ranchers traveled to Denver to attend the funeral. Iliff had provided a tantalizing model for Cheyenne's would-be cattlemen. In addition to being a shrewd judge of cattle, he purchased just enough land to provide him control of surrounding ranges. At the time of his death he owned title to only 15,558 acres of land in 105 parcels. There were fifty 160-acre tracts; twenty-seven tracts of eighty acres; forty-four tracts of just forty acres; and others as small as fourteen acres. These tracts were strategically placed for ranch headquarters and line camps and, of course, to control water sources. F. E. Warren, always alert to profitable enterprises, aggressively followed Iliff's example. Warren and his business partner, A. R. Converse, began ranching, branding "CW" on Converse & Warren livestock. When their partnership was dissolved in 1877, Warren purchased their lucrative mercantile business, along with their ranch property and sheep, while Converse kept their cattle. Warren emulated Iliff on a large scale, acquiring ranch properties in several Wyoming counties, as well as in northern Colorado and western Nebraska. The Warren Livestock Company soon encompassed vast rangelands, although Warren began to favor sheep over cattle. (Sheep provide two crops per year, fleece and lambs, as opposed to an annual calf crop.) Warren eventually served as president of the National Woolgrowers' Association.[2]

A. R. Converse stuck to cattle ranching while running the First National Bank of Cheyenne. In 1884 Converse erected "a magnificent residence" at Eighteenth and Warren for his wife and daughter. But the millionaire banker-cattleman already suffered health problems, and while seeking medical help in New York City he died in June 1885. A founding businessman of Cheyenne, Converse was only forty-three when he was lost to the Magic City.[3]

Judge Joseph Carey, while still a bachelor practicing law and dabbling in real estate, plunged into cattle ranching, accumulating a herd of 6,000 by 1875. But while F. E. Warren centered his ranching efforts south of Cheyenne, Carey looked to the vast unclaimed ranges to the north, where he would establish a magnificent ranch when the army stamped out Indian trouble. Carey entered public life, began a family, erected a $20,000 brick residence at Seventeenth and Ferguson in 1877–78, then moved a few blocks north to an even more splendid mansion seven years later. But for the rest of his life, Carey spent large amounts of time at his big CY Ranch outside Casper, christening the headquarters "Careyhurst."[4]

Surveyor Henry G. Hay entered the livestock business in 1871, raising cattle, horses, and sheep, while engaging in banking and other enterprises. Wealthy merchant Erasmus Nagle invested in cattle ranching, and so did young businessman R. S. Van Tassell, who built the Running Water Ranch and Cheyenne's stockyards, capable of holding 5,000 head of cattle. Former mayor A. H. Reel established a ranch at Carbon, and hard-working attorney W. W. Corlett enjoyed leaving Cheyenne to check his cattle. Wyoming's first two governors, John Campbell and John Thayer, invested in the cattle business and used their influence to promote ranching.[5]

In 1876 twenty-four-year-old W. C. "Billy" Irvine, already an experienced ranch foreman, bought 4,000 Texas longhorns and drove them to Wyoming's open ranges. Locating a ranch on the North Platte River near Fort Fetterman, Irvine doubled the size of his herd within two years. He also helped to organize, and agreed to manage, two big outfits created by investors, the Converse Cattle Company and the Ogallala Land and Cattle Company. Seeking proximity to other stockraisers and to banks—as well as social and material amenities, unavailable on his isolated ranch—this dynamic cattle baron built a home in Cheyenne.[6]

Another visionary cattle-

Rancher A. H. "Heck" Reel was treasurer of the powerful Wyoming Stock Growers' Association for thirteen years, and he also served a term as mayor of Cheyenne. (Courtesy Wyoming State Archives)

man, twenty-five-year-old Englishman Moreton Frewen, moved to Wyoming in 1878 determined to build a cattle kingdom on unclaimed grasslands. Combining his inheritance with that of his brother, Dick, he commenced a ranch on the Powder River, erecting a hulking two-story log residence—"Frewen's Castle"—along with outbuildings and corrals. Raising more capital from English investors, Moreton soon grazed 70,000 cattle on a range that extended about eighty miles north to south and fifty miles east to west. Like Billy Irvine, the Frewen brothers built a residence in Cheyenne, on a hill on Twenty-third Street, in the northeastern part of town.[7]

Alexander H. Swan, another tireless promoter of the cattle industry, reached Cheyenne in the early 1870s. Already in his forties, Swan had considerable experience as a stockraiser in the Midwest, and he saw enormous opportunity in the open ranges of the West. "He stood about six feet and an inch, and wherever he went he made an imposing figure," related the Scottish cattleman John Clay after meeting Swan. "At Cheyenne groups of men sat round him in his office and wor-

Clay Allison's Toothache

By 1886 rancher-gunfighter Clay Allison had established a spread in Lincoln County, New Mexico. According to the June 26, 1886, issue of the *Las Vegas Daily Optic*, Allison drove about 1,500 steers up the old Goodnight-Loving Trail to Cheyenne. A tooth was dealing him misery, so Allison went to an unnamed dentist. (Dr. F. L. Warren, who had been in town for nearly two decades, and Dr. Rees Williams were practicing dentistry in Cheyenne in 1886.) But the dentist drilled into a sound tooth and "inadvertently broke about half the tooth off."

Allison stormed out of the office and sought another dentist, who called his competitor "an arrant quack." Dental repairs cost Allison twenty-five dollars, and he marched back to confront the first dentist. Allison seized an extractor, wrestled the dentist to the floor, and forcibly (and, it may be assumed, inexpertly) extracted "one of his best molars." Then Allison "grabbed for another and caught one of the front teeth together with a large piece of the upper lip." Finally, the den-

tist's shrieks attracted a restraining crowd to the scene.

A few days later, while returning to his ranch, Allison told this tale in Raton, and it was picked up by the *Optic*. "The story is said to be absolutely true," concluded the *Optic* in its account. On August 5, 1886, the Cheyenne *Leader* reprinted "the following piece of newspaper fiction," which also had been copied by Eastern newspapers. The *Leader* sniffed that Easterners "probably regard Cheyenne as just the sort of place" where the gunman's misadventure might have occurred, "but this community now looks back upon such a period as belonging to a remote part which it has long outgrown."

This incident has proved a persistent part of the lore of Clay Allison, and by association, the colorful past of the Holy City of the Cow. In *The Man Who Shot Liberty Valance*, famed Western director John Ford expressed his attitude through a journalist character: "This is the West, sir. When the legend becomes a fact, print the legend!"

shipped at his feet. In Chicago he was courted by bankers, commission men, breeders of fine cattle; in fact, all classes of people in the livestock business."[8]

This ambitious promoter operated on a grand scale, organizing cattle companies while participating fully in the civic affairs and social life of Cheyenne. In 1883, backed by a Scottish syndicate with abundant capital, he organized the Swan Land and Cattle Company. Corporate offices were located in Edinburgh, Scotland, while the ranching headquarters was the Two Bar Ranch at Chugwater, forty-five miles north of Cheyenne. Rapid expansion led to the occupation of more than one million acres of land, with 200 cowboys working a reported 113,000 head of cattle. Also in 1883, Swan established a Hereford breeding ranch six miles southeast of Cheyenne, which produced champion bulls and remains in operation today.[9]

In 1870 just 8,143 cattle were assessed in Wyoming Territory. But herds of Texas cattle were scattered onto open rangelands, and by 1878 there were 300,000 cattle in Wyoming. Seven years later the number had exploded to nearly two million. The Texas Trail stretched north from Cheyenne to Miles City, Montana, and in the peak year of 1884 more than 800,000 cattle were shoved northward from the Magic City. The cattle boom began to affect Cheyenne during the local expansion generated by the Black Hills gold rush. Although the gold rush leveled off during the late 1870s, the Beef Bonanza accelerated Cheyenne's growth as the Holy City of the Cow.

Banker M. E. Post was one of the shareholders in the Luke Voorhees Cattle Company. Post and Voorhees were among many Cheyenne businessmen who invested in cattle ranching. (Warren Papers)

By 1876 A.H. Swan was dubbed "the stock king of Laramie county." The comings and goings of the big ranchers, as well as cattle shipments and range conditions, were regularly reported in the *Leader* under such column headings as "CATTLE TALK," "LIVE STOCK NOTES," "LIVE STOCK GOSSIP," "LIVE STOCK MATTERS," "LIVE STOCK TALK," and "RANGE & HERDS." It was news when the Frewen brothers bought 20,000 pounds of provisions for their Powder River Ranch from Erasmus Nagle's Union Mercantile Company. It was news when W.C. Irvine spent $15,000 on his new home in Cheyenne, and when A.H. Swan built a new brick carriage house, "the costliest in Wyoming Territory." The Union Mercantile and other Cheyenne firms sold vast amounts of supplies to Wyoming ranches. And as his fellow ranchers built handsome residences in Cheyenne, F.E. Warren sold them furniture and carpets, wall paintings and pianos. In July 1882 the *Leader* reported that Cheyenne's "hotels are full of cattle raisers and buyers, and the lobbies are animated" as stockmen negotiated deals. The annual meetings of the Wyoming Stock Growers' Association (WSGA) were covered in detail.[10]

The WSGA originated at a meeting in Cheyenne on November 29, 1873, when ten ranchers formed the Laramie County Stock Growers' Association. The next year the association introduced the practice of cooperative fall and spring roundups, dividing the range into districts to be worked by the combined crews and chuck wagons of member ranches. As ranching boomed in Wyoming, these roundups grew along with the association (there were six roundup districts in 1880—and thirty-one just four years later). In 1879 the expanding organization renamed itself the Wyoming Stock Growers' Association.[11]

Prominent Cheyenne residents served the WSGA in leadership roles. A.H. Swan was president for five years (1876–81), and Judge Joseph Carey proved to be an especially skilled president (1883–87), while concurrently serving Wyoming

The Carey Block featured the Stock Growers National Bank. (Courtesy Wyoming State Archives)

as territorial delegate to Congress. Judge William Kuykendall was the first secretary-treasurer (1873–75). He was followed as secretary by Thomas Sturgis for more than a decade (1876–87) and as treasurer by A.H. Reel for thirteen years (1876–89). Reel was succeeded for another thirteen years by Henry Hay, while William C. Irvine began a notably effective fifteen years as president in 1896.

Membership grew rapidly, by 1885 swelling to 363 paid members, including out-of-state ranchers who did business in Wyoming. John Clay joined the WSGA in 1883 and found his fellow members to be "generally an exceedingly bright set of men. They were young, courageous, possibly wanting in conservativism. In their idle hours they drank too much and did other naughty things, but the western folks forgive them for their hearts were true and leal [loyal]. In adversity they showed up better than in success and this feature is to their eternal credit."[12]

During the early 1880s, the WSGA operated a stock exchange in Cheyenne, providing market reports and other financial information from June 1 to November 15 each year to eastern capitalists who ventured west to visit their ranches. WSGA members exercised great influence in Wyoming because they provided most of the capital invested in the territory. Association members were elected to the legislature and to county and local offices, and they served Wyoming as judges, congressmen, and governors. When

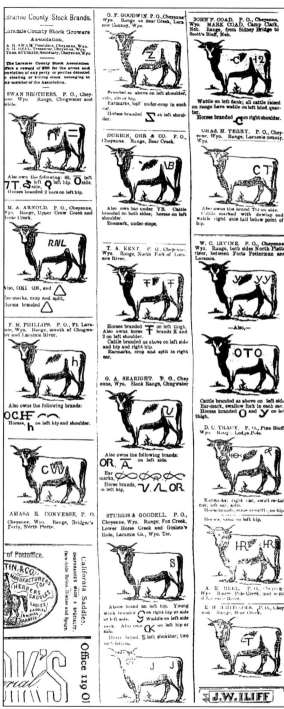

Periodically, brands and markings were published in the Leader. *These are Laramie County brands, and include such Cheyenne leaders as A. H. Swan, A. R. Converse, T. A. Kent, W. C. Irvine, Heck Reel, and E. W. Whitcomb. (*Leader, *August 31, 1878)*

cattlemen needed legislation or official action, more often than not they got it. WSGA members dominated the economy and, consequently, the politics of Wyoming. In 1882 Thomas Sturgis, the enormously influential secretary of the WSGA, pushed a bill through the Legislative Assembly establishing a territorial veterinarian. Aided by a score of WSGA inspectors, the veterinarian would try to keep infected cattle from entering Wyoming. In 1883 a hospital for cowboys and other range workers was opened in the old post hospital at Fort Fetterman. In 1884 a WSGA committee traveled to Washington, D.C., to lobby for changes in

Bird's Eye View of Cheyenne, 1882. (Author's collection)

the Animal Industry Act. The rulers of Wyoming's cattle kingdoms were comfortable with the exercise of power, even in the nation's capital.[13]

The WSGA held its annual meeting each April in Cheyenne. Association members first convened in the Laramie County Courthouse, but later found it necessary to move to the larger Opera House auditorium.

"It was sort of a free for all," described John Clay, who first attended in 1884. "We did not in those days have prepared papers over which the author had labored for days." Instead, committee reports triggered impromptu discussions

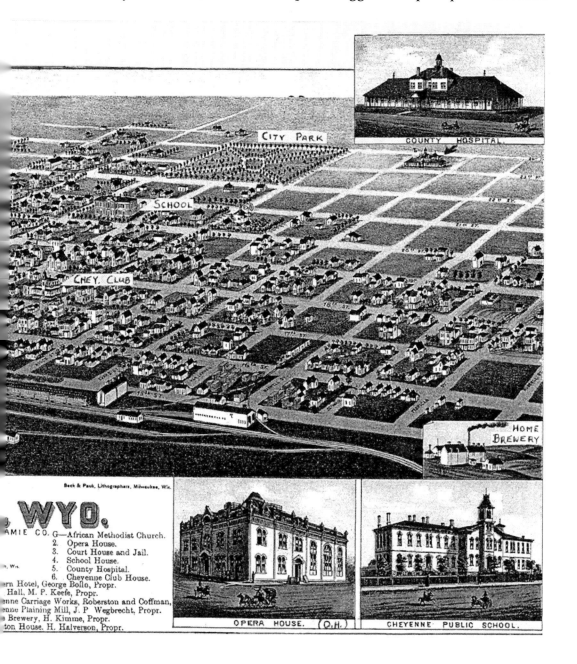

Beck & Paul, Lithographers, Milwaukee, Wis.

WYO.

AMIE CO. G—African Methodist Church.
2. Opera House.
3. Court House and Jail.
4. School House.
5. County Hospital.
6. Cheyenne Club House.

rn Hotel, George Bollo, Propr.
Hall, M. P. Keefe, Propr.
nne Carriage Works, Roberston and Coffman,
nne Plaining Mill, J. P. Wegbrecht, Propr.
Brewery, H. Kimme, Propr.
ton House. H. Halverson, Propr.

OPERA HOUSE. (O.H.)

CHEYENNE PUBLIC SCHOOL.

CITY PARK

COUNTY HOSPITAL.

SCHOOL

CHEY. CLUB

HOME BREWERY

about such subjects as railroads, cattle rustling, public stockyards, livestock diseases, and the leasing of public domain. The most important topic was roundup information, diagrammed on large sheets of paper, fixing the date and place of rendezvous for each roundup district.[14]

In addition to ranch owners and managers, a number of cowboys were present, many hoping to find work. The *Leader* described "the hilarious cow boy with jingling spurs and broncho pony [who] cavorts up and down the streets of the city." In 1880 a well-known black cowboy, "Broncho Bill," was tried and convicted for assault and battery after "seriously beating one of the sergeants at Fort Russell." Two years later, a less violent encounter occurred on the baseball grounds, when a team of "Cow boys" defeated a Fort Russell nine, 23–12.[15]

Also in town each April were numerous representatives from railroads, stockyards, and packing plants, along with managers of feed companies and "Chicago

The Wyoming Hereford Ranch

The world-famous Wyoming Hereford Ranch was originated in 1883 by cattle king Alexander Swan, who was determined to introduce Herefords at a time when Shorthorns dominated breeding in Wyoming. In conjunction with his cattle business, Swan was vice-president of the First National Bank of Cheyenne, and he located his breeding ranch six miles southeast of Wyoming's capital. Crow Creek meandered through the ranch, and adequate precipitation produced fine grasses. An elevation exceeding 6,000 feet enhanced the quality of the grasses.

Swan sent an English-born associate, George F. Morgan, to England to purchase foundation stock. Morgan brought back 146 Herefords, including a 2,600-pound bull, Rudolph. Although Rudolph died in 1885 of injuries incurred while being loaded, he produced eighteen sons and twenty daughters during his brief tenure, and his commanding frame and 1884 show prizes went far in spreading acceptance of Herefords. Morgan helped form the American Hereford Cattle Breeders Association, and Swan would become its fifth president.

The conditions which wrecked the open-range cattle industry after 1886 would thrust Swan into bankruptcy in 1887. The Hereford Ranch went into receivership, and the appointed receiver was Colin Hunter, who intended to keep the herd and ranch intact. Will Rossman, trained by George Morgan, was hired as foreman. Hunter finally sold the outfit in 1890, to Cheyenne businessman Henry Altman and his partner, Dan McUlvan, who retained Rossman. "The best today, not good enough for tomorrow" was the motto of the progressive Altman, who operated the Wyoming Hereford Ranch for more than a quarter of a century.

Although the famous property has since changed hands several times, today the Wyoming Hereford Ranch is a major attraction of the Cheyenne area. Self-guided tours are available to visitors, while group tours, picnics campouts, and hayrides may be scheduled. Well into its second century of operation, the Wyoming Hereford Ranch is a tangible link to the ranching heritage of the Cowboy State.

Looking north on Carey Avenue in the early 1880s. Note the freight and delivery wagons, and the steeple of the First Presbyterian Church on the northeast corner of Carey and Eighteenth. (Courtesy Wyoming State Archives)

The Depot Exchange Cafe, owned by leading Cheyenne restaurateur and caterer, Leopold Kabis. (Courtesy Wyoming State Archives)

commission men." These visitors provided an annual bonanza to Cheyenne's hotels and restaurants, as well as saloons and sporting houses. Visitors socialized throughout each day in saloons, with Luke Murrin's establishment drawing the greatest patronage. At night the Cheyenne Club "was a brilliant scene," related John Clay. "Wine flowed freely, tongues got limber, the different cliques broke away from one another. It was a sort of love feast."[16]

The famed Cheyenne Club was an ideal site for a cattleman's convivial love feast. Gentlemen's clubs abounded in the East, as well as in London, and the Easterners and Englishmen who ventured west to engage in cattle ranching brought with them an aura of sophistication. Western ranchers who carved cattle empires from a primitive land wanted to prove that they could be gentlemen, like Easterners and Englishmen, and enjoy amenities in the proper setting. Soon gentlemen's clubs began to be organized across the West. Among the better clubs were the Denver Club and the Montana Club, in Helena. Most notable of all, however, was the Cheyenne Club.

Twelve Wyoming cattlemen formed the Cheyenne Club Association in 1880. The club originally admitted fifty members, but demand for entry quickly raised the membership to two hundred, with an initiation fee of $100. Lots were purchased on Seventeenth Street adjacent to the home of Henry Hay, and soon "work began upon the Cheyenne club house." A full basement was built of stone, with two brick stories above. The top floor, containing sleeping rooms for members

The famous Cheyenne Club on Seventeenth Street. On the main floor were double parlors, a dining room, library, and billiard room. Sleeping rooms were on the top floor, with an observatory above. Two wine vaults and a kitchen were in the basement. (Courtesy Wyoming State Archives)

Cheyenne Club dining room. (Courtesy Wyoming State Archives)

and their guests, was encased in a mansard roof. The main floor boasted a sweeping veranda. There were two wine vaults and a kitchen in the basement, while a dumbwaiter sent gourmet meals up to the dining room. Adjacent to the dining room were twin parlors, a billiard room, and a library which featured the leading newspapers and magazines. Members would play chess on the veranda and tennis on the Cheyenne Club court, and stage harness races and polo matches.[17]

"No wonder they like the club at Cheyenne," approved the cultivated and widely traveled Owen Wister, who belonged to a club in Philadelphia. "It's the pearl of the prairies." Opening with a gala reception on April 7, 1881, the Cheyenne Club thereafter would stage annual receptions and other splendid social events. In August 1883, for example, the British members of the club hosted a dinner for the American members who were in town. The forty-one men who participated in the event consumed twenty bottles of red wine and sixty-six bottles of champagne. Such occasions at the Cheyenne Club demanded black evening wear with stiff white shirt fronts—attire which the ranchers nicknamed "Herefords."[18]

The annual reception for 1887, staged on the last evening of June, was proclaimed "The Most Brilliant Social Event of the Season." Nearly two hundred guests attended, greeted by a veranda decorated with flags and "brilliantly lighted with incandescent lamps." Nearly thirty army officers, attired in dress uniforms, and their wives were present. "Ex-governor Warren and Mrs. Warren" headed the guest list of prominent businessmen, bankers, political leaders, physicians, lawyers, ministers, and their wives and grown daughters. "It was perhaps the best dressed assemblage ever gathered in Cheyenne," according to the *Leader*. "Many of the ladies who are ordinarily charming were last night superb. Female beauty, flashing diamonds and brilliant garniture fascinated the eye at every turn." Stationed in an alcove was "Inman's full orchestra," and dancers swayed in the parlors and the large hallway.[19]

"Socially, Cheyenne is as lively as the liveliest could wish," observed the *Leader* in 1882.[20] The men and women who led Cheyenne society had strong ties with the East and enjoyed fashionable dress and social activities. When Cheyenne became driven by the range cattle industry, many of the new cattle barons came from the East or from England, and eagerly joined — and enriched — the congenial social life they found in the Holy City of the Cow.

"Cheyenne is the dressiest city in the west," was another 1882 observation by the *Leader*.[21] For Westerners, stylish attire indicated the attainment of success, and Cheyenne men and women liked to prove their prosperity with fashionable clothing, as well as with fine Victorian homes and "knobby" horse-drawn vehicles.

Cheyenne's penchant for appropriate dress soon extended to local policemen. In February 1887 the city council ordered uniforms for the police force, complete with helmets that sported a gold cord with two tassels in front. Within a year the night policeman at the Burlington & Missouri depot also acquired a sharp uniform. And by 1889 the Cheyenne Police Department had a set of summer uniforms to relieve their heavy winter outfits.[22]

Western cattle towns always employed policemen to control violence, especially gunplay, on the assumption that Eastern cattle buyers would shy away

The famous Wyoming Hereford Ranch was founded in 1883 by Cheyenne cattle king A. H. Swan. The ranch is located a few miles southeast of Cheyenne, and the fine old horse barn is pictured here. (Photo by Karon O'Neal)

from rawhide communities where they might be shot. In 1881 Mayor Joseph Carey, a leading cattleman, appointed Wyoming's most effective peace officer, Thomas Jefferson Carr, to the post of city marshal. A Union veteran of the Civil War, Carr had served three terms as sheriff of Laramie County during the 1870s, intimidating criminals and troublemakers with hard-nosed physical action. He also worked for a time as a special detective for the Union Pacific, and for more than two decades (1874–1907) he was vice-president and chief detective of the Rocky Mountain Detective Agency. Carr lived on Sixteenth Street with his wife, Jennie, and two daughters. He served with his usual effectiveness as Cheyenne's chief of police until 1884, when he resigned to devote himself to detective work. In 1885, however, Carr was appointed U.S. marshal of Wyoming Territory, serving until 1890. His successor, Joseph Rankin, appointed Carr chief deputy U.S. marshal, and in 1893 Carr accepted another appointment as chief of police of Cheyenne.[23]

With a professional police force patrolling Cheyenne in professional uniforms, violence was held to a minimum. Cattle buyers came to the Holy City of the Cow without worrying about their personal safety, and so did large numbers or other men associated with the cattle industry when the WSGA held their annual meetings. But the Wyoming Stock Growers' Association was staggered by the vicious winter of 1886–87. Membership plummeted, and one of many Wyoming cattlemen to go out of business was longtime WSGA secretary Thomas Sturgis. Sturgis had served as secretary for eleven years, and like many cattlemen he had installed his family in a fine brick home in Cheyenne. But Sturgis was lost to Cheyenne and to the WSGA. He was not present at the sparsely attended WSGA meeting in 1887; neither were the president and vice-president. The WSGA stock detective bureau had to be dissolved because of lack of funds.

The *Leader* lamented the departure of the Sturgis family for New York City in July 1887: "The family will be greatly missed in social circles, and Mr. Sturgis' presence in the western business world will be greatly missed." The new leadership of the WSGA was headed by A.T. Babbitt, who assumed the presidency in 1888. Babbitt, a Union colonel during the Civil War, moved to Cheyenne in 1878 and was president and general manager of the Standard Land and Cattle Company. A fine orator, he had served in the Territorial Legislature and possessed the leadership skills to rebuild the WSGA. But in June 1889, Colonel Babbitt, only fifty-one years of age, died suddenly at his Cheyenne residence. The funeral march from the Congregational Church to Lakeview Cemetery was led by a company of the Seventh Infantry.[24]

When Babbitt's successor as president of the WSGA, John Clay, assumed office in 1890, membership had plunged to a mere 68, from a high of 443 in 1886. But Clay was unusually capable, a university-educated Scotsman who had been employed in 1883 to manage Wyoming's largest ranching operation, the Swan Land and Cattle Company. Clay would ably lead the WSGA for five years. Throughout his term the vice-president was George W. Baxter, who briefly had served as territorial governor in 1886. As a twenty-five-year-old cavalry lieutenant, Baxter brought his bride to his new station in Wyoming in 1880. Excited by the opportunities offered by cattle ranching, Lieutenant Baxter resigned his commission. Although Baxter would center his ranching activities twenty miles east of Cheyenne, where he built a big log ranch headquarters, he and his wife established a residence in Cheyenne. Margaret Baxter was a cultivated woman who had been educated in Europe, and she plunged into Cheyenne society, supporting charitable and educational causes as vigorously as her husband involved himself in ranching and politics.[25]

Under the leadership of Clay and Baxter, the WSGA began to rebound. Western cattlemen were resilient and resourceful, and the ranchers who survived the crisis of 1886–87 fought to maintain their Wyoming empires. Carloads of cattle again were shipped from R. S. Van Tassell's stockyards to Chicago or Omaha. The Cheyenne Club continued to accommodate cattlemen and their guests. The Association once more placed stock detectives on the range, and the rejuvenated WSGA occupied an office in the west wing of Wyoming's new capitol. When Cheyenne entered the 1890s, there were telephones and electric lights and a population of more than 11,000 — and the city maintained its recognition as the Holy City of the Cow.

F. E. Warren bought the impressive log ranch house of former governor George Baxter and moved it to the east end of Eighteenth Street, overlooking Lake Minnehaha. (Photo by Karon O'Neal)

11

Runaways and Wrecks

The streets of Cheyenne teemed with horses and horse-drawn vehicles. Like Westerners everywhere, many Cheyenne men rode horseback, even along the relatively short distances from their homes to downtown. Cheyenne's women also were fond of horseback riding, as the *Leader* remarked: "A larger percentage of ladies ride horseback in Cheyenne than in any city in the country." During good weather men and women were out in great numbers, riding horseback or in carriages up and down the streets, through the city park, around Lake Minnehaha, and to Fort Russell and back. Men bought fine horses and matched teams for their carriages, phaetons, buggies, surreys, and cabriolets. F. E. Warren, of course, had "a team of fine iron-gray horses" for his family conveyances. These same animals were used to pull sleighs when the streets were covered with snow. In addition to light private vehicles, horse-drawn freight wagons constantly plied the downtown streets, along with the delivery wagons of many Cheyenne firms.[1]

With so many horses, as well as mules and oxen, Cheyenne's unpaved streets were liberally adorned with piles of dung. (When automobiles began to displace horses early in the twentieth century, the initial effect was to clean up the atmosphere, despite the introduction of carbon monoxide.) Modern city-dwellers face the constant danger of automobile crashes, but even though life was slower paced during the nineteenth century, horse travelers also were in constant peril. Even horses with placid temperaments can be startled into a stampede, while other equines with an ornery streak are constantly on the lookout for an excuse to bolt. The high winds which regularly gust through Cheyenne often sent scraps of paper whipping in front of horses, and the legions of dogs that prowled the city sometimes yapped at the heels of the larger beasts. Runaways constantly erupted in the streets of Cheyenne, with bruises and broken bones and wrecked vehicles—and occasional fatalities—the inevitable result.

Cheyenne newspapers reported on more than two hundred runaways during the thirty-six years covered by this study. The first runaway covered by the *Leader*

159

occurred on an August afternoon in 1868, when "a couple of mules attached to a wagon, renounced their allegiance to any master," and stampeded northward from the railroad tracks up Ferguson Street. After one block the mules, dragging a riderless wagon, collided with a buggy at Sixteenth Street. The buggy was knocked over and the two men on the seat tumbled onto the street. Startled, the buggy horse bolted toward the railroad tracks, with the upended vehicle in tow, while the mules continued to ramble up Ferguson Street. This incident was a preview of many more to come.[2]

Buggy drivers enjoyed showing off the speed of their horses, but speeding vehicles could be just as dangerous then as now. Cheyenne policemen, like modern traffic cops equipped with radar, attempted to control unsafe drivers. In 1870, for example, a man was arrested "for driving his horse furiously in our city streets." The previous year, when a similar step was made by Cheyenne officers, the driver reacted with the same belligerence sometimes displayed by automobile drivers who have been drinking and speeding. Like many Cheyenne men, this driver packed a gun. Although the arrest was made without gunplay, the man was fined not only for fast driving but also for "reckless drawing of arms against officers."[3]

When the Cheyenne population dropped after the initial boom, traffic and runaways also declined. But the Black Hills gold rush of the 1870s brought an-

Carey Avenue in the early 1890s, bustling with a variety of vehicles, including a street railway car (center) and a dogcart (right). A dogcart was inexpensive and used only one horse. With so much traffic it was only a matter of time until a horse or team stampeded. The Idleman Building is at right, the Union Mercantile Company is at left, and the steeple of the First Presbyterian Church is visible two blocks to the north. (Courtesy Wyoming State Archives)

other boom to the Magic City, along with a corresponding jump in runaways. In May 1876 two officers from Fort Russell were riding behind a team of horses on Cheyenne's crowded streets. Turning onto Seventeenth from Eddy, the team suddenly became frightened. Lieutenant Johnson, the driver, was thrown out of the vehicle. When Lieutenant Robinson jumped up to seize the reins, his foot slipped and was caught in the forward spring, and he lost his balance. "The horses fairly flew down 17th street, over the rough ground, the hapless man being held fast, his head and back bumping along over the loose rocks and earth in a manner horrible to behold." As hundreds of seemingly paralyzed onlookers watched, the horses and buggy of Lieutenant Robinson cornered at Ferguson Street. Robinson's head narrowly missed a pile of lumber in front of a building site. Running south, the horses turned again on Sixteenth, then made another corner and dashed into open ground near the Railroad House. A young man named Ellsworth, a recent arrival from Illinois, sprinted after the careening vehicle, and with a final leap he grabbed the bits and halted the crazed animals. Lieutenant Robinson, badly bruised and lacerated, was carried into the Railroad House and doctors were summoned.[4]

The lieutenant recovered, but the next year a runaway horse resulted in tragedy. Cheyenne's Catholic priest, Father Pease, died late in July 1877. On July 31, as the funeral procession formed, the city sexton saddled a horse in his stable so that he could unlock the cemetery. Eight-year-old Willie Kuykendall, youngest son of Judge William Kuykendall, turned up and asked if he could perform the chore. Knowing Willie to be a good horseman, the sexton handed over his keys. Once seated in the big saddle, the boy could not reach the stirrups, instead slipping his feet between the stirrup straps. Willie rode to the cemetery, unlocked the gates, then remounted. But the horse became startled and broke into a gallop. Willie stayed in the saddle when the horse jumped a ditch, but he lost his seat at a second ditch. With one foot tangled in the straps, he fell downward, his head alternately bouncing on the ground and being kicked by flying hooves. The maddened horse ran for four blocks before Willie finally fell to the ground.

The boy was carried to the nearest house and placed on a sofa. "Almost immediately he straightened out, gave a last agonized gasp, and expired," reported the *Leader*. "Conveyed to his home amid the heart-rending sobbing and wailing of his deeply stricken mother, brother, sisters and friends, the disfigured remains were tenderly bathed and cared for." A telegram was sent to Judge Kuykendall, who was in the Black Hills, and Willie's funeral was delayed until his father could return to Cheyenne.[5]

Six months later Mrs. Kuykendall and a friend, Mrs. D. V. Barkalow, were thrown from a phaeton on Seventeenth Street. A man quickly secured the horse, and although Mrs. Barkalow suffered "a painful contusion," Mrs. Kuykendall was unhurt.[6]

This mishap was the first of numerous runaways in 1878. Two weeks after Mrs. Kuykendall's accident, several men crowded into a carriage drawn by "a fine large bay team" for a pleasure ride around Cheyenne. But when one end of the neck yoke became unfastened and began to strike the team, the bays broke

The front vehicle is a Drop Front Phaeton, or Park Carriage, with room in back for a foot-man, while ladies in front drove an elegant team. There were many varieties of phaetons (from Greek myth, Phaeton nearly set the world on fire while recklessly driving the chariot of the Sun God). As the lineup suggests, by the late 1880s the U.S. was the world's leading producer of carriages. The Studebaker plant covered more than twenty acres, and by 1875 turned out a finished vehicle every seven minutes. (Photo by the author at Cheyenne Frontier Days Old West Museum)

into a run. The passengers leaped overboard, but the driver tried—in vain—to control the team. The bays raced around a corner and headed back to their livery stable. The lower doors had been closed, but the bays barreled into their home. One door was torn from its hinges, while the other was thrown open "with a crash that shook the building." When the team emerged from the rear of the sta-ble, the tongue struck a board fence and snapped. The team and carriage halted, but the driver was sent flying over the team. Back in the stable the other horses "snorted, plunged and kicked . . . , and chaos reigned supreme for a few minutes." The acrobatic driver was not injured, and only the carriage was damaged.[7]

More harm was suffered several days later, when Charles Russell escorted a Miss Smith to an afternoon funeral. When rounding a corner the buggy went out of control, spilling the passengers. The horse stumbled, the fall breaking its neck. Russell was only slightly injured, but Miss Smith suffered a dislocated shoulder and severe internal injuries.

The other runaways of 1878 failed to produce serious damage, except to vehi-cles. But this type of accident became so commonplace in Cheyenne that, when vehicles hit the streets after a long winter, a mishap in June 1879 was labeled by the *Leader* as: "The first runaway accident of the season." This runaway, incidentally, involved a milk delivery wagon. When the horse stampeded, the two employees leaped to safety, but the wagon overturned, and milk splattered "promiscuously." Fifteen years later, when a runaway team rampaged through downtown Cheyenne with another milk wagon, the "racket of milk cans made people believe a switch engine was running amuck."[8]

During the 1880s, when the population grew from 3,412 to 11,690, the steady increase of horse-drawn vehicles meant a corresponding increase in runaways. Two occurred on the first day of July 1881, including an overturned buggy that injured A. R. Converse. There were also two runaways on Wednesday evening, April 25, 1883, and two more the next year on November 25 (one out-of-control wagon destroyed a fire hydrant). Runaways occurred two days in a row in late June 1883. In 1884 a balky team of horses began "smashing things up" near the Opera House corner. "A large crowd gathered ... to witness the fun," since no one seemed in jeopardy.[9]

Often people jumped or were thrown from out-of-control vehicles and were not hurt. Sometimes there was not even any damage to the vehicle. But often a buggy was left in splinters, the horses were maimed, and passengers were badly injured or even killed. In March 1880 James Childs "drove a horse and gig" from the country on a shopping expedition. When Childs was ready to leave Sixteenth Street with his loaded vehicle, the horse bolted. Childs was thrown and his lower jaw was broken on both sides. A little girl was hurt in a Saturday runaway in 1881. During a Sunday afternoon funeral procession in 1882, a team became unmanageable and broke into a run. The driver, who had four female passengers, skillfully avoided other vehicles in the procession, even straddling a ditch to miss a buggy on a bridge. But this maneuver caused the wheels on the left side to come off, spilling all five aboard. Three of the ladies were injured, and one broke a collarbone. During an 1885 runaway, one of the team of horses snapped a leg, and a policeman had to shoot the agonized animal. Harry Kuykendall broke a leg when his carriage overturned at midnight following an 1888 party at Fort Russell. And during an 1886 runaway, the unruly team turned over their carriage, then dragged it into a livery barn and damaged several other vehicles. Also in 1886, eight-year-old

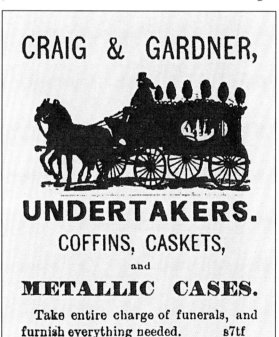

By 1880 deceased Cheyenne residents could be transported in style to Lakeview Cemetery. The military band at Fort Russell often was engaged for funeral services. (Ad was run in the Leader *during October 1880.)*

Charles Dale (the same age as Willie Kuykendall) was trampled to death by two horses.[10]

Another 1886 accident affirmed Cheyenne's cowboy image. The horse pulling a delivery wagon became unruly and ran north up Ferguson Street. In front of the courthouse the wagon became detached, but the driver had twisted the reins around his wrists, and he "was jerked out of the wagon bed and dragged behind the now terrified horse." At the court house Deputy Sheriff Joe McDonigle cut the strap holding a hitched horse, then leaped into the saddle and galloped in pursuit. McDonigle, who clearly had worked on the range before pinning on a badge, shook loose the rope fastened to the pommel, formed a loop, then lassoed the runaway horse, saving the entangled driver from serious harm.[11]

On Sunday morning, June 5, 1887, Mrs. Colin Hunter took her little boys, six and three, for a pleasure drive. But near the cemetery the team spooked and, out of control, headed westward. Mrs. Hunter tightened her grip on the reins and ordered her sons to cling to the seat. "Down the boulevard swept the maddened horses like a tornado," reported the *Leader* with descriptive excitement, "but when they reached the head of Ferguson street they turned into and dashed wildly down it toward the heart of the city." Men who saw the runaway ran out to stop the team to no avail. As the carriage careened downhill, the oldest boy fell out, but was instantly picked up by two nearby women. Hauling on the reins, Mrs. Hunter managed to turn the unruly team toward the Presbyterian church, where the front steps brought the horses to a momentary halt. Before they could make a fresh start, their bridles were seized by Judge Willis Van Devanter and Dr. W. J. Stevens. The fallen boy was taken to Dr. Stevens's office, where it was determined that he had suffered nothing worse than bruises.[12]

A less common runaway occurred in snow-covered Cheyenne in January

The Cheyenne Carriage Works

According to the tax assessment roll for 1889 (published in the *Leader*, August 6, 1889), there were 779 "carriages and vehicles of every description" in Laramie County, valued at $36,368. Most of these carriages, wagons, and delivery vehicles regularly plied the streets of the Magic City, and many of them were built at the Cheyenne Carriage Works.

An old business in Cheyenne, the Carriage Works had grown into a "mammoth establishment" in a complex of buildings at Eighteenth and O'Neil. In 1882 the company incorporated and issued stocks, purchased by such local investors as F. E. Warren (twenty shares at $100 each). One of Cheyenne's few industries which produced anything substantial that was sold outside Wyoming, the Cheyenne Carriage Works built phaetons, top buggies, buckboards, ranch wagons, and miscellaneous other vehicles. When the Cheyenne Street Railway was opened, the passenger cars were crafted by the Cheyenne Carriage Works. (See the *Leader*, August 13, 1887, and November 4, 1893.)

1884, when a four-in-hand sleigh stampeded. The animals were controlled with no damage. Four years later there was another winter runaway involving Wyoming's entire Territorial Council. During the 1888 session of the legislature, the legislators rode the horse trolley from their hotels to the capitol and back. One day at noon, with a blizzard raging and snowdrifts everywhere, all twelve members of the Council boarded a waiting car. When the driver, whose position was outside in front to handle the reins, lost his hat to a gust of wind, he wrapped the reins around the brake handle and went in pursuit. As the driver failed to return, Council member Charles Guernsey announced that he would drive downtown. "All went well until we struck the down grade," reminisced Guernsey, "when, not being used to driving a vehicle without a tongue, and neglecting to manipulate the brake, the car ran on the horses' heels and they began kicking and running. The dignified senators, knowing well what would happen when we reached the sharp curve at 19th Street, stampeded and fell over each other jumping straight out the back door, landing without regard to dignity, in the deep snow." Frank Hadsell

A Wire Wheeled Top Buggy, one of the great variety of horse-drawn vehicles on the streets of Cheyenne. (Photo by the author at the Cheyenne Frontier Days Old West Museum)

did not jump. He came forward and wrestled the brake lever, and the two men brought their car under control. "The senators walked to their different hotels," related Guernsey, "and the driver, after a fruitless chase after his hat, found the horses safely tied to the car brake at the Inter Ocean Hotel corner."[13]

F. E. Warren owned numerous vehicles and horses, for business as well as private use. He maintained a large stable behind his home, and on one occasion he purchased three teams of horses at the same time. Warren company wagons constantly plied the city streets. Inevitably his vehicles were involved in accidents. On a Sunday afternoon in August, with typical generosity, Warren loaned his new phaeton to an employee, Joseph Muenchen, for a family drive. But the horse began acting up, and Muenchen pulled his wife and child from the phaeton. The horse "then galloped madly down Sixteenth street," leaving the vehicle "in a terribly battered condition," according to the *Leader*. "Luckily no damage was done, except that of leaving F. E. Warren to mourn over the well-scattered fragments of his nice new phaeton."[14]

Warren would have other occasions for such mourning. In 1883 a Warren & Co. delivery wagon, drawn by a new team of "fine gray horses," was proceeding toward town along Lake Minnehaha. The animals became frightened and bolted. Since the driver could not halt the team, he tried to pull them to one side. The horses ran into trees beside Sixteenth Street, shattering the wagon and skinning

F. E. Warren invested $2,000 in the Cheyenne Carriage Company. (Warren Papers, Box 63)

the driver's face. Both horses were injured, and Prince, with a broken leg, had to be destroyed.[15]

In 1886 Perry Smith, a cousin of Mrs. Warren, was driving a Warren & Co. delivery wagon, loaded with furniture, on Warren Avenue just south of the railroad tracks. An engine startled the horses, and the team stampeded. In the ensuing wreck Smith suffered a broken collarbone and wrist. Two years later a wagon and team from the Warren Live Stock Company was struck by a switch engine at the Eddy Street crossing of the Union Pacific. "A leg of one animal was severed just above the fetlock, and a shot ended its misery." The next year, in May 1889, Warren even experienced a runaway with the Shetland ponies and junior-sized vehicle he had bought for his children. "Little Miss Frankie fell from the phaeton but was not injured," reported the *Leader*. Fortunately, the nine-year-old did not have far to fall.[16]

During the 1890s, as Cheyenne's population moved toward 14,000, runaways continued to mount, and a popular new vehicle—bicycles—added to the traffic mix and, surprisingly, to the accident total. There were scores of runaways during the 1890s, including two on Monday, June 13, 1892, on Saturday, April 13, 1895, and on Friday, February 12, 1897. Three runaways occurred on Thursday, October 23, 1891, with the principal casualties a smashed buggy and an injured driver, who was "intoxicated and drove through the streets in a reckless manner." In 1890, at the Eddy Street crossing where a switch engine had fatally injured a Warren Live Stock Company horse, another switch engine struck another conveyance. A female passenger narrowly escaped death when she was thrown beneath the cars, while the buggy "was reduced to splinters." A month later, in April 1890, a team of horses standing on Sixteenth Street became frightened by an aggressive bulldog. When the team began to run, the bulldog darted underneath, then leaped up to sink its teeth high into the foreleg of one of the horses. The horses stopped and began rearing and kicking at the dog, who hung on tenaciously. The violent scene "drew an immense crowd, every member of which was thrilled with the unusual spectacle." Several men darted forward to hold the horses' heads, as the crazed animals kicked and leaped. Finally, one man managed to pull off the bulldog, but the fierce canine leaped back to the attack. The man then seized the dog's collar, waved it around in an overhead circle, and hurled the bulldog to the ground. "The dog lay still a moment, recovered, arose with difficulty and slowly and painfully ambled to the sidewalk," related the *Leader* after a detailed description of the fight. "He had enough."[17]

In June 1892 sisters Lizzie and Jennie Walker hitched "a very spirited black" horse to the family buggy for an evening drive. But when they reached downtown their excitable horse stampeded, soon capsizing the buggy. Lizzie Walker was thrown face forward into a corner of Keefe Hall, and both girls were knocked unconscious. The horse kicked free of his harness and galloped to freedom, while the sisters were placed in a carriage and carried to their Eighteenth Street home. "Drs. Hunt and Marston were telephonically summoned," and soon the physicians were able to announce that the girls would recover. Late in the year three men piled into a wagon for a winter journey to a ranch fifty miles to the north.

But the horses, which had not been driven in a great while, quickly became unmanageable. All three men hauled on the reins, but when the wagon struck an obstruction they were thrown onto the frozen ground, while the team headed out Iron Mountain Road with a passengerless vehicle.[18]

A few months later Judge C. F. Miller "was driving a spirited team and four young ladies were in his carriage." Near the Cheyenne Club the harness broke, and when the neck yoke slipped from the pole the horses began to plunge wildly. While the judge wrestled with the reins, one of the young ladies fearlessly descended, seized the bridles, and ended the skirmish. In a similar incident a couple of weeks later, a Mrs. Tew was returning from a drive when a piece of wire caught in the spokes of a wheel. "As the wheel revolved, the wire began swishing about and frightened the horse into a mad run." The phaeton overturned and was "badly smashed," and Mrs. Tew suffered a sprained ankle. The next month, in July 1893, the horse hauling a Troy Laundry wagon bolted down Capitol Avenue, until a sudden turn into Seventeenth Street resulted in a collision with the wagon of O. H. Rhoads. "For a minute the air was full of kicking, plunging horses and wildly swaying wagons." After order was restored, the Rhoads wagon was taken to a blacksmith shop for repairs.[19]

In October 1893, with Senator Joseph Carey in Washington, Mrs. Carey was driven to a reception at Fort Russell. Her driver and a lieutenant escorted her, but in the darkness the carriage ran off the road, spooking the horses. As the team stampeded, the driver lost control, but Lieutenant Dowdy seized the reins and finally stopped the horses. Mrs. Carey had been badly tossed around inside, and she was taken to the fort in a military ambulance. Returned to her home, she was badly bruised and, by the next day, suffering intense pain. She was confined to her bed. The same would happen to her husband four years later. Carey and his youngest son, Charlie, were injured in a runaway in September 1897. Charlie soon recovered, but the senior Carey would not sleep for several days, and his physician forbade him to see visitors.[20]

In March 1894, less than a year after experiencing a similar problem, Judge C. F. Miller again had "a wild run" when his buggy horse was frightened by broken harness. The judge and a female companion were thrown into the street, and he was badly cut over the eye. The "spirited horse" raced on until the buggy was a complete wreck. Another buggy was destroyed the next year when two "drunken women from town"—almost certainly the degraded western end of town—were driving around Fort Russell so recklessly that their team stampeded, overturned their buggy, then ran over the teenaged son of Captain Corliss. In a similar incident, a couple of "west end girls" were thrown from a runaway buggy just west of Fort Russell, which was a primary source of their customers. In February 1899 "several members of the demi-monde residents of the west end" were riding in a sleigh when the horses stampeded. The sleigh was wrecked, but the girls were uninjured.[21]

An out-of-control saddle horse plunged and bucked in downtown Cheyenne in May 1895 and "delighted a crowd of bystanders." But when the bronc reversed his course, his wild antics "scattered the crowd in all directions." A few months later a horse hit and injured nine-year-old Toney Corey, son of a Cheyenne constable. The boy apparently was careless, because it was "the third time he had been injured by a horse or team." In 1897 R. S. Van Tassell, a renowned horseman, was knocked unconscious when his mount fell with him. While Van Tassell was working cattle in the pasture adjacent to the stockyards, his horse stepped in a gopher hole and took a hard fall.[22]

A couple of weeks after Van Tassell was able to leave his bed, tragedy struck in his neighborhood. Mrs. Sam Finch finished supper with her husband and four children, then left on an errand. One of her daughters was scheduled to participate in the Catholic fair, and a cousin on Seventeenth Street had made her a dress. Intending to pick up the dress, Mrs. Finch went to the home of a neighbor, Mrs. L. R. Pettigrew, who would provide transportation and company. The two women rode off in the Pettigrew buggy, secured the dress, then headed home. But a dog barked at the Pettigrew horse, and when the big animal jumped, one of the shafts loosened. With a shaft hitting his back, the horse bolted, turning over the buggy and dumping the women. When the horse reached home trailing a scattered vehicle, Finch and Pettigrew quickly saddled up and raced toward the

An Albany Cutter, one of many winter vehicles used on the snow-covered streets of Cheyenne. (Photo by the author at the Cheyenne Frontier Days Old West Museum)

cousin's house. At the corner of Seventeenth and Maxwell they found their wives sprawled in the street, with a crowd beginning to gather. Mrs. Pettigrew's ear had been nearly severed, and blood was streaming from the mouth of Mrs. Finch. Mrs. Pettigrew was helped into the hack and driven home, where her ear was sewn back. Gasping for breath, Mrs. Finch was loaded into a wagon, with her husband and Dr. Barber at her side. She died before she reached home, and her funeral was held at the Catholic church.[23]

During the 1890s, the bicycle craze that swept across America was embraced by Cheyenne. Bicycle clubs were formed, youngsters rode juvenile "wheels," and businessmen, doctors, and lawyers and their wives bought more expensive models. With so many "wheelmen" cycling around the streets of Cheyenne, inevitably bicycles began to be involved in accidents. In July 1891 a Western Union messenger boy tried to ride over the viaduct. His wheel tipped, however, throwing him over the low wall, and he fell eight feet onto a pile of stones. "He was picked up by those who saw him fall, had the blood washed off and was soon as chipper as ever...."[24]

Within a few years there was a proliferation of accidents involving bicycles. "The habit of Cheyenne's speedy wheelmen to indulge in rapid riding about the streets down town has become an unmitigated abuse," complained the *Leader* in

The Canopy Top Surrey, an American invention, was the most popular family vehicle of the era. (Photo by the author at the Cheyenne Frontier Days Old West Museum)

March 1895. Reporting on the latest pedestrian to be run down by a wheelman "who shot down the streets like a bullet," the *Leader* called for a city ordinance and for bicycles to carry bells and lamps. "Under the wheel oligarchy that now dominates Cheyenne, a pedestrian to have even a fair show to avoid being killed or maimed must be an athlete and able to turn somersault in the air."[25]

A month later a horse tethered in front of a downtown business was spooked by a passing wheelman, and a stampede ensued. A few days later Max Idleman, Jr., began learning to ride on "a fine new bicycle," but when he ventured downtown he suddenly encountered two horse-drawn vehicles in his path. Trying to avoid a wreck, he collided with another bicycle. When he fell he "swallowed a whistle he was carrying in his mouth," but the whistle was retrieved "with the aid of a fish hook and line." Undiscouraged, young Idleman again rode out the next day, and again he lost control, after lifting his foot onto the handlebars on a downgrade. Encountering a stone carriage block at breakneck speed, the rider "was severely bruised and the wheel is a wreck."[26]

The bicycle carnage continued. Several weeks after the Idleman mishap, Dr. Amos Barber and his wife were riding bicycles one evening "when out of the gloom dashed a bicyclist, riding as if for dear life." Dr. Barber called out a warning, but the speeding wheelman crashed into Mrs. Barber. She was scratched and bruised and "had a couple of teeth loosened," and the hit-and-run bicyclist remounted his wheel and sped away. Within a couple of weeks, another reckless wheelman ran over a four-year-old boy, knocking out several of the child's teeth. In the fall of 1897 Mr. and Mrs. E. O. Christie, who were visitors staying at the Inter Ocean Hotel, obtained bicycles for a ride around town. But a "rattle-brained idiot" driving a buggy ran down Christie, who had steered onto a sidewalk in an attempt to escape. Perhaps the horse was out of control, because the buggy raced off after the accident. Christie suffered a variety of injuries "and is otherwise badly used up, besides having his clothes torn almost off his body." Several days later, Dr. A. A. Holcombe was bicycling back to town from Fort Russell when he decided to look at his pocketwatch. While checking the time, Dr. Holcombe "suddenly struck something and was hurled with great force to the ground and rendered unconscious." Taken to his home and office in the Opera House Block, another physician determined that Dr. Holcombe had sprained a shoulder and broken his nose.[27]

In November 1893 Les Snow proved that a bicycle could be a positive factor during a runaway. Snow was a courthouse clerk whose desk was on the first floor. Through an open window "he heard the clatter of a runaway team" and a scream. Looking outside, he saw a buggy careening down Nineteenth Street, with a woman and a small child aboard. Snow leaped through the window, jumped onto a bicycle, and pedaled furiously after the runaway. He pulled alongside the horse, "seized the rein and stopped the frightened animal." The *Leader* reported that Snow "is easily the hero of the county building."[28]

Another form of Cheyenne traffic often proved lethal to travelers and residents. Cheyenne's busy railroad yards featured enormous vehicles that maimed and killed those who were careless around them. In 1878, for example, a cattle car near the Cheyenne freight depot severed the legs of Tony Pastor, Jr. Tony was with his father's dramatic troupe when Pastor played Cheyenne in August. But when Pastor's company headed back to New York, his son stayed behind to tour the West. Within a few weeks Tony, Jr. was out of money, and he persuaded two friends to join him in "beating their way on the cars from Nevada to New York." Their train reached Cheyenne on Thursday night, September 12, and the trio of illegal riders tried to jump off before the cars stopped. Tony fell beneath the wheels, and his legs were cut off at the knees. He was taken to the county hospital but died within an hour. Funeral services were held at St. Mary's Catholic Cathedral the next day, and young Pastor was buried in the Catholic cemetery.[29]

The next year ten-year-old Dell Davis, son of a Union Pacific conductor, suffered the same fate as Tony Pastor's son. An only child, Dell lived with his mother and father in Cheyenne, and he often played around the railroad yards—a dangerous playground. On Sunday, October 19, when Dell's father was in Texas with a train, the boy climbed aboard a group of flatcars that was being moved slowly around the yards. When Dell decided to jump onto the ground, his jacket caught on a projection, throwing him beneath the wheels. Doctors Corey, Gray, and Maynard amputated both legs above the fractures but below the knees, and for a time it was hoped that Dell would recover. Five days after the accident, however, the boy died.[30]

On another Sunday morning a decade later, a UP switchman named E. J. Purney toppled from the roof of a moving freight car, then was crushed between two cars. "Suspended in mid-air was the shapeless body," wrote a horrified reporter, "with distorted black face and blood flowing from ears, eyes, mouth and nose." Purney was married and the father of three children, but recently he had secured a life insurance policy. Also insured was Olaf Johnson, a resident of Cheyenne for nearly two decades who had a wife and two children. Outgoing and cheerful, he was a member of the Odd Fellows Lodge and was well known all over town. Unfortunately, only a short time after taking a job in 1890 with the UP, he was crushed to death in front of the big depot.[31]

On a Sunday morning in 1892, another UP switchman, bachelor Lee Peeke, was coupling freight cars in the yard when he failed to make a connection, and the link mangled his left leg. Peeke was carried on a UP stretcher to his room on Sixteenth Street, and a company doctor was summoned. Constantly attended by fellow workers, the agonized Peeke died that night. The next year switchman Claude Glade was dragged by a freight car, shattering his collarbone and breaking his jaw. But Glade was rushed from Cheyenne to the UP hospital in Denver, where he recovered. Less fortunate was twenty-six-year-old Lee Swan, a cousin of Mrs. Stephen Bon. Working in the Cheyenne yards in 1897 as a switchman, Swan was trying to complete a "flying switch" on a moving coal car beneath the viaduct. Losing his grip, he fell under the wheels and was dragged until the switch engine could be halted. With a mangled leg and internal injuries, Swan was taken to Denver's UP hospital but died within a few hours.[32]

Passengers also could find danger in moving on or off the cars. Mrs. J. M. Deamon, a seventy-three-year-old widow whose home was in Honolulu, was traveling in 1890 with a son and a daughter-in-law to Springfield, Massachusetts. At the Cheyenne depot she tried to descend before the train was fully stopped. She fell beneath the step, and a wheel passed over her arm. She also struck her head and remained unconscious while being driven to the county hospital. Her arm was amputated at the elbow, but soon she died quietly. Her remains were embalmed in Cheyenne and returned to Honolulu for burial beside her husband. A few months later a middle-aged woman, member of a party of tourists bound for California, fell from a sleeper platform. Wheels passed over her arm, and she underwent amputation at the county hospital. A nonpaying passenger, A. D. Allen, tried to board a night freight train at Cheyenne in May 1897. Freight trains accelerated rapidly upon leaving the depot, attempting to discourage tramps from seeking a free ride. Undeterred, Allen tried to jump aboard the swift-moving train, but he lost his footing and was dragged by his right foot. His cries brought help, and Allen was taken to the county hospital, where his leg was amputated below the knee.[33]

Just as Cheyenne experienced a large number of railroad accidents, there also

The Landau, a luxury carriage developed in Europe during the sixteenth century, was popular among Cheyenne's elite. (Photo by the author at the Cheyenne Frontier Days Old West Museum)

were drownings because of nearby waterways. In March 1892 Nicholas Conlon, a four-year-old boy looking for his older brother, broke through the ice on Crow Creek and was swept away by the current. Within moments his father began searching for Nicholas, and he broke through the ice himself. The little boy was found dead beneath the ice. In December 1878 Hill Logan, a Cheyenne business-man, failed to show up at his store. He lived more than a mile east of downtown, near Lake Minnehaha, but he was not at home. A large number of concerned cit-izens conducted a search, and tracks were found leading to the lake—where ice was broken—and his cap lay nearby. Grappling hooks were employed, and Logan's body soon was pulled ashore. His funeral, largely attended, was con-ducted at the Masonic Hall. In 1882 several immigrant families camped beside Lake Minnehaha. Fifteen-year-old Frank Griffin skated too far from shore and the ice broke beneath him. His friends tried to throw ropes to him, but he disap-peared below the water. Frank, "a very promising lad," was the oldest of five chil-dren of Alderman J. W. Griffin.[34]

Cheyenne was a large western community, which guaranteed that there were a great many guns in town. Peace officers kept violent altercations to a minimum, but inevitably there were accidental shootings. For example, in 1881 a recently discharged soldier stood in front of Joe Rose's saloon on Seventeenth Street, demonstrating the action of his new pistol to butcher Ed Betlach. The little gun was a .22, with four stationary barrels, and was "said to discharge at merely being looked at." Predictably, one barrel went off, sending a .22 ball into Betlach's right wrist. A decade later, at a shooting gallery adjacent to the Western Hotel, a man named Davies was cleaning a .22 target rifle. The gun unexpectedly discharged in the direction of the hotel. Inside the hotel office, Mrs. Herman Kimme exclaimed, "I am shot!" Then she fainted. "Mrs. Kimme is rather fleshy and, owing to that fact, escaped what might have been a bad wound," pointed out an ungallant re-porter. A doctor found the little bullet about an inch beneath the flesh of her back. In 1892, the notorious Frank Canton, a WSGA stock detective under very loose custody related to the Johnson County War, drunkenly shot himself in the leg with his own revolver.[35]

Nevertheless, there were far more injuries in old-time Cheyenne from run-away horses and from bicycles than from guns, just as modern Cheyenne experi-ences more automobile wrecks than shooting incidents. While nineteenth-century Cheyenne was no haven for gunfighters, there were frequent runaways on the streets, along with dangerous railway traffic, drownings, and other hazards. Like hardy citizens everywhere in the West, the men and women of Cheyenne nursed their injuries, buried their dead, swallowed their grief, and went on with life in the Magic City.

12

From Victorian Mansions to the Capitol Building

Historical architecture is our most tangible link with the past. Architecture, like any art, is a reflection of life — of the people and of the period and place in which they lived. Cheyenne developed during the Victorian era, a time in America of explosive growth and change. Society was in upheaval after the Civil War, while industrialization and urbanization added to the turmoil. But the unregulated economy produced vast wealth, along with a sense of power and progress and optimism.

All of these qualities were expressed in Victorian architecture. The stability of pre-Civil War society had been reflected by Greek Revival homes featuring stately columns and balanced, predictable floor plans (central hallway, usually with two rooms on either side, both upstairs and downstairs). But after the Civil War, with slavery ended and with countless opportunities beckoning in the nation's new cities and in the last West, successful individuals turned to a new style of architecture — in their homes and churches, as well as in their commercial structures and public buildings. The expansiveness, exuberance, and vitality of the late nineteenth century found architectural expression in a multiplicity of Victorian styles: Queen Anne, General Grant, Second Empire, Gothic Revival, Richardsonian Romanesque, Italiante, Shingle Style, Mansardic, Carpenter Gothic, and Gingerbread. And when the components of several of these styles were combined in one building, the result was termed "Bastardian." Victorian residences expressed the owners' individuality and prosperity. Shunning Greek Revival conformity, Victorian homes bristled with turrets and bay windows and gingerbread decorations. As many different materials as possible were used, inside and out-

175

side, as a demonstration of affluence. In Cheyenne many spectacular homes were "built by cattle," but many more were built by fortunes amassed through real estate and commercial ventures.

One of the first brick homes in Cheyenne was erected by Erasmus Nagle, the "Merchant King of Wyoming." Nagle moved to Cheyenne early and did well. As he rapidly amassed a fortune, he married Emma Houseman in 1876, and their son, George, was born two years later. For his family he built a two-story brick residence on Seventeenth Street, just a few blocks from the business center. The Nagle home featured gingerbread decoration, a two-story tower, and a bay window in front with a Juliet porch above.[1]

Seventeenth became a fashionable residential street. Maj. Herman Glafcke built a two-story frame house on the corner just west of Nagle but soon sold it to F. E. Warren. The three-story Cheyenne Club, complete with prominent tower and mansard roof, was on the next corner to the west. On the diagonal corner from the Cheyenne Club, and across the street from Warren, rancher W. C. "Billy" Irvine built a three-story frame Georgian residence in 1882. Reputed to be the first home in the United States with incandescent lights, the structure included a three-story entrance tower and a mansard roof. Irvine soon sold his Victorian gem to L. R. Bresnahan, longtime mayor of Cheyenne.[2]

Half a block to the east of Nagle, on the corner of the 300 block of Seventeenth,

Wealthy Erasmus Nagle, the "Merchant King of Cheyenne," erected one of Cheyenne's first brick residences, on fashionable Seventeenth Street. (Courtesy Wyoming State Archives)

I.C. Whipple built a splendid home that featured bay windows, a three-story tower, and handsome gingerbread design. A large carriage house —a standard feature—was built behind the house. The property was enclosed with a low iron fence atop a base of cut stone. Other fine homes went up on other streets.[3]

Erasmus Nagle's two-story brick home had been quickly eclipsed, but soon he decided to

Rancher W. C. Irvine built this home on Seventeenth Street in 1882, diagonally across from the Cheyenne Club. The first home in the United States to boast incandescent lighting, it soon was bought by Mayor L. R. Bresnahan. (Courtesy Wyoming State Archives)

The Whipple Mansion on Seventeenth Street, across House Avenue from the Nagle-Warren Mansion (to the west, or left). A wealthy merchant, Whipple and his wife were leaders of Cheyenne society, hosting various events in their handsome home. (Photo by Karon O'Neal)

erect a showplace. Acquiring the corner lot next door to the east, in 1885 he cleared the site prior to the start of construction. On the lot was the U.S. marshal's office, but the building was moved down the street to the property of F. E. Warren, the territorial governor whose home was serving as Wyoming's executive mansion. Construction took two years and cost $35,000, in addition to the expense of the property and a handsome stone carriage house. Nagle served as chairman of the Wyoming Capitol Building Commission, and for his Romanesque mansion he used building stone that had been rejected by the Capitol contractor. (Decades later the rejected stone crumbled so badly that the mansion exterior had to be plastered over with cement.)[4]

At a large reception on Thursday night, July 26, 1888, "the new residence was thrown open to the roof," related an awestruck *Leader* reporter. Guests began arriving at nine o'clock, with Chinese lanterns "giving a gala appearance to the surroundings," and a dance orchestra playing in the first Nagle home next door. "Little groups of people quickly found their way all over the house" while partaking of the lunch catered by Leopold Kabis. Guests "feasted their eyes with pleasure on the artistic beauties of the lower floor," which included mahogany woodwork, stained glass windows, walls faced with stamped leather or rich paneling, and massive fireplaces topped by mirrors which extended to the ceiling.

Cheyenne merchant king Erasmus Nagle built the first two-story brick residence (left). Several years later he moved the U.S. Marshal's Office from its adjacent location so that he could erect a more opulent home. The Seventeenth Street mansion (right) was completed in 1888 at a cost of $50,000, but Nagle died just two years later. His widow, Emma, sold the splendid house in 1910, and in 1915 Senator F.E. Warren bought the property as his final home. Today the Nagle-Warren Mansion is an elegant B&B. (Photo by Karon O'Neal)

Upstairs, "the ladies particularly had a chance to go into ecstasies" over such luxuries as three tin bathtubs, each encased in polished walnut. In the basement men inspected the large Smead furnace, "the big filtering apparatus, the scientific plumbing, sewerage and ventilating system." The exterior was distinguished by a formidable tower and by stone gargoyles.[5]

Mr. and Mrs. Nagle were showered with compliments, and the last guests did not leave until after midnight. Sadly, Erasmus Nagle was able to enjoy his grand residence for only a year and a half. He died early in 1890 of peritonitis at the age of fifty-six. Emma Nagle and her son George stayed in the mansion for a time, rented it for a few years, then sold it to the Cheyenne Realty Company in 1910. In 1915 F. E. Warren purchased the stately dwelling, making it his home for the last fourteen years of his life.

While impressive Victorian houses were being built on Seventeenth Street, even more spectacular mansions were erected on Ferguson, soon called "Millionaire's Row," and renamed Carey Avenue in 1910. In 1885 Joseph M. Carey, then serving as Wyoming's congressional delegate and as president of the Wyoming Stock Growers' Association, erected a splendid, ornate home at 2119 Ferguson. The three-story mansion presented an elaborate façade of bay windows and porches, of brick and cut stone. Carey imported an Italian artist to decorate the ceilings with frescoes. Other interior features included massive fireplaces, crystal chandeliers, gold embossed wallpaper, and parquet floors adorned with Oriental rugs. This magnificent residence became a social center of Cheyenne. By the time Carey became governor in 1911, a Governor's Mansion

Looking north on Carey Avenue, sometimes called Millionaire's Row, from Twentieth Street. The house in the center was built by Joseph Carey, then sold in 1885 to Henry G. Hay when Carey built a larger mansion across the street and a block north. (Courtesy Wyoming State Archives)

had been built at 300 East Twenty-first Street. The Carey home was considerably larger, though, and was a little closer to the Capitol, so Governor Carey used his own residence as the executive mansion.[6]

At 2020 Ferguson, on a corner lot a block south of the Carey mansion and on the opposite side of the street, Judge Carey earlier had built a two-story brick dwelling for his bride. When the family moved to their new mansion in 1885, Carey sold their first home to banker Henry G. Hay. With Carey and Tom Sturgis, Hay had organized the Stock Growers National Bank, which he served as president. When Hay moved his family into the substantial residence, a windmill on the property provided the household with fresh water. Cheyenne houses with a windmill in the yard had a water tank in the attic that supplied the taps. Because insects were attracted to these tanks, a basin or glass filled with tap water often contained floating bugs.[7]

Another prominent banker, M.E. Post, bought a large brick home at 2204 Ferguson, diagonally across from the Careys. The exterior was painted dark red (many brick houses were painted, because the quality of bricks produced in Cheyenne was poor). Post had arrived at Cheyenne in 1867, and his wife traveled to the frontier in a covered wagon. By the time the Posts moved into a two-story brick residence on Seventeenth, she was able to travel in better style. Regularly Mrs. Post climbed into the family carriage, so that her coachman could drive her throughout the city.[8]

Home of Col. E.A. Slack and, at times, of his mother, Mrs. Esther Morris, famous as the first woman to hold public office. This residence was erected at 1916 Carey Avenue but later was moved to 1300 East Twenty-first, where it stands today. (Photo by Karon O'Neal)

A block to the north and across the street, at 2223 Ferguson, stood the large frame house and barn of rancher E. W. Whitcomb. An early Wyoming pioneer, Whitcomb and his Sioux wife outfitted a room in their home with an excellent collection of fine beadwork, feathered headdresses, weapons, and other tribal artifacts. One block north, on a prominent corner facing the Capitol grounds, was the magnificent Victorian mansion of Max Idleman.[9]

But the largest and most impressive mansion of all was a massive stone structure at 1920 Ferguson. The mansion, featuring castlelike towers and crenelations, was erected by cattle baron A. H. Swan as a wedding gift for his daughter, Louise. Louise would marry R. S. Van Tassell in December 1886, but by that time Swan's ranching empire was in the throes of collapse because of disastrous winter losses and unsound management. ("His operations had one and all been of the most reckless character," stated cattleman John Clay, adding that Swan had pyramided "one debt on top of another, borrowing from Paul to pay Peter.") Swan was unable to finish the mansion, which was acquired by banker David Dare. The stone edifice was completed in luxurious fashion, becoming known as "Castle Dare." In addition to lavish interior appointments, Castle Dare was especially noted for its three bathrooms, complete with marble washbasins.[10]

The businessmen who inhabited the Victorian mansions on Ferguson and Seventeenth and other streets also built substantial commercial structures downtown. Although most of these businesses and office buildings had relatively plain façades, a few boasted the ornate features favored by Victorian architects. On the north side of Sixteenth, adjacent to the big, but comparatively plain, Idleman Block, F. E. Warren's three-story Commercial Block had a faux tower high on the

Fashionable Terrace Row, built in 1883 on Eighteenth between Capitol and Carey. (Courtesy Wyoming State Archives)

left side and a second-floor bay window. (Behind this bay window was an office suite rented by the U.S. marshal, and here in 1901 the controversial "confession" of Tom Horn would be manufactured.) Next door to the east, the First National Bank building was erected by Warren in 1882, with an especially decorative sign atop the third story. On the opposite side of Sixteenth, and a block to the west, the three-story Tivoli was built, replacing a more modest structure of the same name. The main floor and basement housed a noted saloon and restaurant, while office space was on the second floor and, it was widely reputed, social recreation was available in the rooms on the top floor. Above the corner entrance was a big round tower which dominates the appearance of the Tivoli. Each of these buildings still stands, with most of their features intact.

The biggest downtown commercial structure during Cheyenne's Victorian era was F. E. Warren's Emporium. Covering most of a block north of the Union Pacific Depot, the Emporium was inspired by London's famous Crystal Palace, built for the Great Exhibition of 1851, and by a similar emporium erected in Philadelphia. In March 1884 Warren's principal mercantile outlet, a three-story building on Sixteenth adjacent to the Inter Ocean Hotel, was destroyed by fire. Warren, who would collect $90,000 in insurance, immediately announced plans to rebuild. Debris was cleaned off the lot within a few weeks, and a new building was begun. The upper two floors of this structure would be utilized by the Inter

Left to right, First National Bank, Converse and Warren, and the Inter Ocean Hotel, which was built in 1875 on 16th, a block north of the UP Depot. The building collapse of 1879 took place just across the street from this important downtown section. (Courtesy Wyoming State Archives)

Ocean, and the Warren Mercantile Company would relocate to a vast and imaginative new edifice diagonally across from the Inter Ocean.[11]

The sprawling Emporium was built in just over five months at an approximate cost of $80,000. Most of the materials and supplies were purchased locally, and carpenters, masons, and other laborers also were local, so that of the $80,000 "fully nine-tenths went into the hands of Cheyenne people." For the foundation, 13,500 cubic feet of stone was used; 300,000 bricks were placed; and 1,500 square feet of heavy plate glass was installed. The building ran for 180 feet along Sixteenth and 132 feet along Hill, facing the three-story Phoenix Block (which Warren had erected in 1882). The entire 132-foot frontage along Hill (later Capitol) was a continuous line of plateglass show windows, and the resulting illumination of the display rooms was supplemented by a skylight sixty feet long by fifteen feet wide. The Emporium was fifty feet tall, but there were three towers that rose above roof level. The roof was adorned with 600 gallons of red paint, while 1,500 gallons of various colors were used throughout the building.[12]

Counting a spacious cellar, the Emporium included 52,000 square feet of floor space. The east side of the building had three floors of workrooms and storage, while the west side featured large display rooms and galleries. An existing brick house was incorporated into the work area and was used to store oils, varnishes, and paints. An elevator "has a lifting capacity of 3,500 pounds, and is fitted up with safety clutches so that heavy weight passengers may make a trip on it without fear." A side track allowed railroad freight cars to enter the south side of the immense structure; delivery wagons also could be loaded and unloaded inside the building. The twelve-foot-wide "elegant walkways" on Sixteenth and Hill streets were paved with 18,000 square feet of flagstone.

The Warren Emporium was the largest structure in town, but within a couple of years two magnificent buildings that would eclipse the Emporium would begin construction. And both of these structures had been needed for years.

Although Cheyenne was a major western stopover on the nation's first transcontinental railroad, the capital city of Wyoming was served merely by a small frame passenger depot dating from 1868. In 1870 the UP announced the construction nearby of a two-story frame express depot, which was built in less than two months. "It ain't two stories high though, unless one of the stories is underground," observed an onlooker. "It may grow to be two stories in the course of time."[13]

By the 1880s these facilities were antiquated and completely inadequate. Cheyenne politicians and newspapers campaigned for a suitable depot. The UP made vague promises about providing a new facility, but nothing was done until competing railroads began building in Wyoming. Finally, in December 1885, Governor F.E. Warren received notification that the president of the Union Pacific, Charles Francis Adams, "has approved the plans for the new depot at Cheyenne, and has ordered the work to be commenced without delay." The cost of this major structure, to be erected near the old depot, would be at least $75,000 (the final total would be close to $100,000).[14]

Construction began with foundation work in March 1886. The old depot was moved, items such as doors and window sashes were assembled in Omaha, and building stone was cut and delivered from quarries near Fort Collins, Colorado. "An endless track" encircled the construction site, so that small flatcars could carry materials to any point as needed. A workforce of seventy men, including twenty stonecutters, was employed, and a boom derrick was set up to swing cut stone and other heavy materials into place. On Monday afternoon, July 19, 1886, the 2,500-pound cornerstone was laid with Masonic ceremonies, following a parade and with a large crowd in attendance, at the northwest corner of the developing structure. In October President Adams and several UP directors came to Cheyenne to inspect the progress of the new depot.[15]

The two-story Pacific Hotel, owned and operated by the railroad and located just east of the depot site, burned to the ground in November, causing one fatality. UP officials promptly decided to build a new railroad hotel, replacing the old frame building with a three-story brick hostelry.[16]

The red sandstone walls of the depot continued to rise. It was hoped that the massive project could be completed in the spring of 1887, after about a year. But even though the workforce was increased, construction went on through the summer and fall. In September, UP officials moved into their upstairs offices: a superintendent's suite, seven rooms for the division superintendent and his staff; four rooms for the assistant general superintendent; records vault; train dispatcher's office; conductor's room; reading room; and toilet. Finally, in November, the railroad palace was opened to the public. The vast waiting rooms, one for gents and a separate room for women, were especially impressive. They were finished with red oak, and the elegant ladies' room featured a fireplace and cush-

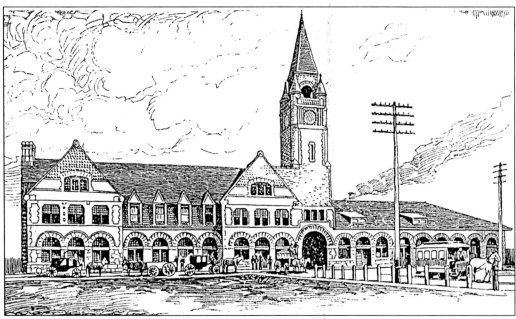

Cheyenne's magnificent UP Depot, sketched while hacks were lined up expecting the arrival of a passenger train. Note the horse-drawn streetcar at right. This view is from the north. (Frank Leslie's Illustrated Newspaper, *January 31, 1891)*

The superb Union Pacific Depot, completed in 1887, as seen from the south. (Courtesy Wyoming State Archives)

ioned furniture. The building was 226 feet long, the exterior was dominated by Romanesque arches and dormer windows on the steeply pitched roof. A clock tower soared to a height of 128 feet, and a clock was installed in 1890. The site was additionally enhanced by the Union Pacific Park, just north of the new building: enclosed by a fence, the grassy park boasted a fountain, four bronze cannon, trees, shrubbery, and fountains.[17]

Almost simultaneously with the construction of the magnificent UP Depot, Wyoming's Capitol went up eight blocks to the north. Cheyenne's two most impressive buildings would face each other on Hill Street, which was renamed Capitol Avenue in 1887.

As the largest town in newly organized Wyoming Territory, Cheyenne had been designated territorial capital in 1869, but biennial legislative sessions were conducted in rented rooms around town. Every other year the Council and the House of Representatives secured temporary space in hotels or vacant commercial buildings. Likewise, the territorial governor conducted business from his hotel room or rented house. In 1885, F. E. Warren was appointed governor. He enjoyed strong support in Wyoming because he was not a political appointee imported from the East. Also, because of his widespread commercial and ranching contacts, he was personally acquainted with most of the influential men of Wyoming. Progressive by nature and having accomplished numerous building projects, most recently the vast Emporium, Governor Warren determined to es-

Parade forming beside the Idleman Building on Carey. This parade would then turn left in front of the Idleman Building, proceed one block east on Sixteenth, then march north on Capitol Avenue to participate in laying the cornerstone of the State Capitol Building on May 18, 1887. (Courtesy Wyoming State Archives)

Laying the cornerstone at the Wyoming Capitol, May 18, 1877. The procession to the building site numbered 2,000, including 500 members of the Seventeenth Infantry in dress uniform. In the background note the rear of Max Idleman's mansion and stable. (Courtesy Wyoming State Archives)

tablish needed institutions for Wyoming. In a message to the Ninth Legislative Assembly in January 1886, he recommended the creation of an insane asylum and a school for the deaf and dumb. Governor Warren also emphasized the need to consolidate the various territorial offices in a public building owned—not rented—by Wyoming.

The Assembly, dominated in both houses by members from Laramie and Albany counties, soon crafted a bill appropriating as much as $150,000 to erect a capitol in Cheyenne, and $50,000 to construct the first building of the University of Wyoming in Laramie. Governor Warren signed the bill on March 4, as well as another bill, five days later, which authorized up to $30,000 to build an insane asylum at Evanston. A separate bill approved $8,000 to establish an institute for the blind, deaf, and dumb in Cheyenne (although the building was erected, the institute never materialized).[18]

Governor Warren appointed a Capitol Building Commission, chaired by Erasmus Nagle and including N. R. Davis, N. J. O'Brien, M. E. Post, and C. N. Potter. The commission hired the architectural firm of David W. Gibbs & Co. from Toledo, Ohio, to develop plans. These plans were accepted by the commission in July 1886, then let out for bids. A month later the low bid of $131,275.13 was submitted by A. Feick & Bro. of Sandusky, Ohio. Meanwhile, potential sites were

The first version of Wyoming's Capitol opened in 1888. Wings were added two years later, then were extended in 1917. As this photo indicates, there was almost no development north of the Capitol in 1888. Year after year in Cheyenne, trees were planted, like those at right. (Courtesy Wyoming State Archives)

considered by the commission. The final selection was just west of the convent—two adjacent blocks at the head of Hill Street (soon renamed Capitol Avenue)—and ground was broken in September 1886. The Ohio firm subcontracted with Robert C. Greenlee of Denver, but the Feicks needed a representative in Cheyenne. George Feick traveled to Cheyenne to start the project. He soon returned to Ohio and was replaced by his brother Adam's son John, a junior member of the construction firm.[19]

John Feick was twenty-four, and because of family obligations his twenty-year-old wife remained in Sandusky. When John arrived in Cheyenne, on the night of February 2, 1887, he promptly wrote home: "It is snowing & blowing bad enough to scare a man to death." Although he frequently wrote about the "very queer weather in this country," he was impressed with the little frontier city. "We have some very nice churches in this city," and he often attended services. He also attended "a very good show" at the Opera House. "They have some finer stores here than there are in the East only that everything is very expensive."[20]

"There are very wealthy people living in this town but they look to me like Cow-boys," observed the young Easterner. "The first day I struck town they told me any man that wore a white shirt would be shot," so he bought a blue double-breasted shirt and wore it every day. Completing his new western image, John confessed to his wife that he now chewed tobacco, like "every body else in town and even every little boy that can walk." He hastened to point out—again—that "I never drink, they tell me the whiskey a man gets here would make a man go home and rob his own trunk." Despite the fact that "the town is made up of Saloons" and that "They have plenty of bad houses out here," John saluted the police force: "You don't see as many drunkards in Cheyenne as you do in Sandusky and the town is kept very orderly." John was taken hunting and to Fort Russell ("I tell you I rode just as fast as I ever want to ride in a buggy") and was otherwise befriended. "People are more liberal & and nicer class of people than you find in the east." Finding room (ten dollars a week) and board (five and a half dollars) to be "very high," John Feick had a "shanty" built on the Capitol grounds. The cabin had an electric light and four bunks, and "almost every body in Cheyenne has been to my room to see it."[21]

The construction site was visited regularly by newspaper reporters who provided progress reports to their readers. In October 1886 a *Leader* reporter discovered a new substance being used on the foundation. "Two large wooden boxes were full of the mixture known as 'concrete,' and this mixture was being vigorously kneaded together by men with suitable tools," while wheelbarrows carried the concrete to foundation trenches. "These trenches, filled with this concrete, form the foundation of the capitol building, and are as firm and solid as rock itself." Teams constantly hauled sand and gravel to the grounds, along with rock from the railroad.[22]

By April 1887 a committee was formed to organize the laying of the Capitol cornerstone: F. E. Warren, Judge Isaac Bergman, Maj. C. W. River, E. W. Whitcomb, Luke Murrin, Governor Moonlight, four other prominent men, and the Capitol commissioners, who planned a gala holiday. John Feicke proudly reported to his wife that he had been asked to serve on two committees: arrangements and receptions. "People here are going crazy over the corner stone … they are going to have Barber Cue, that is something that you or I never saw in the East." He tried to persuade her to attend the event. "If you ever come out here and stay till fall you can vote, all women have the right to vote when in the Territory 3 months."[23]

Although Lizzie Feick did not attend the cornerstone ceremony (she did come later for a visit), many other people came, from all over Wyoming, as well as from Colorado and Nebraska. On May 18, 1887, as many as 4,000 spectators lined the streets to watch Cheyenne's biggest parade, with fully 2,000 men in the procession. From Fort Russell 500 soldiers of the Seventeenth Infantry marched in columns of four. Three bands were interspersed throughout the long procession: the Seventeenth Infantry Band, the Cheyenne City Band, and the Laramie City Band. Members of the G.A.R. and the Sons of Veterans marched in formation, "wheelmen" rode their bicycles, fire companies paraded their vehicles, lodges turned out in large numbers, and carriages were filled with federal, territorial,

The Cheyenne Street Railway

Horse-drawn streetcars were common in American cities during the 1880s, and in 1887 the Cheyenne Street Railroad Company was organized by community leaders, who bought stock—at $50 per share—to fund the enterprise. Tracks were laid through the business district and north to the state capitol building, which was under construction at this same time. Four streetcars, costing $1,000 apiece, were ordered from the Cheyenne Carriage Works. Many Cheyenne businessmen were stockholders in both companies, and even through a Denver firm routinely built streetcars, it was decided to do business locally.

On Tuesday, January 10, 1888, Car. No. 1, "a substantial and beautifully decorated piece of rolling stock," was boarded by company officials at the town's major intersection, in front of the Inter Ocean Hotel at Sixteenth and Capitol (formerly Hill). Several hundred bystanders watched as a draft horse was led from the livery stable of J.C. Abney, across the street from the Inter Ocean. Abney was manager of the street railway, and as soon as his horse was hitched, the inaugural ride of the Cheyenne line commenced. The cars would run until nine at night, and even later on special occasions.

By 1889 the line was extended east along Nineteenth from Capitol Avenue to Lake Minnehaha, and northwest to the fair grounds. Also in 1889, the city council and the Union Pacific agreed to erect a viaduct across the network of UP tracks and buildings, connecting the south side with downtown Cheyenne. The growth of Cheyenne during the 1880s had included a large population addition south of the tracks, and most of these residents were railroad employees and their families. A South Side School already had been built, and by 1890 a streetcar would go back and forth across the new viaduct. (See the *Leader*, August 12, 1887; January 11, 1889; June 18 and December 18, 1889; and December 16, 1892.)

and city officials. This procession started at the corner of Eddy and Seventeenth streets, and wound its way by a circuitous route to the Capitol grounds. The program included prayer, choir and band music, and speeches by congressional delegate Joseph M. Carey and Governor Thomas Moonlight. Judge W. L. Kuykendall read a list of more than fifty items inside the metal box that would be put inside the cornerstone, which then was dedicated with Masonic ceremonies by lodge members from Cheyenne, Laramie City, and Greeley and Fort Collins, Colorado. Tables were set up on the west side of the Capitol grounds, and 4,000 citizens ate barbeque meat and "corner stone pickles" and drank lemonade. The day was regarded as "the greatest one ever known to Cheyenne."[24]

By the next month the second story was going up: "the structure is visible from almost every part of the city," observed a *Leader* reporter, "and while standing on the massive walls every house in the city is visible." As the months passed, the dome, which capped a handsome rotunda soaring from the ground floor, reached a height of 144 feet. The building was 124 feet wide, but the 218 feet of length was abbreviated to save money. The east and west walls were bricked up, to facilitate later construction. Indeed, by the time the Capitol opened in March 1888, the Tenth Territorial Legislative Assembly had appropriated $125,000 to add the east and west wings. Local contractor M. P. Keefe agreed to build these additions for $117,504, and the wings of "the pride of Wyoming" were completed in April 1890.[25]

Cheyenne's two most important and impressive buildings faced each other in full function by 1888. "Reputation is spread by travelers quite a lot," stated historian Neil Harris, "and it's the public facilities of a city — the railroad stations, the hotels — that would supply a lot of the reputation that they spread."[26] Harris was speaking in reference to nineteenth-century Chicago, but application can be made to Cheyenne. Because of the railroad, Cheyenne experienced countless travelers, who must have been impressed by the magnificent UP Depot. A block to the north was Cheyenne's best hotel, the three-story Inter Ocean, which was not exceptional when compared to other grand hotels of the time. But within sight, a few blocks farther to the north, was Wyoming's Capitol, with its columns and dome. Visitors to Cheyenne always took in the new Capitol, which, along with the UP Depot, helped to spread Cheyenne's reputation, already enhanced by its Victorian houses and churches and commercial blocks. Today the Capitol and the UP Depot, as well as many Victorian houses and commercial buildings and two of the churches, remain as tangible testimony to the vigor and confidence of Cheyenneites of the late 1800s.

13

The Cheyenne Opera House

By the spring of 1881, Cheyenne's leading citizens had determined to build "one of the finest opera houses in the west" in the Magic City. Theater always had been a highly popular form of entertainment in Cheyenne, as it was in every western town of any size. But even though a major railroad ran through Cheyenne, top-tier performers and troupes rarely played there because the theaters were inadequate. Small variety halls aside, Cheyenne's best theaters had been, in order, McDaniel's, then Recreation Hall, and finally the short-lived Dramatic Theater, converted by Inter Ocean Hotel owner John Chase from the old Gold Room gambling hall. Stage areas in these theaters were too small, however, and seating capacities limited.

"The only theater [Cheyenne] has at present is a dingy hall over a livery stable," sniffed the Denver *Tribune*, "and the performances are frequently interrupted by the braying of the mules down stairs." When "the fair cantatrice" Emily Melville and her company played Cheyenne in 1881, they were shocked that when the curtain closed on their last act, the regular variety show and dance began. "Will you believe it," said the horrified Emily, "a coarse, fat creature came out on the stage in a shockingly short dress and began singing one of the solos from my opera, and the audience applauded her more than they had applauded me. I shall never get her shrill, harsh voice out of my ears, and that is one of the reasons why I am sorry I ever allowed myself to be induced to appear in Cheyenne."[1]

Clearly it was time for Cheyenne to have a proper opera house. An opera house conferred a certain status on a community. Furthermore, many of Cheyenne's most prominent men and women attended legitimate theater and opera while on family or business trips in the East. Theater lovers also took the southbound train to patronize Denver's big opera houses, but they longed to don evening attire and attend quality performances at home. Although Cheyenne's population was less than 4,000 in 1881, there was a progressive leadership class which knew how to get things done.

The public-minded men who met to consider the project represented a who's who of Cheyenne businessmen and politicians. These men decided to raise start-up money among themselves, with no contribution to exceed $1,000. The target was $15,000, which soon was subscribed. Then, at a called meeting at city hall on April 15, 1881, the Cheyenne Opera House and Library Hall Company was incorporated. Capital stock of $20,000 was issued, divided into 400 shares of $50 each. Mayor Joseph Carey was elected president, Thomas Sturgis of the Wyoming Stock Growers' Association was vice-president, Judge Isaac Bergman was secretary, and banker Henry G. Hay was treasurer. The other five directors were F. E. Warren, W. W. Corlett, M. E. Post, A. H. Reel, and Tim Dyer. Other initial stock-

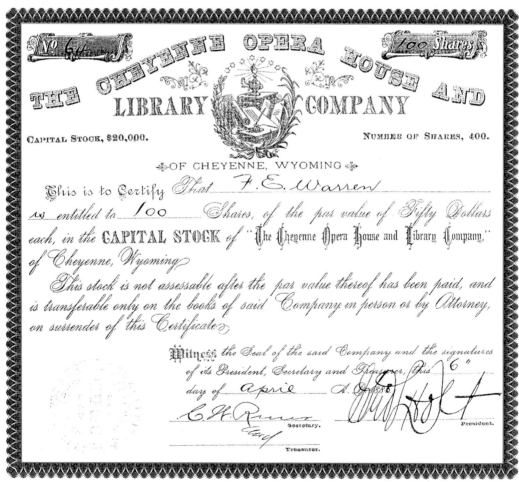

F.E. Warren bought 100 shares of stock in the Opera House Company. Other Opera House stock purchases by Warren included fifty shares, three purchases of ten shares each and one purchase of two shares. (Warren Papers, Box 63)

holders included Professor N. E. Stark, Stephen Bon, W. C. Irvine, Col. E. A. Slack, R. S. Van Tassell, Luke Voorhees, the Idleman brothers, and other key business leaders. To ensure that the opera house would be a true community project, brick for the structure would come from Cheyenne brickyards, stone would be quarried within Laramie County, and decorative woodwork would be fashioned at "the shops of our fellow townsman, Mr. Weybrecht." J. P. Weybrecht was selected as the contractor, and the architectural firm, Cooper & Anderson, also was local. F. E. Warren, appointed to the site committee, sold the corporation a big lot at the southeastern corner of Seventeenth and Hill (one block north of the Inter Ocean Hotel) for $2,500. For years the residence of Judge J. R. Whitehead had stood on this corner. Before construction began in October, an extra twenty-five feet was added to the west side, at a cost of $1,600.[2]

The opera house went up amid a Cheyenne construction boom of residences and brick commercial buildings, as well as a new Presbyterian church. The *Leader* expressed the opinion that the real estate boom had been triggered by the opera house project: "a rise of fifty percent... has been experienced since the opera house became an assumed fact. The reason of this is plain. It shows a thorough confidence in the prosperity of the city—such an investment of so much capital." But the "thorough confidence" was not thorough enough to sell out all the shares of opera house stock. Eight months after $20,000 in stock had been issued, $3,200 worth of shares remained unsold. The building eventually cost $50,000, but director Henry Hay arranged financing.[3]

An opera house in a small city would produce only irregular revenue—the philanthropic backers were providing a noteworthy but unprofitable institution for their community. If it was unrealistic to expect nightly opera house performances in Cheyenne, part of the big building therefore should be utilized to produce regular income. The northern portion, more than sixty percent of the structure, would house the great theater, but the southern end, facing Seven-

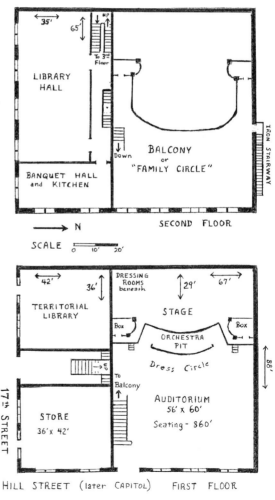

Author's diagram of Cheyenne Opera House.

teenth Street, would be used for miscellaneous purposes. The ground floor comprised two store areas measuring 36 feet by 42 feet each. The Territorial Library rented one of these sections for $800 per year, while the other segment was rented for $900 annually (at first to a millinery shop, but in June the *Leader* moved in with its printing presses.)[4]

The second floor housed a banquet hall, 20 feet by 35 feet, and Library Hall, 35 feet by 65 feet. With a small stage at one end, Library Hall (named for the Territorial Library directly below) could host performances, dances, fairs, and various other activities. While the new Presbyterian sanctuary was being built, the congregation rented Library Hall on Sundays. The telephone exchange rented the large southeast corner room on the third floor. There were eleven smaller rooms on the third floor, beneath the mansard roof, that would be rented as lodgings.[5]

This southern portion was completed in February 1882, nearly three months earlier than the more elaborate theater. The Territorial Library was moved into the building, along with other rental customers. On the last night in February, Library Hall was the scene of the inaugural ball and banquet. Tickets were ten

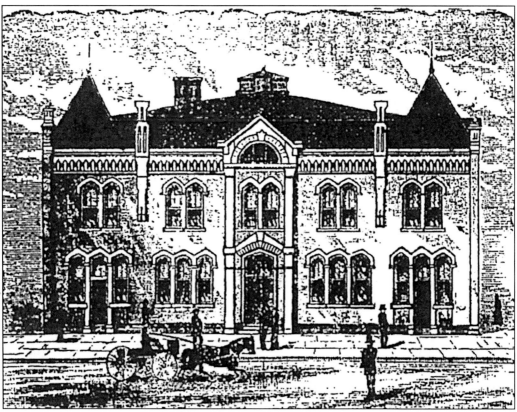

The south side of the Cheyenne Opera House on Eighteenth Street, as pictured by the architect. The left entrance led to the Terrtitorial Library, while the large double room behind the right entrance was rented to a millinery shop. Above the millinery shop was a 20 by 35 banquet hall, while the 35 by 65 Library Hall took up the rest of the second floor on the south side. The telephone exchange was above the banquet hall, and the remainder of the third floor beneath the roof held eleven rented lodging rooms. The Opera House took up the entire north side of the building. (From the dedication story in the Leader, *May 25, 1882)*

dollars, and "Cheyenne society appeared at its best," reported the *Leader*. "The gentlemen were all clad in the regulation evening dress," and the attire of every woman was described: "Mrs. F. E. Warren, white silk and oriental cashmere, trimmed with Spanish lace, diamond ornaments" or "Mrs. H. G. Hay, black silk, trimmed with black passementrie." The floor was "waxed as smooth as glass," and the Third Cavalry string orchestra provided dance music. Carriages began arriving before nine, and couples danced until midnight, when everyone filed into the banquet hall for a "magnificent supper." Dancing then resumed until a late hour.[6]

The "celebrated" Comley-Barton Opera Company was engaged to open the theater on Thursday, May 25, 1882. Western audiences, somewhat incongruously, welcomed opera performances, and the Comley-Barton company would present the French comic opera *Olivette*. The company was scheduled to perform Thursday, Friday, and Saturday nights, with a Saturday matinee as well. The event was widely advertised, attracting visitors from Laramie, Denver, and other northern Colorado communities. In Cheyenne there was a run on opera glasses.[7]

"Cheyenne is the dressiest city in the west," proclaimed the *Leader*. "Silks and satins appeared in every fashionable shade and color, . . . made up with all the skill and taste of the finest dressmaking." The opening night audience "was by far the largest and finest ever gathered in a Cheyenne theater." After the orchestra completed the overture, Mayor Carey was called to the stage, and he publicly thanked Henry Hay and others crucial to the opera house project. The audience responded warmly to the performers, and called for several encores. After the applause ended a ball began in Library Hall. A "large number of invited guests" strolled a couple of blocks eastward to the Cheyenne Club, which had been opened only a few weeks earlier. After refreshments the elite group rejoined "the swaying crowd" at Library Hall, and the ball continued until nearly dawn."[8]

The new theater seated "860 persons comfortably, and can be made to seat 1,000 when occasion requires." This seating capacity included a balcony, or "family circle." Two proscenium boxes, one above the other, flanked each side of the stage. Box seating was part of the opera house ritual. Those who purchased these prized seats were on display as members of the elite. And the "dress circle" beyond the orchestra pit earned its name because formal dress was expected in this location. Audience members were seated in "the latest pattern of opera folding chairs, comfortable, convenient and strong." A "special gas machine" provided gas lighting throughout the hall, including an "immense 52-light chandelier" suspended from the ceiling, with "an immense gas reflector" above, throwing illumination to every corner of the auditorium. Ornamental touches included railings "with red silk plush upholstery," rich carved woodwork, and three large cathedral windows at the rear of the balcony, with 600 colored glass panes. The grand stairway to the balcony was built of hardwood, ash and black walnut.

The arch of the stage was supported by Corinthian-Doric columns, and there was a magnificent drop curtain from Chicago portraying Roman chariot races. The stage was inclined, with footlights across the carved front. The maximum depth was 29 feet, with 67 feet of width backstage. Dressing rooms were beneath

Looking across Capitol Avenue at the east façade of the Cheyenne Opera House. The entrance to the auditorium, which takes up the wing at right, is through the arched doorway. (Frank Leslie's Illustrated Newspaper, January 31, 1891)

the stage, along with a "green room," where actors gathered to go onstage. Eleven sets—prison, kitchen, street scenes, etc.—had been purchased, along with "numerous extras, which makes possible any number of combinations." Careful attention had been paid to acoustics in designing the hall, "and the weakest voice can fill it easily."

The Cheyenne Opera House was leased and managed by D. C. Rhodes, who previously had administered Recreation Hall and the Dramatic Theater. On Friday night, June 2, 1882, Rhodes booked three events: a lecture in Library Hall, "the Automatic City" in the banquet room, and a musical comedy in the opera house. In August *Uncle Tom's Cabin* played the opera house. A perennial favorite, the stage version of Harriet Beecher Stowe's melodramatic novel would appear almost every year of the two-decade existence of the Opera House. The 1899 company advertised "20 Coloreds, 20 Whites." Minstrel shows also brought big crowds to the Opera House. Whites often performed in these shows in blackface, but an 1882 appearance of *The Moss Grown Region of the South* proclaimed "30 Genuine Darkies." *Davy Crockett*, popular for decades in western performance halls, played the Cheyenne Opera House in November 1882. High school commencement exercises would pack the house every year.[9]

Doug Rhodes attracted three spectacular performers in 1887. In April, Edwin Booth, "the world's greatest actor," arrived on the eastbound train "to which his elegant special car was attached." Rhodes met him with carriages and the Seventeenth Infantry band. Installed at the Inter Ocean, Booth received callers throughout the day. That evening he starred in *Hamlet* "before an immense audience at the opera house."[10]

Sarah Bernhardt arrived early in June, also in a private railroad car. Rhodes again engaged the Seventeenth Infantry band, which serenaded Bernhardt after she was escorted to the Inter Ocean. The internationally famous actress appeared "several times on the balcony bowing her acknowledgements for the compliment." Bernhardt and her company staged *Fedora* at the opera house. She spoke only French, but Cheyenne theatergoers were accustomed to French and Italian operas. Bernhardt departed the next morning for an engagement at Denver's Tabor Opera House.[11]

A week later the celebrated English singer-actress Lillie Langtry reached Cheyenne in the "Lalee," the "gorgeously blue" luxury car which had been built for her five-year tour of the United States. Langtry appeared before a full house in the comedy *A Wife's Peril*. But a few days later an even larger crowd attended *The Devil's Auction*, which had played Cheyenne three seasons earlier. The spectacular crowd-pleaser featured "grotesque comedians," a ballet, and "gorgeous scenic arrangements." An eager audience "filled every seat in the opera house, occupied chairs in several aisles and comfortably packed the lobbies upstairs and

Sketch of the Opera House stage and box seats. (Frank Leslie's Illustrated Newspaper, January 31, 1891)

down." Doug Rhodes had achieved the greatest booking triumph the Cheyenne Opera House would ever enjoy. Within a two-month period, Edwin Booth, Sarah Bernhardt, and Lillie Langtry performed on its stage, followed by a dynamic show which produced a standing-room-only crowd.[12]

Rhodes continued to book attractive shows, such as *Dr. Jekyll and Mr. Hyde* in 1888 and Shakespeare's *Much Ado About Nothing* the next year. Minstrel shows continued to draw well, while vaudeville companies suddenly became popular. But now the Opera House had competition: M.P. Keefe expanded and improved his performance hall, and in 1891 Turnverein Hall, designed to accommodate performances, dances or banquets, was erected. By this time the Opera House was nearly a decade old and "showed every evidence of neglect," observed the *Leader*. Shareholders did not want to spend renovation money on what was never expected to be "a directly remunerative investment." F. E. Warren, now a U.S. senator but always interested in real estate, quietly bought up a great deal of stock from various shareholders.[13]

However, Joseph M. Carey, Warren's fellow senator, also was active in Cheyenne real estate, and he saw potential in the big Opera House building on a prominent downtown corner. The population of Cheyenne had tripled—from 4,000 to 12,000—since the Opera House was erected. The expanding business district demanded office space, and Carey contemplated the renovation of the structure he had been instrumental in creating. Senator Carey and his brother Robert approached Senator Warren, who now controlled "a large majority of the stock." The Carey brothers negotiated an outright purchase for $30,000.[14]

The Careys announced plans to spend $15,000 to $20,000 in remodeling the south end of the building. Library Hall and the banquet room would be eliminated in favor of second-floor offices, and renovation of the third floor would include installation of a skylight in the roof. In all there would be twenty-six offices, and the two big store spaces on the first floor would be divided into four commercial rooms. The Carey brothers hired J. P. Weybrecht, who had built the Opera House a decade earlier, to carry out these renovations.[15]

The Devil's Auction Base Ball Club

The large troupe that brought *The Devil's Auction* to the Cheyenne Opera House included enough athletic young performers and crew members to fill a baseball lineup. Upon arriving in Cheyenne, the "Devil's Auction Base Ball Club" issued a challenge, and a local nine of "printers and railroad boys" was hastily assembled. The afternoon of the performance there was time to play five innings, and the Cheyenne boys were "simply tremendous," reported the *Leader* (June 16, 1897). Cheyenne led, 18–3, when the visitors had to report to the Opera House. "A good sized audience witnessed the exhibition and everyone enjoyed it."

Vague plans simultaneously were announced to remodel and expand the Opera House theater. A "gallery," or second balcony, could be installed above the existing balcony for additional seating. Sight lines would be improved; there would be new scenery and perhaps a new drop curtain; and all manner of interior refurbishments would be made. The hall might be expanded to the north, although the existing wall was a support wall. In any event, work on the auditorium would "not be touched until such time as the rest of the building is ready for tenants." When the tenants began moving in during February 1892 (the Opera House "block" proved especially popular with doctors), auditorium renovations remained in the planning stage.[16]

Sarah Bernhardt appeared at the Cheyenne Opera House in June 1887. (From an ad in the Leader, June 19, 1897)

With commercial and office space beginning to produce significant revenue, the Carey brothers chose not to make a major investment in remodeling an auditorium that had never produced profits. So the seating capacity, which could accommodate one-quarter of Cheyenne's population when the Opera House was built, remained unchanged. Therefore, when Doug Rhodes booked a blockbuster act, there could not be enough tickets sold to attain blockbuster profits, the kind of profits that would help make up for off nights. Furthermore, the stage was increasingly obsolete. From the front of the curved stage to the rear wall measured only twenty-nine feet. A serious drawback to this lack of depth was that sets could not be "flown"; that is, raised or lowered. The best stages could raise and lower at least three or four settings, but at Cheyenne it probably was possible to fly only a single set. Large theatrical companies could not adequately stage their shows in Cheyenne. In 1892, after ten years of managing the Cheyenne Opera House, Doug Rhodes decided it was prudent to sell his lease to another management team.[17]

Despite its drawbacks, the Opera House continued to offer excellent entertainment on occasion. In 1894 Gentleman Jim Corbett, heavyweight champion of the world, was a resounding hit in *Gentleman Jack*. Two years later the Tavery Opera Company, fifty-seven strong, arrived in three railroad cars to present *Carmen*. For both nights of the 1900 Frontier Days, a company was brought in to stage grand opera. In 1897 De Wolf Hopper, "the king of American comic opera," appeared with his company in John Philip Sousa's new comic opera, *El Capitan*. Hopper also delighted the Opera House audience with his trademark recitation

OPERA HOUSE PROGRAMME

STAHLE & BAILEY, MANAGERS.

Saturday, January 12. 1901.

Liebler & Co's Production of Hall Caine's

THE CHRISTIAN

Originally produced under personal supervision of Author.

Neatness.   Completeness.

Sweetness

The City Market

Waiter M. Clark, Prop.
214 W. 17th St.

Politeness.

Promptness.   Carefulness.

Have Just Finished

INVOICING

and find we have too much stock on hand.

We need some of your money.

Do you need any of these goods?

Everything First Class.

Prices are Right.

DINNEEN BROS.

Phone. 40.

Brookhart and Bruner, Printers, 1712 Ferguson Street.

Program cover for a 1901 performance at the Cheyenne Opera House. (Warren Papers, Box 300) of "Casey at the Bat." *Uncle Tom's Cabin* continued to attract enthusiastic crowds every year, and each June the Opera House overflowed during Cheyenne High School commencement exercises.[18]

Year after year, the Cheyenne Opera House continued to provide memorable evenings for the community. "It is one of the great attractions of our city," proclaimed the *Leader* twenty years after it was erected.[19] The men who had built the Opera House wanted to create a proper home in their city for first-class entertainment. For two decades Cheyenne's elite was able to dress in evening finery and attend operas or noted plays, just as if they lived in New York or Chicago. The Cheyenne occasions were less regular than those in eastern cities, but when a famous performer played Cheyenne for a single night, the event seemed more special. Less prominent citizens also attended these events, by the hundreds, and everyone enjoyed commencements and local concerts and amateur theatricals. At the Opera House, Cheyenne's citizens laughed and cheered together for twenty years. Through scores or even hundreds of shared evenings across two decades, the Opera House noticeably elevated the cultural level of the Magic City and helped to bind the citizens into a community. The goals of the founders were richly fulfilled as the Cheyenne Opera House became one of the city's most important institutions of the late nineteenth century.

De Wolf Hopper, "the king of the American comic opera," appeared in Cheyenne in El Capitan in 1897. Hopper also delivered his trademark recitation, "Casey at the Bat." (Leader, April 24, 1897)

14

Flood, Fire, Lynching— and Shopping

Cheyenne had survived fires and blizzards, but the Magic City of an arid plain never expected a devastating flood. Late in the morning on Saturday, June 16, 1883, a mass of dark clouds gathered over Cheyenne. "It was evident that a rain of no ordinary magnitude was pending," reported the *Leader*. A cloudburst dumped volumes of water, and "Crow Creek became an angry, raging river." As the unrelenting deluge continued into the afternoon, the streets became flooded. Then, from the high country to the north and west, a torrent of water roared toward Cheyenne. "It rushed on like a living monster," reported an astounded eyewitness at the foothills, "in waves fifteen feet high, and carried all before it."[1]

This overwhelming surge of water swept away boardwalks and eroded sidewalk foundations, upending slabs and threatening brick walls. Downtown basements, used primarily to store merchandise, began to fill with water. Merchants threw up makeshift dams to protect their buildings. "The number of bales of hay used for dams yesterday was uncountable," related the *Leader*. "Five hundred sacks of bran, flour, chop feed and salt were used to dam back the water around the Phoenix block," which housed a grocery. Across the street another dam was hastily erected to protect the Inter Ocean Hotel, which created a powerful funnel in the middle of Sixteenth Street.

A trench between Fifteenth Street and the Union Pacific tracks overflowed, sweeping away several footbridges. As floodwaters coursed wildly between the embankments of Crow Creek, an expectant crowd gathered near the big bridge leading south of town. "Suddenly she shivered," described a *Leader* reporter, "swayed to and fro for an instant . . . , and with a crash she went down, the flood carrying it some two hundred yards down stream where it rests broad side up."

202

At the intersection of Eighteenth and Ferguson, two young ladies headed their horse-drawn buggy toward home. But the horse suddenly disappeared into a hole—only his ears appeared above water. The girls were carried to safety, and "by great efforts the horse was saved from a watery grave." Another buggy, moving south on Eddy Street and carrying a man and two girls, overturned in a ditch. "A bystander waded out and rescued the girls," and the frantic horse was brought to high ground. A boy standing on an embankment of Crow Creek tumbled into the swirling waters when the bluff collapsed. Fortunately, the mishap was seen by a man who was trying to rope some loose horses. The cowboy ran to the embankment and expertly dropped his loop over the boy's head, pulled it tight around his waist, and hauled him out of the creek.

The flood swirled into the new railroad shops, upending everything inside. "It undermined the immense oil tank, which contained several thousand gallons of oil, and lifted it up." Oil from the overturned tank oozed out to join the floodwaters.

Mayor Joseph Carey, who had just seen the brick walls collapse on the new block he was erecting, offered five dollars an hour to each of fifty men who would dig a ditch that would divert the floodwaters into Crow Creek. Such enormous wages quickly attracted a work gang. About a mile northwest of town the drenched workmen hastily produced a ditch, "which turned the volume of water and probably saved the town."

The southward spread of water was halted by the UP track embankment, which extended east and west across the entirety of Cheyenne. But all of downtown and most of the surrounding residential neighborhoods were flooded by waters from one to ten feet in depth. Near the Railroad House Hotel a small lake

The Phoenix Block was built in 1882 by F. E. Warren on the southwest corner of Sixteenth and Hill (Capitol) streets. (Courtesy Wyoming State Archives)

had formed, and boys floated around on rafts made from broken pieces of board-walk. As night fell a sound "was heard in the streets of Cheyenne that never was heard before—the croaking of frogs."

The Phil Sheridan steamer was sent down from Camp Carlin to pump out cel-lars. The Durant Hose Company brought out their steamer for the same purpose. At an impromptu meeting at city hall, covered by the *Leader*, "F. E. Warren said that the man who needed the steamer most could pay the most, and offered $50 an hour for its use. He got it." The Warren Mercantile Company on Sixteenth Street stored furniture and other merchandise in six cellars, and only two days earlier they had brought in a carload of goods that had cost $600 in freight charges alone. Despite the efforts of the Durant steamer, most of the furniture in the cellars was ruined, and Warren estimated his losses between $20,000 and $25,000.

On Sunday, as the waters receded, the two steamers went from cellar to cel-lar. "Articles of every description were being rapidly removed from their wet bath in the cellars and placed upon the boardwalks and streets to dry." Sheets were spread around the Inter Ocean Hotel, and roasted coffee was set out to dry in the sun. "Huge piles of merchandise, dripping with water, were piled up or carted away to dryer quarters," observed the *Leader*. "Huge stacks of meat, boxes of crackers, barrels of sugar, bags of potatoes, flour, bran and salt, all soaked with water, ornamented the sidewalk around the Phoenix block." Total losses were es-timated at $150,000. Men went to work, at a dollar an hour, to repair damages around town.

On at least four occasions in previous years, large volumes of water had cas-caded down the slopes north of Cheyenne, although there had never before been a flood of such proportions in town. Following the great flood, the city council au-thorized construction of a long, permanent ditch across James Talbot's property a mile north of town to divert future floodwaters. But on Saturday, May 24, 1884—less than a year after the flood of 1883—Crow Creek swelled into a river. For several days heavy rains had soaked the region, and on Saturday evening there was "a terrible thunder storm." At Fort Russell and Camp Carlin, located above the Talbot ditch, heavy waters coursed through both posts. There was con-siderable damage at the Camp Carlin stables, which were near Crow Creek.[2]

The Talbot ditch was constructed with the idea of channeling floodwaters from the slopes into Crow Creek, and the idea worked. By nightfall on Saturday, Crow Creek was a raging torrent, and the stream overran its banks; however, floodwaters did not reach downtown Cheyenne. Several modest houses south of the UP tracks and near the creek were flooded or washed away.[3]

There was severe wreckage among the bridges across Crow Creek. A new iron bridge at the foot of Nineteenth Street had been constructed at a cost of $3,000. James Talbot was still working on approaches at each end, but the end sec-tions were swept away, leaving only the central portion in place. The flooded creek carried off the entire Seventeenth Street bridge, and the Sixteenth Street bridge was badly damaged. "The Eddy Street bridge is past talking about," ob-served the *Leader*.

The rain subsided Saturday night, but on Tuesday afternoon a ferocious hailstorm struck Cheyenne, followed by hours of torrential rain. That evening the city council met with the board of equalization. The meeting soon adjourned, however, as the officials "turned out with others armed with picks and shovels and went to work." F. E. Warren was among those who ventured into the rain to rip up wooden street crossings that were acting as dams. Although Seventeenth Street became "one mass of water," the storm abated before flooding could occur—and before any more frogs could be heard.[4]

If flooding was an uncommon calamity in Cheyenne, a more familiar menace did not spare the 1880s. About an hour past midnight on Tuesday morning, March 25, 1884, the cry of "Fire! Fire!" was shouted, followed by several pistol shots. Railroad whistles soon added to the alarm, along with the bell at city hall. Firemen from all three companies turned out with their vehicles, "tugging nobly through the snow and the slush." On Sixteenth Street flames were "shooting furiously up in the air" from the city's largest mercantile house, the three-story Warren Mercantile Company. Soldiers at Camp Carlin hitched horses to the "government steamer, Phil Sheridan," and hurriedly came into town."[5]

But the fire, which apparently started in the rear of the third floor, quickly enveloped "the whole of the interior in one vast seething sea of flames." Merchandise "of the finest description fell a helpless prey to the wild fury of the devouring element." The upper floors contained several lodging rooms, some utilized by Warren employees. A soldier named Mike McCarty bravely helped to rescue some of the residents, until he was severely gashed by a shattered plate-glass window. "Faint and bleeding he was picked up and carried to Dr. Corey's office, where surgical aid was speedily and efficiently rendered," the *Leader* reported.

Firemen scrambled up their ladders to force open iron shutters, and many citizens offered their help. But as it became obvious that the Warren Mercantile was lost, efforts were concentrated on saving adjoining buildings. The Inter Ocean Hotel on the east was threatened, and many guests "packed their trunks and valises hurriedly" as flames "beat furiously against its side." Yet there was no wind to fan the conflagration, and "a splendid firewall" did its job. Within two hours the fire was under control. Although the Warren Mercantile was a smoldering shell, there were no fatalities, and no other buildings were damaged, except for plate-glass windows across the street that were cracked by the intense heat.

The next day F. E. Warren announced his intentions to rebuild. The Warren Mercantile Company quickly rented stores on Seventeenth and Ferguson streets, stored goods in warehouses around the city, filled up the old Congregational Church with goods, and resumed business. Unfazed by the destruction of the fire (and of the flood of the previous March), Warren typically decided to turn adversity into opportunity. While the lot was being cleared of debris, he was formulating plans for a spectacular expansion.[6]

At forty, Warren was at the height of his business career. As president of the Warren Mercantile Company, he had expanded the firm into a great retail and wholesale outlet that served a vast area. He also was president of the Warren Live

Stock Company, which controlled 200,000 acres of land, all fenced and stocked with cattle, sheep, and horses. Warren was president of the Brush-Swan Electric Light Company, with more than $100,000 invested in providing electric lights to Cheyenne. In addition, he served as president of the Cheyenne Carriage Company and the Cheyenne Opera House, and as vice-president of the First National Bank (next door to the Warren Block, which had just burned). He already had built substantial three-story buildings on Sixteenth Street: the Warren Block, the Phoenix Block, the Commercial Block, the Atlas Block, and the First National Bank building. His Cheyenne real estate holdings brought him $30,000 annually in rental income. A gifted and highly successful capitalist, Warren had learned to think big. Not only would he rebuild the Warren Block; he also would erect Cheyenne's largest, grandest commercial structure: The Warren Emporium.

Warren commissioned well-known architect J. S. Matthews to design a business headquarters that would cover almost an entire block on Sixteenth just north of the UP Depot. The eastern third of the Emporium would house three floors of workrooms and storage space, while the western two-thirds of the building (118 feet by 132 feet of floor space, plus spacious galleries) would feature one of the largest and most impressive retail palaces in the West. (Construction details are described in Chapter 12.)

Warren stayed abreast of the fast-changing mercantile world of the late nineteenth century. Such innovative merchant kings as Marshall Field of Chicago, R. H. Macy and A. T. Stewart of New York, and John Wanamaker of Philadelphia were developing urban department stores. The industrial revolution produced goods in great quantity at reduced prices, and the mass availability of merchandise transformed shopping habits from those of colonial shops and rural general stores. At the same time, Marshall Field catered to the moneyed women of Chicago, providing them with elegant surroundings that encouraged a leisurely, recreational shopping experience.

Warren's Emporium opened in 1884 and provided the women of Cheyenne with a shopping palace. (From Frank Leslie's Illustrated Newspaper, *January 31, 1891)*

Field's Chicago was the nearest major city to Cheyenne, a frequent destination for upper-class citizens of the Magic City, and Warren incorporated many of the latest developments into his company. The Warren Mercantile Company bought merchandise by the carload, delivering to stores all over Wyoming and beyond. Warren was keenly aware that there were many well-to-do women in Cheyenne who had plenty of time to engage in recreational shopping, as well as tourists in town for one of the gatherings frequently held in Wyoming's capital. Less affluent customers of the Warren Mercantile could buy on credit, paying "in monthly installments or weekly installments." Because the income of farmers was sporadic, installment purchasing was not possible until the industrial revolution created a growing class of salaried workers who were paid every week or every month. In Cheyenne the wives of the UP employees or of army officers or of clerks would be able to shop in the Emporium and buy, on new-fangled credit terms, items that would not otherwise be affordable. Pianos, organs, and sewing machines also were available "at reasonable terms of rental."

The Warren Emporium opened in late October 1884. Warren always had invested heavily in newspaper advertising, and a full-page ad announced: "THE WARREN EMPORIUM is Now Fully Completed and is Beyond Question the Largest and Most COMPLETE MERCANTILE ESTABLISHMENT in the West. It is Fully Stocked

J. C. Abney's Livery Stable was directly across from the Emporium, on the northwest corner of Sixteenth and Capitol. The Inter Ocean Hotel was across the street to the west (left), and the UP Depot was a block to the south. Abney's Stable was used for Cheyenne Street Railway horses. (Courtesy Wyoming State Archives)

with Selected Goods Bought in Very Large Quantities." The rest of the page was devoted to lists of goods in the various departments.

The most attractive of these goods were displayed behind a long row of plate-glass windows. The principal entrance led through a 52-foot-tall clock tower on the northwest corner of the Emporium, diagonally across from the Inter Ocean Hotel. Entering the Emporium across the tile floor of a hexagon-shaped vestibule, customers beheld a vast array of miscellaneous goods, across the main floor and on galleries above. Each department—Furniture, Carpets, Sewing Machines, Pianos and Music, Wallpaper and Pictures, Glassware and China, etc.—was supervised by its own manager. The *Leader* headlined that the Emporium offered a "Bewildering Display of Pretty Articles for the Ladies," and that sales were "Made by the Single Dollar or by the Thousand." The second floor of the entry tower "is fitted up with an elegant carpet, piano and other furniture, and will be used as a reception and waiting room for the pleasure and convenience of the customers." Customers also could enjoy "elegantly fitted up toilet apartments, provided with hot and cold water and all modern conveniences."[8]

Cheyenne already boasted an excellent business section, and not another town in the United States with a population of 7,000 had a business house to compare with the Warren Emporium. The *Leader* crowed that "Mr. Warren may well be called the A. T. Stewart or the John Wanamaker of Wyoming."[9]

Warren's private office inside the Emporium was "handsomely furnished" and featured "a beautiful fireplace which has a border of illuminated tiles." Adjoining offices served the Warren Mercantile Company managerial staff and, in a separate suite, the Warren Live Stock Company, which had telephone connections to each of the firm's fourteen ranches. This office complex was the nerve center of an economic empire that included a major mercantile operation, large-scale ranching, real estate, and investments. Warren had declined the office of territorial delegate to Congress because he did not want to leave Cheyenne for long periods of time in faraway Washington. The growth of his diverse enterprises demanded his attention and personal presence.

But now there was little more to accomplish in the business world of Cheyenne or the ranching world of Wyoming. Warren was wealthy; he owned fourteen ranches, and had built his Emporium. He had a gracious, loving wife, a bright little girl, and a baby boy. Despite all of this, Warren was too young and ambitious to be satisfied for long. His political gifts were as formidable as his business talents. Already he had served as mayor and territorial treasurer when, in February 1885, he was appointed territorial governor. Warren became governor only a few months after the opening of his Emporium, but now he began to see what he could accomplish from high office. His business career inevitably began to take a back seat to his political rise. Having learned how far he could go in business, he would now see how far he could go in politics. In 1887, when he had the opportunity to sell the Emporium as a depot to the new Cheyenne and Southern Railroad, he took the cash, leased part of the Emporium for two years, then moved the Warren Mercantile Company to a less notable building (which he owned, of course).

Flood and fire were not the only sudden upheavals that occasionally interrupted the pleasant and progressive Cheyenne lifestyle of the 1880s. In September 1883 Cheyenne's veneer of law-abiding respectability gave way for a few days to murder and lynching, demonstrating that frontier violence and retribution remained close to the surface in the Holy City of the Cow. At dawn on Wednesday, September 12, 1883, three men were camped three miles northwest of Cheyenne near Fort Russell. They had four mules and a covered freight wagon, coupled to a small trail wagon. The outfit was owned by twenty-five-year-old John H. Wensel, who had picked up two travelers, James Knight and Henry Mosier.[10]

Mosier, a brother-in-law of Cheyenne's Thomas Cahill, had committed violence in the past. Noticing a satchel of Wensel's containing fifty or sixty dollars, Mosier determined to murder his companions and steal the money. At daybreak he seized an ax and hit the sleeping Knight on the head. Turning to Wensel, Mosier struck twice with the ax. Despite a fractured skull, Wensel grappled with his attacker, wrestled the ax away, and threw it out of the wagon. But while Wensel tried to awaken the unconscious Knight, Mosier found a revolver and shot his victim through the lungs.

Wensel clambered out of the wagon and began running toward the fort. Mosier gave chase, shooting Wensel in the left arm and left hand. When a soldier came into view, Mosier turned and fled into the hills. The badly injured Wensel was taken to the post hospital, and Cheyenne authorities were notified "of the butchery" by telephone. Prosecuting attorney J. C. Baird and Justice of the Peace J. W. Fisher came to the fort and questioned Wensel. Preparing a statement from his remarks, the officials asked Wensel to sign it as an ante-mortem declaration. But Wensel replied that "he thought he might live and therefore it could not be called his ante-mortem statement."

Meanwhile, Knight had been discovered beneath the blankets in the wagon. Dazed, he did not realize what had happened. Knight was taken to the courthouse, where he was tended by Dr. Maynard, the county physician. After providing a description of Mosier, Knight was installed in a boardinghouse on Sixteenth, where he slowly regained his senses and balance.

During Wednesday afternoon, Wensel was interviewed by a *Leader* reporter. That evening J. C. Baird returned to Mosier's bedside. Now recognizing that he was dying, Wensel made his mark on Baird's document, "and said it was his ante-mortem declaration." Wensel breathed his last about half past eight that night, and he was buried the next day in the Cheyenne Cemetery. He avoided potter's field because funeral expenses were taken from the fifty-three dollars in the satchel that the fleeing Mosier had not taken time to steal.

Governor William Hale offered $500 for the capture of Mosier, while Laramie County and the City of Cheyenne added $100 apiece. "I also order the printing of 300 postal cards containing a copy of this reward," stated Governor Hale. Cards and telegrams were sent to a wide expanse of county sheriffs and city marshals. With $700 in rewards offered for Mosier, hundreds of bounty hunters scoured the countryside for a bald, bearded fugitive in his forties, accompanied by a black dog.[11]

Still wearing bloodstained clothing, Mosier was arrested on Saturday at Louisville, Colorado, northwest of Denver. Word reached Cheyenne about nine on Saturday evening, and immediately there was talk on the streets of lynching. "Little knots of resolute men, with compressed lips and frowning faces could be seen here and there," reported the *Leader*, "and it needed no great wisdom to tell what was the subject of their conversation." Within two hours Sheriff Sharpless and several officers took a special train—a locomotive, tender, and caboose—to pick up Mosier at Fort Collins. To his arresting officer, Sheriff John Sweeney of Larimer County, Mosier "predicted that he would not live 5 minutes after reaching Cheyenne."[12]

When the special train returned to Cheyenne on Sunday, a waiting wagon whisked Mosier five blocks to the courthouse and jail on Nineteenth. At nine o'clock, a large crowd collected in front of the jail, calling for Sheriff Sharpless and shouting, "Haul him out and hang him." The gang had no leader, however, and these men soon dispersed. At midnight another mob, better led and organized, ran to the jail, "discharging their weapons and shouting at the top of their voices." Surging into the jail, the mob ordered the officers to hold up their hands. Judge Fisher defiantly refused to raise his hands "at the behest of any mob," and he snatched a long iron bar from a mob member.[13]

The bar was quickly retrieved, then used to pry open cell doors until Mosier was found. "Two men seized him, one by each ear, and dragged him into the corridor, when he was laid hold of by as many hands as could reach him and hurried along on his fateful journey." Someone struck him in the face, and several guns were discharged inside the jail. "The crowd was disorderly and boisterous," observed the *Leader*. The mob hustled Mosier half a block west to the corner of Nineteenth and Eddy, where a rope was noosed around the killer's neck. The other end was strung over a spar on a telegraph pole.

At this point E.S.N. Morgan, secretary of Wyoming Territory, rushed into the midst of the crowd and delivered "an impassioned plea" on behalf of justice and mercy. "The crowd listened to him

E.S.N. Morgan, highly capable territorial secretary (1880–87) who filled in as acting governor during the long absences of Governor William Hale. Morgan tried to stop the lynching of Henry Mosier. (Courtesy Wyoming State Archives)

good naturedly, if not very patiently, but his appeal was of no avail." Mayor Joseph M. Carey also tried to head off the mob, but "his eloquence" was ignored. Mosier was hoisted upward, then came down. Once again he was swung up, only to drop to the ground. The third time he went up and stayed in the air. "The hanging was evidently done by inexperienced hands," reported the *Leader* in an understatement, "and was not performed scientifically by any means."

The mob numbered at least five hundred, "and they represented nearly all grades of society." Although Mayor Carey and Secretary Morgan tried to stop the lynching, at least some members of Cheyenne's leadership class apparently supported the extralegal execution. Despite strong expectations of a lynching attempt, neither Sheriff Sharpless nor other officers had tried to defend the jail. A few days after the lynching, the *Leader* expressed editorial approval: "Exigencies may arise in any community which make it necessary to visit swift and condign

Tramps

"The town is overrun with tramps," began a *Leader* story on April 6, 1888. Tramps constantly came into Cheyenne on freight trains. These "pests" fanned out into town, looking for handouts or engaging in petty thievery. In between sorties into the neighborhoods, they loitered around the vast railroad yards. The *Leader* reporter found twenty or more tramps "sunning themselves" on Fifteenth Street, just north of the tracks.

"There were tall tramps, short tramps, fat tramps, lean tramps, dirty and ragged tramps and a few of the shabby genteel order." The *Leader* reporter interviewed a garrulous vagabond, asking how he covered so much territory with no funds. "If you're thrown out of one car, climb in the next one," the tramp explained. "If you're put to rout entirely, wait for the next train. Never walk."

"Yes, but how about eating?"

"Simplest thing in the land. Beg, but use judgment. When you approach a house see that the inmates burn nothing but coal [cutting wood in exchange for a meal was a hazard to be avoided] and have no dog. Always knock at the back door. Sometimes they'll close the opening

in your face," he shrugged, "but that's nothing. If a good talker can secure an audience with the domestic, he is sure of getting something. If she's Dutch, tell her your father was killed in the Franco-Prussian War; if she's Irish, quietly put her on to the fact that you're a thoroughbred Fenian; if she's a Swede, just make the announcement that your uncle, Yon Yonson, has moved from Dakota to California and you want to join him."

The interview was cut short by the approach of a uniformed constable on horseback. The tramps scattered, "half a dozen squads disappearing in as many directions." Although tramps kept a sharp lookout for officers in uniform, there were frequent roundups of "vags" through the years. After an arrest they were quickly brought before a city judge and fined for vagrancy. Since tramps never had money for fines, they often were ordered to leave town immediately. However, if the city had a project in progress—street improvements or cleaning out the water ditch, for example—the tramps were forced to serve out their fines, then were assigned to a work gang.

[deserved] punishment on a murderer like Mosier." And the Denver *Tribune* of-fered hearty support: "Nobody is sorry that the cold-blooded murderer has met his just reward. Cheyenne is to be congratulated for this summary visit of retribu-tive justice."[14]

Lynching remained common in the South and West during the 1880s, and the men of Cheyenne had abruptly demonstrated that, like Cheyenneites of the late 1860s, they would not tolerate certain crimes. But Cheyenne was not reverting to its boomtown past of street shootouts and vigilante hangings. The vigorous busi-ness climate of Wyoming's capital precluded a return to frontier violence, and the Mosier lynching proved to be Cheyenne's final excursion into extralegal justice. For the remainder of the nineteenth century, law and order prevailed in Cheyenne. Potential troublemakers were intimidated by Cheyenne's uniformed and helmeted policemen, whose professional appearance suggested a more urban environment than that of most Western communities.

Other uniformed men around Cheyenne were soldiers from Fort Russell, which avoided the fate of most Wyoming military posts. By 1880 the increasingly peaceful behavior of Native Americans, except for Apaches in the Southwest, dic-tated the closure of many frontier outposts. Fort Fetterman was closed in 1882, and so was Fort Sanders at Laramie. During the next few years, the military would abandon most of the other Wyoming forts. But late in 1882 the War Department decreed that Fort D. A. Russell, positioned at the juncture of three railroads running in three directions, would be maintained and upgraded. Most of the fort's wooden structures would be replaced with brick buildings, creating a permanent post that would accommodate eight troops. The new construction program would employ contractors and large numbers of Cheyenne workmen. At the end of 1882, Camp Carlin still had 300 civilians on the payroll, with 800 mules hauling supplies, mostly to remaining forts and reservations in the north, where railroads did not yet extend.[15]

In August 1883 Fort Russell provided an escort to Yellowstone Park for President Chester A. Arthur and a party that included Lt. Gen. Phil Sheridan and Secretary of War Robert Lincoln, son of the Civil War president. Cheyenne planned to greet President Arthur with its customary celebration, but General Sheridan telegraphed ahead "that the stop here would be but momentary." Even a momentary stop (it turned out to be twenty-five moments) was better than no stop, and Cheyenne prepared to meet another president.[16]

President Arthur's train pulled in on Friday morning, August 3, 1883. A large crowd awaited, and the official delegation was led by Secretary E.S.N. Morgan (Governor William Hale was on a leave of absence because of illness). Morgan and other leading citizens, accompanied by officers from Fort Russell, came aboard to welcome President Arthur and his entourage. Outside the Fort Russell brass band played, while the cheering crowd called for the president.

President Arthur emerged onto the rear platform and began speaking in a loud voice: "I am glad to see you, and thank you for your warm welcome. I am sorry I cannot stop longer with you. Let me introduce you to Secretary Lincoln."

Robert Lincoln reminisced briefly about visiting Cheyenne during the first year of its existence. General Sheridan, who often had visited Cheyenne and Fort Russell, "was greeted with great warmth." Then prominent citizens "and their ladies" were allowed to ascend the platform and introduce themselves to Secretary Lincoln, who presented them to President Arthur. One of the last men to pass across the platform was a *Leader* representative, who found himself questioned about Cheyenne. President Arthur "said he had no idea that it was anything of a city, but had thought he was far out on the frontier." Reflecting on the opera house, the brick business blocks, the stately residences, Arthur indicated surprise "to see so much advanced civilization so far away out on the plains."

As the train pulled away, "amid prolonged cheering," President Arthur stood alone on the platform. He soon proceeded by rail 220 miles to Green River, where an escort of thirty-eight men and 178 mules from Fort Russell awaited. The presidential party employed three army ambulances and a baggage wagon as the expedition headed north for more than a month. Yellowstone had been designated America's first national park in 1872, and Arthur was the first president to visit the spectacular site. (When James Knight was axed by Henry Mosier near Fort Russell the next month, no military ambulances were available to take him to Cheyenne because the vehicles had not yet returned from Yellowstone.)

Throughout 1885 new brick buildings took shape at Fort Russell, many located south and east of the original parade ground. During the rest of the nineteenth century, a number of old frame structures were sold and moved into Cheyenne, often to the western part of town nearest the fort. (Several frame houses from the fort still stand in Cheyenne just north of the 1905 Governor's Mansion, as well as elsewhere around town.) Perhaps the most impressive new structure was the sprawling, two-story brick hospital. Another important element of the building program was a post waterworks. For nearly two decades a daily soldier detail manned a water wagon and filled barrels behind each quarters, barracks, and company mess hall. The water was pumped from Crow Creek by a steam engine into a storage tank. But in 1885 more than 5,000 feet of four-inch pipe was laid beneath the post grounds, with connecting pipes to each major building, and nine double-nozzle fire hydrants. A 30,000-gallon elevated metal tank provided pressure.[17]

In January 1887 Fort D.A. Russell received its own post office, halting the daily journey of a mail courier to the Cheyenne Post Office. Mrs. Lucinda Lester, wife of the sergeant major of the Seventh Infantry, was appointed postmistress. A few months later, in June, a troop of black cavalrymen was assigned to Fort Russell. All the barracks were filled, so the "Buffalo Soldiers" camped in tents between the fort and Camp Carlin. Black soldiers comprised two regiments of cavalry and two regiments of infantry in the U.S. Army, but these troopers were the first Buffalo Soldiers to be stationed at Fort Russell. It was a racist age, and Cheyenne citizens "solemnly resolved to hate and detest the colored troops before their arrival," related the *Leader*. Yet Buffalo Soldiers were among the most dependable members of the U.S. Army (the nickname, referring to the black, curly hair between the horns of a bison—the staff of life to Plains Indians—was conferred by horseback warriors as a gesture of respect). While "frequently visiting the city," the Buffalo Soldiers "conducted themselves admirably." The black troopers returned to Camp Robinson, Nebraska, in October 1887, causing the *Leader* to point out that while Cheyenne citizens "first tolerated" the "colored troops," their initial "contempt soon turned to respect."[18]

The acceptance of the black troopers was an indication that Cheyenne was more cosmopolitan than the citizenry realized. Former slaves had been part of the community since Cheyenne was founded. The city's biggest hotel had been built and managed by a black man; another had served in the Territorial Legislature; Cheyenne High School's Class of 1888 included a black graduate; and in response to demands from the Third Ward, a black policeman (who had a dog called "Nig") was hired in 1881.[19] Chinese had come with the railroad and had stayed to operate laundries and restaurants, as well as opium dens. A large number of European immigrants added to the mix: Irish, German, and Swede, along with British-born cattlemen such as Moreton and Dick Frewen and John Clay. While the casual racial epithets of the day were heard on the streets and frequently printed in newspapers, no African Americans or Chinese were lynched in Cheyenne—only whites. By standards of the late nineteenth century, Cheyenne was a community of comparative racial tolerance.

A significant military development of 1889 was the closure of Camp Carlin. With future campaigning against hostiles unlikely, with most of the small posts once supplied by Camp Carlin closed, and with a growing network of western railroads, there was little need for the big Quartermaster Depot. For a time Camp Carlin served as the central training post for the army's pack mule service. Longtime Chief Packer Thomas Moore was assigned to Fort Russell but continued to live with his wife and daughter at his old quarters at Camp Carlin. In 1896 Moore died in his home at the age of

Cheyenne High School graduating class of 1882. Fewer than seven percent of American teenagers attended high school during this period, and with high school diplomas this quartet had an inside track when seeking employment positions. (Courtesy Wyoming State Archives)

Camp Carlin in 1880, looking toward the north. The stables and a corral are in the foreground, with storehouses, shops, quarters, and support buildings in the background. (Courtesy Wyoming State Archives)

sixty-four. There was a large funeral in Cheyenne for "Colonel Moore," a local institution for nearly three decades. He was buried at Lakeview Cemetery.[20]

The closure of Camp Carlin had an economic effect on Cheyenne, costing many commercial firms a great deal of business and eliminating hundreds of civilian employees. But it was of some consolation that in September 1888 soldiers at Fort Russell began to be paid every month.[21] In earlier years the paymaster arrived only at intervals of three months or more. The newspapers always announced paydays at the fort to an expectant business community, and now those printed announcements came each month.

Fort Russell was saddened in August 1888 by the news that Gen. Phil Sheridan had died at the age of fifty-seven. Sheridan, who had visited Fort Russell and Cheyenne on numerous occasions through the years, had been commander-in-chief of the army since 1883 and recently had been awarded a fourth star. But Sheridan had grown stout in middle age, and he died of heart failure at his summer home in Massachusetts. General Sheridan had acquaintances in Cheyenne and, of course, at Fort Russell. His death was also mourned in Cheyenne by a great many middle-aged men, Union veterans who felt a nostalgic attachment to the renowned Civil War cavalry leader.

A death a few years earlier had an even more significant impact on Cheyenne. On Tuesday, January 13, 1885, Governor William Hale became the first Wyoming chief executive to die in office. A Republican lawyer and politician from Iowa, Hale was appointed territorial governor in 1882 by Republican President Chester A. Arthur. Governor Hale moved his wife and three sons into a brick house on Eighteenth Street, which became the executive mansion. Although he was befriended by F. E. Warren and Joseph Carey, there was a general displeasure around Wyoming that Hale was another outsider appointed to the governorship. Governor Hale was afflicted with Addison's Disease, and on the advice of his physician he repeatedly departed Wyoming on sixty-day leaves of absence to

Governor William Hale, whose term in office (1882–85) was interrupted by long leaves of absence and was cut short by his death at forty-seven. (Courtesy Wyoming State Archives)

take extended mineral bath treatments at faraway locations. The water cures had little effect, though, and the governor died at his home at the age of forty-seven.

On a bitterly cold January day, Cheyenne's businesses and schools closed, and public buildings were draped in mourning. For two hours the governor's corpse lay in state amid floral arrangements in his drawing room, while mourners filed past. The afternoon funeral was held at the Congregational church, with interment following at Lakeview Cemetery. Every fraternal and civic organization in town participated, along with eight companies of the Ninth Infantry, including the regimental band. As the impressive funeral procession marched past large crowds toward the cemetery, an artillery battery stationed nearby blasted out a salute. The widowed Frances Hale would remain in Cheyenne, a stalwart of the Episcopal church and of community affairs. She died in 1927 at eighty and was buried beside the husband who had died more than four decades earlier.[23]

President Arthur, scheduled to leave office in favor of President-elect Grover Cleveland, a Democrat, wasted no time in making another Republican appointment. The new territorial governor would be F. E. Warren, who had been elected mayor of Cheyenne on the same day that Governor Hale died. At last, one of Wyoming's own, an extraordinarily capable citizen of Cheyenne, was governor. The popular new governor had past dealings with most of the prominent men of Wyoming, and in 1886 both legislative houses were Republican. Governor Warren seized this opportunity, skillfully passing a comprehensive program with the same progressive, collaborative vision that had built the Magic City. Aggressively campaigning for a northbound railroad out of Cheyenne, Governor Warren secured a bill authorizing Laramie County commissioners to call a bond election to provide $400,000 in funding. The bond issue passed, and tracklaying on the Cheyenne and Southern Railroad began in 1887. Governor Warren also engineered a bill authorizing construction of a capitol in Cheyenne, which virtually ended the occasional attempts to move Wyoming's capital elsewhere.[24]

Late in 1886 President Cleveland replaced Warren with a Democrat, but before the decade ended he would return to the governorship. In 1889 Benjamin Harrison, a Republican, replaced Grover Cleveland as president. In Wyoming, Governor Thomas Moonlight, a Democrat from Kansas, was replaced by F. E. Warren, who took office for a second time on April 9, 1889. On a chilly, drizzly Tuesday afternoon, a bugle sounded, signaling an inaugural parade to start toward the Capitol. "The pavements were packed with men, women and children,

F. E. Warren's second commission as territorial governor. (Warren Papers)

and many were standing in the street," reported the *Leader*. The Eighth Infantry led the way, followed by the Wyoming Militia, and martial music filled the air. The end of the long procession was brought up by eleven mounted cowboys. Three thousand people already had gathered in front of the Capitol when "Mrs. Warren, Mrs. Ex-Governor Hale and Mrs. Delegate Carey reached the building a trifle in advance of the marching column." The column was led by Warren's four-in-hand landau, carrying the governor-elect, Territorial Delegate Carey, and Justice Saufley, who would administer the oath of office. When the landau approached the Capitol, the crowd erupted in cheers.[25]

After taking the oath, Governor Warren gave an address anticipating statehood, listing in painstaking detail, point by point, the financial benefits of becoming a state. "Hail to the Chief" then was played by the military band, and the procession marched from the Capitol to the Warren residence on Seventeenth. A flag-draped platform had been erected in his yard, from which Governor Warren and his party reviewed the parade. "Several hundred prominent people did their sightseeing from the spacious veranda" of the nearby Cheyenne Club. "The cowboys were cheered when they dashed past."[26]

That evening Governor Warren staged a reception and gala inaugural ball at the Capitol. "Wyoming has never before witnessed a sight equally elegant." A pair of locomotive headlights flanked the main entrance. "The whole interior of the building was ablaze with light." The Seventeenth Infantry band was stationed in the rotunda, while the city orchestra performed from the old Territorial Council chamber. Couples danced in these areas, while other couples peered from the flag-draped balconies of the rotunda. Looking down, "the scene was like some never-ending panorama," as hundreds of men and women came and went until midnight. The *Leader* published a list of scores of women and their regalia: "Mrs. J. M. Carey, petticoat roe point, court train, cream colored moiré antique with riveres of cream brocade of satin and moiré, with deep Bertha point lace. Diamonds and pearls." And "Mrs. R. S. Van Tassell, heavy cardinal satin rhadimer with black flouncing, en train. Extremely handsome."[27]

"Everywhere was a gala air," and part of the day's celebratory exuberance was the feeling that, at last, Wyoming had a leadership team that would achieve the long-sought prize of statehood. Governor Warren and Delegate Carey had been laying groundwork, in Wyoming and in Washington, since 1885, and in 1889 they launched a final, rapid push. The governor arranged for a July election of fifty-five delegates to meet at the Capitol in September to draft a state constitution. Several key members of the constitutional convention were from Cheyenne: E.S.N. Morgan, attorney and longtime territorial secretary; Henry G. Hay, cattleman and banker; George W. Baxter, cattleman and, for six weeks, former territorial governor; and cattleman H. E. Teschemaker. Governor Warren, Delegate Carey, Judge Willis Van Devanter, and Territorial Engineer Elwood Mead exerted strong guidance as consultants. Within twenty-five days a constitution was adopted and signed, then approved across Wyoming by a special election in November.[28]

With Carey lobbying energetically in Washington, Wyoming statehood passed the House of Representatives the following March, then won Senate approval three months later. President Benjamin Harrison signed Wyoming's statehood bill on July 10, 1890, with Governor Warren and Delegate Carey proudly in attendance. Each federal endorsement of statehood triggered celebrations in Wyoming's communities (on the evening of July 10 an "enormous crowd" watched a tightrope walker perform his act above Eddy Street). Cheyenne hosted the official celebration on July 23, staging a parade—a familiar assignment for the Magic City—as well as a ceremony at the Capitol, followed by a "Grand Free Ball" in the evening. The parade featured a float carrying forty-two little girls representing as many states, with nine-year-old Frankie Warren, daughter of the governor, representing Wyoming in the next rig: "a boat mounted on wheels and drawn by Shetland ponies." The guard of honor for these "cars of state" was Company H of Wyoming's girl militia, "and the pretty soldiers were quite fetching in their new black uniforms."[29]

The day before the statehood celebration, forty-eight-year-old W.W. Corlett died at his Cheyenne home. Arriving in Cheyenne in August 1867, the young lawyer had served Cheyenne in a variety of political positions and was a popular community leader. "Nervous exhaustion brought on by overwork was the fatal ailment," and he was survived by his wife and five-year-old son. Funeral services, conducted the day after the statehood ceremony, were attended by hundreds of mourners. The following day Joseph Carey arrived by train from Washington, occasioning yet another statehood celebration in his honor, held by Republicans at Keefe Hall.[30]

Delegate Carey soon was Senator

W.W. Corlett was interred in Lakeview Cemetery, and his untimely death was mourned by the community he had helped found. (Photo by Karon O'Neal)

Built in 1889, the West Side School was named after W.W. Corlett, prominent attorney, postmaster, and delegate to Congress. (Photo by Karon O'Neal, from memorial display in yard of contemporary Corlett School)

Carey. At a special election called by Territorial Governor Warren for September 11, he was elected state governor, and Republicans won both houses of the legislature. This Republican-dominated legislature promptly appointed Carey as one U.S. senator and, after considerable maneuvering behind the scenes, F. E. Warren as Wyoming's other member of the Senate. Less than three months after election as the first state governor, Warren resigned to accept the Senate appointment. "F. E. AND ME TOO," headlined the *Leader*.

Dr. Amos W. Barber, a physician from Douglas with no political experience, recently had been elected secretary of state and now would succeed Governor Warren as acting governor. (The new state constitution required Barber to serve simultaneously as secretary of state and as acting governor—while being paid only his secretarial salary.)[31]

Political historian Lewis Gould concluded that Warren wanted "to avoid the chores of being governor," recognizing that from Washington he could more fully achieve "the two objectives of his political creed, his own enrichment and the development of Wyoming." As a politician "he practiced the art with a zest and ability unmatched by any of his colleagues." In Washington, Senator Warren would prove to be "a matchless artist of the pork barrel process, an adept and gifted master of intrigue, and an outstandingly successful political leader." During a Senate career that spanned nearly four decades, "Warren campaigned ceaselessly for more forts, buildings, and appropriations.... As a senator after 1890, he badgered presidents and cabinet members to appoint deserving Wyoming Republicans to every imaginable federal office."[32]

In Warren and Carey, Cheyenne had provided both U.S. senators, and now the Magic City was a state capital. Growth during the 1880s had been impressive. The Census of 1880 had credited Cheyenne with 3,450 residents. But the population more than tripled during the decade, and the next census recorded a total of 11,690 Cheyenneites, almost double the second-largest Wyoming community (Laramie, 6,338). Cheyenne could begin the 1890s with high expectations and confidence in the future.

The
1890s

"Cheyenne was definitely a 'city' with many spacious homes, good streets, good churches and good schools.... One never thought of it as a town, always a city."
Alice Richards McCreery

"I sincerely believe Cheyenne is the finest summer town in the world. I have been everywhere, and your cool and pretty little town just strikes me right and that city park is simply grand. I intend to camp here awhile."
Mr. Walton, Chicago mining man

"[Cheyenne's] residents look forward to the future with no misgivings and confidently predict that the 'magic city' will be no misnomer in all time to come."
J. A. Breckons

"Cheyenne, the once famous cattle centre of the west, renowned for its general liveliness, street brawls and 'tough' residents, I found to be an unusually quiet little city of nearly 10,000 souls, much like any of our eastern towns of the same size."
L. L. from Pennsylvania
(Guest of F.E. Warren)

"Cheyenne is in a land of perpetual sunshine, of strange birds and of unknown flowers; where high mountains and boundless plains, elevate, broaden and make healthy the narrowest views of men—"
George S. Walker

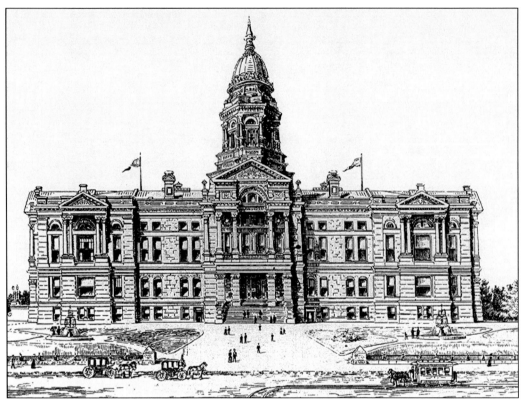

The Wyoming State Capitol in 1890, after the east and west wings were added by M.P. Keefe. (The wings were further extended a quarter of a century later.) Note the horse-drawn streetcar in the right foreground. (Illustrated Leader, July 1890)

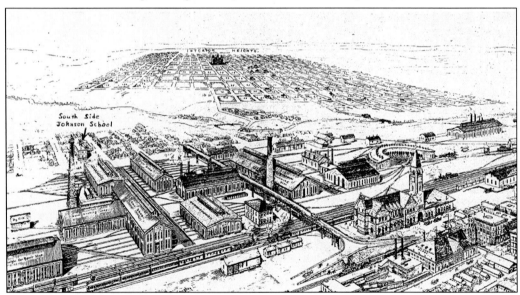

This artist's view, in the Illustrated Leader of July 1890, depicts a projected development, "Interior Heights" (which did not materialize) by the Interior Land and Immigration Company. Note Cheyenne's south side, just beyond the impressive complex of Union Pacific shops (most of these UP structures are now gone). Note the viaduct, the UP Depot, and the Burlington Depot. The Burlington Depot, just north of the UP Depot, had been built as the Warren Emporium.

15

Cheyenne in the Nineties

Cheyenne swaggered eagerly into the 1890s. With more than 11,000 residents, the population at last had reached and exceeded the boomtown total of more than two decades earlier. By mid-1890 Wyoming was a state, and there was a real estate boom in the capital city. Cheyenne boasted handsome public buildings, churches, schools, and stores, along with elegant Victorian homes. And the long-delayed Union Pacific shop expansion finally was in progress, with a projected $1 million expenditure in construction and equipment costs.

The Union Pacific was building a roundhouse with ten stalls, an enormous "car erecting shop" (95 by 275 feet), a woodworking shop (80 by 200), a paint shop (150 by 191), a warehouse (48 by 178), a two-story office building, and various lesser structures. Several hundred more workers could be hired, and by August 1891 the monthly pay envelopes from UP totaled over $70,000—an average of more than $2,000 per day. Small wonder, then, that the city fathers authorized a viaduct across the UP yards to connect the growing south side—populated primarily by railroad families—with Cheyenne's business district. Another regular payday, once every two months, brought more than $20,000 to Fort Russell.[1]

Just four days into 1890, Harry Kuykendall, son of charter settlers Judge and Mrs. W. L. Kuykendall, married Blanche Irene Moore at St. Mark's Episcopal Church. Following the wedding, "the prettiest that has ever been seen in Cheyenne," and reception, the couple left by train for a Chicago honeymoon. Exactly one year earlier Harry's brother, John Kuykendall, married Anna Thomason in an equally splendid ceremony at St. Mark's, attended by Governor Moonlight and almost everyone else of prominence in Cheyenne. A tragedy occurred between the weddings of the Kuykendall brothers. In July 1889, "Happy Harry Kuykendall, always light-hearted, jolly and full of fun," fatally wounded an employee at the family horse ranch at Saratoga, sixty miles west of Laramie. Several young men were target shooting with rifles when the accident occurred, and Harry's grief was "inconsolable," although he recovered sufficiently to marry a few months later.[2]

Less than three weeks after the Kuykendall-Moore nuptials, St. Mark's was the scene of another notable wedding ceremony. Frank Kemp, manager of the Dakota Land & Cattle Company, married Ida Bergman, daughter of Judge and Mrs. Isaac Bergman (Isaac Bergman had first appeared in Cheyenne in 1867 at twenty). The noon wedding was signaled by the church's pipe organ, and "Miss Bergman made one of the daintiest brides ever seen in Cheyenne." The *Leader* provided a column-long "List of the Most Costly Presents Ever Given in Cheyenne." (For reasons never made clear, Judge Bergman tried to commit suicide before the end of the year. The bullet only blinded him, and he learned to get around town with the aid of a hired man. During the 1890s, he was elected a commissioner of Laramie County and a state legislator, before he died at fifty-two of Bright's Disease, in March 1899.)[3]

The two gala weddings held in the first month of the 1890s symbolically ushered in, with ceremony and celebration, an exciting new decade for Cheyenne. St. Mark's, the site of both of these ceremonies, was itself a tangible symbol of the prosperity of the Holy City of the Cow. The Episcopalians decided to erect a new church in 1885, construction began the next year, and the first services were held in August 1888. In January 1890 the magnificent stone edifice was only a few

At the southeast corner of Seventeenth and House, the Union Pacific built a brick facility to house a UP doctor and his offices. Today the building is an art gallery. (Photo by Karon O'Neal)

months into its second year. And during 1890, just east across Central Avenue, the sandstone walls of an equally impressive sanctuary began to rise. The First United Methodist Church was dedicated on Easter Sunday in 1894. By the 1890s Cheyenne's ten churches hosted 2,000 worshipers each Sunday. On a typical Sunday late in 1889, 773 Catholics attended one of the three services conducted by Father F. J. Nugent. First Methodist had 249 in their old frame building; First Baptist had 230; St. Mark's, 200; First Presbyterian, 163; and First Congregational, 134. Hosting fewer than 100 apiece in Sunday school and worship services were the South Side Congregational, African Methodist, Second Baptist, and Lutheran churches. These ten churches offered virtuous balance to merely a couple of dozen saloons (as opposed to seventy whiskey mills during Cheyenne's Hell on Wheels era). "Perhaps the influences for good exerted by Cheyenne church people have not a little to do with the observance of the laws and the maintenance of order," remarked the *Leader*. Although the west end brothels of "Chicago" continued to resist the forces of virtue, "Cheyenne hasn't been a really bad town for fifteen years or more."[4]

Like Cheyenne's Sunday schools, public schools were proliferating across the Magic City in response to escalating student population growth. In February 1890, with the spring term well under way, total enrollment in Cheyenne's public schools was 897, with an average attendance of 727. In 1890 construction began on Cheyenne High School, a $25,000 brick building which would face east at Central and Twenty-second. High school classes had been conducted upstairs in the big, sprawling Central School, a block to the southwest. Now secondary stu-

A workingman's hotel, restaurant, and saloons, facing south on Fifteenth, a block west of the Union Pacific Depot. These modest structures stood across from the UP tracks. (Courtesy Wyoming State Archives)

dents in grades nine through twelve would attend a proper high school with a library, chemistry lab, drafting room, lecture hall, and classrooms, placed in two stories and a full basement. The superintendent's office suite was in a tower that soared above the main entrance, and other picturesque Victorian features included an ornate corner turret. The superintendent was "Professor" J. C. Churchill, who had succeeded longtime superintendent N. E. Stark in 1885.[5]

As the population grew during the 1880s, the Central School was supplemented by the Johnson South Side School and the West Side School, renamed the Corlett School after the 1890 death of dynamic community leader W. W. Corlett. These three neighborhood schools offered grades one through seven, and an East Side School was added in 1892 at a cost of $11,000. The Academy of the Holy Child Jesus taught pupils in a four-story brick convent. With the University of Wyoming in Laramie, Cheyenne's nod in the direction of higher education was the "Wyoming Business College," which rented downtown commercial space.[6]

During the 1880s, Cheyenne High School fielded a baseball club on a few occasions, playing other nines around town. Every spring and summer the young men of Cheyenne played baseball: West Siders vs. South Siders, the Fort Russell nine vs. the Cheyenne Red Stockings, Fort Russell or the Red Stockings vs. visiting teams, etc. But with the wings on the State Capitol completed, and with state-

Looking north on Capitol Avenue from the tower of the Union Pacific Depot. The Burlington Depot, formerly the Warren Emporium, is in the right foreground. At left is the three-story Phoenix Block. Across the street is the Inter Ocean Hotel, and north of the hotel is the Opera House. North of the Opera House is the First Congregational Church, and at the end of the street is the State Capitol. To the right of Capitol Avenue in the distance is the Central School. Note the streetcar in the foreground. (Courtesy Wyoming State Archives)

hood pending, Cheyenne's best baseball squad was named the Capitols. The Capitols were backed by Cheyenne's leading sportsman, Harry Hynds, who purchased the team's uniforms and played second base. The uniforms cost Hynds $150.25 from A.J. Reach & Co. of Philadelphia. With blue padded pants and shirts, red striped caps, red stockings, and tan shoes, the Capitols were dressed for success. Victory followed victory, and in May Cheyenne enjoyed a delicious athletic moment: the Capitols swept a double-header from a Denver nine, 6–2 and 29–3.[7]

Although Harry Hynds was only seven when Cheyenne was founded, he would prove to be a throw-

The beautiful First Methodist Church was completed in 1894 at a cost of $25,000. Contractor M.P. Keefe, who built the exterior walls and roof, burned a $5,000 note he held as his contribution. (From the Illustrated Leader, July *1890)*

In January 1886, St. John's Catholic School moved to this new brick edifice on a block bounded by Twenty-fourth and Twenty-fifth, Central and Warren. The name of the parochial school was changed to St. Mary's, but in 1891 the operation became a boarding school called the Academy of the Holy Child Jesus. (Courtesy Wyoming State Archives)

Cheyenne High School, built in 1890. Note the bicycles parked in front. (Courtesy Wyoming State Archives)

"Fourteen of the brightest youth of Cheyenne," the Cheyenne High School Class of 1895 as described by the Leader on June 1, 1895. Elaborate graduation exercises "filled every nook and corner" of the Opera House, where a standing-room-only crowd numbered over 1,000. (Courtesy Wyoming State Archives)

back to the ambitious, visionary young men who built the Magic City, and he would head the second generation of civic leaders. One of eight children of an Irish immigrant family, Harry P. Hynds was born in December 1860 in Iowa. After mastering the blacksmith's trade, nineteen-year-old Harry arrived at the Holy City of the Cow in 1882 looking for opportunity. He worked for a couple of years for noted blacksmith and wagonmaker Herman Haas, then opened his own shop with a partner.[8]

The young blacksmith eagerly embraced Cheyenne's lusty saloon life. Hynds was a skilled gambler and, literally, a two-fisted drinker, combining traditional Irish conviviality with a volatile temper. He was only five-eight, but he had the muscular build of a blacksmith and was quick to swing his fists. On May 25, 1885, Hynds and another novice prizefighter, James Lavin, squared off at the Rawlins Opera House for "the championship of Wyoming." Before a crowd of 500, Hynds knocked out Lavin in the eleventh round, earning $500 plus side bets. "About $15,000 changed hands," reported the *Leader*. The champ had a trainer and a backer, and this Hynds combination accepted a bout with the middleweight champion of Colorado for August 1 in Rawlins. For this match the crowd totaled 800, including "large delegations" from Cheyenne, Denver, Laramie, and Salt Lake City. "Fully $20,000 changed hands," but this time Hynds was badly battered, then knocked out in the sixth round. He ended his career in the ring after two bouts, but in the future he avidly followed prizefighting and sometimes backed pugilists.[9]

In 1886 Hynds opened the Capitol Saloon. He thrived in the saloon business,

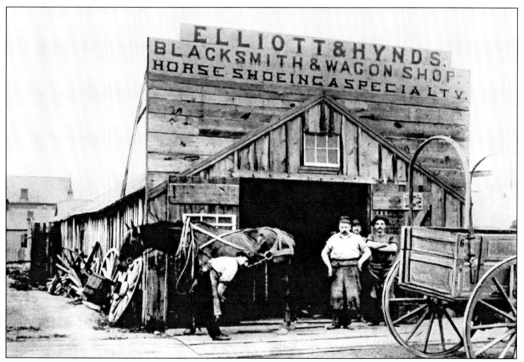

Harry Hynds, with crossed arms, came to Cheyenne as a two-fisted young blacksmith with a penchant for gambling. (Courtesy Wyoming State Archives)

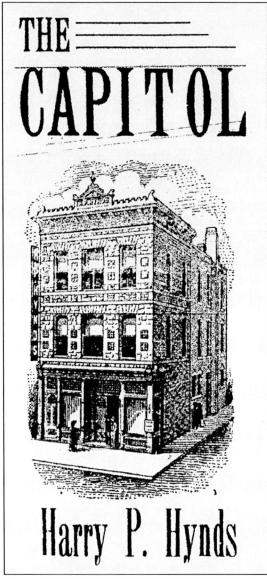

THE CAPITOL

Harry P. Hynds

Harry Hynds built a handsome home for his Capitol Saloon at 1608 Carey. The bar was on the ground floor, gambling rooms on the second level, and female companions on the third floor. (From a long-running ad in the Leader)

starting drinking/gambling establishments in Laramie, Rawlins, Rock Springs, and Salt Lake City. To properly house the Capitol Saloon, he erected a three-story, brick and sandstone building at 1608 Carey Avenue. The saloon, complete with a carved back bar sporting three mirrors, was on the ground floor; the second floor offered club rooms for gambling; and the third floor provided rooms for feminine entertainment. Hynds also invested successfully in mining (and later, oil) ventures. As he prospered he also proved to be philanthropic and community-minded. Popular and prominent, his frequent travels were mentioned in the newspapers. Hynds was a ramblin' gamblin' man, and he constantly was boarding a train bound for the scene of action, perhaps a prizefight or a race. His beautiful wife, Maud, often went with him, to Denver or Salt Lake City or somewhere in the East.

In 1894 Harry and Maud moved their home to Salt Lake City, although Harry continued to travel to Cheyenne and elsewhere to oversee his business interests. In March 1896 Harry returned home a day early from a trip to Butte, where he was establishing another saloon/gambling hall. In his wife's closet, Harry discovered Walter Dinwoodey, twenty-five-year-old son of a prominent local family. Half-clad, Dinwoodey was leaving the premises when he foolishly blurted, "Come with me, Maudie, I'll take care of you."[10]

Walter should have kept his mouth shut. The explosive Hynds whipped out a revolver and shot Walter three times. Harry calmly turned himself in, and a few months later a jury declared him "Not guilty," on the grounds of justifiable homicide. He divorced Maud and moved back to Cheyenne, to the delight of everyone in town except those who objected to drinking and gambling—and killing. But the shooting of his wife's paramour served to raise Harry's stock among the men of Cheyenne. And soon after returning to Wyoming, Hynds was "jumped" by a "Laramieite," who was so badly pummeled by Harry that he had to be carried away on a cot. Back in Cheyenne for good, Hynds enjoyed more respect and popularity than ever, and he put a great deal of his wealth and influence back into the community.

Cheyenne citizens devoured newspaper accounts of the Hynds killing and trial. But two other shootings were of greater local concern. On Friday, November 13, 1891, the Cheyenne National Bank closed its doors (the First National Bank, Stock Growers National Bank, and T.A. Kent's Bank remained sound). The Cheyenne National

Harry Hynds, Cheyenne's leading sportsman, had a volatile temper and could be dangerous with fists or guns. Hynds amassed great wealth and became Cheyenne's leading philanthropist. (Courtesy Wyoming State Archives)

Bank had been founded in 1886 by John W. Collins, who later moved to California to establish another bank. The failure of his California operation caused the fail-

Ice and Horse HQ

"Cheyenne is recognized as ice headquarters for the entire mid-West," bragged the *Leader* in 1889 (February 12). Three contractors cut ice each winter from the lakes around Cheyenne, and the Union Pacific Railroad delivered "the congealed cakes" to the East by the hundreds of carloads.

During this same period the British cavalry decided to purchase 50,000 horses from the American West, and the *Leader* reported (June 26, 1890) that

Cheyenne would be "headquarters" for purchasing agents and rail delivery.

As Cheyenne entered the 1890s, these activities did not measure up to the economic impact of the new Union Pacific shops, or of Fort Russell. Ice harvesting, of course, was seasonal, and large-scale horse purchasing for the British cavalry was a one-time occurrence. Nevertheless, both activities were building blocks, part of the growing and diversified economy necessary to sustain a much larger population.

ure of his Cheyenne bank. Cashier George L. Beard ran the Cheyenne National Bank, and he felt personally responsible for the failure. At thirty, the dapper Beard had been in Cheyenne for ten years, and even though he designated his personal fortune of $40,000 (mostly in insurance policies) as a bank asset, he could not bear the public humiliation. On Saturday night he shot himself in the head, a "tragic sequel" to the bank failure. Another fatal shooting was less lamented in Cheyenne. The following March, John W. Collins, facing arrest for embezzling $200,000 and causing the bank failures, died after shooting himself in San Diego.[12]

On Saturday night, September 27, 1890, two young tramps were shot to death while they slept in a boxcar at Hillsdale, about fifteen miles east of Cheyenne. "I killed them for their money," confessed Charley Miller. "I was penniless, hungry and desperate. I killed both of them with an old 32-caliber pistol which I bought in Kansas City for $1.25." Born in 1875 in New York City, Miller was orphaned by the time he was five. As a teenager, he devoured dime novels, and made his way to the Wild West. In Nebraska, Miller hooked up with two drifters who were only a few years his senior. The next night he shot his slumbering companions and took from them $47, a watch, knife, and revolver. The bodies soon were discovered and taken to Cheyenne, and Miller followed on the next passenger train. He read about the killings in the Sunday newspaper, then left town and began to make his way eastward. The young murderer soon grew remorseful, however, and confessed to some new companions. "Kansas Charley," as he began to call himself, was arrested and taken to the county jail in Cheyenne.[13]

Kansas Charley was tried and convicted of murder in district court. Sentenced to hang, he escaped jail with a fellow inmate in September 1891. Heading east again, he stopped at a tramp campfire about ten miles out of town. "Did you hear of the jail delivery in Cheyenne last night?" he asked the tramps. "Don't say anything about it, but I am the Miller boy murderer." The boy murderer was promptly turned in by the tramps, who wanted a reward. A few months later, on New Year's Eve, Miller escaped again, this time with two fellow prisoners. But the escapees were on foot, and midwinter temperatures hovered around

"Kansas Charley" Miller, the teenaged killer who attracted considerable local attention while awaiting execution in the Laramie County Jail. (From the Leader, April 23, 1892)

zero. One fugitive froze to death, and Charley was found huddled beside him, nearly dead (the third escapee was captured a few days later).[14]

In his cell, Charley read dime novels and played checkers with jailors. He was so fond of doughnuts that he was nicknamed "Doughnut Charley." Sympathizers tried to win him clemency because of his youth. But most citizens were unmoved, and 500 signed a petition "to let the law take its course." The *Leader* harshly opened an editorial: "There probably never has been confined in the Laramie county jail a more thorough criminal than Charley Miller, the youthful double murderer upon whom some sympathy has been heretofore wasted." Insisting that "Miller is by no means such an idiot as he has been credited with being," the *Leader* pointed out that he "possesses a good deal of low grade cunning."[15]

Acting Governor Amos Barber refused to grant a reprieve: "I cannot, without yielding to mere sentimentalism, interfere with the sentence of the court." A scaffold was erected in the jail yard, with a device that would, in effect, make Charley his own hangman. By stepping on the trap door of the gallows, his weight (he was five-four and only 110 pounds) would trigger a water flow that would release the trap door through a system of pulleys and weights. (This same gallows and water device was used eleven years later to execute Tom Horn.) On Friday morning, April 22, 1892, about sixty selected witnesses were ushered inside the small stockade that surrounded the gallows. A crowd of several hundred gathered outside the courthouse and jail, "while several mounted adjacent telegraph poles," and about twenty people took high positions on the nearby mansion, Castle Dare. When Charley emerged from the jail, he was holding a crucifix and was accompanied by Father McCormick, who had just administered Catholic baptismal rites in the cell. The noose was placed on Charley's neck, and he was guided onto the trap door at 11:28. "The automatic action of the trap could be plainly heard," and following an "ominous click," the door collapsed beneath Charley's feet and he plunged downward "with fearful velocity," snapping his neck.[16]

At the same time that Charley Miller was awaiting execution, the infamous Johnson County War erupted in northern Wyoming. Political influence exerted by Wyoming's governor and senators was instrumental in saving cattlemen and their hired gunmen from violent consequences. Cheyenne was the center of months of legal maneuvering, and the cattlemen exercised wealth and political influence to win exoneration.

The politicians who aided the cattlemen were Republicans, and the party suffered a backlash in the November 1892 election. John Osborne became the first Democrat elected governor of Wyoming, and Democrats took unaccustomed control of the legislature. The abbreviated charter term of Republican Senator F. E. Warren expired in 1892, but blundering Democrats could not agree on an appointee to succeed him. For the next two years Joseph W. Carey was Wyoming's only senator. During those years F. E. Warren and his close political lieutenant, Judge Willis Van Devanter, reorganized and revitalized Wyoming's Republicans. Republicans triumphed in the election of 1894: W. A. Richards was swept into the governor's office; Henry G. Hay and Estelle Reel of Cheyenne were elected state

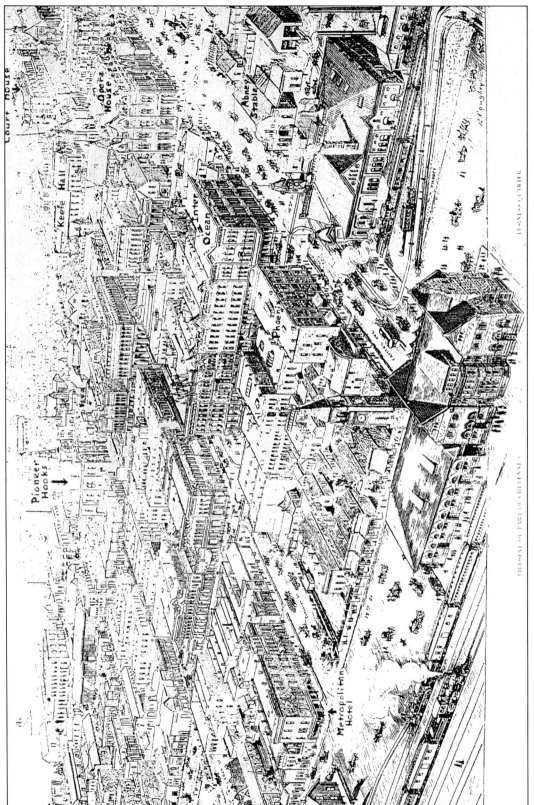

Drawing of downtown Cheyenne for the Illustrated Leader of July 1890.

treasurer and state superintendent of education, respectively; and both legislative houses were dominated by Republicans. Senator Carey's term was up, and Warren outmaneuvered his old ally for the legislative appointment as senator. Carey, of course, deeply resented his ouster from the Senate. But F. E. Warren, after an absence of two years, would serve in the Senate until the end of his long life — to the continuing benefit of Wyoming and Cheyenne.[17]

The year of the comeback of Republicans and Senator Warren also was the year that football was introduced to Wyoming and Cheyenne. On the first day of 1894 at the fairgrounds in Cheyenne, the Cheyenne Bicycle Club defeated a team from Laramie. "The first game of foot ball ever played in the state of Wyoming" was witnessed by "about 500 spectators," half of whom had never seen football played. "I don't understand anything about the game," chirped one young lady, "but isn't it just too sweet for anything the way they knock one another down."[18]

Cheyenne won the coin toss and took the ball, while Laramie had a strong wind at their backs. Cheyenne rumbled downfield with a flying wedge, then used "a criss cross" to gain more yardage. "Full back" Dennis M. Michie scored the first touchdown in Wyoming sports history, less than two minutes after the kick-off, but his dropkick failed "owing to the strong wind that was blowing." Michie, a second lieutenant at Fort Russell, was the star of the game. He had played at West Point (Class of '88), and he acted as player-coach for the Cheyenne Bicycle Club. Touchdowns counted four points, and Cheyenne defeated Laramie, 20-4.[19]

The next month two teams — a Fort Russell eleven captained by Lieutenant Michie, and a Cheyenne High School (CHS) club — took a train over the hill to play a doubleheader at Laramie. The teams were accompanied by 200 Cheyenne supporters. A Laramie delegation and a brass band united at the depot to escort the visitors to the University of Wyoming campus, where the games would be played. "The weather was a trifle cold for football," remarked the *Leader*. The thermometer hovered only a few degrees above zero. Female undergraduates served free coffee to the players. The Fort Russell team, uniformed in blue and white and averaging 163 pounds per man, outscored a Laramie eleven. But the game was rough, and Michie called Laramie's referee a cheat and demanded a new official. "Capt. Michie declined to go on with the game, which was then declared forfeited by the referee." There had been heavy betting by sportsmen from Cheyenne and Laramie, but the bets were called off.[20]

The Fort Russell team brought a "colored mascot" attired in "the most fantastic suit imaginable. It was of red, white and blue and on it multitudinous stars sparkled. His high hat was trimmed with blue and white ribbons—." Adding to the color that would mark football games of the next century, the high school players incessantly chanted a cheer for themselves: "Razzle, dazzle, hobble, gobble, sis, boom, ah; Cheyenne high school, rah, rah, rah."[21]

Clad in red and yellow, the CHS club played the University of Wyoming eleven. During the 1890s it was common practice everywhere for college clubs to play nearby high school teams, even though the college men inevitably were older and more mature physically. "The play on both sides was savage and fast throughout, the home team having the best of it from the start." One of the CHS players who was knocked out was the son of Henry G. Hay. "Dr. Barber, who was surgeon-in-chief to the team, had his hands full taking care of the patients as they were carried from the thick of the fray." The University of Wyoming defeated CHS, 14–0, and the high school players were taunted: "Rah! rah! rah! rah! rah! ray! Who got beat so bad today?"[22]

During the next few years CHS usually fielded a team for a game or two each season. Fort Russell put together a club for a couple of games, and often a Cheyenne team would be formed to play the military eleven or Laramie or some squad from Colorado. Although baseball long remained Cheyenne's most popular sport (the National Pastime was the dominant game everywhere in America), football began to grow in popularity.

Throughout the 1890s Cheyenne shared America's growing passion for sports. For example, a six-hole golf course was created north of Lake Minnehaha in 1899. Charles Erswell set the course record with a 39 on six holes. Membership in the newly organized golf club included "some of our most prominent citizens," and Cheyenne's women were enthusiastic players on the "Lake Minnehaha links." That summer Cheyenne golfers began to use caddies, who had to register and make themselves available at certain hours. "They got 5 cents for every round of six holes and make quite a little spending money." Tennis also became popular and was played at "grounds" on East Seventeenth. By the end of the decade there were competing clubs, such as the Lakeside Club and the Bayside Club.

By 1890 the Inter Ocean Hotel had expanded to the west, incorporating the former Warren Mercantile Building into the hotel. At far right, the single-story structure just behind the Inter Ocean was the first home of F.E. Warren and his bride. (From the Illustrated Leader, July 1890)

Sporting their club colors, they played against each other and against clubs from other communities.[23]

The bicycle craze that swept across America during the 1880s and 1890s became a major form of transportation, as well as recreation, in Cheyenne. The bicycle was invented about 1790 in France, and in the 1870s the "high-wheeler"(a five-foot-tall front wheel, with a small rear wheel) reached the United States. The high-wheeler was difficult to ride, but the "safety bicycle" (both wheels of the same size) became widespread after 1885, and by 1890 the pedal-powered vehicles had air-filled rubber tires. By 1890 there were more than 150,000 American bicyclists, and more than a few of them resided in Cheyenne.[24]

Safety bicycles became a popular curiosity in Cheyenne during the late 1880s. Shops opened to sell and repair "wheels" for local "wheelmen." Wheelmen admired and discussed the latest models: Ariels, Ben Hurs, Clippers, Fleetwings, Columbias, Deeres, Hunts, Tribunes, and the Phoenix. It was of interest to newspaper readers that the '96 model Kearney could be purchased from John Schuneman, "the cycle dealer." The Erswell Cycle Co. at 1709 Ferguson erected a "railing" for bicycles in front of the shop, which "is a good thing and will keep the wheels from being knocked down and broken by ice wagons, coal wagons, drays, etc."[25]

The Wyoming Cycle Manufacturing Company was organized in 1896 by "a number of leading business men." Established in the Carey Block on Ferguson, the bicycle plant employed eight or ten men to manufacture "a limited number of special high grade bicycles, both ladies' and gentlemen's models." The Cheyenne Bicycle Club and the Knickerbocker Wheel Club were organized, renting downtown rooms and raising money with frequent hops and balls. There were excursions to and from ranches several miles out of town. "Ramblers" sometimes took a train to Laramie or Greeley, then rode their wheels back to Cheyenne. In 1893 an annual road race was begun at the Fairgrounds. In 1896 a "Saloon Men's Road Race" was staged."[26]

The *Leader* published information about wheelmen under such headings as "NOTES OF THE WHEEL" and "WHEELS AND WHEELING." There were fifty bicycles at

A Fine Work of Art

Early football games in Cheyenne generated enthusiastic cheers, and on November 17, 1896, the *Leader* published a catchy chant which supported the Knickerbocker Club eleven:

"Wow, wow, wow
Ali-ki-zu-ki-zow

Knickerbocker, Flipflopper
Wow, wow, wow."

The *Leader* urged everyone to cut this chant from the newspaper and use it on Thanksgiving Day. "It's a fine work of art," the reporter declared.

Cheyenne High School by 1897, and a bicycle path at Lake Minnehaha was laid out. Doctors and lawyers and businessmen rode wheels from home to downtown. Cheyenne women, of course, acquired their own bicycles, and in 1895 ten lady cyclists organized the Mishap Club.[27]

There were accidents involving speeding bicycles, and in 1895 the city coun-

Stephen Bon's Shoe Store was a fixture for decades at 345 Sixteenth. (Courtesy Wyoming State Archives)

cil enacted an ordinance against "irresponsible 'scorchers.'" Following drinking bouts in town, soldiers sometimes appropriated the nearest bicycle to make the three-mile ride back to Fort Russell. (These "stolen" bicycles could be picked up by their owners where they were abandoned at the fort.) At the end of the nineteenth century, the *Leader* observed, "Bicycle parties are all the go these lovely evenings."[28]

With escalating interest in outdoor recreation and team sports, Cheyenne produced and took pride in a standout athlete, Johnnie Green. By 1896 Green was recognized as "Wyoming's fastest bicycle rider, and one of the speediest men in the west." In bicycle races staged on the Fourth of July in Cheyenne, Green won four out of five events and set a new record in the Quarter Mile for Wyoming and Colorado. Charles Erswell, a cycle shop owner in Cheyenne, and other sportsmen backed Green as he rode for purses at numerous races. Wearing the orange and green colors of the Knickerbocker Wheel Club, he won a $200 purse in a five-mile race at Cheyenne on Christmas Eve in 1896. Also that year he ran track in Denver, and in 1897 he was a corner man during a prizefight near Cheyenne. Green increasingly channeled his athletic talents into the era's most popular sport. In 1899 he pitched and played second base for the Cheyenne Indians, and he was named team captain. Early the next year, the *Sun-Leader* proudly announced that "John Green, the expert athlete," was in training so that he could "play ball with the Kansas City League team." But Green did not make the pros, instead returning to Cheyenne to play for the Indians. Although Green did not enjoy a professional baseball career, he undoubtedly was paid as the star of Cheyenne's team.[29]

Cheyenne firearms merchant Pete Bergersen became famous as a champion marksman. A crack shot, Bergersen began to attract notice in the 1880s for his hunting exploits. An 1888 hunting trip to the mountains in Carbon County produced a 1,000-pound elk, for example, and he shot game birds by the hundreds. He liked to ride a bicycle to an out-of-town lake in search of ducks. In 1896 a rifle range was opened at 310 Sixteenth, and Bergersen dominated competition there, winning a prize rifle in December. The next year he won a gold medal at the Second Annual Tournament of the Colorado Rifle Association with a score of 242, 16 points higher than the second-place total.[30]

In 1899 Bergersen, firing off-hand at 200 yards without a palm rest, shot a 97 out of a possible 100. It was the highest score ever recorded, and after authentication, Bergersen was declared the Champion of the World. *Outdoor Life* presented him a magnificent engraved target rifle, "the finest gun ever seen in Cheyenne." Immediately, Bergersen, "with no rest, put five successive shots in the bull's eye with it." Harry Hynds, Cheyenne's leading sportsman, issued a challenge to "any and all comers, offering to back Bergersen in sums from $1,000 to $10,000." Bergersen was hired by the Union Pacific as an express guard, and he headed Wyoming's rifle team in national competitions. He taught his two sons to shoot, but tragedy struck in 1903. Eleven-year-old Peter, Jr., accidentally shot his brother Harry, three years older, in the leg with a shotgun while hunting. Harry seemed to recover and, after a couple of months, discarded his crutches. Almost immediately the CHS freshman joined friends in skating at Lake Minnehaha, where he had been wounded. After Harry returned home his leg began to hurt, "and an examination showed that it was darkly discolored from the knee up." Harry was put to bed, but died a few nights later.[31]

The *Leader* proudly and frequently proclaimed Pete Bergersen "the champion rifle shot of the world." Another man whose reputation grew during the 1890s was Cheyenne peace officer Bob Ingalls. Ingalls was not famous outside Cheyenne, but within the Magic City he was well known and respected. A big, good-looking man, Officer Ingalls had patrolled the streets of Cheyenne since the mid-1870s. For a time during the 1890s, he patrolled on a bicycle. Ingalls had a low-key approach to law enforcement. He was a helpful presence around town, trying to head off trouble whenever possible.

On Thursday night, January 3, 1895, Ingalls was patrolling the west end following a recent "epidemic of crime." Hearing a disturbance coming from "May Foster's house of ill fame at 612 West Eighteenth Street," he opened the door and walked into the midst of a disturbance between angry soldiers. "He talked quietly" to the soldiers, but when they would not cool down, "Ingalls began to clear the house." He hustled one soldier outside, but when he seized another man "two more grabbed him." Ingalls pulled his billy club and laid out one of his attackers. Simultaneously another soldier assaulted Ingalls with a knife, slashing him badly on the neck and face, and nearly severing his ear.[32]

Bleeding badly, Ingalls staggered downtown for help. Although it was ten o'clock, he found the Palace Pharmacy open and several friends inside. "Call a doctor, Dick," he announced. "My head is half cut off." Ingalls was taken to a back room, where doctors worked for nearly an hour to stitch his wounds, with no anesthetic except a single shot of whiskey. Ingalls never flinched during the ordeal: "His grit was wonderful." He was taken to his apartment above the First National Bank, and a nurse was provided by his fraternal order, the Knights of Pythias.[33]

Ingalls took weeks to recover. When he presented $260 in medical charges to the city council, "that body refused by a unanimous vote to pay the bills," fumed the *Leader*. Council members justified the miserly action because they were reluctant "to establish a precedent." Ingalls shrugged off his mistreatment at the hands of the city council and returned to the police force. A few years later he was appointed acting city marshal during a vacancy, then was promoted to lead the force on a permanent basis. Cheyenne entered the twentieth century with a steady, trusted, uniformed presence of Bob Ingalls as city marshal. For more than a quarter of a century, Officer Ingalls was one of the most familiar and reassuring figures on the streets of the Magic City.[34]

One of Cheyenne's best-known citizens moved to Washington, D.C., in 1899. State Engineer Elwood P. Mead had worked diligently for eleven years on behalf of Wyoming, and already had achieved national recognition before leaving for Washington. Educated at Purdue University and Iowa State College, in his twenties Dr. Mead served on the faculty of Colorado State Agricultural College in Fort Collins. He spent his summers as Colorado's assistant irrigation engineer, learning firsthand that eastern water policies were totally inadequate in the arid West.[35]

In 1888 the thirty-year-old Mead was appointed territorial engineer of Wyoming, and he quickly impressed Francis E. Warren, who received his second appointment as territorial governor the next year. Governor Warren assigned Mead to write the implementing legislation for what became Article VIII of the Wyoming State Constitution. In Article VIII Mead established a system in which water was "hereby declared to be the property of the state," and in which "the public interest" would be a principal determinant in allocation. Water policy would be administered by a state engineer, a board of control, and four administrative water divisions. Mead's system became a model for the West, and also spread to Colorado, Australia, New Zealand, and South Africa. He traveled constantly and became recognized as a leading authority.

"Prof. Mead," as he was regularly called in Cheyenne newspapers, made the Magic City his home for more than a decade. Mead and his wife, Florence, had three children. After Florence died of toxic goiter in 1897, Mead remarried, but the couple divorced within a year. In 1899 Senator F. E. Warren engineered Mead's appointment as head of the newly established Office of Irrigation Investigations in the Department of Agriculture. Although he departed Cheyenne for broader horizons, Cheyenne long maintained a possessive interest in Prof. Mead. In 1902, when he fell from a Washington trolley and suffered the loss of his left arm, Mead's recuperation was followed closely in the *Leader*. He later married a surgical nurse who had assisted in his amputation, and he remained vigorous

The clothing store of William Myers on Ferguson Avenue. (Courtesy Wyoming State Archives)

and productive until he died at eighty-seven. His final professional triumph was the construction of Boulder Dam on the Colorado River, and Lake Mead was named in his honor.

Prof. Mead was one of the most prominent of a great many Cheyenneites for whom Senator Warren obtained federal appointments, and unlike Mead, most appointees were able to remain in the Magic City, or wherever else in Wyoming they lived. The year that Mead left Cheyenne for Washington, 1899, Senator Warren secured for the Magic City a $250,000 appropriation for a massive federal building to be erected a short distance south of the State Capitol. Local contractor M. P. Keefe would head the project, and upwards of one hundred local workmen would enjoy a couple of years' steady employment. On Saturday morning, June 17, 1899, a "Grand Parade of Masons and Citizens" and imposing ceremonies attended the laying of the big cornerstone. "All business was suspended. Everybody was in holiday dress," reported the *Sun-Leader*. "All nature seemed auspicious and in beautiful harmony with the festivities of the hour."[36]

The workforce and delivery vehicles of the Cheyenne Steam Laundry. (Courtesy Wyoming State Archives)

16

The Johnson County Warriors

wo days after the execution of Kansas Charley Miller, on Sunday after-noon, April 24, 1892, a special train from the north pulled into the little frame depot at Fort D.A. Russell. A large crowd awaited the train, and on the parade ground the regimental band was playing the customary Sunday concert. Two lines of soldiers were stationed as armed guards to receive more than forty men who were to be incarcerated at the fort. Many of these men were prominent in Wyoming's cattle industry, and they were welcomed by family members and friends. The cattlemen and more than a score of hired gunmen from Texas had formed an extralegal force which, early in April, had headed north out of Cheyenne in pursuit of rustlers. In Johnson County violence erupted, and by the end of the month, expedition members were brought back to Cheyenne in army custody. During the next several months, Cheyenne became the scene of the controversial aftermath of the Johnson County War.

This infamous conflict had a long background. By the mid-1880s big cattle-men had badly overstocked Wyoming's vast ranges. Wyoming cattle were in poor condition by 1886, and the vicious winter of 1886–87 devastated the ranch-ing industry. Although a number of cattle barons, especially absentee owners, were driven out of business, many Wyoming ranchers tenaciously fought to re-build. But these ranchers were plagued by cattle theft. On the open range it was always easy for homesteaders and cowboys to take a few stray cattle, and now such losses were more damaging to cattlemen who were struggling to rebound. Stock detectives were hired by the Wyoming Stock Growers' Association (WSGA), but there proved to be little satisfaction in the courts.

"Hundreds of arrests for horse and cattle stealing and other depredations

243

were made," claimed John Clay, who served as WSGA president from 1890 through 1895, "but the judges of the territory of Wyoming ... were lenient and the juries in the northern part. ... were friendly to all classes of crime, but more so to live stock depredators. The miscarriage of justice came to be so notorious that in some counties if a prisoner pleaded guilty he was not punished."[1] Homesteaders and other small operators sat on juries and grand juries, and they had scant sympathy for big ranchers. Despite the accumulation of evidence and the efforts of WSGA attorneys, few convictions were made, and rustlers therefore became bolder.

Ranchers who had built pioneer cattle empires in Wyoming soon became inclined to resort to extralegal action. Justice beyond the law met with general approval in Wyoming, as in most other sections of the United States. Furthermore, many Wyoming cattlemen, with roots in the East, felt a kinship to captains of industry who battled labor disruptions by hiring private armies of strikebreakers. On July 20, 1889, two homesteaders, Ella Watson and Jim Averell, were brutally lynched by six ranchers in Carbon County.

Ella is usually referred to as "Cattle Kate," a prostitute who traded her favors to cowboys for stolen cattle. This false image was created by Ed Towse, one of two newspapermen who would be permitted to ride with the Johnson County Invaders in 1892. He wrote a pro-cattleman account of the lynching for the Cheyenne *Daily Leader* which appeared three days after the hangings, on Tuesday morning, July 23, 1889. Subtitles beneath the bold headline "A Double Lynching" emphasized that "They were tireless Maverickers who defied the law" and "The man weakened but the woman cursed to the last." Towse called Ella "a virago" and "a holy terror." The six ranchers escaped legal consequences, although there was public disapproval of hanging a woman.[2]

The double lynching of 1889 triggered a series of violent events, each of which was reported in sensational detail in Cheyenne newspapers. In 1890 George Henderson, a ranch foreman and stock detective, was shot to death by an accused rustler. The next year Thomas J. Waggoner, a large-scale horse thief, was lynched by a WSGA stock detective and a deputy U.S. marshal. Also in 1891, five or six WSGA stock detectives jumped Nate Champion, regarded as a leader of the rustler faction, at an isolated log cabin in Johnson County. Champion courageously routed his attackers, and it was becoming evident that the small operators would not buckle. "In 1891, we made up our minds to do something," wrote prominent Cheyenne cattleman W. C. Irvine.[3]

Late in 1891, Ranger Jones and John A. Tisdale, two suspected rustlers, were ambushed within a few days of each other on the road south of Buffalo, the seat of Johnson County. Their killer was thought to be Frank Canton, a WSGA detective and former sheriff of Johnson County. Not satisfied with individual murders, some cattlemen decided to lead an expedition into Johnson County to seize control of the county government and eliminate large numbers of suspected rustlers. John Clay, president of the WSGA, advised against this armed invasion of Johnson County, and he extended his annual trip to Europe (to report to British stockholders of the Swan Land and Cattle Company) so that he would not be present if the expedition actually occurred. But other cattlemen contributed generously to a "war chest," and many owners, ranch managers, and foremen agreed to participate.

In addition to Frank Canton and other stock detectives who would ride with the expedition, gunmen from outside Wyoming were enlisted. WSGA detective Tom Smith, a former Texas law officer, returned to the Lone Star State to recruit more than a score of men, many of them U.S. deputy marshals or experienced possemen. These men were told that they were being hired to serve warrants on cattle rustlers, at a wage of five dollars a day, plus all expenses and a bonus of fifty dollars for any thieves who had to be killed. Smith and his Texas recruits boarded a train headed for Cheyenne.

On Monday, April 4, 1892, the Wyoming Stock Growers' Association held its annual meeting in the county courtroom in Cheyenne. Although there are no WSGA records which refer to the expedition, several members were observed buying guns and ammunition. Railroad officials, who did a great deal of business with WSGA members, had agreed to cooperate and assembled a special train at R. S. Van Tassell's stockyards on Tuesday. With Van Tassell supervising, three new supply wagons—purchased locally from the firm of Arp & Hammond— were loaded onto a flatcar, recently purchased saddle horses were led into three stock cars, and personal belongings of the participants were placed in a baggage car. "The word was passed for us to meet at the Cheyenne Stock-yards at five o'- clock in the afternoon," said Dr. Charles Penrose, a visitor to Cheyenne from

Philadelphia. Dr. Penrose had been "advised" by his friend and fellow physician, Acting Governor Amos Barber, to accompany the expedition as surgeon, and Penrose borrowed the medical bag of Dr. Barber. Late on Tuesday afternoon the cattlemen "walked singly and in twos and threes to the stockyards and gathered in the horse stable there."[4]

These activities, of course, were witnessed by various Cheyenne citizens, along with the arrival of the train carrying the Texans. When the train from Texas pulled into Denver earlier in the day, several cattlemen from Cheyenne met the travel-weary Texans. The cattlemen presented new Winchesters to the Texans, welcomed Tom Smith and his men, and completed the journey to Cheyenne with them. After arriving in Cheyenne late on Tuesday afternoon, their passenger car (with window blinds drawn) was uncoupled, backed to the stockyard, then coupled to the special train. Soon the special

Dr. Amos W. Barber, acting governor of Wyoming during the Johnson County War and a partisan of the cattlemen. (Author's collection)

train pulled out and headed north. During the night the train stopped at old Fort Fetterman for a brief meeting with Ed David, ranch foreman for Senator Joseph Carey. David had two additional saddle horses, which were loaded onto one of the stock cars. He also had carried out the assignment of cutting telegraph wires into Johnson County.

The train pushed on to Casper, where the Invaders unloaded before dawn on Wednesday morning, then rode toward Johnson County. During the ensuing week, the Invaders cornered Nate Champion and a companion, Nick Ray, in a cabin at the KC Ranch in Johnson County. Following a daylong siege, Champion and Ray were killed. The Invaders resumed their northward march toward Buffalo but were forced to fort up at the TA Ranch, thirteen miles south of the county seat. The men of Buffalo and the surrounding area turned out in large numbers to defend their homes. Hundreds of riflemen besieged the TA, surrounding ranch headquarters and sniping at long range for three days.

With telegraphic service from the north interrupted, the expedition had been in the field for three days before Cheyenne learned of the startling events. Two articles from the Denver *Times* were reprinted on April 8 in the *Leader*, which featured a lead article headlined: "GONE UP NORTH, A Mysterious Expedition About Which Are Many Rumors." Aside from these rumors, the *Leader* printed hard information about the departure of the "Mysterious Expedition." Crew members of the special train, which had returned to Cheyenne after delivering the expedition members to Casper, "refused to say a word" when interviewed by a reporter.

The next day the *Leader* published an interview with Acting Governor Barber, but he was as noncommittal as the train men: "The matter has not been brought to my attention officially." Behind the scenes, Barber was working frantically to ensure the safety of the besieged cattlemen. He fired off telegrams to President Benjamin Harrison, Senators Carey and Warren, Gen. John R. Brooke, commander of the Department of the Platte, and various lesser officials. On Tuesday night, April 12, the two senators from Wyoming, accompanied by the acting secretary of war, paid a visit to the White House. President Harrison already had retired to bed, but he responded to his fellow Republicans. The urgency of the situation was impressed upon the president, who began dictating telegrams. At Fort McKinney, just outside Buffalo, the commandant received a telegram in the middle of the night, and at two hours past midnight a battalion of the Sixth Cavalry rode toward the TA Ranch.[5]

The cavalry arrived shortly after dawn on Wednesday, with 400 besiegers preparing to rush the Invaders. Outnumbered ten to one, the Invaders were readily persuaded to surrender to the cavalry, and were escorted through the lines of the unhappy besiegers. After three days of firing, the only serious casualties were two Texans who accidentally shot themselves, with fatal consequences to both.

Incarceration at Fort McKinney lasted only a few days. The War Department ordered the military to move the prisoners from Fort McKinney to Fort D. A. Russell. Sentiment against the Invaders was bitter in Buffalo, but most of the Wyoming ranchers had family and friends in Cheyenne, where Governor Barber and WSGA lawyers could provide on-site assistance. The Sixth Cavalry and their prisoners trekked cross-country through an April blizzard, finally linking up with a battalion of the Seventeenth Infantry from Fort D. A. Russell. The infantrymen had come up on a special train from Cheyenne, and family members and friends had been permitted to ride along. At old Fort Fetterman there was a happy reunion, and a few bottles of liquor were slipped to the prisoners, along with food and newspapers, before the train ride back to Fort Russell. There was a stop at little Uva, where the wife of rancher-prisoner H. E. Teschmacher provided a barbeque for everyone on the train. Finally, on Sunday afternoon, April 24, nineteen days after leaving Cheyenne on a special train, the Johnson County warriors returned on another special train.

At Fort Russell the cattlemen and Texans all pitched in to unload their baggage, equipment, and saddles, and then piled everything into army wagons for the short trip to a makeshift guardhouse. They would be incarcerated in a frame building measuring 300 by 50 feet, which previously had been used as a bowling alley. Guards and a rope fence were placed around this building, and written permission was required for civilians to be admitted. Throughout the afternoon buckboards and carriages drove up, bringing well-wishers, as well as clothing, linens, and miscellaneous supplies. Visitors were not permitted into the bowling alley while the Invaders bathed, shaved, and changed clothes. In addition to setting up bathing facilities, soldiers carried cots into the building, lining them up between alley rails and the long side walls. A sergeant and two privates were detailed to hang chandeliers from the rafters. The Texans tossed their warbags onto cots at the rear of the building, while the cattlemen established themselves at the front.[6]

After being brought to Fort Russell, the Johnson County Invaders were photographed by Cheyenne photographer E. D. Kirkland. The most prominent Cheyenne residents were W. C. Irvine and E. W. Whitcomb. (Courtesy Wyoming State Archives)

During the afternoon, longtime Cheyenne resident E. W. Whitcomb, the oldest member of the expedition, enjoyed a "tearful reunion" with his family and "a levee" with his local friends. That evening Maj. Frank Wolcott, who had acted as expedition leader in the field, welcomed a large crowd of visitors. (Although Wolcott now lived on a ranch, he had served as U.S. marshal and headquartered in Cheyenne from 1872 to 1875; subsequently he often visited the Holy City of the Cow on business.) Other prominent cattlemen accepted invitations to the homes of army officers who were personal friends. Gifts "of all kinds" were sent out to the Invaders, and congratulations were expressed. The Texans donned new clothing provided by their employers, but with no friends or family in Cheyenne, they played cards and kept to themselves. When they went outside for exercise, the hired gunmen were accompanied by a guard detail.[7]

In the ensuing days, cattleman Fred de Billier tried to keep the Texans busy by organizing baseball and football games. While baseball had been played in Texas since the 1860s, football as yet was little known in the Lone Star State. But de Billier, with his Ivy League and New York background, was familiar with both sports. He coached the Texans in "the fine points of baseball and football,"[8] and there were enough men for two teams. Balls and bats were available at every military post, since companies played each other, and any needed equipment could be purchased in Cheyenne.

Photographer E. D. Kirkland was summoned from Cheyenne, and the cattlemen and their Texas gunmen gathered for a group photo. Forty-three men, dressed in suits and ties and a variety of hats, lined up in front of a building which might have been a warehouse or stable (or perhaps the bowling alley). This famous photograph shows a proud, fine-looking group of men who seem little intimidated by their incarceration. The photographer shot another pose with all hats removed.

These men of the West required stronger diversions than simply posing for photographs and playing ballgames. The Invaders were allowed to patronize the post canteen, an enlisted men's club which sold beer, wine, tobacco, and sundries (the profits were used for the benefit of the soldiers). On Monday, May 9, Texans Buck Garrett and Cliff Schultz were drinking at the canteen and began quarreling with Fred Fisher, a former trooper who had been dishonorably discharged. Buck, "a hell-diver with his fists," hurled a bottle or a brickbat or some other object at Fisher. The missile whizzed past Fisher and struck a guard in the nose. With blood spurting from his nostrils, the guard dropped his rifle and collapsed to the floor. As a melee erupted, Fisher's brother, Charles, snatched up a rifle, which had a fixed bayonet, and charged. The bayonet ripped into the shoulder of Schultz, exerting a sobering effect on the brawlers.[9]

The Texans now were forbidden to enter the saloon area of the canteen, but this prohibition failed to dull their fighting instincts. One afternoon some of the Texans began playfully knocking the hats from one another's heads, and this roughhouse quickly accelerated into another brawl. One Texan went to the post hospital with two knife gashes in the neck, while seventeen-year-old Starl Tucker, nicknamed "The Texas Kid," sported two black eyes. Army officers responded to the obvious combativeness of the Texas Kid, and they began taking Starl along with them when they went into Cheyenne for a night on the town. "They evidently enjoyed his antics when he was drunk," remarked Starl's half-brother, veteran Texas lawman George Tucker.[10]

While the idle Texans restively tried to pass the time, their employees conferred on legal strategy. The large legal team would be led by thirty-three-year-old Willis Van Devanter, a superb lawyer who had distinguished himself since arriving in Wyoming Territory in 1884. Van Devanter was a native of Marion, Indiana, where his father was a prominent attorney. After graduating from Cincinnati Law School in 1881, Willis returned to Marion to practice with his father. Willis married Dollie Burhans in 1883 (they would have two sons), and the next year they moved to Cheyenne, where a brother-in-law and future partner, John W. Lacey, had been appointed territorial chief justice. A brilliant and energetic lawyer, Van Devanter thrived in private practice and became close friends with Territorial Governor F. E. Warren. In 1886 Van Devanter drafted an appropriations bill which resulted in the construction of the capitol, as well as the establishment of a university. Warren and Van Devanter became close allies in Republican politics. During the late 1880s, Van Devanter served as Cheyenne's city attorney, as a territorial legislator, and as chief justice of the Territorial Court—the first chief justice who was a resident of Wyoming.[11]

In private practice some of Van Devanter's most important clients were cattlemen, and he was chief counsel for the Wyoming Stock Growers' Association. On April 20 Van Devanter, who had corresponded with Senator Warren since early March about the worsening situation in Johnson County, wrote a long letter to Warren in Washington. He described the expedition as "poorly managed" and plagued with "griev-

Willis Van Devanter, former Chief Justice of Wyoming Territory, and future associate justice of the U.S. Supreme Court. The best attorney in Cheyenne, he long had been on retainer by the WSGA. Although Van Devanter disapproved of the Johnson County Invasion, he loyally devised a legal strategy to win exoneration for his clients. (Courtesy Wyoming State Archives)

ous" errors in judgment—"none, however, so grievous as the error of going at all."[12]

Despite Van Devanter's stern disapproval of the Invasion, he was committed to the defense of his clients, the Invaders. Johnson County officials were clamoring to have the prisoners returned to Buffalo. Van Devanter reported to Senator Warren that Sheriff Red Angus was in Cheyenne trying to take the prisoners into custody. "Angus has been in a great state of drunkenness lately and said the other day that" the people of Buffalo would "make short work of them." Van Devanter and his law partner, John W. Lacey, were absolutely convinced "that it was certain death for these prisoners to return to Buffalo."[13] The lawyers determined to move the proceedings to a southern county, where a fair jury might be seated. Such a strategy should cause delays and open up other legal possibilities.

The cattlemen had arrived at Fort Russell supremely confident after being delivered safely from Johnson County. But the day after arriving they met at length with their lawyers, who offered sobering counsel about the virulent public opinion that was building in Wyoming. A blizzard of editorial criticism erupted from numerous Wyoming newspapers, especially those in the area near the path of the Invaders. Regardless of public criticism, the cattlemen's legal team and influential supporters maneuvered relentlessly on behalf of the prisoners, foiling repeated efforts to move the Invaders back to Johnson County. Lawyers developed a strategy of prolonging legal proceedings. The resulting court costs would overwhelm the coffers of Johnson County, forcing them to break off legal action which could no longer be afforded.

Senators Warren and Carey maintained a steady correspondence with Willis Van Devanter, Henry Hay, and other attorneys for the cattlemen. Warren agreed that "the sooner Johnson County begins to have the burden of guarding and maintaining the prisoners, the sooner things will come to a head." Discussing the overall situation with Henry Hay, Warren mentioned that "radically wrong and stupendous mistakes" were made by the Invaders. "By mistakes," he added revealingly, "I do not mean that to 'eradicate' the rustlers was a mistake, but the general plan and execution of it."[14]

The cattlemen faced a pressing need to raise money, for the mounting legal expenses of a platoon of attorneys and for the daily upkeep of more than forty men. The army had protected the Invaders in Johnson County and agreed to house the prisoners at Fort D. A. Russell, but the cattlemen were required to provide their own meals. Numerous Wyoming ranchers contributed more than $1,000 apiece, but more fundraising was necessary. According to John Clay, president of the WSGA, "It cost the cattle-owners around $100,000."[15]

Although their attorneys and various other officials were working to delay legal proceedings, the cattlemen were increasingly anxious to resume their lives. The Texans, after being confined at Fort Russell for more than two months, became dangerously restless, engaging in fights and talking about escape. "The stockmen at Fort Russell are chafing in their imprisonment," reported the *Leader*.[16]

There was a change of scenery in July, when the prisoners traveled by train to Laramie City, site of Wyoming's Second Judicial District Court, where Judge T. A.

Blake presided. Although there were plans to house the prisoners in a vacant wing of the old territorial prison, the cattlemen instead rented two-story Hesse Hall. Mattresses were placed on the second floor, while meals would be brought to the ground floor. Two guards were hired to oversee a rather loose confinement—more expense for Johnson County, which also was expected to provide sixty cents per prisoner for daily upkeep. Legal proceedings made it clear that only in Laramie County, with more than 2,600 potential jurors, would it be possible to find twelve acceptable or unbiased jurors. Judge Blake "therefore ordered the change of venue from Johnson county to Laramie county."[17]

The trial thus would be held in Cheyenne, stronghold of Wyoming cattlemen, and "their joy at the outcome was unconcealed." When they returned to Hesse Hall "many of them made a rush for the telegraph office to send the news to their friends." But nearly two more weeks passed while the prisoners grew bored and restless. Billy Irvine wrote a scathing letter to Senator Warren, complaining bitterly that martial law had not been imposed by the federal government, questioning Warren's friendship, and accusing him of everything from "double dealing" to "cowardice." As requested, Senator Warren passed the letter on to Senator Carey, who had just visited the president and attorney general on behalf of the cattlemen. Senator Carey mentioned the vicious letter to Henry Hay: "Irvine censures me because martial law was not declared. Why, Van Devanter understood before I left the State, that the United States would not under any circumstances go into a state and declare martial law."[18]

Rancher W. C. "Billy" Irvine, shown here as president of the WSGA, was a principal leader of the Invasion of Johnson County. (Author's collection)

Senator Warren wrote a ten-page reply to Irvine. Graciously allowing for strain and confinement "and finally your transfer to the high altitude of Laramie City, I consider you must be in a morbid state of mind and hardly responsible for what you say." Among many other things, Warren pointed out "that Wyoming is but one of 44 states . . .; that it has 60,000 people out of the 60,000,000 in the United States; that we have only 1/100,000 of the population. We cannot ask and if we did ask, cannot get the President to ignore all other business matters at home and abroad to take up Wyoming alone. . . . The President has burned the midnight oil on our account and so have other officers."[19]

Senator Warren could not resist a few counterpunches: "Billy, if you will permit me to suggest it, had there been a little more time used, perhaps maturer judgment and better reinforcements, etc., your expedition would have terminated differently." After all of his efforts, Senator Warren felt unjustly accused: "you have seen fit to take a position inimical of me, because of your groundless suspicions and semi-insane imaginations." Senators Warren and Carey had been roundly criticized by Wyoming newspapers, and now they were attacked by cattlemen. "Having both sides blaming my position is not pleasant," Warren complained. "Now, yourself and your friends do your worst with me," he closed. "I shall do the best I can for you all notwithstanding."[20]

On Monday, August 1, Judge Blake ordered the prisoners to return to Cheyenne. The prisoners quickly packed their belongings and bedding, then boarded an east-bound train. The train pulled into the big depot at Cheyenne at four that afternoon. Johnson County Deputy Sheriff Howard Roles officially turned over the prisoners to Laramie County officers, who gave the men the run of the town. As the "prisoners" descended from the train, they enjoyed handshakes and subdued greetings from friends. "The prisoners straggled up town in small squads with acquaintances," reported the *Leader*. The War Department had directed that Fort Russell no longer would house these troublesome inmates. The county jail could not accommodate such a large number of prisoners, so Keefe Hall was hired as an incarceration center. Indeed, during four months of incarceration, the cattlemen were never behind bars. Instead of the jail at Buffalo or Cheyenne, or the penitentiary at Laramie, they managed to arrange loose confinement at Fort McKinney, Fort Russell, Hesse Hall, and Keefe Hall.[21]

Contractor M. P. Keefe built Keefe Hall across from the courthouse in 1886, later incorporating the old Presbyterian church into the complex. For several weeks in 1892 Keefe Hall was rented as an incarceration center for prisoners of the Johnson County War. (Courtesy Wyoming State Archives)

Sheriff A. D. Kelly employed four men at two dollars per day apiece to cook, wait tables, and wash dishes at Keefe Hall. Twenty-five to thirty-five dollars daily would be spent on meat, bread, milk, and other groceries. Soon after the inmates arrived, "a corps of barbers was summoned and the prisoners were trimmed up." Seventeen guards were hired at three dollars per day to work in three shifts at Keefe Hall. On the first evening, prisoners who had families in Cheyenne were permitted to spend the night at home, on condition that they "return to the bastile" at eight o'clock the following morning. An hour before midnight a *Leader* reporter approached the deputy in charge of Keefe Hall. Seventeen prisoners were out for the night, but the deputy emphasized that on the second day "the rules will be more stringent, and those leaving the hall will be usually accompanied by a guard."[22]

The promised new stringency did not develop. "The guards at Keefe hall have a perfect sinecure," observed the *Leader* only two days after the prisoners arrived. "Just who and what they are guarding is seldom apparent to anybody, for all the prisoners roam about day and night at will and unattended by guards." The cattlemen slept at their homes or in hotels, and provided their Texas employees with funds to enjoy the robust entertainment available in Cheyenne. George Tucker related that "the cattlemen were not stingy with their money. They gave us the best that money could buy.... We could not have asked for nicer treatment in this respect than we got from them."[23]

"A bunch of our young fellows went to a whore house one night and smashed all the furniture in the place," related Tucker. "It cost the cowmen three hundred dollars to repair the damage." During another night of revelry, Frank Canton shot himself. "He got drunk," explained Tucker. "He was out on the street flourishing his gun. He dropped it and it went off and the bullet went through the fleshy part of his leg." One evening a group of cattlemen-prisoners took a train to Denver, more than a hundred miles to the south, to attend a Templar meeting.[24]

On another memorable night, the cattlemen hosted a champagne dinner for the Texans. Each participating rancher brought two Texans to dinner, and the guests included Governor Barber, several cattlemen, and Maj. Harry C. Egbert, a personal friend of several cattlemen and the officer who led the infantry battalion from Fort Russell. As the champagne flowed freely, recalled Tucker, "Major Egbert got so far along that he fell out of his chair." Tucker had his own battle with the bubbly liquor, which he had never before consumed. "I started out taking the champagne in gulps. I expected a breathing spell, but every time I emptied my glass, some flunky would fill it up again. Pretty soon things began to go round."[25]

"Boys," announced cattleman Charley Campbell, "everything goes tonight except the top of the house." Campbell had brought George Tucker and Jeff Mynett to the banquet, and these two Texans hauled out revolvers with the intention of "going after the top of the house." The cattlemen hastily confiscated their guns, but it all was part of "the general hilarity of the occasion." Tucker warmly regarded the ranchers as "real sports" and "gentlemen in the grand manner." During the evening, Governor Barber approached Jeff Mynett and pinned a boutonniere on him. "Everybody there knew that the Governor was merely thanking Jeff for having killed Champion," observed Tucker.[26]

While the prisoners enjoyed the nightlife in Cheyenne, during the day they spent considerable time in the district courtroom of Judge Richard H. Scott. "The big square room with its old-fashioned furniture, grim, dreary, uninteresting, a relic of frontier days, is not an inviting place." Forty-two men, each charged with murdering Nathan D. Champion and Nick Ray, appeared before Judge Scott on Saturday, August 6. Their attorneys were Willis Van Devanter, Hugo Donzelman, M. C. Brown, and Walter Stoll, a bright young lawyer who a decade later would lead the prosecution against the notorious assassin Tom Horn. Judge Davidson and another attorney led the prosecution. A large crowd watched as each of the forty-two defendants answered "Not guilty" to the charges of murdering Nate Champion, then to the charges of murdering Nick Ray. "The reading of the information consumed the greater part of the day," reported the Cheyenne *Leader*, "and as they were identical . . . sitting there was rather tiresome."[27]

Late in the day, counsel for the defense presented a petition from the sheriff of Laramie County. Because keeping the prisoners cost about one hundred dollars a day, and because Johnson County was unable to reimburse him for the expense, Sheriff Kelly asked "that the court grant the necessary relief to protect him from incurring loss." The prosecution "suggested" that if the defendants would apply for bail there would be no opposition. Defense counsel countered with a proposal for personal recognizance, but following a consultation with Billy Irvine, the defendants agreed to "remain in the custody of the sheriff until the time of the trial."[28]

Of course, exhausting the slender financial resources of Johnson County was a key to the defense strategy. "Johnson County has no funds to carry the thing to an end," wrote John Clay to Henry Hay. "We know that Johnson County is pretty sick already," added Clay, "and we must force the matter to an end with them." Clay, Hay, and former governor George Baxter "held an informal meeting," and Clay "was deputized to call on Judge Scott." A key point was that prisoner meals, rent for Keefe Hall, even wages for the guards, was paid for by the incarcerated ranchers, "and other cattle-owners." Clay told Judge Scott "that we proposed to cut off the money supplies, and throw the prisoners into the actual charge of the sheriff. At the time I was talking to him the so-called prisoners could be found at any place but the hall they were supposed to be confined in. Three guards were there, but nobody else. The judge knew this as well as anybody else." As a result of these confidential conferences, Sheriff Kelly filed his petition of relief on August 6.[29]

On Wednesday morning, August 10, Judge Scott handed down his decision regarding the relief petition. Although Johnson County "was practically bankrupt" and had refused to reimburse Albany County for legal expenses incurred at Laramie City, Judge Scott decided that he could not issue an order compelling Johnson County to pay Sheriff Kelly's more recent disbursements. Therefore, since he could not provide for the sheriff's expenses, and since the defense had declined bail, the only remaining alternative was to admit the prisoners to bail "on their own individual recognizances." Immediately, the prisoners entered into their own recognizances in two sums of $20,000 each, there being two indictments against each defendant. "The ranchers had no trouble in raising the money for our bonds," said George Tucker.[30]

The prisoners promptly were released from custody. Keefe Hall was quickly deserted, "and express wagons were kept busy carrying away the paraphernalia with which it had been littered." The bedding and cooking gear were removed, and the building was turned over to Mr. Keefe's representative. The Cheyenne *Leader* commented that many of the prisoners had "never slept in the hall at all, and the guards were an elegant superfluity except whenever it was necessary to preserve the peace among the Texans."[31]

The Texans departed for home before the end of the day. Most of them carried "a brand new gripsack, a Winchester rifle and a cartridge belt." Many of the cattlemen "and a number of spectators were gathered together to see the party off. There was a great deal of hand shaking and a number of congratulatory expressions." A few of the cattlemen also boarded the eastbound train. After a journey of five hundred miles to Omaha, the Texans were paid seven hundred dollars apiece and placed on a train to Texas.[32]

When legal proceedings resumed on January 2, 1893, none of the Texans returned to Cheyenne; twenty-three of the cattlemen appeared before Judge Scott. Willis Van Devanter and the rest of his legal team had been able to plan for five months for the successful conclusion of the trial. For more than two weeks the jury candidates were examined. Eleven men were seated, but the twelfth juror could not be agreed upon. By noon on Saturday, January 21, a total of 1,064 veniremen had been examined, but the jury still was incomplete.[33]

By now Johnson County was virtually bankrupt and unable to bear legal expenses. When the county attempted to pay with warrants, they were considered "scarcely worth the paper they were written on." The prosecuting attorneys, unable to work up much enthusiasm for a case in which they were paid in worthless warrants, took turns being absent from court.

Following Saturday's noon recess, the sheriff of Laramie County informed Judge Scott that he had been told by Johnson County officials, including Prosecuting Attorney Alvin Bennett, that Johnson County was unable to reimburse him for maintaining the prisoners and for the expenses of securing jurors. Although directed to deliver fifty or more potential jurors, the sheriff said that he already had brought to court virtually every eligible juror in Cheyenne, as well as many in the countryside, and he no longer could afford the costs of sending deputies to the far reaches of the county. After Judge Scott turned to the prosecuting attorney with this matter, Bennett moved to dismiss the cases. But Willis Van Devanter contended that since the trial was being conducted in Laramie County, his clients still could be prosecuted in Johnson County, so he insisted that the case continue.[34]

The defense lawyers then conferred with Bennett, while everyone in the courtroom strained to overhear them. After the lawyers returned to their tables, Bennett asked Judge Scott to continue impaneling the jury. The judge declared an open venire for the single remaining jury member. A deputy sheriff summoned a spectator, Adam Adamsky, who was approved by both sides without examination. Van Devanter insisted that the jury be sworn in with instructions to return a not-guilty verdict. Bennett would not agree without consulting his fellow prosecutors, Davidson and Ballard, who were absent. Judge Scott granted a recess, but Bennett returned without having located either of his partners.

When court reconvened, Bennett entered a motion of *nolle prosquei* — formal notice that prosecution in the case now would end. Indictments of each defendant, including the absent Texans, were dismissed. A previous motion to forfeit bail bonds of the missing defendants was rescinded. After concluding formalities were finalized, the jury was dismissed and Judge Scott adjourned the proceedings. The case had not been tried, and the defendants had not been acquitted, but they could never again be arrested for the murder of Nate Champion and Nick Ray. Now free men, the ranchers shook hands and exchanged congratulations with each other and with a sudden swarm of friends.

It was a dramatic ending to the most dramatic and important trial that had ever taken place in Cheyenne. Few citizens of the Holy City of the Cow could have been surprised that the cattlemen, backed by wealth and political power, by the WSGA and Cheyenne's finest legal minds, had won exoneration for themselves and their hired gunmen. But the great age of cattle kings was virtually at an end throughout the West. Cheyenne, always progressive, was growing beyond its colorful past. The lengthy drama of the infamous Johnson County warriors was the last major triumph of western cattle barons, and the final chapter of the Holy City of the Cow.

17

Women of the Magic City

In 1894 Estelle Reel of Cheyenne became the first woman in the United States elected to a statewide office, an achievement that would lead to a national appointment. Also living in Cheyenne during this period was elderly Esther Morris, who was being referred to in print by her son, Col. E. A. Slack, as the "Mother of Woman Suffrage." In 1870, when she was fifty-seven, Mrs. Morris served for several months as justice of the peace in South Pass City. She later moved to Cheyenne and lived quietly with Colonel Slack or another son, court re- porter Robert Morris. But even though she was not an active suffragette, for many years Esther Morris was a living symbol—the first woman to hold office in the first U.S. province to permit women to vote and to serve on juries and in public offices. On July 23, 1890, during the official celebration of Wyoming statehood, Esther Morris agreed to present a forty-four-star U.S. flag to Governor Warren, in front of a crowd of 5,000 at the State Capitol.[1]

Unlike Mrs. Morris, who served less than nine months and heard just twenty- six cases as justice of the peace, Estelle Reel was a hard-driving career woman. Not many American women of the late nineteenth century devoted themselves to careers outside the home. But females who were bold and adventurous enough to go West often demanded the vote and otherwise tried to stretch the confines of a woman's world. "As the 19th Century neared its close," mused one historian of western women, "women savored a self-reliance, freedom and sense of equality unknown to their Eastern sisters."[2]

"Miss Estelle Reel," as she was referred to in the newspapers, carved out a groundbreaking career through grinding work and determination. Estelle was a sister of Heck Reel, a rancher and Republican politician who served as mayor of

Cheyenne and as a Wyoming legislator. Beginning as a teacher—a common occupation for women who worked—Miss Estelle became Laramie County superintendent of schools, regularly visiting all of the rural schools in the big county. Wyoming's Republican convention of 1894 met in the Opera House at Cheyenne. There were parades and bands and speeches, and behind the scenes Estelle Reel outmaneuvered her female opponent, also a county superintendent, for nomination as state superintendent. When her name was announced there was wild cheering, and after a vigorous campaign she resoundingly won the election as state superintendent of public instruction.[3]

During the next four years, there were frequent newspaper items about the incessant travels of Miss Estelle. In visiting schools across a large state she traveled by train, buggy, and horseback, acquiring a special riding habit made of leather for protection from barbed wire fences. During a trip to two remote schools in December 1894, "Miss Reel faced a blizzard, driving forty-two miles in the face of the storm." She handled voluminous correspondence and designed a uniform curriculum, working for years without a vacation. In 1896 she was mentioned for governor, and in 1898 Republican President William McKinley named her to fill the vacant position of Superintendent of Indian Education. Guided through the Senate by F. E. Warren, Estelle's nomination won unanimous approval. When she moved to Washington, she assumed the highest position ever held by a woman in the federal government.[4]

Like Estelle Reel, many other women seeking a career turned to education. Although underpaid, teachers were on a higher professional plane than housekeepers, cooks, and laundresses. (During the 1880–81 school year, "Professor" N. E. Stark received $1,800 for working as superintendent and teacher; the other teachers were unmarried women, and they each earned $750. Salaries increased slightly as the years passed, but males

Esther Hobart Morris, first woman in the U.S. to hold public office. (Photo by Karon O'Neal)

always were paid more than double their female colleagues.)[5] Although young ladies who had graduated from Cheyenne High School (CHS) sometimes were hired to teach locally, the majority of teachers in the Magic City schools were spirited women who wanted to experience the West.

During the 1892–93 school year, for example, three-fourths of the teachers were from the East. Only half a dozen faculty members called Cheyenne home. Professor J. C. Churchill served as superintendent and high school teacher, and one other male also taught at CHS. The other teachers, at Cheyenne's four elementary schools and CHS, were single females. At the end of the school year, the *Leader* ran an article listing twenty-four teachers and their summer plans. Churchill intended to take his family to the Chicago World's Fair, then spend the rest of the summer in Cheyenne. Throughout 1893 the *Leader* regularly listed citizens who traveled to Chicago's "white city," and "to admit that one has not made up his or her mind to go to the world's fair is decidedly unfavorable these bright summer days." Some of the teachers intended to go to Chicago or were planning other "tours," and one adventurous young woman "will take part of her holiday outing on a ranch." But most of the ladies had only enough money to return to their homes for the summer. Four were from Iowa communities; three were from Nebraska towns; two were from Minnesota. One was from Jackson, Mississippi; another from North Tetford, Vermont. Others were from New Haven, Connecticut; Athens, Pennsylvania; Cambridge, Ohio; and Wichita, Kansas.[6]

Cheyenne's teachers were from New England and the South and the Midwest. Year in and year out, with a majority of teachers from every section of the United States, the Cheyenne faculty was decidedly cosmopolitan. Cheyenne pupils were regularly exposed to teachers whose background and experiences ranged far beyond Wyoming. The ladies who sought novelty and excitement by coming to the Holy City of the Cow to teach inadvertently broadened the horizons of their classrooms and community. Often enough, during the summers Cheyenne teach-

Estelle Reel, Laramie County superintendent of schools, in 1894 won election as Wyoming superintendent of schools, and became the first woman in the U.S. elected to a statewide office. (Courtesy Wyoming State Archives)

ers found positions nearer to their homes, or they married[7] and left teaching to become wives and mothers. They would be replaced by other young ladies excited to be professionals in a Wild West city.

Even bolder were women who elbowed their way into professions dominated by men. Some of these female professionals gravitated to the western city where women's suffrage had originated. In 1884 Dr. Jennie Buchanan, M.D., a "graduate of Woman's Medical College, Chicago," opened a practice in Cheyenne. She shared an office with her husband, a dentist, on the second floor of the Wyoming Block, 307 Seventeenth, Room No. 14: "Calls answered day or night." Two years later, when "graduates in the profession" organized the Territorial Medical Association, there were nine medical doctors in Cheyenne, led by Dr. W. W. Crook, and including Dr. Jennie Buchanan and Dr. Antonette Williams. There were five doctors from Laramie, two from Rock Springs, two from Evanston, and one from Rawlins—all male. Of nineteen medical doctors, the only two women were practicing in Cheyenne.[8]

When a female physician moved her practice to Cheyenne in 1902, the community was accustomed to women doctors. Dr. Hawk of Green River was a recent state senator from Sweetwater County and was "one of the best known physicians." Dr. Hawk's wife, "also an able practicioner," was coming to Cheyenne to open an office, with her spouse soon to follow. "Cheyenne is to be congratulated on this double addition to the medical fraternity here," remarked the *Leader*. Also in 1902 a husband and wife dentist duo moved to Cheyenne. Dr. G. E. Glaze and his wife, "both being graduates of excellent schools," paid $1,000 for the practice of Dr. R. D. Robinson, who was moving to Los Angeles. The Doctors Glaze left Portland, Oregon, and moved into Robinson's office on Capitol Avenue.[9]

Isabella Wunderly, who would become Wyoming's "first" first lady, married Territorial Governor (1869–75) John A. Campbell in 1872 in Washington, D.C. The lovely Belle Campbell made her home in a suite at the Converse House, which rented for $32 a month. Belle played the organ at the Presbyterian church and was a leader in Cheyenne society. The Campbells' only child, a daughter, was born in 1873. Widowed in 1880, Belle's last visit to Cheyenne was in 1914. (Courtesy Wyoming State Archives)

A different kind of professional team, two female evangelists, preached and sang to a street corner crowd in Cheyenne in 1888. In 1902 the South Side Congregational Church welcomed a female pastor, Rev. Annette Beecher-Gray. A woman barber set up shop in

Cheyenne in 1889. And in 1891 Miss Marie Trocum, a well-dressed female drummer, was reported to be "doing well" in Cheyenne.[10]

Such career women were drawn to Cheyenne, in large part because female suffrage existed almost nowhere else. In 1870 Utah Territory authorized women's suffrage, but for more than a decade women could vote only in Wyoming and Utah. Washington Territory extended the right to vote to women in 1883; however, four years later, a court decision rescinded female suffrage in Washington. Also in 1887, Congress disfranchised women in Utah because of Mormon polygamy. For the next six years (1887–93) only Wyoming women could vote. After a long campaign, women finally won the vote in Colorado in 1893. Two years later Utah, having eliminated plural marriage, became a state with female suffrage in the constitution. In 1896 Idaho approved women's suffrage. Even so, as the nineteenth century came to an end, only four western states—out of forty-five United States—offered women the right to vote.

Wyoming was widely regarded as "The Paradise of Women Suffrage." An 1883 article published in Illinois rhapsodized that "the heart of every true advocate of woman suffrage beats faster at the name 'Wyoming.'" At this same time, Governor William Hale testified: "The women generally take a lively part in the elections, and proportionately fewer women than men neglect to exercise their right to vote." Estelle Reel, during her travels around Wyoming in the 1890s, noted the proliferation of Women's Republican Clubs, and she estimated that 95 percent of the state's women voted. In June 1889, with Wyoming moving toward statehood, 100 Cheyenne women met at Keefe Hall to take action that would preserve the right to vote when a state constitution was adopted. "The ladies seemed

Scarlet Women

Female professionals in Cheyenne included physicians, dentists, teachers, and preachers. But in any given year of the nineteenth century, female professionals in the Magic City were outnumbered by members of the oldest female profession—"Scarlet Women," according to the *Leader* (March 15, 1902).

Scarlet women led sad lives. In 1895 twenty-three-year-old Daisy Shaw turned up in Cheyenne after being deserted by her husband. She became "an inmate in the house in the west-end known as '333.'" Daisy "had numerous soldier lovers" and a great many quarrels with them. After one soldier stole her money and jewels, the young prostitute committed suicide by gulping dose after dose of morphine. Some of her "associates" contributed money for a funeral, and one associate bought a cemetery lot for Daisy's burial. (*Wyoming Tribune*, January 12 and 14, 1896)

A few months later, another scarlet woman from the west end, "crazed by opium and morphine," ran screaming into the street, where she was arrested by two policemen. (*Wyoming Tribune*, June 7, 1896) Year after year, Cheyenne newspapers related accounts of prostitute suicides or other melancholy tales about the "Scarlet Women of the Magic City."

very much in earnest and talked nothing but politics. Mrs. M. E. Post and Frances Hale, widow of Governor William Hale, addressed the crowd, and resolutions were drawn up for appropriate distribution. Committees were appointed to attend party primaries, and one woman insisted that "ladies should continue active in politics."[11]

Lucy Ellen Gannett, the youngest of three daughters of James Whitehead, charter settler of Cheyenne, proudly reminisced about his role in the 1869 passage of female suffrage. "My father, Judge Whitehead, was a member of the Legislature and helped draft the Women's Suffrage Bill that was passed at that time." Judge Whitehead then instructed his daughters: "Now that you have the privilege I hope you will consider it your duty to use it intelligently for the 'Best Man,' be he Democrat or Republican."[12]

At least one Cheyenne woman cast her first vote after being driven to the polls by a candidate. Margaret Thomson Hunter, a native of Scotland, came to Cheyenne in 1880, when she was thirty-two. Her husband, Colin Hunter, was the same age. Colin had left Scotland for America when the sweethearts were seventeen, and he arrived in Cheyenne in 1867 as a Union Pacific construction worker. Colin soon became a freighter, then prospered as a rancher, returning to Scotland to marry Margaret. The couple made their home in Cheyenne, where their two sons were born. At first Margaret was jolted by Cheyenne: "there were no trees, no birds, no lights, no walks, in fact no improvements." She especially missed trees. "When someone remarked that due to the purity and thinness of the air, one could see tremendous distances, I replied what good to see long distances if there is nothing to see?"[13]

Soon after her arrival in Cheyenne, the Masonic Lodge sponsored a dance. Margaret wore a formal dinner gown, but "every woman present was attired in street clothes—even to hats," and her husband observed, "Maggie, you aren't dressed right." He insisted that they could not go in-

Frances Hale, first lady of Wyoming, was widowed when Governor Hale died in 1885, during the third year of his term. Only thirty-eight, Francis remained in Cheyenne, active in community affairs and in St. Mark's Episcopal Church. (Courtesy Wyoming State Archives)

side. "Of course, that was the very time any woman *would* go in. And how everyone stared." She enjoyed herself immensely. A woman of such spunk was a good fit in Cheyenne, and she lived in the Magic City for more than half a century.[14]

Margaret first voted in 1890. As "all the women were plunged into politics," she attended a political meeting. Her husband was the leader of the Democratic Party in Cheyenne, but she did not know the distinction between Democrats and Republicans—including her neighbor, a Republican politician. "When election day rolled around, Mr. Hellman stopped by and asked me to go and vote for him. I was busy making pies and hadn't intended voting, but after all Mr. Hellman was a neighbor and also a very good friend of my husband's. So I pushed my pies aside, removed my apron, and tidied myself up a bit. Then I got into the buggy with Mr. Hellman and he drove me to the polls. Well, I voted and as we turned to leave we came face to face with my husband. When I explained to him that I had just voted for Mr. Hellman, I thought he would have a fit."[15]

In addition to offering women the right to vote, serve on juries, and hold office, western states learned to attract female citizens with another device. Since colonial times, American women had found it difficult to extract themselves from an unhappy marriage. In an era when most women could not earn a living in the workplace, society frowned upon divorce and erected legal barriers to it. Offering women a legal opportunity to escape an unpleasant husband proved to be a good way to make up the female population deficit that plagued all western territories and states. And certainly most newly divorced women could find new husbands in the West. Nevada became famous for easy divorces, but at one time Wyoming was notorious as a "Divorce Mill."[16]

As early as 1886, the *Leader* reported that there was a "Divorce mania in Cheyenne last year—nearly 30." In 1896 Walter Stoll, one of Cheyenne's finest attorneys, filed for divorce after only two years of marriage. A few years later, Elwood P. Mead, Wyoming's longtime state engineer who now worked for the U.S. Department of Agriculture, returned to Cheyenne to divorce his second wife after just one year.[17]

By 1899 Wyoming's divorce law was so liberal that the New York firm of Hoggatt & Caruthers, "one of the most prominent divorce firms in the United States," established a branch office in Cheyenne, setting up in a suite in the Kent Block. "Wyoming's divorce law is now the best in the United States," stated the senior member of Hoggatt & Caruthers to the *Sun-Leader*. Wyoming granted a divorce following a residence period of six months, and Hoggatt & Caruthers expected Cheyenne to become a "divorce colony," where "the majority of principals" settle permanently after their waiting period. "I believe this will be especially true of Wyoming and Cheyenne," said lawyer Hoggatt. "With the best climate on earth, undeveloped resources and boundless opportunities, the client leaving the east to adjust domestic difficulties will have no desire to return."[18]

There was no waiting period in Wyoming for remarriage after a divorce. The *Leader* announced that "Cheyenne has the prize for the most marriage licenses and divorces granted" during the previous nine months. The majority of marriage licenses were from couples from Colorado, while the greatest causes of divorce were desertion or lack of support. In Cheyenne during 1902, 333 marriages were performed, and 197 of the couples were from Colorado. The State Supreme Court of Colorado ruled "that the marriages solemnized in Wyoming of those who had been granted a divorce in Colorado within less than a year prior thereto, are void."[19] No doubt hundreds of couples married in Cheyenne ignored Colorado's envious ruling. By the start of the twentieth century, the Holy City of the Cow had become a divorce—and marriage—colony.

Of course, most Cheyenne women led stable married lives, and their major concerns centered around their homes and families, rather than suffrage and politics. Prominent women worked together and with their husbands to improve Cheyenne schools for their children, and to create a cultured community that would enrich the lives of everyone in the Magic City. By 1894 there were twelve churches in Cheyenne, and women formed the backbone of every one of them.

There were church organizations, such as the Baptist Willing Workers, St. Mary's Altar Society, the Episcopal Guild, the Christian Endeavors, and the Daughters of the King, through which women served Cheyenne. But many groups formed outside the church. Indeed, during the heyday of the Holy City of the Cow, the famous Cheyenne Club admitted no female members, inciting many women "to talk of organizing a club especially for ladies and buying the large building opposite the Cheyenne club house for their headquarters."[20]

Through the years there were many Cheyenne clubs "especially for ladies." Several of these organizations helped to raise money and volunteers for a public library. In the winter of 1873 the Cheyenne Library Association was formed, with Joseph M. Carey as president and Rev. Josiah Strong as secretary. Books were purchased and a reading

Louisa David moved with her family to Cheyenne in 1876, when she was twenty. The next year Louisa married Judge Joseph Carey, who was becoming wealthy in ranching and business. Witty and educated, Louisa was an advocate of women's suffrage, and long was prominent in Cheyenne society. (Courtesy Wyoming State Archives)

Cheyenne had the first county library in the United States. The Laramie County Library opened in October 1887. (Photo by Karon O'Neal at the Cheyenne Frontier Days Old West Museum)

room was opened — then closed, due to public indifference. The books had to be mortgaged to pay off library debt. In 1879 Governor John Hoyt reorganized the library, but interest fluctuated. A pay library was tried in 1886, the same year that the legislature provided a small tax to establish and provide a public library at every county seat. The Laramie County Library opened in October 1887. By 1895 the library occupied a room in the Central School, loaning an average of 100 books a day (175 on Saturdays). In October 1895 a free reading room opened, with magazines and newspapers made available as "the gift of a number of spirited women."[21]

When wealthy industrialist and philanthropist Andrew Carnegie began donating large sums of money to build public libraries, a committee headed by Joseph M. Carey, and including Henry G. Hay, Robert Morris, John W. Lacey, T. E. Burke, and John A. Riner, began working to secure a grant for Cheyenne. A site had to be provided as a condition of the grant, and a quarter of a block was donated at Capitol and Twenty-second. By 1900 Carnegie had agreed to provide $50,000, and Cheyenne's busy young architect, William Dubois, was given another assignment. Completed early in 1902, the Carnegie Public Library had a spacious reading room and a children's room on the main floor, along with a stack room that could accommodate 50,000 volumes. Upstairs were two sets of double parlors for women's and men's clubs, and the basement boasted a semicircular auditorium with a seating capacity of 350. F. E. Warren, "who is always to the front when there is anything handsome to be done," donated "a magnificent mahogany piano."[22]

An especially useful organization was the Ladies' Relief Association, founded in 1886 by leading women of the city. Four ministers attended the organizational meeting, and the Relief Association always worked closely with various men's groups. The Ladies' Relief Association channeled relief to needy families and causes. In 1895, for example, there were twenty-one active members who dispensed aid to twenty-seven families, and the Relief Association sent "comfort and cheer into over thirty homes" at Thanksgiving and Christmas. In 1902 another charitable group, the Women's Hospital Aid Society, raised more than $500 to purchase a "handsome ambulance" for the Laramie County Hospital, in northwest Cheyenne. Soon afterward, the Society provided the hospital with invalid tables, bed trays, and head rests, ordered by Mrs. R. S. Van Tassell from Chicago.[23]

The steady stream of contributions and accomplishments, large and small, by the women of Cheyenne had a marked impact on the community. Alice Richards McCreery, daughter and private secretary of Governor William A. Richards (1895–99), described Cheyenne during the 1890s as a city with culture and amenities: "Cheyenne was definitely a 'city' with many spacious homes, good streets, good churches and good schools. The best of the plays and some opera were given in the Cheyenne Opera House. It was a very sociable town with much social life—the women being as well dressed as anywhere in the nation. The stores were good, train service to Denver was efficient, any food delicacy could be easily procured.... One never thought of it as a town, always a city."[24]

During her school days, Alice experienced a rivalry between "east-siders" and "west-siders." Like many others, she remarked on the close social ties be-

Horse-drawn ambulance, St. John's Hospital. (Photo by author at the Cheyenne Frontier Days Old West Museum)

tween Fort Russell's officers and wives and Cheyenne's upper class. The military wives "were very cordial and friendly with the town ladies, who, often, were from the same social strata in the east as the fort ladies." Alice spoke fondly of the dances at the fort. "Many young officers came to town dances" and found brides among the girls of Cheyenne.[25]

"The officers and civilians were very congenial, most elaborate functions exchanged," agreed Lucy Ellen Whitehead Gannett. "The army blue and gold making an attractive setting among the full dress black and white of the civilians, the young ladies in beautiful, fluffy dresses, low neck and short sleeves, very good to look at." After her two older sisters married, "I was the only girl at home having such fun—teas, cards, dancing, horseback riding and driving." Lucy Ellen was one of the many observers who related that women of the Magic City "were not behind in being well-dressed. Cheyenne had good modistes and stores with fine materials." She pointed out that many Cheyenne women "were ladies of refinement and education, beautifully gowned, giving a cosmopolitan air to this city of ten or fifteen thousand people."[26]

Lucy Ellen was only one of a great many Cheyenne females who rode horseback. In 1881 an equestrienne school opened in Cheyenne, "and many of the ladies of this city are taking lessons." In April "Miss Addie de Vere broke a leg while riding," but few of her female friends were frightened. Two months later the *Leader* claimed that "a larger percentage of ladies ride horseback in Cheyenne than in any other city in the country." At the 1894 State Fair in Cheyenne, one of the horseraces pitted two young women against each other. Cheyenne girls often rode astride instead of sidesaddle, and they enjoyed skating and sledding during

The Sad Saga of Little Rosebud

"She was pretty little Levira Perry, an innocent laughing school girl fifteen years ago, or perhaps it was only ten years ago," recalled the *Leader* (May 12, 1889). Charming as well as beautiful, Levira was nicknamed "Little Rosebud."

While quite young, Little Rosebud married "a brute" named Thorn. She soon divorced him, then accepted an offer to go onstage in her hometown. "Little Rosebud became the favorite of patrons of the variety theater at the corner of Eddy and Seventeenth streets." But "Cheyenne was too small for a vaudeville queen," and Rosebud departed for Leadville, where she soon became "the reigning favorite"

of the mining boomtown. "All men paid homage to the sweet little beauty from Cheyenne," including famed millionaire Horace Tabor.

Little Rosebud collected numerous gifts and a great deal of money, "which she managed to spend as rapidly as it was forthcoming." There were other problems, and she moved back to Cheyenne, "broken in health and minus charms put to flight by dissipation." She was involved in frequent "scraps," but in May 1889 she married a man named Boggs. Sadly, on her honeymoon night Mrs. Boggs took an overdose of morphine: "Death came quietly and gently."

268 *Cheyenne*

the winter. When Cheyenne entered the twe
was invested into the new sport of basketball
school team. Cheyenne High School had no g
Keefe Hall for practices and games.[27]

In 1884 a burglar found that Cheyenne w
orous but "plucky" as well. On a May eveni
band was not at home, was visiting with a
confidently took her husband's six-shoote
Sighting the burglar, she squeezed off a rour
Leader labeled her "A PLUCKY WOMAN" and

On Monday night, August 30, 1897, Mr
her home by a party honoring the thir
Cheyenne. Julia was considered the second
boomtown, and her friends wanted to hono

But during the 1890s a number of beloved women were lost
1892 Minnie Slaughter, who had succeeded her father as state librarian, died at
the age of forty-two. As the daughter of charter settler John Slaughter, she had
spent all of her life in Cheyenne. Minnie Slaughter was mourned as "a woman of
lovable disposition who found her greatest delight in doing good for others."
Judge Slaughter's son, Johnny, had been murdered in 1877 while driving a Black
Hills stagecoach during a robbery attempt by the Sam Bass Gang. In 1897 Judge
Slaughter, now in his late eighties, lost his wife.[30]

Early in November 1895, Mrs. Henry G. Hay was informed by Dr. Amos
Barber that she was dying. She calmly gave various instructions to her prominent
husband, who at that time was serving as state treasurer, then consulted with
Rev. George Rafter of St. Mark's Episcopal Church. "She was fully prepared for
death and feared it not," although she was just forty-eight. The mother of a son
and daughter, she and her husband were honored by the closure of all state offices during the funeral. The pallbearers were led by Senator F. E. Warren and
State Engineer Elwood Mead.[31]

Two years later Amelia Post, wife of Morton E. Post, died in her home. One
of the first females to settle in the Magic City, in 1867, she long held a "conspicuous position" in Cheyenne society and "dispensed a generous and elegant hospitality." Amelia represented Wyoming at the National Women's Suffrage
Convention in 1871, and that same year she was instrumental in the defeat of a
bill to repeal female suffrage by the Second Territorial Legislature. The following
month Elwood Mead's wife died, and Henry G. Hay was one of her pallbearers.
A few years later Mead remarried, but the union proved unhappy and brief.[32]

Perhaps saddest of all was the critical illness of Mrs. F. E. Warren. Helen Smith
Warren moved to Cheyenne in 1871 as a twenty-seven-year-old bride. For years
the couple lived in a house just behind the Inter Ocean Hotel. Then Warren bought
a two-story frame house built by Herman Glafcke at 200 East Seventeenth, where
Helen and Emroy (she called him by his middle name) raised their son and daughter. Warren became the wealthiest man in Cheyenne and Wyoming and the state's
ablest politician. He was mayor of Cheyenne, twice governor, then a U.S. senator.

In Cheyenne, therefore, Helen was the city's first lady, then twice the first lady of Wyoming. She was a gracious, capable hostess. ("Mrs. Governor Warren gave an elaborate dinner of fourteen courses to some friends in the city last evening," reported the *Leader* in 1885. "Each course was illustrated with an appropriate quotation from Shakespeare.") Prominent in Cheyenne society, Helen was involved in almost every worthwhile organization and cause, and she was a stalwart of the First Baptist Church. After her husband settled into the U.S. Senate, the family spent as much as half of each year in Washington. Helen wrote a letter to "My Dear Wyoming Friends" that was published in a twelve-page "Women's Edition" of the *Leader* in November 1895. She had just served as Wyoming's delegate to a national meeting of the Women's Christian Temperance Union. "But before I write of this inspiring meeting, let me tell you that we are located at 1725 Q street, and that our latch string will always be out to all Wyoming friends...."[33]

Helen Smith Warren was bright, sweet, cultured, and devoted to the First Baptist Church. Helen was first lady of Cheyenne and of Wyoming, and she was a leader of society. (Courtesy Wyoming State Archives)

A month later Helen was interviewed by a Washington *Post* reporter, and the article was reprinted in the *Leader*. After complimenting the Warren children and their richly appointed home (the senator, of course, had been in the furniture business since 1868), the reporter turned to Helen. "Mrs. Warren is well versed in political movements, and has voted ever since going west.... Mrs. Warren is fond of society, but is at the same time a domestic woman. She is a brunette, with a plump figure and easy manner."[34]

During 1899, Helen began suffering from a mysterious illness. Writing to "Dear Emroy" in Washington, she tried to describe her condition: "About my health. I consider myself in a very bad way because my mind is not acting well. I have such a confused feeling sometimes. My will power is extremely weak.... I find I am too sick to do anything." Cheyenne physicians had prescribed medicine to reduce swelling in her limbs. "I had no sleep to speak of last night and am exceedingly melancholy. I try to shake it off and to be cheerful.... I do not care to meet people any more—I used to love it. I am so changed that I do not recognize my old self. Now dear, I have tried in my previous letters not to tell you this.... I now think you ought to know my condition."[35]

After joining her husband in Washington, Helen's condition worsened, and doctors suggested that she should be admitted to an "asylum" near Baltimore, Sheppard & Enoch Pratt Hospital. In a letter to her elderly father in Massachusetts, she expressed the hope that she could visit him for his birthday. "My daily routine is about the same, i.e. I get up, dress, eat breakfast about 8, medicine about half past, doctor at nine, reading, writing until nearly one, dinner, than a long afternoon with the same occupation as in the morning. Once in a while a drive—and go out doors a little while after supper after taking more medicine."[36]

But she experienced hallucinations, her periods of normalcy were brief, and she responded little to visits from her family or such old friends as the Van Devanters. Between visits she wrote to "My dearest husband," thanking him for a number of gifts, then expressing despair. "I am dangerously near collapse, dear.... Isn't it horrible to be in such a condition and fully realize it!... Why is it that I cannot rally! Dearest, as usual I think this is my last letter—and I love you so."[37]

With her husband and her children at her hospital bedside, fifty-eight-year-old Helen Warren died on March 28, 1902. She was returned to Cheyenne for funeral services in her beloved First Baptist Church, then buried at Lakeview Cemetery. In her memory, Senator Warren erected a large, brick shelter house in Cheyenne's City Park.[38]

For three decades Helen Warren had been at the forefront of a remarkable generation of lively, progressive Cheyenne women. No one in the succeeding generation of Cheyenne females radiated more outstanding qualities than

NEW REST HOUSE

F. E. Warren built this "rest house" of brick and stone, with a red-tiled roof, for the city park in honor of his deceased wife. (From the Leader, September 16, 1903)

Helen's daughter. The namesake of both parents, Helen Frances Warren was born in 1880. She was a charming, confident little girl, and the activities of "Miss Frankie" were noted in the *Leader*. Her affluent parents provided her with piano lessons, a pint-sized phaeton drawn by Shetland ponies, and all manner of other advantages. Smart and popular, Frankie attended Cheyenne schools through her junior year at Cheyenne High School. In 1895 the family began spending a major part of each year in Washington, D.C., where she graduated from Central High School in 1896.[39]

Frankie was high-spirited, in the tradition of many Cheyenne females, and in an 1896 letter to his wife, Senator Warren disapproved of his daughter's "immature years." When she went away to college, Warren intended for her to board with a "matron or chaperone." Frankie went to Wellesley College, in Wellesley, Massachusetts, and soon her father became concerned that she would "fool away" his money. There was another typical parental complaint, at least partially due to her upbringing among women of Cheyenne: "Whatever may be Frankie's ideas of liberty of action and no interferences with her liberty, etc., she is not old enough to run wild and completely unchecked."[40]

During summers and holidays in Cheyenne, Frankie plunged back into community activities. "Miss Frankie Warren will entertain a few friends at a bicycle party this evening," related the *Leader* in the summer of 1900. And that same summer: "Don't fail to hear Frances Warren in her inimitable recitations at the Opera

Frankie Warren, one of Cheyenne's favorite and most accomplished young women, married Captain—later General—John J. Pershing. General and Mrs. Pershing are shown here with three of their four children. The little boy in the uniform, Francis Warren Pershing, was named after his grandfather. (Courtesy National Archives)

House Monday" (she was part of a program presented by violinist Marie Buchanan and other local young people). Before returning for the fall semester at Wellesley, she traveled to California: "Frances Warren, the accomplished daughter of Senator F. E. Warren, has been selected to christen the monitor *Wyoming* — to be launched in San Francisco, September 8."[41]

Frankie studied piano at the Chicago University of Music, offered piano lessons in Cheyenne, graduated from Wellesley, then met and fell in love with a dashing cavalry officer. Capt. John J. Pershing, although twenty years older than Frankie, was handsome and rugged, a decorated veteran of the Apache Wars and of combat in Cuba and the Philippines. They married in 1905.[42]

Frankie often played concerts in Cheyenne with Marie Buchanan, a gifted violinist. The daughter of Cheyenne physician W. T. Buchanan, Marie studied in Denver, where she "surprised the musical people of that city by her proficiency on the violin and promises to become famous as a soloist." Accompanied by her mother, Marie followed Frankie to Chicago for advanced studies. At sixteen she played a solo with the Chicago Symphony Orchestra and "created a sensation in the musical circles of Chicago." When the orchestra toured western states early in

1902, Marie traveled as violin soloist. And when she appeared with the orchestra in Denver, a number of her fans came over from Cheyenne. The *Leader* proclaimed her "the most talented virtuoso in the state and probably in the western country." She played to standing-room-only crowds and was given enthusiastic ovations. Following a final concert in August 1903, the seventeen-year-old violinist left Cheyenne for Europe and studies at the Berlin Conservatory. The Olympian Club gave Marie a sendoff with a dance in her honor at Keefe Hall.[43]

Another popular young lady in Cheyenne was Fannie Crook, daughter of

longtime Cheyenne physician W. W. Crook. During a dreadful scarlet fever epidemic in March 1880, Fannie's sister Ruby died, followed a few days later by her brother George. Little Fannie was the only surviving child of Dr. and Mrs. Crook, who devoted themselves to her upbringing and activities. Fannie attended social events with her mother, assisted at receptions and weddings, and was involved in a series of parties and picnics with her school friends.[44]

Built by Dr. W. W. Crook, this Victorian residence was the home of popular Fannie Crook, his daughter. In 1904 Wyoming's first Governor's Mansion was erected on the corner lot just west (left) of the Crook home. (Photo by Karon O'Neal)

As a girl, Dazee McCabe moved with her family from North Platte to Cheyenne. Vivacious and fun-loving, Dazee graduated from CHS in 1897. Three years later she married Lt. Charles A. Bristol, who had just returned from the Philippines with the Alger Light Artillery. Bristol's father had founded Wyoming's oldest book-binding and printing firm in 1868 in Cheyenne. Dazee became an institution in Cheyenne, deeply involved in civic affairs and responsible for colorful floats ("Dazee's Dance Hall") for Frontier Days parades.[45]

In 1902 twenty-five-year-old Nellie Tayloe Ross moved from Omaha to join her new husband, William B. Ross, who had begun a law practice in Cheyenne. While Nellie gave birth to three sons and involved herself in Cheyenne society, her husband held a succession of political offices. In 1923 Ross won the Democratic nomination for governor, triumphed in the fall election, and was inaugurated on January 1, 1924. But within a few months Governor Ross became ill, and he died on October 2, 1924. Democrats nominated Mrs. Ross to succeed him, she won a special election, and Nellie Tayloe Ross was inaugurated on November 7 — sixteen days before Miriam A. Ferguson became governor of Texas. It is fitting that another groundbreaking Cheyenne woman was the first female governor in the United States.[46]

18

Frontier Days

In 1897 Cheyenne community leaders threw together a one-day festival dubbed Frontier Day. A celebration of Cheyenne's frontier and cowboy past, the festival attracted an excited local crowd as well as many tourists from other towns. Elated by the enthusiastic response and by the economic impact on their community, city leaders immediately began planning an expanded festival for 1898. Soon Frontier Days was a wildly popular Cheyenne institution, well on the way to becoming the largest and most famous rodeo in the American West.

Many elements, past and present, went into the first Frontier Day, but the catalyst was Frederick Angier, traveling agent of the Union Pacific. Angier's primary job was to arrange excursion trains, at special ticket rates, to one event or another. Angier had a gift for inspiring leaders in various communities with a vision for creating events that would attract tourists. Late in August 1897, Angier stepped off a train at Cheyenne's depot, hoping to promote passenger traffic to the Magic City. The UP general agent in Cheyenne offered little hope, pointing out that local business was sluggish.[1]

Angier was not easily discouraged, and he knew the power of enlisting newspapermen. Walking to the office of the *Daily Sun-Leader*, he was ushered to the desk of the publisher. Col. E. A Slack was an inveterate promoter of Cheyenne, and he had been mulling over the possibilities of staging a festival. Although Slack had attended such events in northern Colorado as Denver's Festival of Mountain and Plain, Loveland's Corn Day and Greeley's Potato Day, he realized that Cheyenne had no agricultural products around which to build a festival. But Angier suggested a cowboy exhibition of "handling cattle and horses" featuring "riding, throwing rope and doing feats that are common to them, mounting wild horses and things of that sort."[2]

Such a festivity was a natural for the Holy City of the Cow, and Slack's imagination was immediately fired by Angier's suggestion that it could be "sort of a Wild West Show." Buffalo Bill Cody's Congress of Rough Riders had become enormously popular, and other Wild West Shows also were entertaining large crowds with hard-riding cowboys and Indians, sharpshooting exhibitions, stagecoach robberies, horseraces, and other exciting activities which evoked the last frontier.

During the same period that Wild West Shows were proliferating, the modern rodeo was in the process of evolution. Working cowboys often raced their cow ponies and held informal roping competitions. When western communities began to stage cowboy competitions in the 1880s, these events were called Frontier Days Celebrations (the term "rodeo" was not yet popularized). Pecos, Texas, celebrated the Fourth of July in 1883 by penning longhorn steers on the courthouse square and inviting area cowboys to rope and to race their horses. The next year Payson, Arizona, began staging "August Races," which also featured cowboy roping contests. On May 1, 1885, a "grand cowboy tournament" was held at Caldwell, Kansas, and cowboy Charles Siringo was awarded "a fine silver cup" for his steer-roping performance. In Arizona the Prescott Frontier Days began on July 4, 1888, and today proclaims itself the "oldest continuous rodeo."[3]

In Wyoming during these years there were informal cowboy contests, and Alex Swan staged an outdoor entertainment for investors after he organized the Swan Land and Cattle Company in 1883. About 150 British stockholders journeyed to Cheyenne, where Swan met them with carriages, wagons, and saddle horses. The entourage headed to the Laramie Plains, where a barbeque was laid out for them, and where every rider on the payroll participated in

Col. E.A. Slack, longtime Cheyenne newspaperman and booster. Colonel Slack played a key role in creating Frontier Days, and his descendants have continued family involvement in the event. (Courtesy Wyoming State Archives)

the Wild West exhibition. Horseracing, roping, and bareback riding—of steers as well as broncs—amused the stockholders and other visitors. Swan had brought Native Americans to add to the western atmosphere, and a tug of war was staged between cowboys and Indians. One cowboy, later rumored to have been teenaged Butch Cassidy, demonstrated his marksmanship with a revolver.[4]

The most unique event placed twenty-five cowboys atop broncs that had never been ridden. Blindfolded and placed in a line, the horses were supposed to race 200 yards. But when the blindfolds were pulled, the broncs began bucking and many of the riders were thrown. It was half an hour before one skilled rider finally managed to guide his raw mount across the finish line. This wild horse race would long be remembered in Wyoming.

In 1897 enterprising leaders of the Holy City of the Cow would combine elements of Wild West Shows with the evolving rodeo to produce a Frontier Day entertain-

Poster printed by Colonel Slack to advertise the first Frontier Day. (Courtesy Wyoming State Archives)

ment that would resonate with the inhabitants of Cheyenne and the surrounding area. E. A. Slack took Frederick Angier to see Mayor William Schnitzer. An insurance agent and coal merchant, Mayor Schnitzer had appointed a Board of Trade to consider ways to improve Cheyenne's business climate. The mayor saw promise in the proposals of Slack and Angier, and he joined them in visiting other community leaders.

On Monday and Tuesday, August 30 and 31, Slack published articles in the *Daily Sun-Leader* boosting the notion that a Frontier Day celebration "could be made one of the big events each year to which new features could be added from time to time." This "unusual and novel" event would feature cowboy races, "good specimens of the noble red men," and "scenes of the frontier days brought back." On Tuesday night there was large attendance at the office of Mayor Schnitzer to enlist support from the business community. It was suggested that a parade should be staged on the morning of Frontier Day, before the anticipated crowd would move to Pioneer Park (in the northwest part of town) for races and other events. A seven-man committee was appointed to solicit funds and arrange an event that "will gladden the hearts of all old timers; will entertain perfectly those who come from abroad and will be a source of profit and pleasure to the community."

Warren Richardson, a thirty-three-year-old businessman who had been in Cheyenne with his family since 1870, agreed to serve as committee chairman. (A lifelong bachelor, Richardson would serve Frontier Days for decades; July 27, 1950, was named Warren Richardson Day, and he died at the age of ninety-four during Frontier Days 1960.) Richardson provided a committee headquarters by turning over his office in "the elegant front room" on the second floor of the Tivoli. Committee members began to seek donations and pledges for prizes, advertising and other expenses, finally collecting $562. Thursday, September 23, was set as the first Frontier Day, which gave Richardson and the committee three weeks to create the event.[5]

Meanwhile, Frederick Angier was arranging excursion trains from Denver and other Colorado communities, charging passengers a mere penny per mile. Two committee members traveled to towns north of Cheyenne to publicize "Wyoming's great annual festival." Cheyenne's Battery A of the Wyoming National Guard scheduled a hop for the night of Frontier Day, engaging Napersick's orchestra and arranging for the governor and his staff to appear in

The Tivoli, still the jewel of downtown, decorated with bunting. The first Frontier Day Committee used Warren Richardson's second-floor office, which overlooked Sixteenth from the bay window over the Tivoli sign. Richardson operated a bar and restaurant on the main floor. (Courtesy Wyoming State Archives)

dress uniforms. "A picked squad is drilling daily on a fancy sabre drill, which will precede the dance." The UP shops, as well as the public schools, agreed to close on the afternoon of Frontier Day. Each new development was publicized in the *Daily Sun-Leader*, and excitement grew rapidly throughout Cheyenne.[6]

Three weeks may have seemed a brief time to put together a major event, but Cheyenne had a long history of staging community celebrations, often on short notice. Within a week the committee hammered out an itinerary. Heading the list was a half-mile Wild Horse Race. The first prize was $50, and at a signal the cowboys would have to saddle and bridle their broncs before trying to mount. There were five cow pony races of distances from 250 yards to two miles. Other events were wild steer roping, "quickest roped and hog-tied," and "the worst bucking bronco produced and ridden." There would be Native Americans who were expected to "give a vivid representation of a massacre and will also give fantastic dances." A stagecoach robbery, staple of Wild West Shows, would be reenacted, and so would "an old-time lynching," although the committee had a hard time finding "a volunteer to act the part of the main character."[7]

Area ranchers "are looking for their swiftest and meanest horses and getting their riders in training." Rancher John Coble, in town from his Iron Mountain spread, shared the general excitement and pledged to send a number of horses and riders, including Otto Plaga, considered "the best rider in the state." The committee anticipated that Frontier Day "will inaugurate an annual state festival."[8]

Admission would be free to Pioneer Park, but those who wanted to sit in the covered grandstand, which would hold 500, would have to pay 35 cents, while a bleacher seat cost 15 cents. Vendors had to pay a fee to sell lemonade, beer, cigars, peanuts, candy, popcorn, soda water, souvenirs, and other items. Mayor

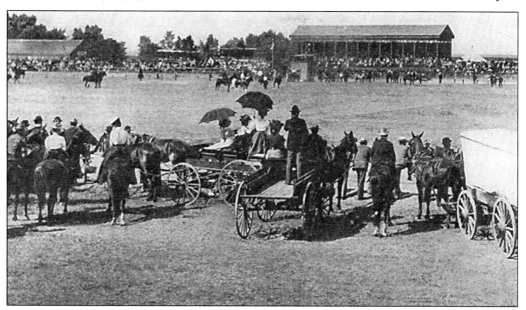

Frontier Day crowds sat in the grandstands or bleachers, or in their carriages, or atop their horses around the racetrack. (Courtesy Wyoming State Archives)

Schnitzer allocated $150 to be spent for special policemen. Pioneer Park would open at one o'clock, and special passenger trains were arranged for one, two, and three o'clock for the two-mile run from the UP Depot to the park.[9]

Tourists and cowboy participants began arriving in large numbers on Wednesday, September 22. Excursion trains were met by a reception committee, while a brass band played popular tunes of the day. Three companies of the Eighth Infantry marched the short distance from Fort Russell to Pioneer Park and set up camp, "pitching their tents in picturesque form." Following the cowboy events, the soldiers planned to enact a sham battle.[10]

At noon on Thursday, Battery A banged out a twenty-one-gun salute, thirty UP shop whistles shrieked, and school and fire bells clanged. Hundreds of citizens fired revolvers and shotguns into the air. The cacophony signaled everyone to finish their lunches and head for Pioneer Park. A stream of horse-drawn vehicles, horsemen, pedestrians, and stray dogs, surged toward the park. More than 4,000 spectators jammed the grandstand and bleachers and stood or sat around the racetrack. The crowd was four or five deep in places, and many people watched from their carriages.[11]

The stagecoach appeared, drawn by six horses and packed with local citizens. A dummy was lynched from a pole and filled with bullets. Although no Native Americans were brought from a reservation, two local men donned war paint and breechcloths and performed their version of a war dance in front of the grandstand — until the breechcloths worked loose and left them prancing "in dishabille duet." Races and bronc-busting events were loudly cheered. Saddle broncs were

Following the first Frontier Day, the Committee took a ride to Fort Russell in the spirit of fun that had characterized the gala celebration. Committee members donned top hats and rode a barouche pulled by a span of oxen and a phaeton drawn by a mule. (Courtesy Wyoming State Archives)

ridden until the horse stopped bucking, or until a revolver was fired indicating the rider had mastered the beast. Bill Jones was awarded the prize for bronc busting, but darkness fell before the steer roping could be staged.[12]

The militia band escorted the happy crowd back to the depot, continuing to play while the special trains were boarded. Many visitors chose to stay over, filling Cheyenne's restaurants, saloons, and hotels for the second night in a row. Some of them attended the Grand Frontier Ball, given by Battery A at Keefe Hall, which was being used as the armory.[13]

The next night another event took place in conjunction with Frontier Day. A meeting at the courthouse resulted in the organization of the Wyoming Pioneer Association. Nearly 100 "old timers" gathered, including one who had pioneered Wyoming in 1849, another in 1854, and several in 1867, when Cheyenne was founded. Trustees were elected, and three levels of membership were established: Pioneer Rank (those who arrived before Wyoming became a territory in 1869); Territorial Rank (those who arrived before statehood in 1890); and Statehood Rank. Wyoming women, never slow to assert themselves, immediately insisted on the formation of a Ladies' Auxiliary.[14]

Praise from visitors to Frontier Day was enthusiastic, and newspapers saluted the event: "a decided success," said the Douglas *News*, for example, and "a 'show' that was interesting from start to finish," according to the Wheatland *World*. A few weeks after Frontier Day, the committee met in Warren Richardson's Tivoli office to settle accounts. Donations, tickets, and vendor fees had produced more than $1,200 revenue. After bills were paid, $150 remained and was deposited for use by the committee in 1898. The committee enthusiastically decided to expand the festival to two days, and Frontier Day became Frontier Days.[15]

"I'm a-leavin' Cheyenne"

When old-time cowboys or bronc busters found themselves aboard an outlaw horse, personal safety sometimes overcame cowboy bravado. If an outlaw could not buck off its rider, the frustrated animal might rear up and threaten to fall backward. If the horse did fall back, the rider could be crushed beneath, suffering injury or even death. When an outlaw reared up precariously, the rider might be prudent to bail out, as in an old cowboy ballad:

"So long, ladies, my horses won't stand,

Goodbye, Old Paint, I'm a-leavin' Cheyenne."

By the time Cheyenne's Frontier Days became an annual event, early rodeo cowboys were using the ballad phrase for any contestant who was thrown from a bucking horse. When a horse dropped its head and arched its back ("swallows his head"), then jumped high and twisted violently ("sunnin' his sides"), and tossed his rider, onlookers often muttered, "Goodbye, Old Paint, I'm a-leavin' Cheyenne."

In 1898 Frontier Days was held on Monday and Tuesday, September 5 and 6, in conjunction with a performance of Buffalo Bill's Wild West and Congress of Rough Riders. Cody's Wild West Show was at its peak, with a troupe of 500 and featuring a large-scale reenactment of Custer's Last Stand. Cody also displayed "battle-scarred, maimed and wounded soldiers" from the recently concluded Spanish-American War. On a chilly Monday, September 5, Buffalo Bill led his superbly mounted troupe in its customary parade, supplemented by 200 members of the Cheyenne Fire Department. The parade through Cheyenne ended spectacularly, with the stagecoach racing up Ferguson Street and Cody's warriors galloping in pursuit.[16]

Buffalo Bill Cody brought his world-famous Wild West and Congress of Rough Riders to the second Frontier Days event, in September 1898. Cody had appeared before, and would appear again in Cheyenne, and he often visited the Magic City. (Author's collection)

Cody's show was held on open prairie north of the Capitol, and a crowd of 6,000 viewed his polished extravaganza. Then many of the spectators proceeded over to Pioneer Park for the rest of the afternoon, although the amateur performance may have seemed anticlimactic following the best Wild West Show ever mounted. On Tuesday, Frontier Days was the only show in town. New features included the wedding of a Denver couple in front of the grandstand, a delivery wagon race won by former mayor L. R. Bresnahan, and a dog chasing a rabbit. The latter event was unexpectedly expanded when a vast number of stray dogs also gave loud pursuit of the frantic rabbit.[17]

The weather for Frontier Days 1898 had been cool, so the festival was moved up to

One Afternoon Performance Only.

Cheyenne, Saturday, Aug. 9.

"Au Revoir, but Not Good-Bye."

Will positively go to Europe this Fall.

BUT THIS YEAR IT WILL TOUR THE AMERICAN CONTINENT.

FROM OCEAN TO OCEAN.

Visiting the Principal Cities and Greater Railway Centers Only, as a Parting Salute to the Great Nation which gave it birth.

BUFFALO BILL'S WILD WEST

And Congress of Rough Riders of the World.

Now in the Zenith of its Overwhelming and Triumphant Success, Presenting a Programme of Marvelous Merit, and Introducing the

World's Mounted Warriors

Such as INDIANS, SOLDIERS OF THE AMERICAN, ENGLISH, GERMAN, RUSSIAN AND CUBAN ARMIES, FULLY EQUIPPED AND

READY FOR WAR

AN EXHIBITION THAT TEACHES BUT DOES NOT IMITATE.

These Are the Men Who Do and Dare and These Are the Events in the Action:

A GRAND REVIEW OF ALL NATIONS.

A RACE OF RACES. In which Cowboys, Cossacks, Mexicans, Gauchos, and American Indians participate.

ARTILLERY DRILL BY VETERANS.

A ROUND-UP ON THE PLAINS, with Incidental Events.

PONY EXPRESS RIDING.

GROUPS OF MEXICAN HORSEMEN AND LASSO EXPERTS.

CELEBRATED CRACK SHOTS AND NOTED MARKSMEN.

REAL ARABIAN HORSEMEN AND ATHLETES.

LIFE-SAVING DRILLS. By Veteran Members of U. S. Life-Saving Service.

GENUINE COSSACKS FROM THE CAUCASUS OF RUSSIA.

INDIAN BOYS IN FAVORITE PASTIMES.

COWBOY FUN WITH THE BUCKING BRONCOS.

U. S. CAVALRY DRILLS AND MILITARY EXERCISES.

THE FAMOUS DEADWOOD STAGE COACH. Attack, Repulse, Victory.

MOMENTS WITH THE BOLAS THROWERS.

ROUGH RIDERS AND NATIVE GAUCHOS.

COLONEL W. F. CODY | Buffalo Bill

IN FEATS OF MARKSMANSHIP.

A BUFFALO HUNT AS IT WAS IN THE FAR WEST.

A HERD OF REAL BUFFALO, the Last of the Race.

GRAND MILITARY MANEUVERS.

EPISODES OF CAMP LIFE, with its Humor and Hardships.

THE BIVOUAC AT NIGHT.

ASSEMBLY OF THE ALLIED ARMIES. Incidental Drill and Action.

REALISTIC SCENES "ON THE FIRNG LINE."

ALL THE EXCITING ELEMENTS OF WARFARE AND BATTLE, IN WHICH OLD GLORY ALWAYS WAVES TRIUMPHANT.

See it while you may.   Enjoy it while you can.

Grand Review of the Rough Riders

IN STREET CAVALCADE AT 9 A. M. ON DATE OF EXHIBITION. THE WHOLE CULMINATING WITH THE GREAT MILITARY SPECTACLE,

The Battle of San Juan Hill

Admission · 50c.   Children under 9 years 25c

Reserved Seats (including admission) $1.00, on sale at Palace Pharmacy.

August 23 and 24 in 1899. "Appropriate and costly prizes" were offered for such winners as the best Frontier Day costume and "the handsomest young lady." The Native American presence planned for 1897 had not materialized, but Buffalo Bill's mounted warriors, along with a delegation of twenty Shoshones from the Wind River reservation, were fan favorites in 1898. Shoshones were back in 1899, delighting audiences with tribal dances and games, and Native Americans became a permanent fixture of Frontier Days.[18]

A significant new feature of 1899 was a half-mile ladies' race, held on the first day. Anna McPhee, a teenager raised on a ranch north of Cheyenne, won a saddle worth $45. The event was popular, and for 1900 a $50 purse was offered, to be divided into $25, $15, and $10 prizes. These turn-of-the-century Frontier Days contestants, therefore, became "the first professional woman athletes in the world." Yet another first for Wyoming women: first to vote, first to sit on juries, first to hold public office, first to compete in games for pay.[19]

By 1900 the Magic City's hotels, boardinghouses, and restaurants could not accommodate all of the visitors, so the Frontier Days Committee solicited the names of

In August 1902, Buffalo Bill returned with his show to Cheyenne just three weeks before Frontier Days. (From the Leader, *July 19, 1902)*

Cheyenne citizens who could provide rooms or meals. More attractions were added for 1900, including Cheyenne's first balloon ascension and parachute jump. Cheyenne boasted an excellent baseball team, and a game was scheduled against a Denver club for each morning before the afternoon events. A bullfight was talked up, but there was considerable opposition and the idea was dropped. The Opera House offered performances both evenings, Wednesday and Thursday, September 12 and 13. The Grand Frontier Ball was held in the open air, along with a crowd-pleasing Cake Walk.[20]

An estimated 6,000 spectators attended the events of 1900, and it was calculated that tourists spent as much as $75,000 in Cheyenne. Businessmen donated more than $5,000 to the Frontier Committee for prizes and other expenses, but these contributions now were recognized as an investment. On Friday, thirty-five Shoshone participants came to the Stock Growers Bank and were paid six dollars apiece. Their spokesman was Charlie Washakie, youngest son of the great Chief Washakie, who recently had died. Charlie said that his men "all had a fine time and all want to come again next year."[21]

For the second year in a row, Hugh McPhee won the steer-roping contest. The winner of the saddle bronc competition was Thad Sowder, a future inductee of

Early Frontier Days parade coming west on Seventeenth and turning north onto Ferguson (Carey). Note the Opera House in the right background. (Courtesy Wyoming State Archives)

The bank of T. A. Kent at the corner of Seventeenth and Carey. For two nights during Frontier Days 1902, a canvas screen was suspended from the side of the building, and crowds estimated at 6,000 watched outdoor motion pictures. (Courtesy Wyoming State Archives)

the Rodeo Hall of Fame. A cowboy from Julesburg, Colorado, Sowder had successfully ridden a bronc called High Five in the inaugural Frontier Day in 1897. Although Sowder was beaten out by Otto Plaga at Frontier Days in 1901, he was named "World Champion" a few weeks earlier at a Denver event, the "Festival of Mountain and Plain World's Championship Broncho Busting Contest." This festival, launched in 1901 by Cheyenne native John Kuykendall, was the first to designate a World Champion while awarding a cash prize and a championship belt.[22]

Sowder joined Buffalo Bill's Wild West and Congress of Rough Riders. But in August 1902 the twenty-eight-year-old "champion rough rider of the world" returned to Cheyenne to marry nineteen-year-old Anna Farrell. Sowder also defended his world championship in Denver, riding Steamboat, a bucking horse from Wyoming dubbed "King of the Plains." Steamboat was foaled in 1896 on the Two Bar at Chugwater, and for fifteen years the fierce black bronc threw riders at the most prestigious rodeos, including Frontier Days.[23]

Otto Plaga rode a bronc named Teddy Roosevelt to the 1901 Frontier Days championship, and the animal was designated as the "worst horse." A skilled competitor of the steer-roping event was stock detective Tom Horn, soon to be implicated in a brutal murder. A new section of 200 seats was added to the bleachers, but thousands of spectators still stood, or sat in carriages around the racetrack. The reputation of Frontier Days had grown rapidly, especially after the spectacular expanded events of 1900. Expecting a record crowd for 1901, the Frontier Committee hired thirty special policemen. Admissions to the grounds were estimated at 10,000 or more, "and next year it is expected 20,000 people will come."[24]

Renewed efforts were made to achieve this optimistic total. Proclaiming Frontier Days "the very best performance in the world" and "by far the biggest event of the west," the 1902 committee advertised widely, with special focus on Denver, which had sent hordes of visitors since the first Frontier Day. The committee spent $400 to import the sixty-piece, prize-winning Cook's Drum Corps from Denver. Several other bands also were paid to come. Young Marie Buchanan of Cheyenne, "the greatest lady violinist for a child her age in the world," was engaged to play at both halls on both nights for the scheduled balls. Arrangements were made for a new sensation, motion picture scenes, to be shown for free on both evenings. Small prizes were offered for the best-decorated residence and commercial building, and a record $3,000 in prizes was offered to Frontier Days contestants. Trains were scheduled to run every half hour between the depot and the arena.[25]

A major part of Frontier Days entertainment now was offered downtown, especially during the evenings. A merry-go-round was set up in a vacant lot, and a "vaudeville" troupe set up a tent on another lot and offered "hooche-kooche and other Midway features." Five bands played on the streets and at the balls, as well as at the arena. The drum corps from Denver was judged "without doubt the best musical organization in the city," while the new Imperial Military Band of Laramie played themselves "into popular favor." The Eighth Infantry band was excellent, as always, and on Thursday night, at the corner of Seventeenth and Ferguson, the Salvation Army Band and the Union Pacific Band—"in their attractive khaki uniforms"—staged an impromptu contest which was "watched by a large multitude of people."[26]

At the same busy street corner, about 6,000 people jostled for room to watch the newfangled motion pictures, projected on a large canvas suspended from the north wall of the Kent Block. A representative of the Selig Polyscope Company presented the program, which consisted of twenty-five flickering black and white scenes: a bucking horse and rider; trains in motion; cattle in the Chicago stockyards; panoramas of various canyons; a "Stage coach hold up"; a view from a hot air balloon; and miscellaneous other brief views. Frontier Days provided Cheyenne with a spectacular exhibition of the "flickers" that soon would become a sensation in America.[27]

Although trains began to depart on Thursday evening after the outdoor competitions ended, many visitors chose to stay over until Friday. Large numbers of tourists were therefore in Cheyenne for four nights, visiting stores and saloons. Hotels and restaurants were "overflowing," and the Baptist ladies sold meals at the big Burlington Depot building downtown. At the arena nearly 400 people participated in producing a "steady succession of events" and in managing the crowds. After bills were paid, the committee deposited $2,000 to carry over, and for 1903 it was decided to expand Frontier Days to three days.[28]

Within only half a dozen years, the citizens of Cheyenne had created an event that tapped into their own pioneer past, reflected the rich heritage of the Holy City of the Cow, and struck a deep response from the people of the West. Frontier Days offered an annual economic boost while providing a link between nineteenth-century Cheyenne and the unknown twentieth century. And all indications — even the weather — promised continued success. "The weather was simply perfect, just cloudy enough to keep off the sun, and the zephyrs from the right direction, and neither too hot nor too cold," rhapsodized the *Leader* on August 29, the morning after Frontier Days 1902. "All nature smiled on the great popular entertainment."

19

Cheyenne Marches to War

CHEYENNE MEN FIGHT" read a bold headline, followed by the subheading, "Participate in One of the Hottest Battles of the Philippine War."[1] This participation by volunteer soldiers from Cheyenne in combat on the other side of the world was part of an unforeseen movement that swept America into international prominence.

As the nineteenth century ended, Americans brimmed with confidence: an exploding economy soon would be recognized as the wealthiest in the world; the American people were the freest in the world; the last and most forbidding West had been conquered. Americans were proud of their accomplishments and wanted the United States to be acknowledged as a great nation. The explosion of the USS *Maine* in Spanish Cuba in 1898 triggered a war with Spain, which American military forces won within a few months. But to everyone's surprise, the first battle of the Spanish-American War took place in Manila Bay, not in Cuba, and after Spain surrendered Cuba and Puerto Rico, Americans found themselves still fighting in the Philippines. Guerrilla warfare in the Philippines lasted into the next century and cost the United States far more casualties than had been suffered in Cuba. When combat in the Philippines finally ended, Americans discovered that their nation had acquired a colony of 7,000 islands and 8 million people. The defeat of a European nation and the acquisition of a large colony halfway around the world suddenly and unexpectedly thrust the United States onto the world stage.

Cheyenne played a colorful role in these momentous events. Westerners in general were highly patriotic, and western men were familiar with firearms and unafraid of hardships and conflict. The martial spirit always had been strong in

Cheyenne; guns, gun shops, and gun ranges were commonplace in the Magic City. The amicable and profitable connection with Fort D. A. Russell heightened Cheyenne's appreciation for the military, and the community long had been willing to support a militia unit.

In July 1876, shortly after learning of the Sioux triumph over George Armstrong Custer's Seventh Cavalry, a "new military company" was organized at City Hall. Cattle baron Alexander Swan was elected captain of the Cheyenne Independent Rangers. But the Sioux scare was short-lived, and so was the Ranger company. In 1884, although Indian troubles were long over in Wyoming, the men of Cheyenne talked longingly of forming another militia company. "This is a good scheme," remarked the *Leader* sarcastically, "as it is impossible to tell at what moment the city may be invaded by the Zulus or some other bloodthirsty outfit."[2]

Within three years, despite the absence of war or rumors of war, the desire for a Cheyenne militia company heated up again. A Territorial National Guard was being organized, and with enough companies Wyoming could field a regiment. When it proved difficult to put together a company in Cheyenne, "public spirited citizens" got behind this project, as they had so many other times for the community. In the summer of 1888 a series of meetings produced the Cheyenne Guards, with F. A. Stitzer as captain. Governor Thomas Moonlight requisitioned guns and equipment from the War Department, while the company purchased kepis and blue wool blouses for fatigue uniforms. Contractor M. P. Keefe leased Keefe Hall "at a moderate figure" to the company as an armory. An Eastern outfitter was engaged, and a representative traveled to Cheyenne to take measurements for tailored dress uniforms. In October the uniforms arrived, dark gray with black stripes, and "much admired by all." A War Department shipment brought Springfield rifles "direct from government armory," along with the regulation belts, swords, bayonets, and 10,000 rounds of ammunition, half of which were blanks. On Friday night, October 2, 1888, a crowd of 500 gathered at Keefe Hall to cheer when Governor Moonlight mustered in the Cheyenne Guards as Company B of the Wyoming National Guard. Fifty-

Led by the regimental band, the Seventeenth Infantry parades past officers' row at Fort Russell in 1890. (Courtesy National Archives)

five men took an oath that prescribed a three-year enlistment, and "over 100 honorary members" were acknowledged. Company B executed "a pretty drill," then with Inman's orchestra playing, dancing "continued until a late hour."[3]

By 1891 there were seven companies of the First Regiment of the Wyoming National Guard (WNG): Co. A, Laramie; Co. B, Cheyenne; Co. C, Buffalo; Co. D, Rock Springs; Co. E, Green River; Co. F, Douglas; and Co. G, Sheridan. Future governor DeForest Richards was regimental colonel. F. A. Stitzer had been promoted to adjutant general, and W. J. Wilkes now was captain of Company B. The roster of Company B had dropped to thirty-six men, and the privates included Charles and Steve Bon, Jr., E. W. Glafcke, and other sons of prominent Cheyenne families. In 1891 Governor Barber, Adjutant General Stitzer, and Colonel Richards planned a weeklong summer encampment for the First Regiment of the WNG. Laramie would host the event, and as part of their summer maneuvers, the Seventeenth Infantry would march overland from Fort Russell and join the encampment. "The boys are ready to go," announced the *Leader*, as Company B went through drills every evening in preparation for this military adventure, and spent the last night before departure in the armory.[4]

Company B left by train for Laramie at six on Friday morning, August 21. They were met at the depot by Company A, and the local troop escorted the Cheyenne men to Camp Barber, on a plain a mile and a half south of town. "We were the first arrivals and did not have anyone to copy after in the pitching of

Regimental headquarters, built in 1893 on the Fort Russell parade ground. A bugler is playing at left. Today this fine old structure serves the base as the Warren ICBM & Heritage Museum. (Courtesy Wyoming State Archives)

tents," explained one of the part-time soldiers. But they figured it out, and soon "the Cheyenne company was safely and securely housed in thirteen tents." Cheyenne ladies had presented Company B "a beautiful banner," and it was placed "in front of company quarters." The Seventeenth Infantry marched into camp, "and in a remarkably short space their tents were in place." A captain from the 17th was assigned to report on the progress of the WNG to the War Department. Companies C and F, from Buffalo and Sheridan, had no rail connection and did not come. The five WNG companies in Camp Barber totaled about 200 men.[5]

Off-duty soldiers were allowed to go into Laramie in the evenings until ten o'clock. When one Cheyenne boy sauntered back to his tent, he was challenged by the guard, a fellow member of Company B. "Who goes there?" came the martial challenge. "Where?" replied the novice soldier. But the militia men learned quickly, marching and drilling throughout the week. One day there was a dress parade, anther day a skirmish drill. Everyone grew whiskers, because their sunburned faces were too sore to shave with straight razors.[6]

"As the days go by company B looms up stronger and stronger as the crack company in the regiment," reported a "Special Correspondent" to the *Leader*. Seventeenth Infantry regulars "swear that our company is head and shoulder above the rest of the regiment." Proud that against other companies "Cheyenne's crowd shines in comparison," not a single member of Company B reported to sick

Dress parade of the Eighth Infantry on Fort Russell parade ground in April 1897. Dress uniforms include white gloves and dress helmets. Cheyenne citizens always attended these exercises, as well as band concerts. (Courtesy Wyoming State Archives)

call during the week. In addition to night passes to Laramie, the boys shot craps and, on two different evenings, enjoyed cigars and beer kegs provided by Governor Barber. On Monday evening in Laramie, officers and the governor's staff, as well as a large number of civilian visitors, attended a dress ball. "The Laramie ladies and visitors from Cheyenne attended in full dress and their handsome costumes with the flashing gilt and glitter of the uniforms of the officers of the Seventeenth and the 1st Wyoming, made as brilliant a picture of light and color as one could wish to see." Senators Warren and Carey were there, and so were Mrs. Carey and numerous other Cheyenne women. The last night in camp, Tuesday, the Seventeenth Infantry held a dance featuring the regimental band. The tents were taken down on Wednesday morning, Governor Barber reviewed the WNG troops, and the men marched to the depot.

"A dusty, sunburned lot of soldiers got off the train [Wednesday] afternoon," reported the *Leader*. "They looked like veterans and from the way in which they lined up and acted after leaving the train might easily have been taken for returning regulars." Company F from Douglas rode on the same train, and Company B invited their new comrades-in-arms to remain overnight as their guests. Fifty-one carriages had been lined up to tour the Douglas men around town and to Fort Russell. There was always a strong social element to Cheyenne's militia companies, and inevitably there was a military hall in the Keefe Hall armory. The Union Pacific band was engaged, and before the dancing began, Company B gave "a short exhibition drill" for the crowd.[7]

Under the scrutiny of statewide newspapers and officials, Cheyenne's Company B had acquitted itself well, while progressing considerably as a military unit. But membership continued to dwindle. The nationwide depression that began in 1893 caused even more defections, as the UP laid off workers and the local economic turndown caused men to move. Cheyenne restaurateur Leopold Kabis replaced F. A. Stitzer as Wyoming's adjutant general, and in August 1893 Kabis informed Captain Wilkes that Company B "is hereby disbanded" because membership had fallen well below the required total. Wilkes was directed to turn in the company's arms and equipment to the office of the adjutant general. Kabis hoped to organize an artillery company in Cheyenne. A few months later Kabis, a member of the Cheyenne Bicycle Club, proposed forming a "cycle company" of the Wyoming National Guard in Cheyenne.[8]

A year after Company B was disbanded, twenty young men petitioned Governor John Osborne with a request to organize another WNG company in Cheyenne. Although they were a dozen signatures short, enough volunteers were recruited before the end of 1894 to form a company. The old Company B designation had been appropriated by the growing WNG regiment, so Cheyenne's new unit was mustered in as Company I. Company I also was called the Governor's Guard, and twelve of the best men were selected to mold into a precision drill team. The AOUW Hall was secured as an armory. Large crowds turned out each week to watch the drill team and to attend the monthly hops. The gray-clad drill team, regarded locally as "without doubt the crack squad of the W.N.G.," helped to revive military ardor in Cheyenne.[9]

More significant was the Cuban rebellion against Spanish colonialism that erupted in 1895. In the face of Cuban guerrilla warfare, Spanish repression revolved around a series of concentration camps, where very young and very old Cubans died by the thousands from disease and starvation. With more than $50 million invested in Cuban plantations, utilities, and railroads, Americans responded sympathetically to lurid propaganda spread by Cuban refugees and by New York newspapers. Growing American anger prompted Congress, early in 1896, to adopt a joint resolution of support for the Cuban insurrection.

By 1896, then, war fever began to grip many Americans, including a number of Cheyenne residents. With Company I thriving, Cheyenne determined to support an artillery company, a key component of the WNG regiment. Rawlins had attempted to form an artillery unit, but the little town proved unable to maintain a company. F. A. Stitzer of Cheyenne again had assumed the office of adjutant general, and he disbanded the Rawlins unit, Battery A of the WNG. General Stitzer had the two light artillery pieces shipped — free of charge by the UP — to Cheyenne, along with miscellaneous equipment and the "bright and showy uniforms," which appeared hardly to have been used. Adjutant General Stitzer enlisted newspaper help to encourage the reorganization of Battery A. "It would greatly strengthen the interest now being taken in Company I," rationalized Cheyenne's *Wyoming Tribune*, "as the members of the latter would, no doubt, endeavor to outshine the battery both in military and social circles."[10]

The battery would require forty men: a captain, two lieutenants, four sergeants, four corporals, a bugler, and twenty-eight privates. A petition with more than forty signatures soon was presented to Governor William A. Richards, who mustered in Battery A at Cheyenne in March. J. K. Jeffrey was elected captain, while bugler Phil Noble proved so talented that "every drill night his calls are listened to by a large number." Keefe Hall was leased for an armory. In addition to its earlier use as a drill arena, Keefe Hall "would furnish a better dance floor as well." Planning began to organize baseball teams from both Battery A and Company I, to play each other as well as "the Cheyenne Bicycle Club, Knickerbocker club and Fort Russell nines." The regular army uniforms were greatly admired, trimmed in red for artillery and topped by a dress helmet which sported a red plume and red cords. Battery A sometimes drilled in the streets to stimulate public enthusiasm, already excited by the Governor's Guards drill team, which performed before each of the company's regular dances.[11]

"Professor" Henry T. Irvine, who headed a popular Cheyenne orchestra, began talking about organizing a regimental band late in 1895. On Wednesday night, June 4, 1896, Irvine assembled an "enthusiastic meeting" of "about twenty Cheyenne musicians." Seventeen men were selected, and they agreed to rehearse on Monday and Saturday evenings. Dress and fatigue uniforms were requisitioned, along with "equipments." Irvine and the band members were mustered in, and a sergeant and secretary were elected. The first concert was given on Friday night, July 24, from the balcony of Keefe Hall.[12]

By 1896 Cheyenne provided a major portion of the First Wyoming Regiment of the WNG: an infantry company, the artillery battery, and the regimental band. But these units did not provide sufficient military outlet for men impassioned over the Cuban insurrection. In December 1896 there was a movement to form a volunteer company to fight in Cuba. Several soldiers from Fort Russell whose enlistments were about to expire indicated a willingness to go—probably while drinking in the West End—and so did "several young men" from Cheyenne. "There is lots of sympathy in Cheyenne for the Cuban patriots," reported the *Wyoming Tribune*, although there was not quite enough sympathy to form a company of Cuban invaders.[13]

Throughout 1897 the Cheyenne companies continued their drills, often under the direction of Maj. Thomas Wilhelm of the Eighth Infantry. Assigned as military instructor of the WNG, Major Wilhelm, who lived on Central Avenue, often opened his home for dinners or smokers for WNG officers. In January 1897 a dress inspection and dance was held at Keefe Hall. Governor Richards and his staff, attired "in full uniform," inspected the soldiers and regimental band and artillery pieces before the dancing commenced. As a February fundraiser, Battery A staged a play at the Opera House. In May, Battery A held a three-day encampment. Artillery pieces were hauled by four-horse teams, followed by a "mess wagon loaded with hard tack and other warlike provisions." Battery A marched out of town, west along Happy Jack Road for five miles to the campsite. "Many

The USS *Cheyenne*

During the Spanish-American War, the U.S. Navy pressed into service a tugboat that was named the *Cheyenne*. The *Cheyenne* was used by the Navy for only two months, July and August of 1898.

There was alarm during the war that coastal cities were vulnerable to attack by the Spanish Navy. Accordingly, in 1899 the U.S. Navy began building big-gun "monitors" to protect the coast. Senator F.E. Warren was chairman of the influential Committee on Military Affairs, and one of the 3,225-ton monitors would be named the *Wyoming*. Governor DeForest Richards and staff members traveled to San Francisco to view construction progress, and he called on the women of Wyoming to raise money for a silver service set for the officers' wardroom. Governor Richards led a Wyoming delegation to San Francisco in September 1900 for the launching ceremony, and Miss Frances Warren christened the ship.

In 1909 the monitor was renamed the USS *Cheyenne*, so that a new battleship could be named the *Wyoming*. By the time that the U.S. entered World War I in 1917, the USS *Cheyenne* was obsolete as a warship. But it was utilized as a submarine tender, then later as a training ship. In 1926 the USS *Cheyenne* was decommissioned but was kept on the reserved list for more than a decade. The navy's last surviving big-gun monitor was sold for scrap in 1939. Decades later, the name was revived for a nuclear attack submarine, and the third *Cheyenne* was launched in 1996.

(See the *Leader*, January 25 and September 8, 1900, and information available at the USS *Wyoming* and *Cheyenne* display at the Wyoming State Museum in Cheyenne.)

citizens on bicycles, horses and in buggies followed the battery to their camp," the *Leader* reported.[14]

During the next several months, "yellow journalism" continued to rouse the American public against Spain through sensational newspaper stories. When the USS *Maine* exploded in Havana harbor on February 15, 1898, 260 officers and men were killed. The furious public assumption was that Spanish operatives had sabotaged the *Maine* (today it is thought that the explosion was internal and accidental). Less than one month after the sinking of the *Maine*, on March 8 Congress responded to public war hysteria by unanimously voting President William McKinley a $50 million emergency fund for national defense. On April 13 Congress overwhelmingly adopted resolutions that recognized Cuban independence, demanded the immediate withdrawal of Spain, and authorized President McKinley to employ U.S. armed forces to carry out these resolutions. Although Spain failed to enlist any European allies, the Spanish government felt honor-bound to declare war, on April 24, 1898.

At the beginning of 1898 there were only 28,000 officers and men in the regular army. A call went out for volunteers, prompting tens of thousands of men to enlist. To outfit the newly organized volunteer units, government warehouses were emptied of uniforms, weapons, and equipment, including Civil War surplus. The War Department organized 182,000 volunteers into seven corps, providing rudimentary training in the East, South, and West—including Fort D. A. Russell.

The U.S. monitor Wyoming *was launched in 1900, christened by Frankie Warren. In 1909 the name of the monitor was changed to* Cheyenne, *so that* Wyoming *could be used on a new battleship. (Courtesy National Archives)*

The most colorful of the volunteer units were three cavalry regiments, popularly called "Rough Riders." Theodore Roosevelt, who ranched in Dakota Territory during the 1880s, developed the idea of cowboy cavalry. Cowboys could ride and shoot, and Roosevelt wrote of raising a company or even a regiment from these "harum-scarum rough riders of the West." During ensuing years other men discussed the concept of cowboy "rough riders" in future wars, including Jay L. Torrey.[15]

A graduate of the Law School of Washington University in St. Louis, Torrey was a skilled attorney who often represented causes in Washington, becoming familiar with congressmen and government officials. Torrey swiftly rose to lieutenant colonel of militia in St. Louis, then assistant adjutant general on the staff of the brigadier general. During a summer vacation to Wyoming, Judge Torrey became "enamored" of life on the range, and he acquired large ranching interests in Fremont County. Torrey was forty-four in 1898, heavyset with a thick mustache. As war clouds gathered, he drew up a bill that was introduced in Congress by Senator F. E. Warren, chairman of the Senate Committee on Military Affairs. In early March, Senator Warren introduced Torrey to President McKinley and General of the Army Nelson A. Miles, who provided an endorsement to the bill: "The services of men whose lives are spent in the saddle as herdsmen, pioneers, scouts, prospectors, etc., would be exceedingly valuable to the government in time of hostilities. They are accustomed to a life in the saddle, most excellent horsemen, fearless, intelligent, enterprising, accustomed to taking care of themselves in bivouac, skillful in landcraft, and as a rule excellent riflemen." The *Sun-Leader* added its own enthusiastic endorsement: "The western cowboy is accustomed nearly every day of his life to ride from 60 to 100 miles a day. What cavalryman has training more conducive to health, strength, endurance, picket duty and expert rifle manipulation than he?"[16]

Three volunteer cavalry regiments of "rough riders" were authorized. The First U.S. Volunteer Cavalry would train in San Antonio under Col. Leonard Wood and Lt. Col. Theodore Roosevelt. The Second U.S. Volunteer Cavalry Regiment would rendezvous at Cheyenne, then would train nearby at Fort D. A. Russell under the command of Col. Jay Torrey. The Third Cavalry, commanded by Col. Milt Grigsby of South Dakota, would muster at Sioux Falls.

While still in Washington, Torrey encouraged recruitment by telegrams and letters to Governor William Richards and to numerous personal acquaintances. Colonel Torrey arrived in Cheyenne on May 16, establishing temporary headquarters at the Inter Ocean Hotel. Western states and territories lobbied Torrey, as well as Wood and Grigsby, to accept troops into their regiments. It was decided that the twelve troops of the Second Cavalry would be composed of seven companies from Wyoming, two from Colorado, and one each from Idaho, Nevada, and Utah. Volunteers streamed into Cheyenne, "singly and in groups," from across Wyoming and the other four authorized states. "Every train added to the throng. Almost every hour in the day and night brought those who had traveled by rail 'to join Torrey.'" Recruits were interviewed by Torrey, who rejected potential troublemakers. "It is a privilege, not a right," he repeated, "to ride in this regiment." Only a few dozen volunteers failed physical examinations, and the regiment reached a total strength of 934 men. With most of Fort Russell's regular army garrison already en route to Florida to prepare for invading Cuba, the volunteers were housed in empty barracks at the fort.[17]

After six days of "fermentation," Colonel Torrey visited each barrack, where the men were loosely grouped into companies. An election by secret ballot was conducted to choose a captain, then two lieutenants. These elected officers appointed sergeants and corporals. On a plain north of the parade ground, the regiment was drawn into a hollow square three ranks deep (seated, kneeling, standing), with officers arrayed in the middle. Colonel Torrey presented each officer his shoulder straps, while Maj. Thomas Wilhelm gave Torrey his straps. After breakfast each morning the newly elected and commissioned officers assembled at the band hall to learn the next drill. The officers then went out to teach the drill to their individual companies. Afterward the novice officers filed back to the band hall to learn another drill. "The intelligence of the officers and men made this rapid work possible," reported a national magazine.[18]

Colonel Torrey secured a two-seat carriage to transport reporters between Cheyenne and Fort Russell. In addition to Cheyenne newspapers, there were reporters from the Denver *Republican*, the Denver *Evening Post*, and the Chicago *Daily Tribune*. Colonel Torrey lunched with the reporters each day, and stories about "Torrey's Rough Riders" and "Torrey's Cowboy Cavalry" were regularly filed, keeping Cheyenne in the news. While a wide search went on for 1,100 horses to satisfy Torrey's exacting standards, the regiment received Krag-Jorgensen carbines and Colt revolvers. On June 9 the regiment enjoyed its first payday when an army paymaster arrived with more than $20,000 for the Second Volunteer Cavalry.[19]

By June 9 the First Volunteer Cavalry was in Tampa Bay, Florida, having left Texas by train late in May. On June 14 the regiment of Leonard Wood and Theodore Roosevelt sailed for Cuba with an invasion force of 17,000, and less than three weeks later Roosevelt led a charge up San Juan Hill that propelled him toward the presidency and immortalized his regiment as the Rough Riders. Meanwhile, it was June 22 before Torrey finally got his regiment aboard two Union Pacific troop trains. The previous day the Second paraded through the streets of Cheyenne on their horses, before loading aboard their trains and heading toward Jacksonville, Florida.[20]

On the second day of the long journey the second train jumped the track, killing the engineer. None of the troopers or horses were injured. The trip soon continued, and in St. Louis a soldier fell from a platform and was fatally mangled. On June 26, at Tupelo, Mississippi, the second train slammed into the lead train, which had stopped for water. Five soldiers were killed and fifteen seriously injured, including Colonel Torrey. The tragic journey finally ended in Jacksonville, following six days and three accidents. But the Second suffered from oppressive heat and camp diseases in Jacksonville, and another three dozen men died in ensuing months. During the time that San Juan Hill was stormed (July 1), Puerto Rico was enveloped (in August), and the Spanish agreed to a preliminary peace

"Torrey's Rocky Mountain Riders" parade south on Carey Avenue in June 1898, just before boarding troop trains. The First Presbyterian Church is in the center of the photo, and the First Congregational Church is visible in the background at right. (Courtesy Wyoming State Archives)

treaty (August 12), the Second U.S. Volunteer Cavalry languished in Jacksonville. (Grigsby's Third Cavalry also was stuck in camp in Georgia, likewise failing to get into the war.) At last, on October 24, 1898, the Second Cavalry was mustered out in Jacksonville. The final payroll totaled about $90,000, including $100 travel money per man, although a number of men remained too ill to travel.[21]

If the fate of the Second U.S. Volunteer Cavalry was sad and anticlimactic, other Wyoming soldiers were about to find themselves in combat. After Comdr. George Dewey destroyed a Spanish fleet in Manila Bay on May 1, 1898, he made contact with Filipino *insurrectos* in rebellion against Spanish authority. While Dewey maintained a naval blockade, Filipino leader Emilio Aguinaldo declared himself president. But a U.S. ground force, totaling 11,000 regulars and volunteers—including the "Wyoming Battalion"—sailed to the Philippines. Victorious over Spain, the United States annexed the Philippines on July 7, 1898. By early 1899, the Filipinos decided they did not want merely a change of masters, and Emilio Aguinaldo led a guerrilla war against the Americans. The jungle fighting was vicious, with casualties from combat and disease. Although American forces in the Philippines eventually totaled 70,000 men, resistance did not end until April 1902.

During the scramble to raise an American army in the spring of 1898, four companies of the Wyoming National Guard were attached to the regular infantry as part of the Philippine invasion force. On May 18, 1898, two days after Col. Jay Torrey set up his headquarters at the Inter Ocean Hotel, the Wyoming Battalion set out by train for San Francisco, where oceangoing troop transports were being collected and provisioned. The 11,000-man force left in three contingents: the Wyoming Battalion steamed west with the third contingent on June 29. The trip across the Pacific took five weeks, with a stopover in Hawaii. At Manila Bay, sunken Spanish ships cluttered the harbor, while Dewey's fleet stood in blockade. The three contingents assembled and marched toward the walled city of Manila. Two weeks of fighting ensued, and "the Wyomings" saw their first combat.[22]

Cheyenne's Battery A, sometimes called "The Wyoming Light Artillery" and "The Alger Light Artillery," also was sent to San Francisco, sailing for the Philippines on November 9, 1898. Arriving at Manila Bay in December, battery members were met by soldiers of the Wyoming Battalion, including Joe Onhaus of Cheyenne, who wrote home: "The battery arrived the day before yesterday, but have not landed yet. We have been out to see them and they are all in good health and spirits." The newcomers were informed that the Wyoming Battalion's baseball team was undefeated, and that there was "a slight earthquake shock the other day and the sensation was novel." Also novel were bananas and coconuts. Battery member William Gauff wrote home that he had been transferred to Battery A of the regular army.[23]

The Wyoming Light Artillery set up "four big field guns" at the end of the peninsula about three miles from Cavite. The Cheyenne artillerymen fired their first shots on February 15, 1899, after *insurrectos* opened fire on outlying guard-posts. "We have fired the guns and are tin soldiers no more," exulted a battery member in a letter to the Cheyenne *Sun-Leader*. "When the insurgents drove in our outposts, and Mauser bullets were flying fast on all sides and whistling over-head, we did some fine shooting. Capt. Clarke, chewing a cigar, coolly gave his orders and behaved like a true soldier. We hit a block house 4,500 yards away and Maj. Rice threw up his hat and said, 'Boys, that was a fine shot.' He now thinks we are somebody."[24]

Two days later, the *Sun-Leader* published a lengthy letter from the battery commander, Capt. Harry Clarke. "Our forces are driving the natives into the interior from the vicinity of Manila," reported Captain Clarke. "The battery up to this time has fired nearly 75 rounds of shells and shrapnel and our organization has already secured quite a reputation for good marksmanship.... Last night we fired two shells at some parties who were making signals with the lights, the distance being about 3,500 yards, but the lights went out very quickly after the first shot." Captain Clarke described in detail the rather comfortable camp enjoyed by the Cheyenne battery. "The surf bathing at our camp is simply elegant, there being a beautiful beach of fine white sand."[25]

Cheyenne newspapers regularly published stories about "WYOMING IN MANILA," along with letters from the soldiers. Cheyenne residents thus experienced vicariously exotic aspects of the Philippines, as well as combat adventures in which "the gallant Wyoming battalion was always foremost." In March, front-page headlines proudly proclaimed: "OUR WYOMING BATTALION LEADS TO

VICTORY," heading a charge on March 7 which dislodged insurgents at San Juan del Monte. No one was hit in this attack, but later in the month Pvt. Ray Weidmer was killed by a sniper's bullet. Weidmer was a Cheyenne volunteer who had worked in the UP shops and whose father, Rudolph, still lived in the Magic City — "his sorrow cannot be described." (Early in 1900 the government shipped "the Cheyenne boys" — Weidmer, William Holden, Charles Rogers, Charles Wilseck, and Clyde Woods — back to the Magic City for final burial at home.)[26]

Governor Richards often pointed out, and newspapers regularly repeated, that Wyoming "has more volunteer troops in proportion to her population than any other state in the Union." (There were fewer than 300 volunteer troops from Wyoming, but the U.S. population was more than 75 million, while the Wyoming population numbered only 92,000.) Patriotic lads from Cheyenne High School formed a unit of cadets, obtaining uniforms from Adjutant General Stitzer and drilling at CHS. Stitzer, anticipating a call for more troops by the government, began planning to raise and equip a reorganized regiment of volunteers. When the Wyoming Battalion and Battery left Cheyenne bound for the Philippines, "they were equipped, as far as possible, with the supplies on hand in possession of the adjutant general." Stitzer applied to the War Department for reimbursement, and in June the adjutant general received "a number of big boxes containing rifles, ammunition, tents, sabers, saddles, blankets, etc." Stitzer hoped to use three companies, at Evanston, Kemmerer, and Sundance, "which have signified

---

142   CHEYENNE. WYOMING TUESDAY EVENING: MARCH 7, 1899.

Our Wyoming Battalion Leads to Victory

PLACED IN THE POST OF HONOR THEY ELECTRIFY THE ARMY BY THEIR VALOR.

Company C Made an Impetuous Dash Upon the Insurgents, Followed by the Other Wyoming Companies and Our Army Closes With Them.

THE INSURGENTS DRIVEN ALONG THE PASSIG RIVER AND SHELLED BY GUNBOATS.

from their earthworks and fled, closely pursued by the Wyomingites.

Retreat was cut off in all directions save toward the Pasig river, and as the insurgents turned that way they were met by the pitiless shelling of the gunboats.

ness not occurred, the Wyoming boys were scheduled to reach home in April. Lieut. Pest was a passenger on the steamer Zealandia, which reached San Francisco after a rough trip, during which she encountered a typhoon of 48 hours' duration. The ship was considerably damaged, several of the men

Headline story in the Leader praised the combat exploits of Wyoming units in the Philippines.

their desire to enlist for service with the general government." To these companies Stitzer would add elements of the disbanded Second Volunteer Cavalry, "seven troops of which were raised in Wyoming," if he could persuade "Col. Torrey [to] undertake the work" of reorganization.[27]

This rather far-fetched regiment never materialized, but Cheyenne men continued to fight in the Philippines. In 1900, even though the Wyoming Battalion and Battery had been brought home, there was a Cheyenne contingent with the Twenty-second Infantry. In the summer of 1900 Fred Hagen wrote to friends in Cheyenne describing the jungle skirmishing during the rainy season, including a pursuit of snipers that inspired a *Sun-Leader* headline: "CHEYENNE MEN FIGHT."[28]

Other Cheyenne men were close to the front as packers, both in the Philippines and in Cuba. If Torrey's Cavalry had been unable to reach Cuba, "at least forty men from Wyoming" landed with the Cuban invasion force as members of the pack service. "Many are from Cheyenne," explained Chief Packer Thomas Mooney, in town during a six-day leave from Cuban occupation in 1899. Mooney long had worked at Camp Carlin and Fort Russell and had made his home in Cheyenne. "You see," he told a *Sun-Leader* reporter, "we have 23 pack trains in Cuba and 13 men to the train, making 299 men.... Of the Cheyenne boys, John Eckhorst took my place as chief packmaster. He is enjoying good health, as is Roy Baxter, Tom Murphy, Billy Mueer and other old Camp Carlin boys. I want to tell you that I have never met an Eighth or Seventeenth infantry man but that he referred to Fort Russell and Cheyenne as paradise, and wished he were back and said he never knew how well off he was when he was here."[29]

The next year Hector Robatille wrote to his sister from the Philippines, where he was in the pack service. "The writer says all the Cheyenne boys are doing well and getting fat and saucy," reported the *Sun-Leader*. "Harry Witt is chief packer, while Will Fisher is in Mr. Robatille's train, No. 38."[30]

Through the artillery battery and other soldiers who fought in the Philippines, along with the cavalry regiment that had trained with such fanfare in their midst, the people of Cheyenne developed a keen sense of involvement in America's turn-of-the-century combat. While fighting still raged in the Philippine jungles, a thirty-foot-tall "Soldiers' Monument" was planned for placement on the Capitol grounds. Entitled "Taking the Oath," the handsome statue stands on a prominent corner of the Capitol, and the base proudly proclaims:[31]

ERECTED TO
THE MEMORY OF
THE HEROES OF
THE SPANISH
AMERICAN WAR

"Taking the Oath," a statue placed on the Capitol grounds to honor the men of Wyoming who volunteered for service in the Spanish-American War. (Photo by Karon O'Neal)

1900–
1903

"Killing is my specialty. I look at it as a business proposition, and I think I have a corner on the market."
Tom Horn

"We, the jury, ... do find the defendant, Tom Horn, guilty of murder in the first degree."
Judge R.H. Scott
Reading the jury's verdict

"The 1902–1903 Cheyenne City directory listed 468 business entities, with several conducting multiple businesses at one location.... Cheyenne was the home of three railroads, four newspapers, 18 restaurants, 14 grocery stores, four churches [at least eight others were unlisted], seven pool table rooms, two banks, two plumbers, and one library. There were 20 active union organizations, and 36 secret and fraternal societies along with 21 clubs listed including ours, the Young Men's Literary Club."
Joseph R. Marek in a 2001 address to the Young Men's Literary Club

"Cheyenne is becoming a metropolitan city."
Cheyenne Daily Leader, August 22, 1903

20

Into a New Century

The Great Man Will Be Given a Rousing Reception by the Citizens of Wyoming." This confident prediction was offered on Monday morning, September 24, 1900, by the Cheyenne *Daily Leader* in heady anticipation of an evening visit by "Teddy, the Rough Rider."[1]

Theodore Roosevelt, the governor of New York and hero of San Juan Hill, was campaigning in the West on behalf of incumbent President William McKinley, and for himself as vice-presidential candidate on the Republican ticket for the election of 1900. A few days earlier, Governor DeForest Richards and Senator F. E. Warren led a Wyoming delegation to Ogden, Utah, to welcome Roosevelt and accompany him on his campaign train. Roosevelt appeared in Salt Lake City, then headed toward Wyoming. A phone call to Wyoming from "The Gallant Soldier" heightened anticipation in Cheyenne, where flags and bunting were displayed all over town. On Monday, while hundreds of people from northern Wyoming streamed into Cheyenne, Roosevelt spoke in the morning at Rawlins, then proceeded to Laramie, with a whistle-stop appearance at Medicine Bow.[2]

In Cheyenne the rousing reception that had been planned was literally dampened by a daylong rain, as well as cold temperatures. When the famous candidate arrived late in the afternoon, he was "greeted by the gubernatorial salute of seventeen guns." A short carriage ride brought Roosevelt to the Inter Ocean Hotel. From the balcony he was scheduled to review an elaborate parade—which had to be canceled because of the weather and sloppy streets. But large crowds gathered inside the Cheyenne Opera House and Turner Hall, with an aggregate total of 3,500 spectators. At seven o'clock Senator Warren introduced Roosevelt at Turner Hall, while simultaneous addresses were being made to the crowd at the Opera

Famed Rough Rider Theodore Roosevelt first came to Cheyenne in 1900 while campaigning for vice-president, and his image appeared frequently in local newspapers. He returned in 1903—spectacularly, on horseback—as president.

House. An hour later Roosevelt stalked onstage at the Opera House and forcefully repeated his campaign speech in his high-pitched, staccato delivery.[3]

The next morning, Dr. Amos Barber rode to the Inter Ocean Hotel leading "one of the best horses that Laramie County can produce." The forty-one-year-old Roosevelt was renowned for his physical vigor, and the two men set out on horseback for Fort Russell. They were joined en route by R.S. Van Tassell and Arthur Porter, a rancher and a distant relative of Roosevelt. After Fort Russell, the riders looped into the countryside, and TR set a fast pace: "The last five miles of the ride were covered in surprisingly swift time." After returning to town, reported the *Leader*, "The quartette galloped down Capitol avenue at a lively pace." Before boarding the train for Denver, Roosevelt exulted, "That was as nice a spurt as I have ever had since I punched cows in Montana."[4]

Citizens of the Holy City of the Cow responded warmly to the former rancher, who had mastered the cowboy's skills and who had avidly hunted across the West. Indeed, there was passionate support for Roosevelt throughout the West, as well as much of the rest of the United States. Within a year of his visit to Cheyenne, Roosevelt was president, following the assassination of McKinley. "Now look," groaned Senator Mark Hanna, "that damned cowboy is President of the United States." But President Roosevelt, bristling with awesome energy and ability, led his fellow Americans into the twentieth century with an aggressive drive toward national greatness.

Less than two years after assuming the presidency, Roosevelt returned to Cheyenne for a memorable western adventure. Senator Warren had developed a friendship with President Roosevelt and often was a guest at the White House. Aware of an upcoming presidential tour through the West, and recalling how much Roosevelt had enjoyed his horseback ride in 1900, Warren suggested a cross-country saddleman's trek from Laramie to Cheyenne. Roosevelt was characteristically enthusiastic, and Senator Warren began working on details in Washington, while in Cheyenne an arrangements committee was formed. The committee included Acting Governor Fenimore Chatterton, Mayor M.P. Keefe,

Col. E. A. Slack, former governor Dr. Amos W. Barber, and other community leaders.[5]

Cheyenne, of course, had enjoyed a long history of hosting celebrities, and the Magic City outdid itself for this occasion. A three-day itinerary was worked out, including not only a fifty-six-mile ride but a scaled-down version of Frontier Days. In Cheyenne a handmade saddle worth $400 was crafted for Roosevelt, as was a set of "finest bluesteel" spurs. Money was raised by the arrangements committee, including a $500 appropriation each from the city and from the state. A presidential platform was erected at Frontier Park, and another for an open-air speech at Eddy and Nineteenth.[6]

President Roosevelt entered Wyoming, as he had done in 1900, from the west in a special train. The presidential train arrived in Laramie before eight on Saturday morning, May 31. A reception party drove President Roosevelt through Laramie to the University of Wyoming, and he spoke to a crowd from the front steps of the main building. Then President Roosevelt and his riding companions mounted nearby horses. Wearing khaki pants and lace-up leggings with his coat and tie, TR settled into his new saddle, then struck out across the mountainous terrain. He was accompanied by Senator Warren, Dr. Barber, R. S. Van Tassell, Arthur Porter, Surgeon General Rixey of the U.S. Navy, U.S. Marshal Frank Hadsell, Deputy Marshal Joe LeFors, W. L. Park, superintendent of the Union Pacific Railroad, and half a dozen other dignitaries. After noon, with an exhilarated Roosevelt in the lead, the riders reached Van Tassell's ranch, where lunch

Halting for a photograph during President Roosevelt's 56-mile, cross-country ride from Laramie to Cheyenne. Senator F. E. Warren is third from left; fourth from left is noted lawman N. K. Boswell; next is deputy U.S. marshal Joe LeFors; in front of LeFors is the president. (Courtesy Wyoming State Archives)

and fresh horses awaited (there were five relays of horses along the route). A rail connection was nearby, and Senator Warren (who was fifty-eight) and a few others finished the trip on the waiting presidential train.[7]

After two o'clock President Roosevelt and the other riders headed out for Fort D. A. Russell. A few miles from the fort, Acting Governor Chatterton, a rancher and expert rider, met the president with a short welcome speech, then accompanied him the rest of the way. Riding into Fort Russell at four o'clock, President Roosevelt was greeted with a twenty-one-gun salute. Following a brief reception at the Commanding Officers' Quarters, the party headed to town along Happy Jack Road, crossing Crow Creek Bridge and on to downtown where a large parade had formed. The president was supposed to ride in the lead carriage, but impulsively he decided to stay aboard his mount, a superbly trained horse from Douglas named Rag-a-Long.

"Roosevelt's entry into the city and his triumphant ride up Ferguson street was typical of a president who was once a cow-puncher in a cow country," admired the *Leader*. "On the hurricane deck of a Wyoming mustang, ... he entered Cheyenne as a MAN."[8]

The parade destination was the speaker's platform at Nineteenth and Eddy, where 10,000 people had gathered in the streets and an adjacent lot. Introduced by Senator Warren, the president energetically began his speech a little after seven o'clock, and soon "cheer after cheer broke from the assembled throng." During this Memorial Day speech, Roosevelt acknowledged the Civil War heroism of Warren, and in discussing the Monroe Doctrine, he cited "a proverb I heard in the old days when I myself lived in the cow country. The proverb ran: 'Don't draw unless you mean to shoot.' (Cheers)" The *Leader* was impressed: "Roosevelt was a cowboy again, speaking to those who lived in cow country."[9]

On Sunday morning President Roosevelt conducted business with his secretaries for a couple of hours in the Inter Ocean Hotel, then was escorted by carriage with Senator Warren and others to the First Methodist Church. A standing-room-only crowd worshiped with the president, and a highlight of the service was a violin solo by Marie Buchanan. Following the service the presidential entourage went to lunch at the Carey mansion, where "Mrs. Carey proved herself a charming and accomplished hostess" — as well as a forgiving one, because F. E. Warren was one of the Carey guests (eight years earlier Warren had derailed Joseph Carey's senatorial career, but the Careys graciously accepted him into their home because of the magnitude of the occasion). During the afternoon TR, mounted on Rag-a-Long, accompanied Warren on a ride to his Terry Ranch, thirteen miles south of town. A crowd of more than 125 had come by horseback, carriages, and bicycle to share a five-course meal under a large tent (the presidential party ate in the dining room of the Warren ranch house). It was nearly nine o'clock on Sunday night before TR and Rag-a-Long returned to the Inter Ocean Hotel.[10]

On Monday morning, Senator Warren arrived at the Inter Ocean in a carriage, escorting the president to Frontier Park. About "12,000 people were gathered around the gigantic oval" as Roosevelt and his party ascended the platform. As the crowd "cheered enthusiastically," Senator Warren presented Rag-a-Long as a gift to the president, then put the horse through some of his tricks. Roosevelt was delighted: "I shall rechristen the horse 'Wyoming' to commemorate this state, and I shall be proud at Washington to be riding so fine a horse, which comes from the cow country I love so well."[11]

Thad Sowder was brought to the presidential stand, and Senator Warren started to introduce the cowboy champion. "You don't have to tell me who Mr. Sowder is," replied TR. "I am glad to meet you." Sowder took off his world championship belt for the president's inspection. Later in the morning Sowder rode Steamboat, "one of the most notorious buckers in the country." Other buckers ridden included "the Warren Live Stock company's famous outlaw Dynamite," a horse called Oh Hell, and another one named Teddy Roosevelt. The bucking exhibition was exceptional, and there also was a bareback ride and a wild steer ride. Three contestants entered the Ladies' Cow Pony Race, and frenetic action broke out during the Wild Horse Race. Although the Steer Roping competition proved disappointing, the Stakes Race was exciting. The *Leader* did not exaggerate: "GREATEST COWBOY CARNIVAL EVER HELD IN THE WEST GIVEN HERE TO-DAY FOR BENEFIT OF ROOSEVELT." Reluctantly Roosevelt departed for his train after noon, "waving his hat and bowing to the crowds as long as he was in sight."

It was obvious that President Roosevelt had reveled in the three days of western experiences that Cheyenne had provided him — "as pleasant a 48 [*sic*] hours as any President ever spent since the White House was built," he proclaimed at Frontier Park. Since its earliest years, Cheyenne had entertained famous generals, beautiful actresses, and other presidents. But in President Roosevelt the Magic City found its most responsive guest, and in turn he brought out the creative best in the people of Cheyenne. The exciting events of the long weekend brought back his years as a "ranchman" during the 1880s, without which, he felt, "I would never have become President of the United States." Despite his nostalgia for the nineteenth-century West, however, President Roosevelt was the embodiment of progressive, hard-driving Americans of the twentieth century. And like Roosevelt, Cheyenne found itself in transition during the early years of the twentieth century — with deep roots extending back to the nineteenth century.

An unwelcome transition occurred one month before President Roosevelt rode into Cheyenne. On Tuesday morning, April 28, 1903, Governor DeForest Richards died at the age of fifty-six. A banker in Douglas, Richards had moved with his wife and two children to Cheyenne after his election as governor in 1898. The Richards family made their home in the magnificent mansion built by Max Idleman on the corner of Ferguson and Twenty-fourth, across the street from the State Capitol. A highly capable executive, Governor Richards traveled extensively, bringing new methods back to Wyoming. He was reelected in 1902 by a large margin, but fell ill of "inflammation of the kidneys" a few months into his second term. Governor Richards died after two weeks bedridden in the Executive Mansion. His remains lay in state in the Capitol rotunda. On Thursday, April 30, funeral services were held in the House chamber, and the funeral cortège to Lakeview Cemetery "was the longest ever seen in the city."[12] Secretary of State Fenimore Chatterton became acting governor.

Graveside memorial in Lakeview Cemetery to Governor DeForest Richards, who died in 1903 during his fifth year in office. (Photo by Karon O'Neal)

Within months Harriet Richards, wife of former Governor W. A. Richards, died at forty-eight in Washington, D.C. After serving as governor, 1895–99, Richards moved to Washington, where Senator F. E. Warren helped him become commissioner of the General Land Office. Mrs. Richards was brought back to Cheyenne for funeral services at the First Baptist Church, where she had been extremely active, and for burial at Lakeview Cemetery. A year or so later Governor Richards moved back to Cheyenne.[13] Another former first lady of Wyoming, Helen Warren, died in 1902 (as described in Chapter 17).

Judge John Slaughter, one of the first settlers of Cheyenne, died on December 5, 1903, at the age of ninety-four. Slaughter had arrived at Cheyenne in 1867 as an agent for a Denver lumber company. He was an early justice of the peace in Cheyenne and a long-time member of the school board. When the Wyoming Territorial Library was created in 1871, Judge Slaughter was appointed territorial librarian, a post he held for thirty years. One of his sons had been murdered during a stagecoach robbery, and Slaughter had been a widower since 1897. State offices were closed during his funeral. A direct link to Cheyenne's founding, Judge Slaughter was borne to his grave by Joseph M. Carey, E. W. Whitcomb, and other distinguished old friends.[14]

A landmark passage occurred the previous year, when Esther Morris died on April 2, 1902, at eighty-nine. The Wyoming pioneer was the first American woman to hold public office, as a justice of the peace in 1869. Another link to the past was lost, but a statue of Mrs. Morris graces the approach to Wyoming's State Capitol.[15]

A related transition took place at the end of 1903. Col. E. A. Slack, son of Esther Morris by her first marriage, was clerk of the District Court and had the pleasure of swearing in his mother as justice of the peace in South Pass in 1869.

He ran a weekly newspaper in South Pass before moving his operation to Laramie. Then he decided to transfer his *Daily Sun* from Laramie to Cheyenne in 1876. Colonel Slack erected a two-story brick building on Ferguson Street and a residence on the northwest corner of Ferguson and Nineteenth. A community booster and leader, he regularly worked in his office until two, three, or four in the morning. In 1895 he bought the *Leader*, and for a time he called his publication the *Daily Sun-Leader*, although later the name reverted to the familiar *Daily Leader*. In 1897 Slack provided key leadership in initiating Frontier Days. But by 1903 he was in his sixties, and he wanted to remain involved in community affairs. "Realizing that the varied demands of the newspaper business were increasing with the growth of the city and the state, and that it called for young men of energy, it seemed prudent to let the work be taken up by others." The others were Capt. Harry Clarke, who had worked as a business manager for twelve years (except for his service in the Philippines as commander of the Cheyenne Battery) and stockholder Wallace Bond. Clarke purchased Slack's interest in the *Leader*, while Bond assumed Slack's duties as editor. Colonel Slack sold out on December 29, 1903, and by coincidence, earlier in that same month Herman Glafcke died — the man who had sold the *Leader* to Slack.[16]

Another important institutional transition took place in 1903, when Prof. J. C. Churchill ended his long tenure as superintendent of Cheyenne's public schools. Churchill had taken over from N. E. Stark in 1885, and during the next eighteen school years, student growth mirrored the steady growth of Cheyenne's population. In the fall of 1901, for the first time more than 1,000 students attended Cheyenne schools. During the 1890s, Churchill superintended the building of Cheyenne High School and a fourth elementary school, hired more teachers, and taught at CHS. As the leading educator in Cheyenne, Professor Churchill was included in numerous civic and social events. But his wife suffered health problems and began spending most of her time in the "milder climate" of California, where Churchill joined her each summer. He also experienced friction with school board members, and in June 1903 Churchill tendered his resignation. Before the month was over the school board selected a new superintendent, thirty-four-year-old Henry E. Conrad of Ohio, a married man with four children.[17]

Professor Conrad acted to relieve overcrowding in the four elementary schools by departmentalizing the seventh and eighth grades and moving them to the high school. Only about 115 students per year had been attending the big high school, which easily accommodated the 159 seventh- and eighth-graders who came out of the elementary schools.[18]

Another Conrad innovation was an increased emphasis on athletics, a precursor of the sports obsession that would sweep across America during the twentieth century. Conrad was aided by the new high school principal, "Professor Ryther," a sports enthusiast who would coach CHS teams throughout the year — "all of the sports which go to make high school life in the cities so attractive," according to the *Leader*. At the start of school a CHS Athletic Club was organized with forty-four members. Uniforms and equipment for football and basketball were ordered, and Ryther, "an old-time football player," began daily gridiron practice. Conrad and Ryther developed a plan to remove the boilers in the CHS basement, "and by installing a steam plant, give sufficient room for the establishment of a modern gymnasium." A gymnasium would allow "physical culture [to] be made a daily part of the high school pupils, not only with the young gentlemen but with the young ladies also."[19]

On Saturday afternoon, October 3, Coach Ryther matched the CHS juniors against an eleven made up of seniors, sophomores, and freshmen. It was the first football game in Cheyenne in a couple of years, and "a large crowd of people" gathered to watch the juniors win, 6–5. Coach Ryther acted as referee, and the spectators admired "many brilliant plays." The Cheyenne Athletic Club also organized a football squad and began looking for games with Fort Russell and Laramie teams. When the seventeen-man squad from Carlisle Indian College stopped in Cheyenne en route to a series of games in California, a crowd of football fans gathered to watch the famous team practice near the depot.[20]

When basketball season began, the local sporting scene was dominated by Cheyenne Business College. The previous year CBC was declared champion of Wyoming, Colorado, and Nebraska, after beating "every team they played." In one home game before 600 spectators at Turner Hall, CBC crushed the University of Nebraska, 42–28. For the 1903–04 season, CBC returned all five starters from the championship team, and also fielded a girls' squad. Almost any occasion in Cheyenne was regarded as a social opportunity, so following every game there was a dance.[21]

In addition to the sudden football craze and interest in the new game of basketball (invented just a dozen years earlier), Cheyenne sportsmen still enjoyed baseball every spring. Aside from the semi-pro Indians, there were neighborhood nines and teams from CHS and Fort Russell. Along with boating, Lake Minnehaha now boasted a launch. In June 1903 "prominent men" incorporated the Rocky Mountain Country Club.[22]

For sportsmen-gamblers, prizefighting exerted the same irresistible appeal that had captivated Cheyenne since the founding of the Magic City. On December 8, 1903, for example, the *Leader* reported that "200 Cheyenne sportsmen assembled near the city at 1 o'clock this morning to witness the ten-round fight between Tom Kinsley of Denver and 'Kid' Gregory of Cheyenne." (Throughout the Progressive reform era, before and after the turn of the century, prizefighting was in official disfavor, which is why boxing matches were held somewhere "near the city.") In the fifth round "Kinsley landed a straight right very low," and Kid Gregory could not continue. The defeat of Cheyenne's fighter was disputed, triggering immediate talk of a rematch.

Fight fans had a novel treat on Monday night, January 22, 1900. Motion pictures, or "flickers," of the heavyweight championship fight between the reigning champ, Jim Jeffries, and challenger Tom Sharkey were shown at the Cheyenne Opera House. The Jeffries-Sharkey match was staged under 400 lamps at Coney Island on November 3, 1899. The first prizefight to be filmed under artificial lighting turned into a brutal brawl, with the powerful Jeffries pounding Sharkey for twenty-five rounds (the challenger had to be taken to the hospital). The Cheyenne audience saw the full twenty-five rounds, and found the film "perfectly clear from start to finish and entirely clear of any flicking."[23]

In July 1901, the First Methodist Church was crowded for two nights when Thomas Edison's Biograph Pictures presented a film of the famous Passion Play of Oberammergau, Germany. Marie Buchanan introduced the program with a violin solo and was "enthusiastically encored and responded with another selection equally delightful." In 1902 Leopold Kabis purchased two Mutoscopes to present pictures with "lifelike motion" at his Depot Cafe. During Frontier Days in August 1902, a representative of the Selig Polyscope Company projected twenty-five scenes onto a large canvas suspended from a wall of the Kent Block. The outdoor showings mesmerized about 6,000 onlookers both nights.[24]

On two consecutive nights in January 1903, "the largest collection of moving pictures ever seen here" was exhibited in Turner Hall. In May 1903 "Prof. E. Clarke" set up a projector on the balcony of the Inter Ocean Hotel and showed films, including "many Cheyenne and Wyoming views," against a wall across the street.[25] That same year *The Great Train Robbery*, an outdoor drama inspired by the Wild Bunch of Wyoming fame, created a sensation among filmgoers. The motion picture industry rapidly became the most popular source of entertainment in America, and during the first few years of the twentieth century Cheyenne was given a tantalizing introduction to moving pictures.

Another invention, one which swept America with even greater effect than

The Eagles Lodge on Thomes Street housed Turner Hall. Built in 1892, Turner Hall was regularly rented out for dances and varied other uses, including theatrical performances. In January 1903 motion pictures were shown. (Courtesy Wyoming State Archives)

movies, also was introduced to Cheyenne early in the twentieth century. In 1901 a wag mentioned that a "horseless carriage" had been purchased by the Union Pacific. It was a push cart for transferring the mail from the depot to the Cheyenne post office. But in early August 1901 UP master mechanic W. R. McKeen bought "a beautiful runabout" from a Denver agency. The automobile was driven to Cheyenne and delivered to McKeen. "It is propelled by a motor operated by gasoline and is attractively built," admired the *Leader*. McKeen drove his auto for the first time on Cheyenne streets on Sunday morning, August 4, 1901. "The genial master mechanic treated a large number of friends to rides about the city and the novelty was greatly enjoyed." Before Henry Ford began mass manufacturing affordable Model T's in 1908, the automobile was regarded as a rich man's toy. But the first auto owned by a Cheyenne resident was purchased, not by a Carey or Warren or Van Tassell, but by a shop mechanic who understood and was fascinated by the potential of the gasoline-powered horseless carriage.[26]

Before the month was out, another Cheyenne resident bought an automobile, and in June 1902, Joe George purchased an auto in parts and assembled it in his bicycle shop. At an auto show held in Chicago in February 1903, Wyoming rancher John D. Morley, who resided in Cheyenne, was carried away by the "new fangled things" and bought two automobiles and two "autobicycles" (motorbikes), while an Idaho rancher also purchased an auto. Show sponsors proudly announced that "this is the first sale of automobiles to western ranch owners for

Vehicles for rent at J. M. Newman's Livery Stable. Note the horse-drawn hearse at right. By the turn of the century, William Dinneen owned five stables around town, but in 1906 he opened an automobile agency. (Courtesy Wyoming State Archives)

practical use." Apparently the sponsors envisioned cowboys working the pastures astride motorbikes.[27]

By June 1903 the *Leader* was moved to write an editorial on "THE AUTO RAGE" in Cheyenne. A month later a story entitled "AUTO CRAZE" revealed that "over a dozen well known business and professional men are victims of the horseless carriage microbe." George Nagle, the youthful heir to the fortune of Erasmus Nagle, was "arranging to exchange his fine touring car, which is a 10-horse power Autocar, for a big 15-horsepower Peerless, which will generate more power and higher speed." Harry Hynds, merchants Myer Frank and Max Meyer, and Dr. J. P. Conway were among several others "who are preparing to order automobiles." Bicycle dealer J. D. Pratt had "ordered a 10-horsepower Conrad machine," and he planned to open an auto agency, which "will doubtless create a new era in Cheyenne." Pratt intended to drive potential customers into the countryside in his new touring car. Livery stable man William Dinneen, who owned five stables around town, within a few years opened an automobile agency.[28]

A large passenger car already made hourly trips between Fort Russell and Cheyenne, providing the city's first bus service. Samuel Corron devised a "turntable for the examination and repair of his auto," which caused other enthusiasts to plan their own. In August 1903 a new Cheyenne physician, Dr. E. E. Hill, purchased "a fine automobile," prompting the *Leader* to herald: "Cheyenne is becoming a metropolitan city."[29]

This metropolitan city began the new century with a population of 14,087, a one-fourth increase over the Census of 1890, and by 1903 the total increased to approximately 16,000. The street accidents and wrecks that regularly occurred in nineteenth-century Cheyenne increased in frequency when the Magic City en-

Cheyenne Clubs

Since its earliest years Cheyenne had offered a variety of clubs which had provided social outlets as well as organized means of furthering causes within the city. On May 8, 1903, the *Leader* published a list of current clubs in Cheyenne, excluding fraternal organizations:

Women's Club
Young Women's Club
Young Men's Club
Alpha Club
Whittier Club
Browning Club
Shakespeare Club

Tuesday Night Club
Hospital Aid Society
Episcopal Guild
Daughters of the American Revolution
The Congregational Bible Study Club
Daughters of the King
Whist Club
T.T. Club
Eastern Star
Saturday Musical Club
Baptist Willing Workers
Epworth League
Women's Relief Corps
Christian Endeavors
St. Mary's Altar Society

tered the twentieth century. There were more people, more vehicles, and more accidents. In July 1901, for example, when Judge Miller drove three women out to Fort Russell, the discharge of the sunset gun startled the horses, which broke the doubletree and spilled the passengers. The pleasure riders, shaken up and slightly injured, were taken home in an army ambulance.[30]

Less than two weeks later, Fred Hagan, coachman for Governor DeForest Richards, was badly trampled by a team of horses he was leading. "The frenzied animals, in their frantic plunges, struck Hagan in the chest with their hoofs and beat him almost into insensibility," the *Leader* reported. Hagan was taken to the county hospital for a long convalescence. Before the end of 1901 the daughter of E. W. Whitcomb was dragged by a colt after a buggy shaft broke. Ida Whitcomb, "an accomplished horse woman," could not hold the inexperienced horse, and she and her female companion tumbled onto the street when the buggy overturned. Both women "escaped by a miracle with hardly a scratch."[31]

On Cheyenne's south side in March 1902, a boy plinked a horse with a beanshooter. The frightened animal stampeded, dragging a wagon behind him. When the horse and careening wagon headed toward two-year-old Edna Miller, the little girl's mother shielded her and was herself trampled and injured. The following month a graveside funeral service for an elderly Civil War veteran featured volley firing, which unnerved the team of horses hitched to a three-seat carriage used by the six pallbearers. On the way back to town the nervous horses bolted, and everyone in the carriage was spilled. Injuries ranged from broken bones to deep lacerations to a dislocated shoulder. In August 1902 there were two wild runaways on succeeding days. Two women were riding in each of the buggies that overturned, and all four women were injured.[32]

In 1903 Margaret Grimes was twenty-five and engaged to a New York businessman. The daughter of Dr. R. B. Grimes, who had died the previous year, Margaret had attended school in Cheyenne and was popular because "of her jovial, genial ways," reported the *Leader*. "She was a peerless equestrienne and used to ride the wildest animals with the greatest ease and grace." But on a winter ride in February 1903, Margaret lost control and her horse fell on her. Her health declined precipitously after the accident, and in September Margaret was seized with convulsions and died.[33]

Cheyenne's leading architect, William Dubois, was bucked off a horse in June, breaking an arm and dislocating his elbow. In October John Smith, Jr., son of a longtime Cheyenne carpenter, was instantly killed during a runaway. A coal deliveryman, Smith was headed home at the end of the day when his team stampeded. As the dray hurtled westward on Eighteenth, Smith was dashed into the street, landing on his head. In his late twenties when he died, Smith left a widow and three children.[34]

Although numerous other runaways occurred in 1903, there were no other fatalities on the streets.[35] The rail yards, however, proved more dangerous than ever. In January, Jesse Jessen, a local air brake inspector, was run over by a freight train. Jesse's legs were amputated, and he died soon after at the county hospital. The next month John Bolin, "an old resident of the south side," was killed when he was struck by an eastbound train while he was gathering discarded coal in the yards. After surviving a serious runaway with permanent injuries several years earlier, Bolin had been reduced to searching for coal around the tracks.[36]

Charles Linn, a resident of Cheyenne for eighteen years and the father of ten children, was killed in April while loading pipe onto a flatcar. There was another work-related fatality in April, although not in the rail yards. Charles Chaffee, an eighteen-year-old orphan, was employed by house mover Frank Joslin. Joslin moved houses by placing them on "mammoth trucks," which weighed a ton apiece and were drawn by a powerful traction machine. Chaffee carelessly let his pants leg become caught in one of the trucks, and he was fatally crushed.[37]

The next month Al Vernon, a middle-aged machinist's helper for the UP, was caught between two cars and dragged a quarter of a mile. One arm was found 100 yards from his mutilated corpse. "Part of the right foot was gone, the left ear torn off, the skull crushed in, the jaw fractured and all of the clothing torn from his body below the waist," related the *Leader*. "He presented a frightful spectacle." In September another UP yard employee, Pete Golden, was found dead: "The wheels had passed over at the abdomen and the body lay in two parts."[38]

A couple of weeks later, an eleven-year-old boy, Clarence Swainson, was playing with two other boys, who slipped between two stationary railroad cars. When Clarence followed, a switch engine caused the cars to lurch, mangling the boy's arms. He walked three blocks to the Idleman building, where his father worked as janitor. Clarence climbed two flights of stairs to find his father, then said simply, "I'm hurt, papa." A nearby physician stopped the bleeding, and Clarence was rushed to the county hospital. He lost his right arm, but the left was saved after surgery which removed a section of shattered bone above the elbow, then wired the separated segments. "Don't cry, papa," said the courageous boy.[39]

On Friday afternoon, November 6, 1903, a different kind of mishap occurred—Cheyenne's first automobile accident. Joe George bought one of the town's first horseless carriages, an "Orient Buckboard" with a five-horsepower engine. In the long tradition of Cheyenne women who eagerly drove their husbands' carriages, Mrs. George soon became "an expert in the handling of automobiles." However, while driving on Eddy Street "at a high rate of speed," she leaned forward to shift the clutch and inadvertently "pushed the steering rod to one side, causing the machine to swerve." Bumping over a sidewalk, the auto collided with a building and hurled Mrs. George to the sidewalk. As onlookers rushed to help, Mrs. George had the presence of mind to turn off the engine. Neither the automobile nor the building suffered damage, but Mrs. George broke her left forearm and dislocated her left wrist. She walked to her husband's place of business "and startled him by announcing that her arm was broken."[40]

With less than two months left in 1903, Cheyenne had experienced another transition. The runaways that had been so common on the streets of Cheyenne soon would be a thing of the past, while increasing safety measures at the rail yards would drastically reduce the ghastly succession of fatalities and maimings along the tracks. On the other hand, the automobile wreck of Mrs. George was a glimpse into a future of dented fenders and shattered windshields.

The future of Fort D. A. Russell seemed questionable during the early years of the twentieth century. When vice-presidential candidate Theodore Roosevelt visited Cheyenne and Fort Russell, he found only a skeleton garrison of two officers and seventy-seven men (most army regulars were in the Philippines in 1900). With the construction program authorized in 1884 still in progress, the remaining old frame buildings were sold in 1901. Most of these structures were bought by F. E. Warren and Joseph Carey, moved into Cheyenne, and refurbished for rent property. In that year a board of high-ranking officers was formed to determine the future of all U.S. military posts. Senator Warren, of course, was artfully lobbying behind the scenes, and in January 1902 the board recommended Fort Russell as a permanent post, garrisoned by a regiment of infantry and a battery of artillery. Soon Senator Warren announced a $230,000 appropriation for ten new buildings that would accommodate two artillery batteries. Mayor M. P. Keefe, Cheyenne's largest contractor, successfully bid on several structures. In December 1903 the *Leader* observed: "Fort Russell is becoming quite a little city with the new buildings that are being constructed."[41]

Fort Russell was not the only "little city" along Crow Creek that was visibly growing. In 1901 walls began to go up on a three-story, $400,000 (Senator Warren engineered a substantial increase of the initial $250,000 appropriation) post office and federal building. After a few weeks the low walls had to be razed because of faulty concrete. But a fresh start went rapidly, and the post office moved into the building on West Sixteenth in 1902, although the upper structure was not completed until the next year. Simultaneously a big, ornate Masonic Temple was built on Capitol Avenue at a cost of $40,000. The cornerstone was laid on June 6, 1901,

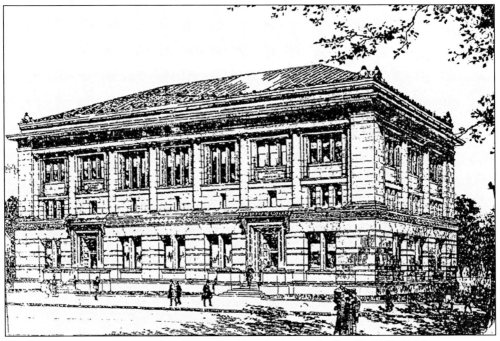

In 1901 construction began on the post office building, built with $400,000 in appropriation secured by Senator Warren. (This view was repeatedly shown in the Leader.*)*

and the next year the Masons moved out of their old temple, built in 1868 on Sixteenth Street. In March 1903 the splendid new temple was gutted by fire, but the walls still stood and there was $35,000 insurance. Rebuilding began immediately, and the Masons moved back in late in 1903. Almost at the same time, the Elks settled into their handsome new lodge on East Seventeenth. The $40,000 structure boasted baths and billiard halls in the basement, lodge rooms on the second floor, a third-floor meeting hall that seated 500, and rich paneling throughout.[42]

"Cheyenne in the past few years has grown at a remarkable rate, the shops are running full blast and almost every day new taps are put in with the water system," explained Mayor Murray at a special meeting of the Cheyenne City Council in August 1901. "The result has been that the city water system, sufficient for all needs a few years ago, has now become too small to supply the increased demand and a more extensive system must be built and built at once." Two new reservoirs were constructed north of town, and the next year new water mains were laid.[43]

In 1901 the Rocky Mountain Telephone Company added 100 phones for new subscribers, and poles and wiring stretched to "every portion of the city." Another operator was hired for the exchange office: "instead of one 'hello' girl two will hereafter respond to calls." The next year pay telephones and booths were installed around Cheyenne (calls cost a nickel). Also in 1902, the company began plans to build a two-story exchange building at the southeast corner of Seventeenth and Capitol.[44]

In 1902 Masons moved into their splendid new Temple, designed by Cheyenne architect William Dubois and erected for $40,000. Soon there was severe fire damage, but the Temple was immediately rebuilt and expanded. (Courtesy Wyoming State Archives)

Construction began on Wyoming's first Governor's Mansion in 1903. (Photo by Karon O'Neal)

A long-needed building began to go up in 1903. A year earlier the legislature appropriated $37,000 for a Governor's Mansion. The two-story, red brick, colonial revival residence would be erected on the northeastern corner of East Twenty-first and House Avenue. Early governors had used their hotel rooms or rented houses as the "Executive Mansion." Governors from Cheyenne used their homes, but governors from out of town had to rent or buy. Although there was a long delay over plans for the mansion, construction finally began in the

spring of 1904 and concluded late in the year. Governor Bryant B. Brooks, who took office in January 1905, and his family were the first to reside in the new Governor's Mansion.[45]

Although important new buildings were being added to the Cheyenne scene, a structure that had provided rich memories in the community for two decades was destroyed by fire. The Cheyenne Opera House was gutted by flames in December 1902. The fire began in the rooms beneath the stage, but a thick brick wall confined the flames to the auditorium. The south part of the building, which housed offices and apartments, was not damaged. The Carey brothers, who owned the structure at that time, had $20,000 in insurance coverage on the auditorium and promised to rebuild the Opera House. But the Opera House had never been profitable, despite hosting a steady bill of entertainment, high school commencements, political meetings, and other community events. The Carey brothers prosaically decided to convert the space to offices and apartments. It was years before another entertainment palace was built in Cheyenne, and the Lincoln Theatre (1927) would feature movies. Ironically, the next attraction scheduled for the Opera House in December 1902 was a program of moving pictures.[46]

In addition to presiding over the transformation of the Cheyenne Opera House, Joseph Carey also witnessed the domestic transformation of his sons, Charles and Robert. In February 1902, twenty-one-year-old Charles visited his sweetheart, Mabelle Myers, in Denver. Mabelle had been in Europe, and impulsively she agreed to marry Charles that day. Charles helped his father supervise rental property, and the young couple made their home in Cheyenne. Robert, a 1900 graduate of Yale, managed his father's ranch near Casper. In August 1903, Robert met beautiful Julia Freeman of Douglas. Following a three-week courtship, like his brother, Robert created "a great society sensation" with a sudden wedding in Douglas. Sixteen years later, Robert and Julia would move into the Governor's Mansion that was being planned while they met and married.[47]

Interior view of the plush new Elks Lodge, built for $40,000 on Seventeenth. (Courtesy Wyoming State Archives)

Henry G. Hay, a business and civic leader since 1870. Hay's daughter married in 1903, and at fifty-seven, Hay left Cheyenne to return to his native Indiana as an executive of the U.S. Steel Corporation. (Courtesy Wyoming State Archives)

Another second-generation marriage in 1903 was more conventional. Mildred Hay, "the charming and accomplished daughter of Henry G. Hay, state treasurer," married an artillery captain from Fort Russell in "one of the prettiest home weddings ever held in the city." Presided over by Dr. George C. Rafter of St. Mark's, the Episcopal service was conducted at the Hay mansion on Ferguson Street. The guest list included a who's who of nineteenth-century society, including Senator Warren, Mr. and Mrs. R. S. Van Tassell, Dr. and Mrs. Amos W. Barber, Mr. and Mrs. William C. Irvine, Mr. and Mrs. Luke Voorhees, Mr. and Mrs. I. C. Whipple, and many others, as well as several officers and wives from Fort Russell. The newlyweds departed for a European honeymoon.[48]

Hay himself soon experienced a major transition. Long prominent as a banker, businessman, and community leader, the fifty-seven-year-old Hay had made the Magic City his home since 1870. But less than three months after his daughter's wedding, Hay resigned as state treasurer and announced that he would move to Gary, Indiana (he was a native of Indiana) as assistant treasurer of the United States Steel Corporation. W. C. "Billy" Irvine was appointed to succeed Hay as state treasurer. At fifty-one, the vigorous Irvine was a wealthy cattleman who was in the middle of a fifteen-year tenure as president of the Wyoming Stock Growers' Association. He had served two terms as a territorial senator and was widely popular. Irvine, though, was forthright and feisty, and he was one of the ranchers who planned and executed the Johnson County War. "It is a wonder that he was not killed long ago," remarked the *Leader*.[49]

Another feisty Cheyenne official was Justice of the Peace Sam Becker, a former railroad employee who had lost a leg. On the last day of January 1902, Judge Becker was standing on Sixteenth Street, Cheyenne's main business thoroughfare, when a drunken switchman made a boisterous remark to a passing woman. Judge Becker "promptly called the man down for his insulting language," reported the *Leader*. The drunken railroad man took offense at interference by a one-legged gent "and applied vile epithets to his honor." But "the doughty judge immediately knocked the man into the gutter and followed this up by a severe thrashing." Judge Becker held his opponent down and summoned a nearby officer, but the man expressed such contrition that he was released from custody. Ten days later the police reported "that no offense of any kind against the laws has been committed in Cheyenne within the past two weeks, even to petty thefts."[50]

A religious transition involving 150 children occurred at St. Mary's Cathedral on a Sunday in June 1903. In "one of the most impressive services that ever occurred in the church history of Cheyenne," one hundred girls and fifty boys were confirmed into the Catholic church. The children marched into the cathedral, with the girls clad in pure white and wearing white veils and flower wreaths on their heads, and the boys dressed in black, with ties and white gloves. Chants and hymns came from the choir loft, while Bishop Keane addressed the crowd.[51]

A long-sought business transition finally took place in August 1901. When Cheyenne was founded, saloons stayed open most of the night, and mercantile businesses also were open to customers until nine or ten o'clock. These enterprises opened their doors at six or seven each morning, so clerks and other mercantile employees spent scant time at home. Saloons were open seven days — and nights — a week, but businesses soon began to close on Sundays. Six days a week, however, married clerks saw their families only at bedtime and breakfast. In July 1884 more than fifty clerks met in an attempt to induce a closing time of "7 P.M. on each night of the week except Saturday." The *Leader* supported the clerks in a lengthy editorial. "The custom of doing business fifteen, sixteen and seventeen hours a day, in Cheyenne, is one which has come to us from the earlier days of the town," explained the writer. It was a hard sell, however, and even the businesses that consented to close at seven, "except on Saturday," still opened early, so that employees continued to put in a work week of ninety hours or more. Finally, in 1901, a "clerk's association" persuaded most of the merchants to "close for the day" at six o'clock. Barber shops continued to operate seven days a week, but in 1902 the tonsorial artists of Cheyenne agreed to close on Sundays. To compensate for such a slothful schedule, the barbers decided to stay open until midnight on Saturdays.[52]

A nostalgic transition was the disbanding of the Pioneer Hook Company in 1900. "The first and most prominent citizens of Cheyenne were 'Pioneer Hooks,'" reminisced the *Leader*. "It was a company of the bravest of the brave, the strong, the hardy, the fearless. To think of them is to revert to the balmy days when money seemed to grow on the sage brush." But now there were "speedier and more scientific methods of coping with flames," and members had died or grown old. "There is $140 in the treasury, which will be devoted to a grand banquet." During the new century the remaining volunteer companies gave way to a professional fire department.[53]

"Senator Warren is back at Washington and hard at work again in the interests of Wyoming," announced the *Leader* in January 1903. Few members of Congress were as skilled at securing federal benefits as Warren, and Wyoming became accustomed to receiving far more government funding than was sent to

Washington in taxes. Warren made sure that substantial federal monies wound up in Cheyenne. In February 1902 the *Leader* stated that Senator Warren had obtained more than $1 million in appropriations for government buildings in Wyoming—a sum that included $400,000 for Cheyenne's new post office.[54] He also continued to work incessantly to obtain federal appointments for Wyoming citizens, and one of the most significant brought honor to Cheyenne.

Warren's close friend and political ally, Willis Van Devanter, was appointed assistant attorney general in charge of Indian and public lands cases in the Department of the Interior in 1907. Van Devanter was courteous, dignified, and a master of his profession, and Warren continued to promote his impressive friend behind the scenes. In 1903, President Theodore Roosevelt promoted him to a judgeship on the Federal Court of Appeals for the 8th Circuit. Van Devanter was elevated to the Supreme Court as an associate justice in 1911. Justice Van Devanter served ably for twenty-six years, and he remains the only Wyoming jurist to have served on the U.S. Supreme Court.[55]

The cattlemen and hired gunmen who had invaded Johnson County were brilliantly defended by a disapproving but professionally loyal Willis Van Devanter in 1892–93. But a decade later, when cattlemen needed an artful defense for a notorious hired killer, Judge Van Devanter was in federal service—and doubtless pleased that he could not be called upon. The events involving Tom Horn during 1901–03 would signify one of the most crucial of Cheyenne transitions in that era.

The Knights of Columbus at a Christmas dinner. (Courtesy Wyoming State Archives)

21

Tom Horn Meets the Twentieth Century

As Cheyenne entered the twentieth century, the notorious Tom Horn was an embarrassing reminder of the violent past of the Magic City and of frontier Wyoming. From 1892 on, Horn was in and out of Cheyenne in his capacity as a Pinkerton operative and as a stock detective for big cattle ranchers. Although he had earned respect as an army scout during the Apache wars, as a Pinkerton detective, as an army packer during the war with Spain, and as a deputy sheriff and deputy U.S. marshal, it was clear by the turn of the century that Horn had become a hired assassin. Horn made little secret of his lethal occupation and, worse still, he headquartered uncomfortably close to Cheyenne.

Horn was a compulsive seeker of adventure, unafraid of danger or consequences. Born in 1860, he was reared on a farm in northeastern Missouri, where he became addicted to hunting, fishing, and outdoor life. Ignoring the certainty of whippings, Tom often skipped church to plunge into the woods with the family hunting dog. As he described, "all the natural influences of the country were against my acquiring much of an education." Walking to school on a snowy day with his siblings, he would spot animal tracks. "Then an overpowering desire to get that rabbit or 'coon or wild cat, as it happened to be, would overcome me," and he would spend another school day hunting in the woods. Tom was a habitual truant from school, although he was "an enthusiastic reader of dime novels," according to his sister Harriett. Recruiting other daring boys, "frequent raids were made on chicken coops and orchards," and Tom was caught shoplifting ammunition from a general store. After a whipping by his father, the rebellious fourteen-year-old ran away to the West. "I had, of course, heard of the West, California, Texas, and Kansas also," he said, but he "had not the faintest idea" of the location of these alluring places.[1]

Like many youngsters after the Civil War, Tom wanted the adventure of cowboy life. Working on ranches in Kansas and Arizona, he mastered the cowboy's skills, later winning steer-roping contests in early rodeos. For four years during the 1880s, with the military battling Apaches, Horn, now in his twenties, worked for the army as a packer, then as a scout, and finally as chief of scouts. He was shot in the arm during a famous engagement in which Lt. Emmett Crawford was slain, and he was present when Geronimo finally surrendered.[2]

A study by the author for a biographical encyclopedia, *Fighting Men of the Indian Wars* (published by Barbed Wire Press in 1991), revealed a correlation between seeking out hostile Indians and hunting wild game. Numerous reports and memoirs reveal the pulsating anticipation of the hunter stalking a dangerous prey, the challenge of detecting a promising trail, the exhilaration of discovery of a favorite watering place or a den, the chilling lust for the kill. There also was a widespread callousness toward the Indian, a casual habit of regarding him as less than human, like an antelope, deer, bear, or wolf. For many nineteenth-century

frontiersmen, fighting Indians was the ultimate sport, offering the maximum in adventure, challenge—and mortal danger.[3]

For four years Tom Horn, an avid hunter since boyhood, pursued the ultimate game, and clearly he acquired a taste for manhunting. But after Geronimo's capture in 1886, Chief of Scouts Horn was required to discharge his scouts, then was himself released. During the next few years, according to Horn, he worked as a deputy sheriff, and a cowboy, miner, and ranch foreman. From 1890 to 1894, Horn was employed by the Pinkerton Detective Agency, headquartering in Denver while pursuing criminals across much of the West. In 1891, while working undercover, he was arrested and tried for theft in Reno, Nevada. The Pinkerton Agency provided defense attorneys and secured supportive depositions from Arizona law officers and judges and

Tom Horn, noted army scout, Pinkerton detective, veteran of Cuba—and hired killer. (Courtesy Arizona Historical Society Library)

from Gen. Nelson A. Miles. William A. Pinkerton, superintendent of the agency, testified on behalf of Horn, who was pronounced not guilty. (A decade later, Pinkerton would admit that he should have extended similar assistance to Horn in Cheyenne.)[4]

Horn left the Pinkerton Agency in 1894, although there would be occasional professional connections in future years. "I then came to Wyoming and went to work for the Swan Land and Cattle Company" as a "range rider," or stock detective, he explained. Only a couple of years had passed since the Johnson County War. Although Wyoming's big ranchers had escaped legal consequences, they still were plagued by rustling and by lack of effective prosecution. Horn almost immediately arrested three members of the "Langhoff outfit," but two of the rustlers were set free, while the third was convicted and then pardoned by Governor John Osborne.[5]

Apparently, this failure of the legal system made a strong impression upon Horn and his employers. Horn soon acquired the reputation of killing rustlers who refused to leave the country. Through the years, he worked closely with John C. Coble, who ran the Iron Mountain Cattle Company in rugged country northwest of Cheyenne. Coble greatly admired the famous Indian scout, but the rancher had a certain notoriety of his own. In 1890, for example, he tangled with Kels Nickell, a nester whose stock often grazed on Coble range, and Nickell cut Coble with a pocketknife. On another occasion, in 1895, Coble went on a drunken spree in the exclusive Cheyenne Club, and he was suspended after shooting up a large painting of a Holstein bull.

William Lewis, an English immigrant who held a 160-acre homestead near the Iron Mountain Ranch, bragged about stealing Iron Mountain cattle. He received a warning to pull out, then in August 1895 his corpse was found on the range, riddled with three bullets fired from a range of 300 yards. It was widely rumored that Tom Horn had killed Lewis.

Not long after the death of Lewis, Fred Powell received a similar warning to leave Wyoming. A known confederate of Lewis, Powell had a homestead about ten miles away, near Horse Creek. Defiantly, Powell invited cowboys from the nearby KYT Ranch to come to his place for a supper of their own beef. Soon a rider shot Powell to death, and those who saw the big assassin were wise enough not to identify Tom Horn.

Horn now cultivated his image as a cold-blooded killer. He was a tall, powerful man who stood over six feet and weighed more than 200 pounds. When not investigating stock thefts, he worked cattle on the ranches which employed him. He always carried a forty-foot lariat and liked to show off his roping skills. Horn usually packed a revolver along with a rifle, and he also readily demonstrated his marksmanship. A cowboy for the Swan Land and Cattle Company was sometimes asked to toss tin cans in the air for Horn, who would drill them twice with revolver bullets before the can hit the ground.[6] Horn's two primary enjoyments were participating in rodeos and drinking in a good saloon in Cheyenne, Laramie, or Denver. He drank heavily whenever in town, and when he was drunk he talked boastfully, often about his murders and gunfights.

Much of his drunken boasting was classic frontier exaggeration. But this murderous braggadocio doubtless added to his sinister reputation. Horn roamed widely through much of Wyoming and Colorado, "working the pastures." The range was mostly fenced, but he would be out for a week or two at a time, riding through the vast "pastures" of his employers, and checking the much smaller pastures of the nesters who were likely to brand mavericks or rustle branded cattle. "Of course," testified Horn, "it is just the least bit embarrassing ... to ride into a man's pasture and look over his pasture and have the man come along."[7] Horn sometimes would spend the night with men whose pastures he would check, but customarily he tried to stay out of sight, riding cross-country rather than on public roads.

He traveled light, carrying only a little bacon and bread, and often going without food if he could not shoot a jackrabbit. In the summers he did not even carry a slicker or coat, sleeping on the ground with only his saddle blanket to make an uncomfortable bed. Nevertheless, he seemed to like these duties. "I don't have any particular place to go, or any particular time. I don't work under any particular instructions at any time. I am supposed to go when I please and where I please, and how I please. The boss or foreman of the ranch, the manager of the ranch leaves that entirely to myself."[8]

Although he skulked from ranch to ranch, no one ordered him off their ranges. Horn's contemporaries understood his purpose: "He was given employment by some of the larger cattle outfits, to rid the country of rustlers and sheep men, to dispose of them in his own fashion; they called him a range rider. These large outfits by whom he was employed were very touchy and did not want it to be known who paid him or whom he was working for. Whenever rustling was evident or maverick calves were stolen and branded Tom Horn was notified so that he could go to the scene, look the situation over, and, when the guilty party or parties were identified by him, he at once disposed of them in such a way that they would never bother again."[9]

Governor William A. Richards, who owned a large number of cattle in the Big Horn country, interviewed Horn in the Wyoming Stock Growers' Association (WSGA) office in the Capitol building regarding a solution to rustling problems. "Whenever anything else fails," stated Horn, "I have a system that never does." Horn went into specifics about his fee, but when he pointed out that there should be no limit regarding the number of men who might have to be gotten rid of, Governor Richards became visibly uncomfortable and indicated that the interview should end. Horn politely excused himself. "So that is Tom Horn!" exclaimed Richards to the WSGA official who had arranged the meeting. Richards described Horn as a "very different man from what I expected to meet. Why, he is not bad looking, and is quite intelligent; but a cool devil, ain't he?"[10]

It is likely that Horn's chilling reputation greatly facilitated his work, persuading rustlers who received warnings to leave the country rather than risk a visit by the mysterious rider with a deadly rifle.

In 1898 Horn interrupted his career as a range rider to seek another combat zone with the army. His quest for adventure undimmed in his late thirties, Horn responded to the War with Spain by journeying to Tampa, Florida, to find a place in the expeditionary force that would invade Cuba. Horn was hired as a packer, and once in Cuba the veteran of the Apache Wars was promoted to chief packer at $133.33 per month. But like thousands of American soldiers, Horn contracted yellow fever, and when he returned to Wyoming he was wracked with illness. John Coble put him to bed at the Iron Mountain Ranch, where he slowly recovered his health. By this time war was raging in the Philippines, and even though Horn still suffered intermittently from fever, he tried to secure an appointment as a packer with an expedition bound for the Pacific.[11]

Although service in the Philippines did not materialize, Horn found himself busier than ever as a range rider. In 1900 he ventured into Brown's Park in the northwestern corner of Colorado. Still isolated even today, at the turn of the century Brown's Park was a notorious haunt of outlaws, from Butch Cassidy and the Wild Bunch to rustlers who regularly relayed stolen livestock. Horn rode into the valley, which is surrounded by vast mountains and dotted with marshy lakes. Even in outlaw country, Horn proved to be a formidable figure, later bragging that "I stopped cow stealing there in one summer."[12] Within three months Horn assassinated two suspected rustlers in the Brown's Park area. Establishing sniper positions overlooking their respective cabins, he killed Matt Rash and Isom Dart with long-range rifle fire, on July 8 and October 3, 1900.

By 1901 John Coble and other large cattlemen were thoroughly disgusted with Kels Nickell. Nickell was born in Kentucky in 1858, but in 1863 his father was murdered by guerrilla raiders. From 1875 to 1880, Nickell served a hitch in the Fifth Cavalry, then took up a homestead on Iron Mountain. Married in Cheyene in 1881 (he was divorced from his first wife in 1877), Nickell raised nine children on his little spread. By the 1890s he had accumulated more than 1,000 head of cattle, but naturally he was suspected of rustling some of the animals. As the range became fenced in, his still small holdings could not support such a cattle herd. Contentious by nature, in the spring of 1901 Nickell brought sheep to his range.[13]

For more than a decade John Coble, who had tried unsuccessfully to file charges against Nickell after the 1890

The author with Tom Horn's rifle. (Courtesy Gatchell Memorial Museum)

knifing, had looked for the opportunity to oust the disagreeable nester. Now Nickell had introduced sheep to the Iron Mountain country and was grazing his band "on the cattle range and watering them out of water holes which had been used for cattle." Ora Haley and the Swan Land and Cattle Company joined Coble in resenting the intrusion of sheep onto range that had traditionally been used by big cattle operations. "This caused a great deal of agitation among the cattle men," observed a Swan rider, "which resulted in Tom Horn being notified of the condition."[14]

On July 16, 1900, John Coble wrote to his partner about the situation: "The Iron Mountain, Wall Rock and Plumbago pastures are filled with sheep and look wooly. Our she cattle are in Iron Mountain and they are doing fine, like in a meadow. When the sheep men attempt to drive or handle our cattle I will at once have them arrested. But they are scared to death, are hiring all the six-shooters and bad men they can find. I want Horn back here [Horn was in Brown's Park]; he will straighten them out by merely riding around."[15]

Horn heard not only from large cattlemen but from small ranchers as well, who said it "was not right," and said so "in very strong terms."

"They say if [Nickell] started in the sheep business," pointed out Horn, "it would be different. Being in the cattle business and deliberately selling cattle and putting sheep in for no other reason than to spite the neighbors about it" would prove intolerable to those neighbors. The consensus of opinion among area cattle ranchers, according to Horn, was that only "the kind of man Nickell is, troublesome and quarrelsome, [a] turbulent man without character or principle," would bring sheep into a cattle haven.[16]

Adding to the tensions was the fact that Nickell had wrangled for years with another small rancher named James Miller, whose home was about three miles northeast of the Nickell homestead. When Miller was brought up on charges of cutting Nickell's fence, the *Leader* complained that their troubles "are becoming rather old and tiresome," and that "it seems a farce to take up the time of courts with such trivialities." Willie Nickell, one of Kel's sons, fought with Miller's sons, Gus and Victor. Even though Gus was two or three years older than Willie, young Nickell was large for his age, and he whipped Gus—much to the chagrin of James Miller. Indeed, in 1900 the senior Miller bullied the thirteen-year-old Willie, beating him with a whip and threatening him with curses and a cocked six-gun. Kels Nickell had Victor and Gus arrested for fence cutting. "They go to the other neighbors with their trouble and tell what kind of ornery people they are," testified Horn. "They are both the same kind of people . . . neither one has good reputations."

James Miller began carrying a shotgun. When the weapon discharged accidentally in a wagon, killing one of the younger Miller boys and wounding a daughter, the embittered Miller blamed the tragedy on Kels Nickell. His reasoning was that he carried the gun only because of the feud with the Nickells. Nickell added to Miller's resentment by grazing sheep close to the Miller house. "I wonder how the son-of-a-bitch feels about it because I left them, right in his door yard," Nickell told Horn. Horn said that he heard of Miller offering a $500 reward to anyone who would kill Nickell.[17]

In mid-July 1901, Tom Horn rode out from John Coble's headquarters to spend several days inspecting the range on behalf of his employers. After a few days he stopped at the Miller ranch, partly to see Glendoline Kimmel, a schoolmarm who roomed with the Millers and who was quite taken with the famous frontiersman. On Monday, July 15, Horn slept with the Miller boys in a big tent in front of the house. On Tuesday he rode off to locate the Nickell sheep. He found them in one of Miller's pastures, then returned for another night in the tent. While with the Millers he fished a bit, yarned with the boys, visited with Glendoline, and engaged in target practice. He carried a .30-30 Winchester but no belt gun. He left the Miller ranch on Wednesday morning, July 17, later testifying that he spent another couple of days checking Swan and Coble ranges before returning to the Coble ranch and on into Laramie for a spree.

On Thursday morning, July 18, thunder and rain slashed across the Iron Mountain country. Breakfast at the Nickell homestead was served before six o'clock. Surveyor John Apperson and Mrs. Nickell's brother, William Mahoney, were on hand to help Kels survey fence lines a mile or so east of the house. Fred Nickell, Willie's younger brother, was assigned to drive a hay wagon to a distant barn. Willie was told to fetch a sheepherder; on Wednesday an Italian herder had stopped by looking for work, and overnight Kels had decided it was a mistake to have sent him away.

Willie was directed to ride his father's saddle horse, and because of the stormy weather he donned Kels's coat and hat. Willie, now fourteen, owned a .22 rifle, but he left on his mission unarmed. Kels led the surveyor and his brother-in-law to the east immediately after breakfast. Fred Nickell drove the hay wagon to the west, passed through a wire gate, and drove past a concealed rifleman. Fred would return home by another route. A few minutes later, Willie rode west about a mile, then dismounted to open the wire gate on his way to Iron Mountain Station, where it was thought the sheepherder had gone. In a cluster of rocks 300 yards in front of the gate, the hidden assassin took aim. The sniper squeezed off three rounds. One bullet slammed into Willie's back and tore out his chest. The stricken youth dashed away from the gate, but another slug ripped through his body. Dying, he fell on his face. The killer came out to check his work. He turned Willie onto his back and opened his bloody shirt to look at the wounds, then rode away.

Kels Nickell, Mahoney, and Apperson heard the three shots echo across the countryside, but they assumed someone was hunting deer. Although Willie did not return by nightfall, there was no particular alarm, since he might not be able to find the sheepherder. The next morning, Friday, young Fred Nickell drove the milk cows west to pasture. When he reached the open gate, he was horrified to find the bloated, discolored body of his older brother. Fred raced back to the house screaming out the terrible news, "Willie is murdered!"[18]

The murder became a front-page story in Cheyenne the next day, and in the first story the feud between the neighboring families was mentioned. On

Monday, July 22, Kels Nickell told the coroner's jury that he first thought "that the killing was done either by his neighbor ranchman, Miller, or his oldest son, but now believes it was done by the second oldest son, Victor Miller." The next day Glendoline Kimmel stated that the entire Miller family was breakfasting at the time of the murder. She also testified "that Tom Horn, the detective," was at the Miller ranch two days before the killing but "rode away in the afternoon on the black horse. He had a pair of field glasses with him."[19] Many people began to think about the dislike of John Coble for Kels Nickell and his sheep, and the possibility that Willie may have been mistaken for his father. Suspicion of Coble's menacing friend, Tom Horn, started to grow.

Willie Nickell was brought to Cheyenne for burial in Lakeview Cemetery. The plate attached to the stone announces that Willie was "MURDERED NEAR HIS HOME AT IRON MOUNTAIN/TOM HORN HANGED FOR HIS MURDER." (Photo by Karon O'Neal)

Kels Nickell received an anonymous note warning him to leave the country with his sheep or suffer the consequences. The bereaved father ignored the warning. But on August 4, 1901, seventeen days after the murder of Willie, Kels was fired upon by concealed riflemen. It was estimated that thirteen to seventeen bullets were triggered. Kels sprinted to his house 600 yards away, zigzagging under fire. He was hit three times, most seriously by a slug which shattered his left elbow, but he escaped with his life. After he disappeared, four riders went to find a band of 1,000 sheep owned by other men but pastured by Nickell. The raiders ran off the Italian sheepherder, then opened up on the sheep, killing about seventy-five animals. Kels Nickell was taken to Cheyenne for medical care, while his sheep ran unattended for several days. Nickell accused the Millers. James, Gus, and Victor Miller were arrested, then released when they produced an alibi. Mrs. Nickell cowered with her children in their ranch house, afraid of the next attack that might come.[20]

The State of Wyoming and Laramie County offered rewards totaling $1,000 for Willie's killer,[21] and the Laramie County sheriff's office engaged the services of an experienced detective, Joe LeFors. LeFors was born in Texas in 1865, moved with his family first to Oklahoma, and then, in 1875, to the Texas Panhandle. As a teenager Joe carried the mails and worked as a bull-whacker and as a cowboy. In 1885 he helped drive a herd of Texas cattle to Buffalo, Wyoming, and soon hired on with a Montana outfit. He was then offered a job as a livestock inspector, with the assignment of locating stolen Montana stock in Wyoming. His efforts

Joe LeFors won fame by extracting a controversial confession from Tom Horn. (Courtesy Wyoming State Archives)

were highly effective, and he moved to Newcastle, Wyoming, in 1895. LeFors even penetrated the lawless Hole-in-the-Wall country, rounding up nearly 1,200 head of stolen livestock in 1897. After a brief stint in private business, LeFors became a deputy U.S. marshal, tracking train robbers and counterfeiters and various other lawbreakers.[22]

On August 5, 1901, LeFors arrived by train in Cheyenne to deliver a prisoner. But Laramie County Sheriff J.P. Shaver was in Los Angeles hoping to recover from a long illness (the sixty-year-old lawman died a month later),[23] so LeFors was asked to begin an investigation of the Nickell shootings. The following morning LeFors and another peace officer took a train to Iron Mountain, then rode horseback seven miles to the Nickell place. LeFors found Mrs. Nickell barricaded inside the house, with three crying children clinging to her skirts. After LeFors calmed her, Mrs. Nickell showed the lawman the bloody coat worn by Willie when he was killed, and the jacket Kels was wearing two days earlier when he was wounded. "We are being shot and killed off one at a time," cried Mrs. Nickell, "and all day yesterday not an officer came."[21]

During the fall, Kels Nickell recovered from his wounds, then sold his ranch and sheep. Nickell moved his family into Cheyenne and found a job as a night watchman with the Union Pacific.

On September 1, 1901, Tom Horn competed in Cheyenne's Frontier Days, winning "honors in the riding and roping contests." Later in the month he helped deliver horses for rancher John Kuykendall to Denver. There Horn engaged in a saloon brawl and suffered a broken jaw which hospitalized him for three weeks.[25]

After he recovered, Tom Horn, along with almost everyone else in the Iron Mountain district, testified at the lengthy coroner's inquest. Results of the proceedings were inconclusive, but there was a growing public demand to find the killer of Willie Nickell. Pinkerton detectives were engaged, including a female agent who spent several weeks doing undercover work in the Iron Mountain area. Little concrete evidence was found, but Tom Horn was overheard talking about the Nickell killing during his drinking sprees. LeFors had a conversation with a cattle rancher who had admitted he had paid Tom Horn "for the jobs committed before" (Powell and Lewis?), and "if Horn got to talking too much they would have to bump him off themselves."[26]

LeFors showed this rancher a letter he had received from the chief livestock inspector of Montana, requesting "a good man to do some secret work." Smith offered $125 per month for several months of undercover work against rustlers, but "He will have to be a man that can take care of himself in any kind of country."[27]

The letter was passed on to John Coble, who informed Horn. Apparently, the ranchers and Horn thought it would be a good idea for him to depart the vicinity. Horn wrote to LeFors, stating that he had received the letter from John Coble, and the offer sounded good. "I would like to take up that work and I feel sure I could give Mr. Smith satisfaction. I don't care how big or bad his men are or how many of them there are, I can handle them."[28]

LeFors continued to act as a middleman between Horn and Smith. In another letter Horn expressed his appreciation to LeFors and stated that he would be ready to depart for Montana within the next ten days. "I will get the men sure," he stated confidently, "for I have never let a cow thief get away from me unless he just got up a[nd] jumped clean out of the country."[29] Horn obviously was eager for the challenge of a new manhunting job, and doubtless his Wyoming employers were eager for him to leave the country.

But LeFors was ready to spring a trap. LeFors and Horn had arranged to meet in Cheyenne at the U.S. marshal's office on Sunday, January 12, 1902. LeFors contacted Charles Ohnhaus, U.S. court reporter, and Deputy Sheriff Les Snow, developing a scheme to take down Horn's remarks. Ohnhaus, of course, would record from behind an inner door, while Snow would be a concealed witness. LeFors told Laramie County Prosecuting Attorney Walter Stoll his plans. Stoll approved and suggested that Ohnhaus bring the transcript to his office as quickly as possible after the conversation with Horn. (Less than three months earlier, the *Leader* noted, Ohnhaus and a Mrs. Gus Jenkins "took the stenographical examination under the civil service.")[30]

On Sunday, LeFors met Horn's train. Later, Horn would refute his "confession" as partially false and partially the empty boasts of a drunk. "I know that he was not drunk," insisted LeFors in his autobiography, but the detective admitted that Horn had been drinking.[31]

When LeFors led Horn into the marshal's office (a second-floor suite on

Sixteenth which still stands), Ohnhaus and Snow were already behind the inner door. LeFors and Horn began to discuss the Montana job, and Tom soon asked, "These people are not afraid of shooting, are they?"[32]

LeFors turned the conversation to the Nickell killing. He asked a number of leading questions, and Horn later testified that he did not take such questions seriously, answering with the kind of absurd statement that he assumed LeFors wanted. LeFors did indeed receive the answers he wanted, including the famous line from Horn about the 300-yard shot that struck Willie: "It was the best shot I ever made, and the dirtiest trick I ever done." Perhaps the dirtiest trick of all, however, was done by the men who manipulated a "confession" that would not be admitted as evidence in a modern court.

A number of other incriminating statements were made by Horn, who planned to leave for Montana by rail the next day. But Ohnhaus typed the transcript Sunday night, and warrants were promptly prepared. On Monday morning Sheriff Edward J. Smalley (who had been appointed to replace the deceased J.P. Shaver) and two other officers arrested Horn in the lobby of the Inter Ocean Hotel. LeFors was nearby, witnessing Horn surrender with no resistance. Horn was placed in a cell in the Laramie County courthouse jail.

"Tom Horn, Detective, Arrested for Murder," screamed the headline in Cheyenne on Monday. "That is the startling news which passed from mouth to mouth on the streets of the city this afternoon." Horn had "many friends" who

Joe LeFors interviewed Tom Horn in the U.S. Marshal's Office—second floor, behind the bay window. The next day Horn was arrested in the lobby of the Inter Ocean Hotel, at far right. (Courtesy Wyoming State Archives)

tried to visit, "either through sympathy or curiosity" but were turned away by jailors. "Even an attorney cannot talk with him unless by order of the district court." On the sidewalks of Cheyenne, and in saloons and stores and hotel lobbies, the "Horn case still continues to be the sensation of the hour and is more discussed than any other topic."[33]

Less than a decade had passed since the Johnson County War and the legal machinations that had occurred in Cheyenne. There was a general perception that big cattlemen still were fighting, through Tom Horn, for the continuation of their domination of the range. Joe LeFors reminisced that cattle barons exerted "enormous political influence" on Horn's behalf. Although there was speculation that many ranchers were afraid of being incriminated by Horn, a hefty war chest was collected for his defense. (It was publicly announced that John C. Coble was "defraying the expenses for defending Tom Horn,"[34] but it seems obvious that more than one man provided funds for the expensive legal team.) As in 1892, the best available legal talent was engaged. Judge J. W. Lacey would lead the defense, along with T. E. Burke, U.S. district attorney for Wyoming, and Burke's partners, Edward T. Clark, R. N. Matson, and T. Blake Kennedy. The obscure Walter Stoll, even though assisted by H. Waldo Moore and Clyde Watts, was given little chance of obtaining a conviction. But Stoll knew that success in this high-profile case could vault him to high political office. And with the "confession" extracted

by LeFors, Stoll possessed a spectacular secret weapon.

The preliminary hearing convened on Thursday, January 23, 1902, before District Judge Samuel Becker. The courtroom was packed when Stoll introduced his surprise "thunderbolt" and brought the crowd to their feet. "Tom Horn is undoubtedly a stoic," described the *Leader*, "but for once he lost his customary equanimity and could not hide the startled look which crept into his eyes." Although Stoll's document had not yet been subject to challenge, the *Leader* announced in bold headlines: "TOM HORN CONFESSES." Joe LeFors was proclaimed "one of the shrewdest and most brilliant detectives in the United States."[35]

Despite a lengthy plea by Lacey, Horn was ordered to be held without bail until trial. But

Judge J. W. Lacey of Cheyenne led Tom Horn's defense team. (Courtesy Wyoming State Archives)

the defense attorneys went to work, conferring with Horn every day. T. Blake Kennedy, youngest member of the defense team, spent weeks inspecting the mur-

der site and surrounding area. Horn was visited frequently by friends, and he devoted a great deal of time to braiding hack-amores, lariats, and other tack. These items were masterfully done and were treasured gifts to his friends, and to Sheriff Smalley and the jailer.[36]

In May, Walter Stoll, "popular prosecuting attorney," took time off to marry a widow from Mil-waukee. She arrived in Cheyenne on Thursday, May 22, and the wedding was conducted by Judge Becker in Stoll's office. Since he neglected "to tell his friends," they hired "a blind man with a grind organ to play all night in front of Mr. Stoll's house." But about eleven o'clock "the crowd insisted on taking Mr. Stoll's house by

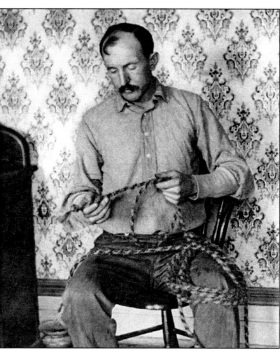

During his long incarceration, Horn braided horse-hair lariats and bridles as gifts for his friends. (Courtesy Wyoming State Archives)

T. Blake Kennedy, youngest of Tom Horn's lawyers, spent weeks inspecting the site vicinity of the murder. (Courtesy Wyoming State Archives)

storm." The couple endured their singing, then were presented an expensive cut-glass set. Less than two weeks later, Sheriff Smalley married Marie Collins in Denver, then brought her to his quarters in the jail before departing on a honeymoon to the East.[37]

Stoll and Smalley had time for weddings and honeymoons because there were few legal maneuvers during the spring and summer of 1902, although both sides competed at length over the selection of a jury. A majority of jury members were small ranchers who would naturally be opposed to large cattlemen, but Horn personally approved half of the men who would hear the case. When the trial finally began on Friday afternoon, October 10, 1902, an eager crowd jammed the courtroom (many spectators would not vacate the room during lunch breaks and other recesses, for fear of losing their seats). More than 100 witnesses had been assembled, and journalists added to the throng. The daily progress of the case was described on front pages in Cheyenne and across the nation.

One of the West's most famous trials would last for two weeks. The trial transcription seems to reveal that Stoll, tenacious and resourceful, outdueled his vaunted opponents. The defense failed to emphasize Horn's service to his country, nor did they stress the extent of cattle rustling in Wyoming, and there was insufficient effort to refute the transcribed document of LeFors.

Stoll opened the trial on Friday afternoon with a masterful address to the jury. On Saturday photographs and measurements of the murder site were introduced, and Willie's wounds were described in graphic detail. Witnesses included Willie's parents, who offered pathetic descriptions of the discovery of their murdered son.

Glendoline Kimmel created great interest in Cheyenne during the trial. (Courtesy Wyoming State Archives)

On Sunday the jurors were permitted to attend church services, and the trial resumed on Monday. As the trial gained momentum, business eventually came to a standstill in Cheyenne. During the early part of the week, exhaustive attempts were made to prove the caliber of the murder weapon. The Miller family appeared as witnesses, and Kels Nickell and his wife were recalled to the stand. On Tuesday the courtroom was electrified when a witness testified that on the day of the murder he had seen Horn galloping toward Laramie from Iron Mountain on a lathered, exhausted horse.

The trial on Wednesday featured two witnesses who told of an

October 1901 drinking bout with Horn in Denver's Scandinavian Saloon. A drunken Horn reportedly bragged about the Nickell shot; said the killing of Willie was the dirtiest work he had ever done; stated that many Cheyenne men were involved; and asked that his drinking partners keep all of this information secret. Then Joe LeFors testified, arousing the spectators as he related details of the transcribed conversation with Horn. Deputy Sheriff Les Snow and Charles Ohnhaus added their testimony, and other witnesses swore that Horn was not drunk when he went to the marshal's office with LeFors.

The next day, Thursday, October 16, the defense provided several witnesses who testified that Horn had been drinking heavily and was "loaded" prior to the meeting with LeFors. Various other witnesses appeared on Thursday and Friday. Then silence fell over the courtroom as Tom Horn took the stand in his own behalf. Judge Lacey questioned Horn at length about his occupation and his activities during the period of the murder. Horn testified that he was hospitalized in Denver when he supposedly was in the Scandinavian Saloon bragging about committing the murder.

Horn was to be cross-examined by Walter Stoll on Saturday morning, and people began trooping to the courthouse in the dawn chill to make sure of having a seat. They were rewarded with a relentless grilling of Horn by Stoll. At one point Stoll pressed Horn regarding a question the defendant earlier had answered vaguely. Stoll asked Horn if he could not "speak more clearly" as to his whereabouts. "I certainly can," replied the beleaguered Horn, "because I have had several things to refresh my memory. The simple fact of your questioning me so closely ... has certainly had a tendency to refresh my mind on the subject."[38]

But when Stoll quizzed Horn about what he was wearing when he returned to Laramie shortly after the murder, Tom dryly commented, "I change clothes sometimes anyhow." The courtroom broke into laughter. Horn brought even more laughter from the spectators with his next remark.[39]

Stoll continued to bear down, repeatedly asking Horn if he was sober enough to remember this or that conversation. "I knew perfectly well what I was saying," replied Horn. The defender insisted that he had "a distinct recollection" of a certain point, and he stated emphatically, "I remember everything that occurred to me in my life." Regarding "the young gentleman, Charlie Ohnhaus, who took down the conversation in short hand," Horn was surprisingly charitable: "I have every reason to believe that he took it down as accurately as he could, and he didn't make any mistake that I know of, and I certainly don't think that he made an intentional mistake."[40] Stoll, by exacting a repeated insistence from the defendant that he always was in control of his faculties, may have caused jurors to feel that even if Horn had been drunk while talking to LeFors, the transcribed statements were not empty boasts.

Horn also admitted making a number of statements, some peppered with profanity ("I am given in a natural way to profanity"), but he insisted that he was just swapping "stories."

Over and over Stoll asked Horn if he had made this or that statement under the influence of alcohol. To one such question Horn replied affirmatively, adding,

"I would have said anything else that pleased him." To a similar question he admitted, "I had been drinking considerably, of course, but as far as that influencing anything I had to say, I knew perfectly well what I was saying." Horn had told LeFors that his horse was far away at the time of the murder, and Stoll asked if that conversation had occurred as stated: "It did and the horse was a long ways off at the time," Horn said pointedly, "and I was with the horse also."[41]

Although Horn continued to insist that he had never killed anyone, Stoll hammered at him throughout Saturday. Sunday brought a day of recess, and on Monday Joe LeFors and Les Snow were recalled to the stand, followed by a series of miscellaneous witnesses. Judge Richard H. Scott delivered instructions to the jury on Tuesday morning, then Walter Stoll spent the balance of the day reviewing the evidence and delivering his summation. On Wednesday, T. E. Burke spoke at length for the defense, followed by Lacey. Lacey concluded his impassioned plea on Thursday, then Stoll began his closing argument to the jury. Stoll dramatically concluded his presentation on Friday morning, and the fatigued jury filed out at 11:30.

The crowd dispersed, betting enthusiastically about the verdict. Joe LeFors "fully believed that the jury would find a verdict of not guilty," and Horn's friends planned a party to celebrate his expected acquittal. But at 4:20 in the afternoon a voice called down from the jury room that a verdict had been decided upon, and spectators scurried back to the courtroom. Horn was pronounced guilty, and Judge Richard Scott sentenced him to hang on January 9, 1903.[42]

Attorneys for the defense soon filed a motion for a new trial, citing twenty-three reasons for their motion. The prosecution blocked the motion for a new trial, but the defense filed a petition of error and won a stay of execution. Ensuing legal

The jury, accompanied by two bailiffs, which convicted Tom Horn. (Courtesy Wyoming State Archives)

maneuvers would cause a stay for at least six months, until the state supreme court could offer a ruling. Many citizens, already appalled at the enormous cost of the long trial, predicted that a new trial would bankrupt the county. Although Horn was dismayed at the prospect of several more months in confinement, the defense was optimistic, and in many quarters it was cynically assumed that the cattle barons would ultimately prevail over the law again. But Stoll resoundingly won reelection in November 1902, an indication of the public's opposition to Horn and his high-powered lawyers.

Rumors of escape plots began to circulate, causing Sheriff Smalley to take precautions: extra arms were placed in the sheriff's office; anyone entering the cell block was carefully inspected; steel gratings were placed over the windows of the sheriff's office; and a heavy steel door was installed at the corridor entrance to the jail area.

In January 1903 an elaborate plan to liberate Horn with a dynamite explosion was exposed by Hubert Herr, a cowboy from Coble's Iron Mountain Ranch who had been jailed as an inside man to facilitate the scheme. Herr fled west on a train, fearing for his life. He told a newspaper reporter, in exchange for travel funds, that he had "ordered a conversation between Horn and another man, in which the deal was arranged for the murder of Kels P. Nickell." Horn's lawyer must have cringed at the revelation of a plan which could only swing public opinion further against Horn.[43]

The stoic demeanor maintained by Horn throughout his long incarceration and trial earned the prisoner grudging admiration for courage. But the public was incensed by allegations made during the trial, and shortly after testimony ended, the *Leader* excoriated "the coward-villain" in a damning editorial. "Tom Horn is no more the debonaire criminal and splendid assassin in the eyes of worshippers

Halloween 1902

Halloween in Cheyenne often had been a night of rough pranks. But in 1902 Halloween occurred immediately after the trial and conviction of Tom Horn, and the mood was ugly. "The police report that never before have they seen such large crowds out on Hallowe'en," stated the *Leader* on November 1, adding that "gangs kept a sharp lookout for officers and evaded them."

A special target was boardwalks and plank street crossings. Between 300 and 400 crossings were overturned, along with boardwalks, all over town. One "gang, believed to have been soldiers, rocked three houses of ill fame in the west portion of the city," including "Mother Curly's." Window panes were shattered, and an officer was assigned to patrol the red light district the rest of the night.

On Seventeenth Street, on a telegraph pole across from the home of Judge J. W. Lacey, "pranksters" hanged Tom Horn and John Coble in effigy. "The dummy was an excellent imitation of a man," and on its chest was attached "a huge white placard bearing the inscription, 'Horn and Coble.'"

of this type of heroes." Horn "is a miserable braggart, a monumental liar, or else a man with a soul steeped in guilty crime," fumed the *Leader*. "From any perspective Horn has ceased to exist as a hero in the eyes of the dime novel reader or the cowboy as a 'bad man.'" Indeed, after Horn's arrest the Omaha *News* published "a full page write up of Tom Horn which is as blood-thirsty as the worst dime novel ever written." And while Horn was awaiting execution, Deputy Sheriff Les Snow, who had been part of the "confession" team, stated that the prisoner "realizes that any break would cost him his life in all probability," and was afraid to act. "Horn is a moral and physical coward when it comes to risking his own life and would never take a long chance to break away." Three days later, Horn broke out of jail.[44]

On Sunday morning, August 9, Horn and a fellow inmate, Jim McCloud, overpowered a guard. The two escapees made their way outside, where McCloud, who was under indictment for bushwhacking a sheepherder, galloped off on the only horse in the jail corral. After a brief chase he was caught and subdued.

Horn, fleeing on foot, was charged by a citizen named O. A. Aldrich. Aldrich fired several pistol shots, one of which grazed Horn in the head. Horn was unfamiliar with the automatic he had seized and could not release the safety, and Aldrich wrestled him to the ground. A swarm of officers beat Horn into submission and dragged him back to jail. Mobs threatened to lynch Horn, further evidence of the turn of public opinion. (However, when Kels Nickell tried to harangue a mob, he was silenced by Sheriff Smalley, who threatened to put him into the cell with Tom Horn.) For his efforts O. A. Aldrich was granted permanent license to run his concession, a merry-go-round, free of charge in Cheyenne. Sheriff

Tom Horn (center) being escorted back to jail along Ferguson Street. Several citizens had given pursuit on bicycles. (Courtesy Wyoming State Archives)

Smalley used the *Leader* "to extend his sincere thanks to all of these brave citizens who assisted him during the escape and recapture of" Horn and McCloud.[45]

Horn's escape attempt damaged his chances for another stay of execution. On October 1, 1903, the Wyoming Supreme Court affirmed the verdict of the trial court in an opinion that required two hours to read. Horn would be executed on November 20 — the day preceding his forty-third birthday — on a complex gallows designed in 1892 for Charlie Miller. No one wanted to execute the teenaged killer, so the design caused the victim to trigger his own gallows. The device was reassembled for Horn's execution.[46] As Horn's lawyers mounted a last-ditch effort, rumors again abounded that cattle barons would sponsor an escape attempt. Butch Cassidy and the Wild Bunch were mentioned as leaders of the jailbreak. A machine

Tom Horn in the cell block doorway. While in jail he lost so much weight that his hangman miscalculated the necessary length of the rope. (Courtesy Wyoming State Archives)

gun from Fort D. A. Russell was set up at the jail, with a sergeant to operate it, and a large arc light was strategically placed to discourage a night attack.

Every possible legal device was attempted by the defense lawyers, but to no avail. "All right," Horn told his lawyers. "But by God, they are hanging an innocent man." Horn wrote numerous letters and finished an autobiography, which would be published posthumously by John Coble. Although the handwritten manuscript filled "four note books of about 125 or 150 pages each," the book closed with 1894, "since which time everybody else has been more familiar with my life and business than I have been myself."[47]

No rescue attempt was made, and on the day of the execution, Horn faced his fate with admirable courage. John Coble broke down as he said farewell, but other cattlemen, holed up at the Cheyenne Club, were rumored to be apprehensive to the last that Horn might talk. Yet Horn denied to the end that he killed Willie Nickell, and he disdained to divulge any information about his employers.

By dawn a crowd began gathering which soon numbered in the hundreds, while two troops of the Wyoming National Guard were deployed to maintain order. Their rifles were loaded "with 'mob' cartridges containing two bullets of .30 calibre and without jackets," reported the *Leader*. "They are intended for use at ranges under 200 yards and are very destructive."[48] A plank fence had been

Acting Governor Fenimore Chatterton, seated at center, resisted pressure from cattlemen to pardon Tom Horn. Next to Chatterton, in double-breasted coat, is Wyoming's longtime adjutant general, F. A. Stitzer. (Courtesy Wyoming State Archives)

erected to shield the gallows area from public view, and only a small number of law officers, journalists, and friends of Horn were permitted to view the execution. Horn ate a hearty breakfast, smoked a final cigar, and met his end impassively.

Many students of the murder trial remain unconvinced that Horn killed Willie Nickell. In 1993 lawyers retried the case in a Cheyenne courtroom, and the verdict was not guilty. After reading the trial manuscript and considering other aspects of the case, one is tempted to conclude that a member of the Miller family murdered Willie Nickell. On the day of the execution, Horn wrote John Coble that when he spent two nights at the Millers' ranch, James Miller and another cattle rancher, Bill McDonald, told him they intended "to kill off the Nickell outfit and wanted me to go in on it." Two other ranchers would pay Horn, but Tom declined. The next day Horn was asked again, and when he once more turned down the offer, McDonald said, "Well, we have made up our minds to wipe out the whole Nickell outfit." When Horn heard of Willie Nickell's murder, "I felt I was well out of the mix up." Several weeks later, he again saw McDonald and Miller, "and they were blowing to me about running and shooting the sheep of Nickell." Horn went on to refute the "supposed confession" on several points of testimony: "Ohnhaus, LeFors and Snow ... all swore lies to fit the case." He closed his final letter with a ringing statement: "This is the truth, as I am going to die in ten minutes."[49]

Whether or not Horn was guilty of the murder of Willie Nickell, there was general certainty that he had killed four other men as a hired killer, along with rumors—which he had done nothing to discourage—that he had slain many others in the course of his work. There was a sense that Horn was a throwback to a more primitive and lawless era, and that Wyoming—and certainly Cheyenne—were well rid of the noted assassin.

A decade earlier, the cattlemen's faction had won legal exoneration following a large-scale effort to invade Johnson County with hired gunmen. For the cattlemen it was business as usual in Cheyenne. But by the twentieth century a civilizing transformation had been wrought in Cheyenne and Wyoming, as profoundly evidenced by the conviction and execution of Tom Horn. Wyoming cattlemen had generously funded Horn's defense, they had exerted political pressure to secure his release—and he had been hanged anyway. Such efforts several years earlier almost certainly would have resulted in the release of a hired gun of the big ranchers.

But the landmark legal events of 1902 and 1903 revealed a permanent change of attitude toward unbridled violence over western rangelands. The most spectacular trial ever held in Cheyenne, a trial followed across the nation, proclaimed that the Magic City no longer should be considered a haunt of Wild West lawlessness. For more than three decades the reputation of Hell on Wheels had clung tenaciously to Cheyenne. But with the dawn of a new century, Cheyenne had presided over the trial and execution of a notorious western killer. While the flavor of the Old West always would permeate Cheyenne, the twentieth century ushered the Magic City into modern America.

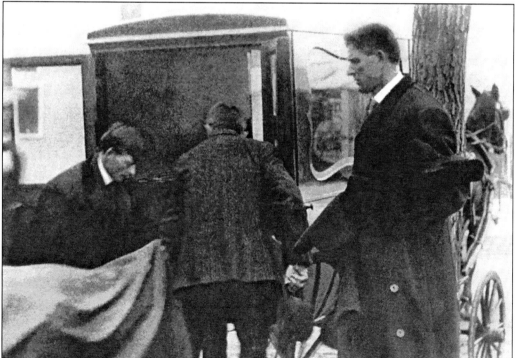

Tom Horn's body being loaded into a horse-drawn hearse. His brother Charles had arranged for the remains to be taken to Boulder, Colorado, for burial. (Courtesy Wyoming State Archives)

22

Echoes

The forces that shaped Cheyenne during the nineteenth century would echo through the years to come. For example, Senator F.E. Warren, a powerhouse in Cheyenne for the last three decades of the 1800s, proved just as potent during the first three decades of the twentieth century.

Senator Warren never ceased to funnel a stream of federal appropriations into Cheyenne and Fort Russell and elsewhere in Wyoming. He served as chairman of the Military Affairs Committee from 1905 through 1911, working with the secretary of war to reorganize the army, raise military pay, and establish a general staff. From 1921 until 1929, Senator Warren was chairman of the powerful Senate Appropriations Committee. In 1905 Frankie Warren married Capt. John J. Pershing, and the next year he was promoted to brigadier general by President Roosevelt, who vaulted the captain over 862 majors, lieutenant colonels, and colonels. There was widespread criticism that General Pershing won his star because of the influence of Senator Warren, even though Pershing had an impressive combat record against Apache warriors, Spanish soldiers, and Filipino insurrectos, as well as service in Cuba alongside Col. Theodore Roosevelt.[1]

General and Mrs. Pershing presented Senator Warren with four grandchildren—three daughters and a son, Francis Warren Pershing. But in 1915, while General Pershing was stationed in Fort Bliss, tragedy struck when Frankie and her three little girls were killed in a fire at the Presidio in San Francisco. Only Warren was saved. Frankie and her daughters were buried beside Helen Warren at Lakeview Cemetery.[2]

Fred Warren assumed management of the Warren Livestock Company after graduating from Harvard. He married and had a son and a daughter; little

Francis Emroy Warren eventually would succeed his father as the head of the family business interests. Senator Warren, a widower since 1902, remarried in 1911 and purchased the mansion on Seventeenth Street built by merchant king Erasmus Nagle.

On July 11, 1929, a thirteen-gun salute welcomed Senator Warren, accompanied by his wife, to Fort Russell. The eighty-five-year-old senator, proudly wearing his Civil War Medal of Honor, was scheduled to review the Fourth Infantry Brigade. The big parade ground was surrounded by handsome brick buildings built with appropriations secured by Senator Warren for his favorite military post. Ignoring concerned pleas that he sit down, the old soldier stood at attention for nearly an hour while 2,000 infantrymen marched past.[3]

A few months after this splendid occasion, F. E. Warren died in Washington, on November 24, 1929, following a three-week illness. He had served in the Senate for a then-record thirty-seven years, and he was the last Civil War veteran in Congress. Brought to Cheyenne, he lay in state in the rotunda of the Capitol he had been instrumental in building. Again the garrison of Fort Russell turned out in his honor, at the head of the long funeral procession from St. Mark's Episcopal Church. In a light snowfall, Warren was borne to Lakeview Cemetery in a flag-draped casket atop a caisson drawn by six black horses. A final artillery salute was fired, "taps" was sounded, and ten enlisted men carried him to the open grave, because it was as an enlisted man that Corporal Warren had won the Medal of Honor. The opening words of the *State Leader* account summarized his contributions:

> He came home today for the last time, our Grand Old Man—home to the state he loved, *home to the city which he more than any other had helped to build*—home to us of whom he was a peerless champion.[4] [Author's italics]

Within days after the funeral service, President Calvin Coolidge directed that Fort D. A. Russell would be renamed Fort Francis E. Warren. Camp Marfa, Texas, became known as Fort D. A. Russell, assuming the designation that had been carried for sixty-two years by the fort near Cheyenne. Fort Francis E. Warren expanded enormously during World War II, with a post population of 26,000 at one point. In 1949 Fort Francis E. Warren became Francis E. Warren Air Force Base. By the next year it was announced in the newspaper that, factoring in payroll for military personnel and civilian employees, along with overall economic impact, the base had become "Cheyenne's Leading Industry."[5] Fort D.A. Russell had provided a steady economic input since Cheyenne's earliest years, a key financial role that was markedly improved upon by F. E. Warren AFB.

The Union Pacific Railroad likewise had performed a crucial economic role since Cheyenne's beginnings. Passenger trains no longer pull in and out of the imposing UP Depot throughout each day. But the UP now is the nation's largest freight carrier, and freight traffic is constant along Cheyenne's vast rail yards. Today, antique steam engines impressively decorate Cheyenne parks, and the old roundhouse is the home of rolling stock that is kept in repair.

"The Union Pacific is the main corporate employer in town," observed historian Stephen Ambrose in his history of the first transcontinental railroad, *Nothing Like It in the World.* "To the uncountable number of train buffs in the United States, and indeed around the world, Cheyenne is a Mecca. There the last steam engines purchased by the UP are housed ..., and today they haul passenger trains to special events. The old depot has been turned into a railroad museum. Dodge's tent site has a marker on it. Everyone with any connection to the UP or to trains knows the simple fact that Dodge picked well, and that Cheyenne remains, as it had been for nearly a century and a half, one of the premier railroad towns in the world."[6]

Cheyenne was designated temporary capital in 1869, and today the Magic City continues to enjoy the prestige and influence and economic advantages which benefit a seat of government. And the one-day Wild West exhibition first staged in 1897 has become Frontier Days, a weeklong celebration of Cheyenne's cowboy past and an annual cash cow. Every year the population of Cheyenne is doubled for a week as the Holy City of the Cow lives again through an incomparable rodeo.

Like F. E. Warren, Joseph M. Carey earned a fortune, built a livestock empire, and gained high political office while making Cheyenne his home. Carey's senatorial career was cut short after one abbreviated term in the 1890s, but in 1910 he was elected governor, even though he had to switch to the Democratic Party to secure a nomination. Governor Carey served with typical efficiency for four years, then declined to run for reelection. Carey had the satisfaction of seeing his son, Robert, elected governor as a Republican in 1919, and Robert also would win election to the U.S. Senate in 1930. Joseph M. Carey died in 1924 at the age of seventy-nine. Louisa David Carey, the wife of a governor and senator, and the

This old locomotive and tender in Lions Park is one of many reminders of the Union Pacific around Cheyenne. (Photo by Karon O'Neal)

mother of a governor and senator, lived for another decade. "Her culture and charm won her a wide circle of friends," eulogized the *Wyoming Eagle* in 1934. "She was noted for her hospitality and was fond of entertaining."[7]

The Carey Mansion, where Louisa staged countless socials, many on a grand scale, no longer stands. But F. E. Warren's last home, known today as the Nagle-Warren Mansion, still strikingly dominates a corner of Seventeenth, as it has for nearly 120 years. The superb Whipple Mansion, now a restaurant, is across the street. The home of Judge Willis Van Devanter continues to house a family, as do the residences of Dr. W. W. Crook and of Moreton Frewen. Many other dwellings built in the late 1800s still fulfill their original purpose.

Although the Warren Emporium is gone, several of the handsome commercial structures he erected on Sixteenth still host businesses. The ornate Tivoli remains a vibrant commercial building on Sixteenth, and so does the two-story structure erected in 1871 by F. E. Addoms, the oldest business building still functioning in downtown Cheyenne. Throughout the old business district are a number of other nineteenth-century commercial structures which, although sometimes altered in appearance, are still open to trade. One of those is Max Idleman's three-story brick building on Sixteenth, and the Idleman Mansion (now a funeral home) is the only one of the grand homes on Carey Avenue that survives.

Of the magnificent church buildings that served nineteenth-century congregations, two of the finest—St. Mark's Episcopal and First Methodist—remain open to worshipers. And the two most impressive edifices built in the 1880s, the

The Eighteenth Street home of Willis Van Devanter. A prominent Cheyenne attorney and faithful lieutenant of F. E. Warren, Van Devanter held numerous positions in Cheyenne and Wyoming, and eventually served as an associate justice of the U.S. Supreme Court for twenty-six years. (Photo by Karon O'Neal)

State Capitol and the UP Depot, continue to be utilized and enjoyed daily by Cheyenne residents and tourists.

Longtime Cheyenne residents lament the destruction of many historic buildings, some of which were replaced by parking lots. But much remains that would be recognized by R.S. Van Tassell, Billy Irvine, Estelle Reel, Jeff Carr, Prof. Churchill, Dr. Crook, Colonel Slack, Marie Buchanan, Henry Hynds, Pete Bergersen, Tom Horn, Judge Van Devanter, the Kuykendall family, Joseph and Louisa Carey and their two sons, Emroy and Helen Warren, and Frankie and Fred—and by a host of their less-well-known contemporaries. They all send echoes into the future.

How Green Was My Valley, the motion picture which won an Academy Award for Best Picture of 1941, opens with an unseen narrator reflecting on memory: "There is no fence nor hedge around time that is gone. You can go back and have what you like of it, if you can remember." It is easy to remember the formative period of the Magic City, because there are so many places in Cheyenne that transmit echoes from the past.

The Tivoli, built in the 1880s, remains a jewel of downtown Cheyenne. (Photo by Karon O'Neal)

Endnotes

Chapter 1: Birth of the Magic City

1. Joseph W. Cook, *Diary and Letters of the Reverend Joseph W. Cook, Missionary to Cheyenne*, 12-13.
2. Dodge, How We Built the Union Pacific Railway, 12.
3. *Ibid.*, 20-21.
4. *Ibid.*, 18-19.
5. *Ibid.*, 23.
6. Seymour, *Reminiscence of the Union Pacific*, 16-17, 20-24; Stetler, "The Birth of a Frontier Boomtown," *Annals of Wyoming*, 7-8.
7. Seymour, *Reminiscence of the Union Pacific*, 24; *Leader*, February 20, 1883.
8. Kuykendall, *Frontier Days*, 108-109; Stetler, "The Birth of a Frontier Boomtown," *Annals of Wyoming*, 9-10; *Leader*, July 20, 1886.
9. Dodge, *How We Built the Union Pacific*, 116.
10. *Leader*, January 26, 1881; Dodge, *How We Built the Union Pacific*, 23; Bartlett, ed., *History of Wyoming*, 550.
11. *Leader*, July 18, 1886; Stetler, "The Birth of a Frontier Boomtown," *Annals of Wyoming*, 10-11.
12. *Leader*, February 20, 1883, July 18, 1886, and April 1, 1896; Kuykendall, *Frontier Days*, 108-109, 117; Stetler, "The Birth of a Frontier Boomtown," *Annals of Wyoming*, 9.
13. Dodge, *How We Built the Union Pacific*, 116-117.
14. *Leader*, July 18, 1886; Stetler, "The Birth of a Frontier Boomtown," *Annals of Wyoming*, 15-16.
15. *Leader*, July 18, 1886.
16. *Ibid.*, September 19, 1867.
17. Mumie, *Nathan Addison Baker*; *Leader*, September 19, 1877.
18. *Leader*, January 28, February 3, May 21, 1868; Cook, *Diary and Letters*, 20, 27, 29, 30.
19. *Leader*, January 11, February 19, March 2 and 9, 1868; January 27 and September 7, 1869.
20. *Leader*, April 24, 1868; September 7, 1869.
21. Kuykendall, *Frontier Days*, 116; *Leader*, April 5, 1887, and August 31, 1897.
22. Ambrose, *Nothing Like It in the World*, 317.
23. *Leader*, November 2, 1867; Simonin, "A French View of Cheyenne in 1867," 241.
24. Dodge, *How We Built the Union Pacific*, 53-54.
25. Bell, *New Tracks in North America*, 254.
26. Dodge, *How We Built the Union Pacific*, 45; *Leader*, November 14, 1867.
27. *Leader*, November 16, 1867.
28. *Ibid.*, November 21, 1867; Union Pacific Railroad Company, *Progress of Their Road*, 11.
29. *Union Pacific Railroad Company, Progress of Their Road*, 11; Dodge, *How We Built the Union Pacific*, 53; Kuykendall, *Frontier Days*, 117.
30. Bell, *New Tracks in North America*, 18; *Leader*, December 21, 1867; August 15, 1877; July 12, 1882; Simonin, "A French View of Cheyenne in 1867," 241.

31. Kuykendall, *Frontier Days*, 117.

32. Simonin, "A French View of Cheyenne in 1867," 241-242.

33. *Ibid.*, 240.

34. Simonin, "A French View of Cheyenne in 1867," 240, 242; *Leader*, December 28, 1867; January 29 and April 1, 1868.

35. Simonin, "A French View of Cheyenne in 1867," 241; J. Jordan to sister, November 24, 1867.

36. Simonin, "A French View of Cheyenne in 1867," 241-242.

37. Dodge, *How We Built the Union Pacific*, 116; Kuykendall, *Frontier Days*, 117; Bancroft, *History of Nevada, Colorado, and Wyoming*, page 733-738

38. *Leader*, September 24 and 28, October 5 and 8, December 31, 1867; Stelter, "The Birth of a Frontier Boom Town," *Annals of Wyoming*, 15-16.

39. *Leader*, January 22, June 22, August 24, September 4, 1869.

40. *Ibid.*, January 15 and May 20, 1868.

41. *Colorado Herald* article cited in the *Leader*, February 17, 1868.

42. *Leader*, October 5 and December 31, 1867; July 18, 1886.

43. *Ibid.*, January 17, 18, 22, and 24, 1868; June 18, 1869.

44. *Ibid.*, January 24 and February 17, 1868; July 14, 1902.

Chapter 2: Fort Russell and Camp Carlin

1. Adams, Col. Gerald M., *The Post Near Cheyenne*, 7.

2. *Ibid.*, 7-8; Hart, *Old Forts of the Northwest*, 110-111.

3. Utley, *Frontier Regulars*, 86; Adams, *The Post Near Cheyenne*, 13.

4. Adams, *The Post Near Cheyenne*, 12-13.

5. *Leader*, February 21 and 28, and March 5, 1868.

6. Adams, *The Post Near Cheyenne*, 103-109.

7. *Ibid.*, 103, 108-109; Heitman, comp., *Historical Register and Dictionary of the United States Army*, Vol. I: 282.

8. Adams, *The Post Near Cheyenne*, 103-108; *Leader*, May 15, 1896.

9. Adams, *The Post Near Cheyenne*, 106-108.

10. *Leader*, February 12, 1869.

11. *Ibid.*, February 20, 1869.

12. *Ibid.*, May 4, 1869.

13. *Ibid.*, February 29, 1869, and July 6, 1868.

Chapter 3: Vigilantes and Peace Officers

1. Ambrose, *Nothing Like It in the World*, 217-220.

2. *Wyoming Tribune*, December 20, 1896.

3. "The 'Magic City' Cheyenne, Dakota Territory — 1867," Annals of Wyoming, 161

4. *Leader*, December 22, 1889; October 8, 1867.

5. *Ibid.*, December 22, 1889; January 1 and February 3, 1868.

6. *Ibid.*, January 1, 1868; September 19, 1867.

7. *Ibid.*, September 24, 26, 28, December 12, 17, 31, 1867; January 14, 16, 31, 1868.

8. *Ibid.*, October 5, 1867; March 27, 1897; Kuykendall, *Frontier Days*, 117-118.

9. *Leader*, November 2, 1867; January 6 and 7, 1868.

10. An extensive history of the vigilante movement was presented by Richard Maxwell Brown in *Strain of Violence: Historical Studies of American Violence and Vigilantism* (New York: Oxford University Press, 1975). Also see Frank Richard Prassel, *The Great American Outlaw: A Legacy of Fact and Fiction* (Norman: University of Oklahoma Press, 1993), W. Eugene Hollon, *Frontier Violence: Another Look* (New York: Oxford University Press, 1974), and Wayne Gard, *Frontier Violence* (Norman: University of Oklahoma Press, 1949).

11. *Leader*, December 27, 1867; January 11, 1868; Kuykendall, *Frontier Days*, 117-118.

12. *Leader*, January 13, 1868.

13. *Ibid.*, January 17 and 18, 1868.

14. *Ibid.*, January 20 and 21, 1868; September 18, 1883; Kuykendall, *Frontier Days*, 120-121.

15. *Leader*, January 22, 1868.

16. *Ibid.*, January 30, 1868.

17. *Ibid.*, February 10, 1868.

18. *Ibid.*, February 11 and 13, 1868.

19. *Ibid.*, February 14 and 15, March 17, 1868; Kuykendall *Frontier Days*, 115.

20. *Ibid.*, February 15, 1868.

21. *Ibid.*, February 26, March 2, 13, 14, 1868.

22. *Ibid.*, March 12 and 21, 1868; Homsher, ed., *South Pass*, 1868, 16.

23. *Leader*, March 17 and 21, 1868.

24. *Ibid.*, March 21 and 23, 1868.

25. *Ibid.*, March 21, 1868; Chisholm, *South Pass*, 1868, 16.

26. *Ibid.*, March 23, 1868.

27. This incident is described in testimony offered to the coroner's jury and printed in the *Leader*, April 6, 1868.

28. *Ibid.*, April 6, 1868.

29. *Ibid.*, August 11 and September 10, 1868.

30. *Ibid.*, September 10 and December 15, 1868.

31. *Ibid.*, January 4, 5, and 6, 1869.

32. *Ibid.*, February 16, 17 and 18, 1869.

33. *Ibid.*, March 17, 1869.

34. *Ibid.*, May 14 and June 9, 1869.

35. *Ibid.*, September 14 and 21, October 2, 1869.

36. *Ibid.*, December 13, 14 and 20, 1869.

37. *Ibid.*, January 3, 1870.

38. Coutant, "Thomas Jefferson Carr," *Annals of Wyoming*; Gorzalka, *Wyoming's Territorial Sheriffs*, 37-42.

39. *Leader*, November 11, 23 and 25, 1869.

40. The execution of Boyer is described in the *Leader*, April 21 and 22, 1871.

Chapter 4: Urban Pioneers

1. Billington, *Westward Expansion*, 6-7.

2. *Leader*, July 23 and 25, 1890; Trenholm, *Wyoming Blue Book*, Vol. 1: 285-286.

3. Flynn, "Renesselaer Schuyler Van Tassell," *Annals of Wyoming*, quote on 4.

4. *Leader*, December 16, 1873.

5. Bartlett, ed. *History of Wyoming*, 132-135, 366-368.

6. Trenholm, *Wyoming Blue Book*, Vol. 1: 108, 117; *Leader*, October 18, 1900.

7. Barton, ed., *Early Cheyenne Homes*, 1880-1890, 27, 59-60.

8. *Ibid.*, 66; Trenholm, *Wyoming Blue Book*, Vol. 1: 105; *Leader*, June 9, 16 and 21, 1885.

9. *Leader*, September 10, 1891.

10. *Ibid.*

11. *Ibid.*

12. *Medal of Honor*, 136.

13. *Salt Lake City Tribune*, December 2, 1917.

14. *Ibid.*

15. Bartlett, ed., *History of Wyoming*, Vol. 1: 5-9; *Leader*, March 27, 1889; Hansen, "The Congressional Career of Senator Francis E. Warren from 1890 to 1902," *Annals of Wyoming*, 2-16.

16. Mabel E. Brown, ed., *First Ladies of Wyoming*, 33-36.

17. Bartlett, ed., *History of Wyoming*, Vol. III, 5-7.

18. Mabel E. Brown, ed., *First Ladies of Wyoming*, 55-59; Barton, ed., *Early Cheyenne Homes*, 1880–1890, 17.

19. *Leader*, May 10, 1869.

Chapter 5: After the Boom

1. *Leader*, October 19 and 24, November 12 and 16, 1867.

2. *Ibid.*, January 6 and February 3, 1868; Joseph W. Cook, *Diary of Rev. Joseph W. Cook*, 12-13.

3. *Leader*, March 16 and 21, 1868; September 27, 1869; Cook, *Diary and Letters*, 32.

4. *Leader*, January 8, 1868; Cook, *Diary and Letters*, 32, 92, 111-112, 115.

5. Malcolm L. Cook, *First Church: A People Called Methodist*, 1-18; *Leader*, October 5 and 12, 1867, and September 22, 1870.

6. Stelter, "The Birth of a Frontier Boom Town," *Annals of Wyoming*, 28-29.

7. The founding of St. Mark's is described in detail in Reverend Cook's *Diaries and Letters* and in Shirley E. Flynn, *Our Heritage: 100 Years at St. Mark's*, 18-25, as well as in various newspaper items.

8. *A History of the First Congregational Church*, 3-5.

9. Morton and Dubois, *A Century of Service: History of the First Presbyterian Church, Cheyenne*, 5-7.

10. *Leader*, May 26, 1870; Cook, *Diary and Letters*, 18.

11. Cook, *Diary and Letters*, 18.

12. *Leader*, August 7 and December 9, 1869; July 17, 1889; January 14, 1899; April 22, 1902.

13. *Ibid.*, January 18, 26 and 30, 1869.

14. *Ibid.*, January 18, February 9, 13 and 16, March 16, July 10 and 12, December 24, 1869.

15. *Ibid.*, March 17, May 8, 20 and 26, June 2, 3 and 4, August 27, November 19, 25 and 27, 1869.

16. Dial, *A Place to Raise Hell: Cheyenne Saloons*, 30-35; *Leader*, January 27 and July 21, 1869; July 17, 1889; January 14, 1899.

17. *Leader*, December 14 and 31, 1867; April 3, 8, 20 and 21, 1868; Dial, *A Place to Raise Hell: Cheyenne Saloons*, 18-19.

18. *Leader*, October 10, 1867; February 10 and 11, 1868; July 15 and 16, and August 30, 1869.

19. *Ibid.*, April 29 and 30, May 14, September 1, 6, 9, 18 and 29, October 9, 1869.

20. *Ibid.*, January 15, 1868.

21. *Ibid.*, July 3 and 6, 1868; July 5, 1869.

22. Bancroft, *History of Nevada, Colorado, and Wyoming*, 741.

23. *Ibid.*, 741-42.

24. Kuykendall, *Frontier Days*, 131.

25. Larson, *History of Wyoming*, 70-71; *Leader*, June 14, 1869.

26. *Leader*, October 12, 1869; Trenholm, *Wyoming Blue Book*, Vol. 1: 150-151; Kuykendall, *Frontier Days*, 132.

27. Larson, *History of Wyoming*, 78-81.

28. *Leader*, December 11, 1869; Kuykendall, *Frontier Days*, 133.

29. *Leader*, December 11, 1869.

30. *Leader*, March 5, 1868; May 23 and September 21, 1869; Kuykendall, *Frontier Days*, 134.

31. Kuykendall, *Frontier Days*, 108; Bartlett, *History of Wyoming*, 651.

32. Kuykendall, *Frontier Days*, 108; *Leader*, February 7, 1868; February 13 and July 22, 1869.

33. Kuykendall, *Frontier Days*, 162-163, 250.

34. *Leader*, December 10 and 12, 1867; February 6, November 8 and 10, 1869.

35. *Ibid.*, September 24, 1867.

36. *Ibid.*, October 10, 1867; April 13 and 24, 1868.

37. *Ibid.*, September 24, 1867; February 25 and April 2, 1868; January 15 and 20, February 13 and 17, May 20, and November 16, 1869.

Chapter 6: Fires, Storms, and Other Disasters

1. *Leader*, January 13, 1870. Most of this issue is devoted to the fire, providing the description and quotes in the next several paragraphs.

2. *Leader*, January 14, 1870.

3. *Ibid.*

4. *Ibid.*

5. *Ibid.*, January 13 and 20, 1870.

6. *Leader*, April 20, 1870; Epps, *Cities on Stone*, 2, 13.

7. *Leader*, May 7, 1870.

8. *Ibid.*, March 27, 1895.

9. *Ibid.*, November 25, 1870; August 3, 1871; July 3, 1873.

10. *Ibid.*, December 13 and 14, 1871; January 11, 1872.

11. *Ibid.*, May 12 and 16, 1873.

12. *Ibid.*, July 3, 1874.

13. *Ibid.*, December 23, 1874.

14. *Ibid.*, February 21, 1872; January 4, 5 and 6, 1875.

15. *Ibid.*, July 6, 7 and 12, October 2, November 11, 1875; July 5, 1876.

16. *Ibid.*, December 11, 1877.

17. *Ibid.*, March 29 and April 18, 1878; March 21, 1895; May 8, 1877; Cheyenne Centennial Committee, *The Magic City of the Plains*, 70-71, 75.

18. *Leader*, July 26, 1875; April 4, 1876; *Wyoming Tribune*, August 13, 1896.

19. The story was reported in detail in the *Leader* on September 6, 1879, and there were follow-up accounts the next day. Further description was added in testimony before the coroner's jury, published in the *Leader* on September 10, 11 and 16.

20. *Leader*, September 10, 14 and 16, 1879.

21. *Ibid.*, December 13, 1871.

Chapter 7: Cheyenne and the Black Hills Gold Rush

1. Kuykendall, *Frontier Days*, 137-140; *Leader*, December 11, 13 and 23, 1869.

2. *Leader*, January 2, 1875.

3. *Ibid.*, October 6 and 7, 1874.

4. Parker, *Gold in the Black Hills*, 47-48; Larson, *History of Wyoming*, 131.

5. *Leader*, March 17, 18 and 23, 1875.

6. *Ibid.*, March 23, 1875.

7. *Ibid.*, March 24, 1875.

8. *Ibid.*, March 26, May 3 and 13, and July 6, 1875.

9. *Ibid.*, July 6 and 7, 1875.

10. *Ibid.*, July 12, 1875; May 14 and June 29, 1876.

11. Kuykendall, *Frontier Days*, 174-177.

12. *Leader*, January 11, 1876.

13. *Ibid.*, January 11, March 5, April 19, and June 6, 1876.

14. *Ibid.*, February 5 and 10, September 10, 1875.

15. *Ibid.*, January 11, March 9, and July 16, 1876.

16. *Ibid.*, January 15 and 29, March 18 and 25, and April 18 and 19, 1876.

17. *Ibid.*, March 19, 1876.

18. *Ibid.*, February 3, 1876.

19. *Ibid.*, February 13, 1876; Parker, Gold in the Black Hills, 119.

20. Moody, *Stagecoach West*, 302-303; *Leader*, December 9, 1875, and March 10, 1876; Parker, *Gold in the Black Hills*, 112-113.

21. *Leader*, April 12 and December 3, 1876; Parker, *Gold in the Black Hills*, 118-120.

22. Kuykendall, *Frontier Days*, 119, 121.

23. *Ibid.*, 220; Parker, *Gold in the Black Hills*, 120.

24. *Leader*, December 2, 1876.

25. Parker, *Gold in the Black Hills*, 119, 197-202.

Chapter 8: Gamblers and Gunfighters

1. *Leader*, February 7, 1876.

2. *Ibid.*, August 31, 1876.

3. *Ibid.*, August 31, 1875; January 24 and 30, 1878.

4. *Ibid.*, February 5 and April 26, 1876.

5. *Ibid.*, June 4, 1876.

6. *Ibid.*, December 19 and 26, 1876.

7. Hickok's life is detailed by his biographer, Joseph G. Rosa, in his authoritative *They Called Him Wild Bill*.

8. Hickok's activities in Cheyenne are covered by Rosa, *They Called Him Wild Bill*, 262-278, and by the local newspapers.

9. *Leader*, April 14, 1876.

10. *Ibid.*, June 8, 1876.

11. *Ibid.*, August 26, 1876; and Rosa, *They Called Him Wild Bill*, 295-296.

12. *Leader*, August 16, 1876.

13. Kuykendall, *Frontier Days*, 185-190.

14. DeArment, *Bat Masterson*, 74-75.

15. Masterson, *Famous Gunfighters*, 35-36.

16. Tanner, *Doc Holliday*, 102-104; Jahns, *The Frontier World of Doc Holliday*, 70-71.

17. A full account of the shooting is in the *Leader*, March 10, 1877. Bat Masterson's remarks about Levy were published in *Famous Gunfighters*, 25-26.

18. *Leader*, March 10, 1877.

19. *Ibid.*, December 15, 1877.

20. *Ibid.*, January 22, 1878.

21. *Ibid.*, January 22, 23 and 29, 1878; and Frye, *Atlas of Wyoming Outlaws at the Territorial Penitentiary*, 53.

22. *Leader*, June 9, 1876.

23. *Ibid.*, June 20, 1876.

24. *Ibid.*, July 7, 1877.

25. *Ibid.*, March 17, 1877.

Chapter 9: Life in Cheyenne during the Seventies

1. *Leader*, October 4, 5 and 6, 1875. Grant's 1873 visit was covered in the *Leader*, April 27 and 30. Also see Haas, "The Story of the Inter Ocean Hotel," typescript.

2. *Leader*, October 31 and November 1, 1879; Mabel E. Brown, ed., *First Ladies of Wyoming*, 19-21.

3. *Leader*, August 24 and 25, 1880.

4. *Ibid.*, February 18 and 23, 1874; October 12, 1875; May 20, 1877; May 17 and 24, 1879.

5. *Ibid.*, August 31, 1878; September 20, 1879.

6. *Ibid.*, August 25, September 3 and 5, 1880.

7. *Ibid.*, September 5, 1880.

8. *Ibid.*, June 21, 1870; May 20, August 2 and 4, October 20, 1877; August 16, 1878.

9. *Ibid.*, August 2, 1877; August 2 and 3, 1879.

10. *Ibid.*, November 3, 1892.

11. Carley, *A History of the First Congregational Church of Cheyenne*, 5; "Josiah Strong," *Dictionary of American Biography*; *Leader*, January 1, 1878.

12. *Leader*, July 5, 1871; July 4, 1876; July 4, 6 and 9, 1878. The *Leader* described each Fourth of July celebration during the decades.

13. *Leader*, January 3, 1870; January 2, 1874; January 3 and December 30, 1877; January 1, 1878.

14. *Ibid.*, December 31, 1878; January 1 and 2, 1877.

15. *Ibid.*, January 3 and 4, 1880; January 1 and 2, 1881.

16. Brown, ed. *First Ladies of Wyoming*, 19-21.

17. *Leader*, December 20, 1876; March 13 and 14, 1877; April 5, 1878; June 5 and 15, 1879.

18. *Ibid.*, July 27, 1871; December 20, 1876.

19. *Ibid.*, December 18, 1878.

20. Gannett, *Lucy Ellen's ... Girlhood Days*, 8-11.

21. *Leader*, January 12, 1875; September 25, 1902.

22. *Ibid.*, June 3, 1871; February 6 and May 26, 1874.

23. *Ibid.*, February 14, 15 and 24, 1878; July 26, November 18, December 23, 1879; May 1, 1881; September 22, 1882.

24. *Ibid.*, March 1 and 8, 1888; August 3, September 17, December 22 and 27, 1882; January 18 and 25, February 8 and 23, 1883; August 7, 1900; Cheyenne Centennial Committee, *The Magic City of the Plains*, 74.

25. *Ibid.*, May 7 and 29, October 8, 1875.

26. *Ibid.*, March 16 and April 17, 1877; October 3, 1878.

27. *Ibid.*, January 1, October 13, and December 18, 1878.

28. Census of Cheyenne City, October 18, 1878; *Leader*, June 2 and 29, 1878; January 4, 1879.

29. *Leader*, April 29, May 2, 16 and 25, June 3 and 15, November 15, December 30, 1871; January 5, 1872.

30. *Ibid.*, March 20, 1873; September 9, 1877; June 1 and September 3, 1878; May 8, 1879.

31. *Ibid.*, December 15, 1877; June 1, September 13, October 20, 1878.

32. *Ibid.*, August 15, 1876; August 15, 1877; August 16, 1878.

33. *Ibid.*, February 7, 1877.

34. *Ibid.*, October 18 and 23, 1877; May 16, 1878.

35. Cheyenne Historic Downtown Walking Tour, 12; *Leader*, October 22, 1896; *A History of First Baptist Church*, 1-20.

36. Dubois, "A Social History of Cheyenne, Wyoming, 1875-1885," thesis, 117-118; *Leader*, October 13, 1878.

37. *Leader*, January 22 and 25, March 2, September 19, and December 25, 1878.

38. *Ibid.*, March 30, 1872; April 8 and July 3, 1877; letter to the editor, *Ellis County Star* (Hays City, Kansas), June 29, 1876, quoted in Miller and Snell, *Great Gunfighters of the Kansas Cowtowns*, 139.

Chapter 10: The Holy City of the Cow

1. *Leader*, February 7, 1868; January 18 and August 6, 1876; March 31, October 9 and December 15, 1877; February 3, 9, 10 and 13, 1878; February 24 and April 10, 1881.

2. Bartlett, ed., *History of Wyoming*, Vol. 3: 5-9.

3. *Leader*, July 24, 1884; June 16 and 25, 1885.

4. *Ibid.*, October 18, 1877; February 15 and 24, 1878; Bartlett, ed., *History of Wyoming*, Vol. 3: 5-7.

5. For a few of the many references to the ranching activities of these men, see the *Leader*, March 8, 1881; June 28 and August 3, 1883; June 27, August 4 and September 22, 1885; May 22, 1886; June 15, 1887. Also see Henry G. Hay, biographical file, Wyoming State Archives, Cheyenne; and Larson, *History of Wyoming*, 166.

6. Clay, *My Life on the Range*, 73, 242, 257, 265, 282; Margaret Hanson, *Powder River Country*, 256-257.

7. Woods, *British Gentlemen of the Wild West*.

8. Clay, *My Life on the Range*, 49-50.

9. Alexander Swan, biographical file, Wyoming State Archives, Cheyenne; Bassford, *Wyoming Hereford Ranch*, 1883-1983.

10. *Leader*, May 21, 1876; July 14 and 19, 1879; April 4, 1880; June 27 and July 11, 1882.

11. There are three institutional histories of the WSGA: Agnes Wright Spring, *A Panoramic History of the Wyoming Stock Growers' Association*, 192; Maurice Frink, *Cow Country Cavalcade: Eighty Years of the Wyoming Stock Growers' Association*, 1954; and John Rolfe Burroughs, *Guardian of the Grasslands: The First 100 Years of the Wyoming Stock Growers' Association*, 1971.

12. Clay, *My Life on the Range*, 245.

13. Spring, *Seventy Years*, 73-74, 84.

14. Clay, My Life on the Range, 114-115.

15. *Leader*, September 23, 1880; June 17, 1881; May 3, 1882.

16. Clay, My Life on the Range, 116-17.

17. *Leader*, August 25 and October 20, 1880; January 15, 1881; January 6, 1882.

18. Wister, 1885 Journal, Owen Wister Collection, American Heritage Center (Laramie, Wyoming), 4; *Leader*, April 8, 1881.

19. *Leader*, July 1, 1887.

20. *Ibid.*, November 18, 1882.

21. *Ibid.*, May 25, 1882.

22. *Ibid.*, February 24 and March 6, 1887; February 4, 1888; May 2, 1889.

23. Carr, biographical file, Wyoming State Archives, Cheyenne.

24. *Leader*, July 2, 1887; June 28 and 29, 1889.

25. Clay, *My Life on the Range*; Mabel E. Brown, ed. *First Ladies of Wyoming*, 29-30.

Chapter 11: Runaways and Wrecks

1. *Leader*, September 25, 1879.
2. *Ibid.*, August, 26, 1868.
3. *Ibid.*, January 20, 1869; July 16, 1870.
4. *Ibid.*, May 13, 1876.
5. *Ibid.*, August 1, 1877.
6. *Ibid.*, January 29, 1878.
7. *Ibid.*, February 12, 1878.
8. *Ibid.*, February 24, 1878; June 25, 1879; September 30, 1894.
9. *Ibid.*, July 2, 1881; April 26 and June 27, 1883; May 3, 1884.
10. *Ibid.*, March 10, 1880; March 10, 1881; June 6, 1882; November 26, 1884; October 18, 1885; March 18, 1886; June 12, 1886; March 1888.
11. *Ibid.*, December 5, 1886.
12. *Ibid.*, June 7, 1887.
13. *Ibid.*, January 17, 1884; The Young Men's Literary Club of Cheyenne Centennial Papers and History, 106.
14. *Leader*, August 5, 1875.
15. *Ibid.*, June 26, 1883.
16. *Ibid.*, February 26, 1886; November 27, 1888; May 24, 1889.
17. *Ibid.*, March 10, 1890; April 13, 1890; October 23, 1891; June 14, 1892; April 14, 1894; February 13, 1897.
18. *Ibid.*, June 2 and December 16, 1892.
19. *Ibid.*, May 12, June 1, and July 23, 1893.
20. *Ibid.*, October 4 and 5, 1893; September 9, 1897.
21. *Ibid.*, March 8, 1894; July 5 and September 30, 1895; February 2, 1899.
22. *Ibid.*, May 17 and September 15, 1895; October 4 and 7, 1895.
23. *Ibid.*, October 21, 1897.
24. *Ibid.*, July 29, 1891.
25. *Ibid.*, March 13, 1895.
26. *Ibid.*, April 14 and 24, 1895.
27. *Ibid.*, June 11 and July 1, 1895; September 20 and October 7, 1897.
28. *Ibid.*, November 16, 1897.
29. *Ibid.*, September 13, 1878.
30. *Ibid.*, October 21 and 25, 1879.
31. *Ibid.*, October 8, 1889; October 10, 1890.
32. *Ibid.*, February 25, 1892; December 9, 1893; July 30, 1897.
33. *Ibid.*, June 20 and October 12, 1890; May 24, 1897.
34. *Ibid.*, March 5, 1872; December 17, 1878; June 22, 1882; December 5, 1886.
35. *Ibid.*, August 16, 1881; August 15, 1891; George Tucker manuscript, 86.

Chapter 12: From Victorian Mansions to the Capitol Building

1. Barton, ed., *Early Cheyenne Homes, 1880–1890*, 60; information provided to the author by Jim Osterfoss, Cheyenne.
2. Barton, ed., *Early Cheyenne Homes*, 64, 65.
3. *Ibid.*, 61.
4. *Ibid.*, 59.
5. *Leader*, July 27, 1888.
6. Barton, ed., *Early Cheyenne Homes*, 17.
7. *Ibid.*, 6, 27.
8. *Ibid.*, 21.
9. *Ibid.*, 15.
10. *Ibid.*, 31; Clay, *My Life on the Range*, 209.
11. *Leader*, March 25 and 26, 1884.
12. The Emporium was described in detail in the *Leader*, May 1 and October 26, 1884.

13. Arnold and Ehernberger, *Union Pacific Depot*, 7-10.

14. *Leader*, December 20, 1885.

15. *Ibid.*, March 17, April 27, May 18, June 17, 18 and 19, July 20, October 8 and 23, 1886.

16. *Ibid.*, November 27, 1886; March 1, 1887.

17. Arnold and Ehernberger, *Union Pacific Depot*, 14-15, 20.

18. Larson, *History of Wyoming*, 144-146.

19. Ewig, ed., "Behind the Capitol Scenes: The Letters of John A. Feick," *Annals of Wyoming*, 3-4.

20. *Ibid.*, 4-6.

21. *Ibid.*, 4-11.

22. *Ibid.*, October 8, 1886.

23. *Leader*, April 14 and May 4, 1887; Ewig, ed., "Behind the Capitol Scenes: The Letters of John A. Feick," *Annals of Wyoming*, 10.

24. *Leader*, May 18 and 19, 1887.

25. *Ibid.*, June 17, 1887; *Cheyenne Landmarks*, 1976, 7.

26. Neil Harris, quoted in *Chicago: City of the Century*, PBS Video, Part I.

Chapter 13: The Cheyenne Opera House

1. Denver *Tribune* story reprinted in the *Leader*, November 3, 1881.

2. *Leader*, April 16, 1881, and January 5 and May 25, 1882.

3. *Ibid.*, December 27, 1881.

4. *Ibid.*, June 21, 1881.

5. *Ibid.*, December 27, 1881; May 25, 1882.

6. *Ibid.*, March 1, 1882.

7. *Ibid.*, May 23 and 25, 1882.

8. A detailed description of opening night and of the new opera house is in the *Leader*, May 25, 1882.

9. *Leader*, April 14, June 3, and August 16, and November 14, 1882; February 20, 1899.

10. *Ibid.*, April 19, 1887.

11. *Ibid.*, June 3 and 4, 1887.

12. *Ibid.*, June 10, 12 and 15, 1887; Langtry, The Days I Knew, 185-186.

13. *Leader*, June 10, 1888; April 6 and July 6, 1889; June 22, 1890; August 4, 1891.

14. *Ibid.*, August 4, 1891.

15. *Ibid.*, August 4 and October 23, 1891.

16. *Ibid.*, October 23, 1891, and February 19, 1892.

17. *Ibid.*, August 5, 1892.

18. *Ibid.*, June 1 and 6, 1894; April 7, 1896; April 24 and 29, and May 1, 1897; September 5, 1900.

19. *Ibid.*, December 8, 1902.

Chapter 14: Flood, Fire, Lynching—and Shopping

1. The flood is described in the *Leader*, June 17 and 19, 1883. These issues provide the source of the description in the next several paragraphs.

2. *Leader*, June 17, 1883; May 17 and 25, 1884.

3. *Ibid.*, May 25 and 28, 1884.

4. *Ibid.*, May 28, 1884.

5. *Ibid.*, March 25, 1884.

6. *Ibid.*, March 26, 1884.

7. *Ibid.*, October 26, 1884.

8. The Warren Emporium is described in detail in the *Leader*, May 1 and October 26, 1884.

9. *Leader*, October 26, 1884.

10. The murder and subsequent events are described in the *Leader*, September 13, 14, 15, 16, and 18, 1883.

11. *Leader*, September 14, 1883.

12. *Ibid.*, September 16, 1883.

13. The lynching is described at length in the *Leader*, September 18, 1883.

14. The Denver *Tribune* commentary was reprinted in the *Leader*, September 18, 1883. The *Leader* editorial was published in the issue of September 23, 1883.

15. Col. Gerald M. Adams, *The Post Near Cheyenne*, 75, 81; *Leader*, December 9, 1882.

16. President Arthur's brief visit was described in detail in the *Leader*, August 5, 1883.

17. Adams, The Post Near Cheyenne, 86.

18. *Ibid.*, 96-97; *Leader*, October 19, 1887.

19. *Leader*, February 3, 1881; June 14, 1888.

20. Adams, *The Post Near Cheyenne*, 107-108; *Leader*, May 15, 1896.

21. Adams, *The Post Near Cheyenne*, 98.

22. *Leader*, January 14 and 15, 1885.

23. *Ibid.*, January 17, 1885; Mabel E. Brown, ed., *First Ladies of Wyoming*, 23-24.

24. Larson, *History of Wyoming*, 159; Gould, *Wyoming: A Political History, 1868–1896*; 83-107.

25. *Leader*, April 9 and 10, 1889.

26. *Ibid.*, April 10, 1889.

27. *Ibid.*

28. Larson, *History of Wyoming*, 236–261.

29. *Leader*, July 11, 23, and 24, 1890.

30. *Ibid.*, July 23, 25, and 30, 1890.

31. Larson, History of Wyoming, 266–267; *Leader*, November 19 and 25, 1890.

32. Gould, *Wyoming: A Political History, 1868–1896*, 80–81, 123.

Chapter 15: Cheyenne in the Nineties

1. *Leader*, January 10 and 15, April 27 and 29, 1890; August 21, 1891; January 24, 1892.

2. *Ibid.*, January 2 and July 16, 1889; January 5, 1890.

3. *Ibid.*, January 24; November 29 and 30, 1890; March 11, 1899.

4. Flynn, *Our Heritage: 100 Years at St. Mark's*, 34-36; Malcolm L. Cook, *First Church: A People Called Methodist*, 103-120; *Leader*, November 12, 1889.

5. *Leader*, February 9, August 2, September 3, 1890; March 24, 1892.

6. *Ibid.*, November 22 and 30, 1890.

7. *Ibid.*, May 3 and 9, 1889; January 14 and May 31, 1890.

8. Flynn, "Cheyenne's Harry P. Hynds," *Annals of Wyoming* (Summer 2001), 2-11; Bartlett, ed., *History of Wyoming*, 300, 303.

9. *Leader*, May 24 and 26, August 2, 1885.

10. *Wyoming Tribune*, March 3 and 5, 1896.

11. *Wyoming Tribune*, March 10, May 3, June 4, 5, and 7, October 13, 1896.

12. *Leader*, November 14, 17 and 18, 1891; February 26 and March 4, 1892.

13. *Ibid.*, October 17, 1890.

14. *Ibid.*, September 29, 1891; January 1, 3, 5 and 8, 1892.

15. *Ibid.*, January 5 and April 22, 1992.

16. *Ibid.*, February 19, March 24, 25, 26, 30, April 22, 23, 1892.

17. The story of the elections of 1892 and 1894, and of the rivalry between Carey and Warren, is told with great insight by Lewis Gould in *Wyoming: A Political History, 1868–1896*, 159–229.

18. *Leader*, January 2 and 5, 1894.

19. *Ibid.*

20. *Ibid.*, December 13, 1893; February 24 and 25, 1894.

21. *Ibid.*, February 24, 1894.

22. *Ibid.*

23. *Sun-Leader*, May 16, June 16 and 29, 1899.

24. Herlihy, *Bicycle: The History*.

25. Wyoming Tribune, February 25 and 26, April 2 and 3, 1896.

26. *Ibid.*, May 13 and December 5, 1896.

27. *Leader*, June 6, 1895; May 4 and 21, 1897.

28. *Ibid.*, June 6, 1895; June 19, 1899.

29. *Wyoming Tribune*, April 21 and 29, May 13 and 29, July 5, September 30, November 7, and December 25, 1896; *Sun-Leader*, May 24, 1897; June 16 and 20, 1899; January 22 and July 9, 1900.

30. *Leader*, September 23, 1888; October 27, 1895; October 19, 1897; *Wyoming Tribune*, November 25 and December 1, 1896.

31. *Sun-Leader*, April 7 and 14, May 23, June 8 and 19, 1899; *Leader*, February 19, May 10, July 6, December 29, 1900; March 3, October 16, December 10, 1903.

32. *Leader*, January 4, 1895.

33. *Ibid.*, January 4 and 5, February 2, 1895.

34. *Leader*, February 21 and May 30, 1895; May 3 and 29, July 7, 1900; June 19, 1901; January 13 and 24, 1902.

35. Mead's life and career are recounted and analyzed by James R. Kluger in *Turning on Water with a Shovel: The Career of Elwood P. Mead.*

36. *Sun-Leader*, May 11, June 17 and 27, 1899.

Chapter 16: The Johnson County Warriors

1. Clay, *My Life on the Range*, 269-70.

2. George Hufsmith, in *The Wyoming Lynching of Cattle Kate*, details how Ella Watson was made into "Cattle Kate."

3. Hanson, ed., *Powder River Country*, 261-262. For details of the Johnson County War, see O'Neal, *The Johnson County War*, and Smith, *The War on Powder River.*

4. Penrose, *The Rustler Business*, 24.

5. The telegrams of April 12 were reprinted in the *Leader*, April 13, 1892.

6. David, *Malcolm Campbell, Sheriff*, 310-11.

7. *Ibid.*, 311-312.

8. *Ibid.*, 340.

9. George Tucker manuscript, 83-84; Adams, *The Post Near Cheyenne*, 97; David, *Malcolm Campbell, Sheriff*, 321-22; Dallas *Morning News*, May 11, 1892; Sheridan *Post*, July 14, 1892.

10. David, *Malcolm Campbell, Sheriff*; Tucker manuscript, 84.

11. Holsinger, "Willis Van Devanter: Wyoming Leader, 1884–1897," *Annals of Wyoming*, 170–206; Bartlett, ed., *History of Wyoming*, 3: 26–29.

12. Van Devanter to Warren (April 20, 1892), quoted in Gould, "New Light on the Johnson County War," *Montana* (October 1867): 22-23.

13. Van Devanter to Warren (May 9, 1892), quoted in Gould, "New Light on the Johnson County War," 24.

14. Warren to Hay, June 28 and July 1, 1892.

15. Clay, *My Life on the Range*, 284.

16. *Leader*, June 14, 1892.

17. *Ibid.*, July 20, 1892.

18. *Ibid.*; Warren to Irvine, July 23, 1892; Carey to Hay, July 22, 1892.

19. Warren to Irvine, July 23, 1892.

20. *Ibid.*

21. *Leader*, August 2, 1892.

22. *Ibid.*

23. *Leader*, August 3, 1892; Tucker manuscript, 86.

24. Tucker manuscript, 80; David, *Malcolm Campbell, Sheriff*, 346.

25. Tucker manuscript, 82.

26. *Ibid.*

27. *Leader*, August 7, 1892.

28. *Ibid.*

29. Clay to Hay, July 21, 1892; Clay, *My Life on the Range*, 280-281.

30. *Leader*, August 11, 1892; Tucker manuscript, 81.

31. *Leader*, August 11, 1892.

32. *Ibid.*

33. See the *Leader*, January 3-22, 1893, for a day-by-day account of the trial. Also see David, *Malcolm Campbell, Sheriff*, 346-348.

34. The dramatic final day in court is described in detail in the *Leader*, January 22, 1893.

Chapter 17: Women of the Magic City

1. Larson, *History of Wyoming*, 84, 85, 86, 88-94, 260.

2. Reiter, *The Women*, 226.

3. *Leader*, November 6, 1894; Bohl, "Wyoming's Estelle Reel," *Annals of Wyoming*, 23-27.

4. *Leader*, December 28, 1894; September 15, 1896; Bohl, "Wyoming's Estelle Reel," 23, 27-36. In later years Estelle married Cort Meyer.

5. *Leader*, July 3, 1880.

6. *Ibid.*, June 3, 1893.

7. On May 16, 1899, the *Leader* made a typical announcement: "Two of our lovely school teachers have fallen in love and are telling their friends about the marriages that are to take place in the lucky month of June."

8. *Leader*, January 15 and September 11, 1884; April 24, 1886.

9. *Ibid.*, July 31 and September 2, 1902.

10. *Ibid.*, June 19, 1888; August 18, 1889; March 25, 1891; August 22, 1902.

11. *Ibid.*, March 20, 1883; June 16, 1889; November 15, 1896; Bohl, "Wyoming's Estelle Reel," 34.

12. Gannett, *Lucy Ellen's ... Girlhood Days*, 13.

13. Dunn, "Reminiscences of Fourscore Years and Eight," *Annals of Wyoming*, vol. 19 (July 1947): 125-135.

14. *Ibid.*, 130-131.

15. *Ibid.*, 133.

16. *Leader*, August 16, 1901.

17. *Ibid.*, February 4, 1886; June 9 and August 27, 1899; September 3, 1901.

18. *Sun-Leader*, June 28, 1899.

19. *Leader*, September 6, 1900; January 16, 1903.

20. *Ibid.*, April 6, 1881; May 27, 1894; May 8, 1903.

21. *Ibid.*, November 28, 1895.

22. *Ibid.*, March 6 and June 16, 1900; November 28 and December 1, 1901.

23. *Ibid.*, April 22, 1886; May 1, 1897; August 13 and December 28, 1901; February 4, 1902.

24. Alice Richards McCreery, typescript.

25. *Ibid.*

26. Gannett, *Lucy Ellen's ... Girlhood Days*, 7-9.

27. *Leader*, April 7 and June 1, 1881; March 28, 1883; October 18, 1894; December 5, 1903.

28. *Ibid.*, May 6, 1884.

29. *Ibid.*, August 31, 1897.

30. *Ibid.*, September 13, 1892.

31. *Ibid.*, November 7 and 8, 1895.

32. *Ibid.*, January 29 and February 23, 1897.

33. *Ibid.*, August 15, 1885; November 28, 1895.

34. *Ibid.*, December 27, 1895.

35. Helen Warren to Emroy Warren, May 14, 1899, Warren Papers, Box 56.

36. Helen Warren to Matthew Smith, August 15, 1900, Warren Papers.

37. Helen Warren to Emroy Warren, December 21, 1901, Warren Papers.

38. Mabel E. Brown, ed., *First Ladies of Wyoming, 1869–1990*, 33-35.

39. *Leader*, May 24, 1889; June 11, 1896.

40. F. E. Warren to Helen Warren, September 15, 1896, and August 8, 1898, Warren Papers, Box 29.

41. *Leader*, July 27, August 10 and 11, 1900.

42. *Ibid.*, November 7, 1901, ad: "Miss Frankie Warren, TEACHER OF PIANO." Also see the *Leader*, May 16, 1899, and Vandiver, *Black Jack*, 1: 332-352.

43. *Leader*, May 16, 1899; February 5, 1900; June 5 and 25, September 1902; May 16, July 27, August 1, 1903.

44. *Leader*, March 30, 1880.

45. Dazee Bristol biographical file, Wyoming State Archives; *Leader*, April 18, 1900; Flynn, *Let's Go! Let's Show! Let's Rodeo!*, 69, 78, 83, 84.

46. Brown, ed., *First Ladies of Wyoming, 1869–1990*, 1-9.

Chapter 18: Frontier Days

1. Flynn, *Let's Go! Let's Show! Let's Rodeo!*, 14-15.

2. *Daily Sun-Leader*, August 30 and 31, 1897.

3. Guy Logsdon, "Rodeo" entry in Lamar, *Reader's Encyclopedia of the American West*, 1027-1031.

4. O'Neal, *Historic Ranches of the Old West*, 186.

5. *Daily Sun-Leader*, September 3, 1897; Flynn, *Let's Go! Let's Show! Let's Rodeo!*, 15, 19.

6. *Daily Sun-Leader*, September 3, 9 and 22, 1897.

7. *Ibid.*, September 9, 1897.

8. *Ibid.*

9. *Ibid.*, September 20 and 22, 1897.

10. *Ibid.*, September 22, 1897.

11. Flynn, *Let's Go! Let's Show! Let's Rodeo!*, 16-18; *Daily Sun-Leader*, October 4, 1897.

12. *Daily Sun-Leader*, October 4, 1897; August 17, 1900.

13. *Ibid.*, September 24, 1897.

14. *Ibid.*, September 24, 25, and October 4, 1897.

15. *Ibid.*, September 24 and October 4 and 20, 1897.

16. Flynn, *Let's Go! Let's Show! Let's Rodeo!*, 21-23.

17. *Ibid.*, 23.

18. *Ibid.*, 24; *Daily Sun-Leader*, June 8 and 16, 1897.

19. Cheyenne *Frontier Days*, 2004 Souvenir Program, 29.

20. *Leader*, July 31, August 1, 20, 21, September 12, 1900.

21. *Ibid.*, September 14, 1900.

22. Flynn, *Let's Go! Let's Show! Let's Rodeo!*, 223; Porter, *Who's Who in Rodeo*, 122-123. Later in his career Sowder was thrown from a horse, causing a partial paralysis which lingered for the remainder of his life. Sowder died at fifty-seven in 1931. The first "World's Champion Broncho Rider" was voted into the Rodeo Hall of Fame in 1960.

23. *Leader*, August 8 and 11; 1902; Porter, *Who's Who in Rodeo*, 123.

24. *Ibid.*, July 13, August 10, 13, 15, 16, 26, 28, 30, 31, September 1, 1901.

25. *Ibid.*, August 6, 19, 20, 25, 26, 27, September 2, 1902.

26. *Ibid.*, August 27 and 28, 1902.

27. *Ibid.*, August 20, 28 and 29, 1902.

28. *Ibid.*, August 28 and 29, September 5, 1902.

Chapter 19: Cheyenne Marches to War

1. *Leader*, August 8, 1900.

2. *Ibid.*, July 16, 1876; May 6, 1884.

3. *Ibid.*, August 5 and October 23, 1888.

4. *Ibid.*, August 15, 1891.

5. *Ibid.*, August 21, 1891.

6. *Ibid.*, August 23, 26, 27, 1891. These issues reported the activities of the week in detail.

7. *Ibid.*, August 27, 1891.

8. *Ibid.*, August 8, 1893; January 31, 1894.

9. *Ibid.*, August 7, 1894; January 17, 1895.

10. *Wyoming Tribune*, January 19, 1896.

11. *Ibid.*, January 28; February 20; March 6 and 18; April 23 and 29; November 25; December 5, 1896.

12. *Ibid.*, October 23, 1895; June 4 and July 21, 1896.

13. *Ibid.*, December 22, 1896.

14. *Leader*, January 23, February 13 and 16, May 15 and 18, 1897.

15. Walker, *The Boys of '98*, 68-69; Westermeir, *Who Rush to Glory*, 37-44.

16. Stevens, "The Story of the Rough Riders," *Leslie's Weekly*, 333 and 335; Westermeir, *Who Rush to Glory*, 38-39; *Sun-Leader*, March 9 and 10, April 1, 1898.

17. Westermeir, *Who Rush to Glory*, 69, 88; Stevens, "The Story of the Rough Riders," *Leslie's Weekly*, 334; *Sun-Leader*, May 4, 1898.

18. Stevens, "The Story of the Rough Riders," *Leslie's Weekly*, 334.

19. Westermeir, *Who Rush to Glory*, 104-114.

20. *Ibid.*, 112-113.

21. *Ibid.*, 230-232; Stevens, "The Story of the Rough Riders," *Leslie's Weekly*, 336.

22. *Sun-Leader*, May 18, 1898; January 6, 1899.

23. *Ibid.*, January 18, June 29, 1899.

24. *Ibid.*, March 27, 1899.

25. *Ibid.*, March 29, 1899.

26. *Ibid.*, February 7 and 9, March 7, 20, 28, April 5, May 5, 1899; February 3, 1900.

27. *Ibid.*, April 19, May 23, June 27 and 29, 1899.

28. *Ibid.*, August 8, 1900.

29. *Ibid.*, June 14, 1899.

30. *Ibid.*, April 5, 1900.

31. *Ibid.*, December 17, 1900.

Chapter 20: Into a New Century

1. *Leader*, September 19 and 24, 1900.

2. *Ibid.*, August 21, September 19, 21, 22, 25, 1900.

3. *Ibid.*, September 24 and 25, 1900.

4. *Ibid.*, September 25 and 26, 1900.

5. *Ibid.*, March 18, 1903.

6. *Ibid.*, April 23, May 9 and 23, 1903.

7. *Ibid.*; June 1, 1903; Cheyenne Centennial Historical Committee, *Cheyenne: The Magic City of the Plains*, 98.

8. *Leader*, June 1, 1903.

9. *Ibid.*; Cheyenne Centennial Historical Committee, *Cheyenne: The Magic City of the Plains*, 98-99.

10. *Leader*, June 1, 1903. This edition gave full coverage to the Wild West Show arranged for President Roosevelt. Also see the June 6 edition.

11. *Leader*, June 1, 1903.

12. *Ibid.*, April 28 and 30, 1903; Mabel E. Brown, ed., *First Ladies of Wyoming, 1869–1990*, 43-44.

13. *Leader*, October 28 and 29, 1903; Brown, ed., *First Ladies of Wyoming, 1869–1990*, 39-41.

14. *Leader*, July 1, December 6, 8, 22, 1903.

15. *Ibid.*, April 3, 1902.

16. *Ibid.*, December 5 and 29, 1903.

17. *Ibid.*, September 3, 1901; June 10 and 29, September 10, 1903.

18. *Ibid.*, September 10, 1903.

19. *Ibid.*, September 10 and 27, 1903.

20. *Ibid.*, October 4 and 18, November 1, December 18 and 19, 1903.

21. *Ibid.*, February 9 and March 25, 1902; April 3, October 30, November 27, 1903.

22. *Ibid.*, September 2, 12, 16, 1901; June 13, 1903.

23. *Ibid.*, January 22, 1900.

24. *Ibid.*, July 13 and 30, 1901; May 16, August 27, 28, 29, 1902.

25. *Ibid.*, January 30 and May 30, 1903.

26. *Ibid.*, August 2 and 5, 1901.

27. *Ibid.*, August 28, 1901; June 19, 1902; February 19, 1903.

28. *Ibid.*, April 24, May 9, June 29, July 29, 1903.

29. *Ibid.*, August 22, December 17, 1903.

30. *Ibid.*, July 31, 1901.

31. *Ibid.*, August 20 and December 30, 1901.

32. *Ibid.*, March 12, April 8, and July 7, 1902.

33. *Ibid.*, September 30, 1903.

34. *Ibid.*, June 24 and October 6, 1903.

35. See, for example, the *Leader*, January 20, May 2, September 22, October 3 and 4, and December 23, 1903.

36. *Leader*, January 26 and February 24, 1903.

37. *Ibid.*, April 2 and 26, 1903.

38. *Ibid.*, May 21, and September 22, 1903.

39. *Ibid.*, October 6 and 9, 1903.

40. *Ibid.*, November 7, 1903.

41. Col. Gerald M. Adams, *The Post Near Cheyenne*, 128-132; *Leader*, December 8, 1900; January 24, March 6, July 31, September 5, 1902; March 19, April 23, September 11, December 18, 1903.

42. Cheyenne Centennial Historical Committee, *Cheyenne: The Magic City of the Plains*, 69; Laramie County Chapter, Wyoming State Historical Society, *Cheyenne Landmarks*, 64-65; *Leader*, July 23, 1901; February 27-28, June 10, 1902; March 2, November 7 and 17, 1903.

43. *Leader*, August 16, 1901; November 8, 1902.

44. *Ibid.*, July 18, 1901; October 10 and November 1, 1902.

45. Mabel E. Brown, ed., *First Ladies of Wyoming, 1869–1990*, 48, 50, 153; *Leader*, September 23, 1903.

46. *Leader*, December 8, 1902.

47. *Ibid.*, February 5, 1902; September 6, 1903; Brown, ed., *First Ladies of Wyoming, 1869–1990*, 73-75.

48. *Ibid.*, September 25, 1902; June 16, 1903.

49. *Ibid.*, September 1, 3, 12, 1903.

50. *Ibid.*, February 1 and 11, 1902.

51. *Ibid.*, June 22, 1903.

52. *Ibid.*, July 3 and 8, 1884; August 5, 1901; August 8, 1902.

53. *Ibid.*, March 21, 1900.

54. *Ibid.*, February 22, 1902; January 27, 1903.

55. "Van Devanter, Willis," Dictionary of American Biography (Supp. 3): 788-789; *Leader*, March 10, 1903.

Chapter 21: Tom Horn Meets the Twentieth Century

1. Horn, *Life of Tom Horn*, 3-6, 8-10. The account of Harriet Horn Miller about her brother was printed in the *Leader*, August 19, 1903.

2. Tom Horn's autobiography, *Life of Tom Horn*, offers insightful material, but must be used with caution. Horn expert Chip Carlson has written *Tom Horn: Blood on the Moon*, an expanded version of his earlier *Tom Horn, "Killing Men Is My Specialty,"* as well as *Joe LeFors: "I Slickered Tom Horn."* Carlson's work concentrates on the final period of Horn's life in Wyoming. Doyce B. Nunis, Jr., has examined Horn's entire career in a brief biography, *The Life of Tom Horn Revisited*. Dr. Larry D. Ball, noted western historian, is preparing a comprehensive biography. Lauren Paine, in *Tom Horn: Man of the West*, provides good background information on the enigmatic frontiersman. Dean Krakel, *The Saga of Tom Horn*, is a detailed chronicle of Horn's last years in Wyoming; Horn's testimony from his trial is presented verbatim, and considerable insight about his background may be gleaned from Krakel's comments. Interesting accounts of Horn were presented by contemporary western writers William MacLeod Raine (who covered Horn's trial) in *Famous Sheriffs and Western Outlaws*, 80-91, and Dane Coolidge, *Fighting Men of the West*, 87-110. Eugene Cunningham provided a worthwhile chapter on Horn in his classic *Triggernometry*, and Dan Thrapp effectively covered Horn's Indian-fighting days in his superb biography, *Al Sieber*. Excellent biographical files on Horn are maintained at the Wyoming State Historical Society in Tucson. In addition, Dean Krakel delivered an illuminating address about Horn in Cheyenne at the 1984 Rendezvous of the National Association for Outlaw and Lawman History, and he wrote "Was Tom Horn Two Men?" in *True West*, January-February, 1970. Surprisingly, an entry in the *Dictionary of American Biography* is devoted to Horn.

3. For a fuller discussion of this subject, as well as substantiating quotes, see O'Neal, *Fighting Men of the Indian Wars*, 1-2.

4. Horn, *The Pinkertons*, 380-383; Carlson, *Tom Horn: Blood on the Moon*, 43-46.

5. Horn referred to his experience with the "Langhoff outfit" three times during his trial testimony, which is on 595-701 of the transcript of *The State of Wyoming vs. Tom Horn*, on file at the Wyoming State Historical Association in Cheyenne. Dean Krakel reproduced Horn's testimony in *The Saga of Tom Horn*, 103-118, 135-197. I have read the trial transcript in Cheyenne, taken notes from it, and photocopied portions of it. But because *The Saga of Tom Horn*, although out of print, is more readily available than the trial transcript, I have noted specific trial quotations from Krakel's book.

6. Henry Melton, "Recollections of Tom Horn," typescript, 3.

7. *Wyoming vs. Horn*, cited in Krakel, *The Saga of Tom Horn*, 109.

8. *Ibid.*, 110. Horn's complaint about his duties as a Pinkerton agent reveals why he liked his stock detective activities. "My work for [Pinkerton] was not the kind that exactly suited my disposition; too tame for me. There were a good many instructions and a good deal of talk given the operative regarding the things to do and the things that had been done." Tom Horn, *Life of Tom Horn*, 222.

9. Melton, "Recollections of Tom Horn," typescript, 2.

10. Krakel, "Was Tom Horn Two Men?" *True West*, 15-16.

11. Quartermaster Pay Records: April, July, September, 1898, National Archives.

12. Horn to Joe LeFors (January 1, 1902), cited in Joe LeFors, *Wyoming Peace Officer*, 190-191.

13. Dennis Trimble Nickell, "Who Were Tom Horn's Victims?" *Yesterday in Wyoming*, 23-38.

14. Melton, "Recollections of Tom Horn," typescript, 4.

15. Letter quoted in LeFors, *Wyoming Peace Officer*, 136.

16. J.C. Best, "More on Tom Horn," *Real West Yearbook*, 40.

17. *Wyoming vs. Tom Horn*, 291; Tom Horn file at Wyoming State Historical Society, Cheyenne; *Leader*, August 22, 1900.

18. The account in the preceding five paragraphs is pieced together from the trial testimony.

19. *Leader*, July 19, 22, 23, 30 and August 6 and 7, 1901.

20. LeFors, *Wyoming Peace Officer*, 132-134.

21. *Leader*, August 28, 1901.

22. LeFors wrote his autobiography, *Wyoming Peace Officer*, while Mabel Brown added considerable information in an article in the *Quarterly of the National Association for Outlaw and Lawman History*, Winter 1983-84.

23. *Leader*, September 6 and 7, 1901.

24. LeFors, *Wyoming Peace Officer*, 132-133.

25. *Leader*, August 30, October 5, and November 1, 1901; Laramie *Daily Boomerang*, September 1, 1901.

26. LeFors, *Wyoming Peace Officer*, 136.

27. W.D. Smith to Joe LeFors (December 28, 1901), cited in LeFors, 190.

28. Tom Horn to Joe LeFors (January 1, 1902), cited in LeFors, 190-191. Horn stated that he could guarantee Smith "the recommendation of every cow man in the State of Wyoming in this line of work." Horn asked LeFors to assure Smith "that I can handle his work and do it with less expense in the shape of a lawyer and witness fees than any man in the business." Horn closed with a final suggestive remark: "Joe you yourself know what my reputation is although we have never been together."

29. Tom Horn to Joe LeFors (January 7, 1902), cited in LeFors, 191-192.

30. LeFors, *Wyoming Peace Officer*, 138-139; *Leader*, October 22, 1901.

31. LeFors, *Wyoming Peace Officer*, 141.

32. The transcript of the Horn-LeFors conversation may be found in LeFors, 140-145.

33. *Leader*, January 13, 14, 15, 16 and 17, 1902.

34. *Ibid.*, March 22, 1902.

35. *Ibid.*, January 23, 24 and 25, 1902.

36. *Ibid.*, May 30, 1902.

37. *Ibid.*, May 26 and 27, June 7, 1902.

38. Horn's testimony cited in Krakel, *The Saga of Tom Horn*, 162.

39. *Ibid.*, 169.

40. *Ibid.*, 173, 175, 179, 184, 196, 197.

41. *Ibid.*, 174-175, 178-179, 184.

42. *Leader*, October 24, 1902; LeFors, *Wyoming Peace Officer*, 145.

43. Tucson *Daily Citizen*, November 1, 1902; January 24 and 26, 1903; *Leader*, January 21 and 22, 1903.

44. *Leader*, May 19 and October 21, 1902; August 6, 1903.

45. The attempted jailbreak is described in detail in the *Leader*, August 10, 1903.

46. *Leader*, October 4, 1903.

47. Horn, *Life of Tom Horn*, 225; *Leader*, October 29, 1903.

48. *Leader*, November 20, 1903.

49. Tom Horn to John C. Coble (November 20, 1903), cited in Horn, *Life of Tom Horn*, 240-241. In another letter to Coble, on October 3, 1903 (cited in *Life of Tom Horn*, 234-235), Horn wrote to other ranchers who had made specific offers "to do something to the sheep."

Chapter 22: Echoes

1. Vandiver, *Black Jack*, Vol. 1: 392-402.

2. *Wyoming Tribune*, August 31, 1915.

3. Col. Gerald M. Adams, *The Post Near Cheyenne*, 200.

4. *Ibid.*, 200-201; *State Leader*, November 28, 1929.

5. Adams, *The Post Near Cheyenne*, 201-230.

6. Ambrose, *Nothing Like It in the World*, 220-221.

7. *Wyoming Eagle*, November 30, 1934.

Bibliography

Books

Adams, Col. Gerald M. *The Post Near Cheyenne: A History of Fort D. A. Russell, 1867–1930.* Cheyenne: High Flyer Publications, 1989.

Adams, Judith. *Cheyenne: City of Blue Sky.* Northridge, California: Windsor Publications, Inc., 1988.

Ambrose, Stephen E. *Nothing Like It in the World.* New York: Simon & Schuster, 2000.

Arnold, Bess, and James L. Ehernberger. *Union Pacific Depot: An Elegant Legacy to Cheyenne.* Cheyenne: Challenger Press, 2001.

Ballentine, F.J. Pablo. *Freund & Bro.: Pioneer Gunmakers to the West.* Newport Beach, California: Graphic Publishers, 1997.

Bancroft, Hubert Howe. *History of Nevada, Colorado, and Wyoming, 1540–1888.* San Francisco: The History Company Publishers, 1890.

Bartlett, I.S., ed. History of Wyoming. 3 vols. Chicago: The S. J. Clarke Publishing Company, 1918.

Barton, William H., ed. *Early Cheyenne Homes, 1880–1890.* Cheyenne: Wyoming State Press, 1962.

Bassford, Forrest. *Wyoming Hereford Ranch, 1883–1983: A Century of Endurance.* N.p., 1983.

Beard, Frances Birkhead, ed. *Wyoming, From Territorial Days to Present.* Vol. I. Chicago and New York: The American Historical Society, Inc., 1933.

Bell, William A. *New Tracks in North America.* Vol. I. London: Chapman and Hall, 1869.

Billington, Ray Allen. *Westward Expansion: A History of the American Frontier.* Fourth Edition. New York: The Macmillan Company, 1963.

Brown, Mabel E., ed. *First Ladies of Wyoming, 1869–1990.* Wyoming Commission for Women, 1990.

Brown, Robert Herald. *Wyoming: A Geography.* Boulder, Colorado: Westview Press, 1980.

Burial Records, Cheyenne, Wyoming, 1868–1956. Cheyenne Genealogical Society, 1959.

Burroughs, John Rolfe, *Guardian of the Grasslands: The First 100 Years of the Wyoming Stock Growers' Association.* Cheyenne: Pioneer Printing and Stationery Co., 1971.

Carley, Maurine. *A History of the First Congregational Church of Cheyenne.* N.p., 1957.

Carlson, Chip. *Joe LeFors: "I Slickered Tom Horn."* Cheyenne: Beartooth Corral, LLC, 1995.

———. *Tom Horn: Blood on the Moon.* Cheyenne: High Plains Press, 2001.

———. *Tom Horn: "Killing Men Is My Specialty."* Cheyenne: Beartooth Corral, LLC, 1991.

Chamblin, Thomas S., ed. *The Historical Encyclopedia of Wyoming.* Vol. I.

Cheyenne Club, By-Laws, Articles of Incorporation and House Rules, with List of Officers and Members. 1888.

Cheyenne Light, Fuel and Power Company. *History of the Gas, Electric and Steam Heating Utilities of Cheyenne, Wyoming.* N.p., 1943.

Cheyenne: The Magic City of the Plains. Cheyenne Historical Committee, 1967.

Clay, John. *My Life on the Range.* New York: Antiquarian Press, Ltd., 1924.

Cook, James H. *Fifty Years on the Old Frontier.* New Haven: Yale University Press, 1923.

Cook, Joseph W. *Diary and Letters of the Reverend Joseph W. Cook, Missionary to Cheyenne.* Laramie: The Laramie Republican Company, Printers and Binders, 1919.

Cook, Malcolm L. *First Church: A People Called Methodist.* Cheyenne: The First Methodist Church, 1993.

Corley, Maureen. *A History of the First Congregational Church of Cheyenne.* N.p., 1857.

Darwin, Robert. *The History of the Union Pacific Railroad in Cheyenne.* Carmel Valley, California: Express Press Limited, 1987.

David, Robert B. *Malcolm Campbell, Sheriff.* Casper, Wyoming: Wyomingana, 1932.

DeArment, Robert K. *Bat Masterson: The Man and the Legend.* Norman: University of Oklahoma Press, 1979.

———. *Knights of the Green Cloth: The Saga of Frontier Gamblers.* Norman: University of Oklahoma Press, 1982.

Dial, Scott. *A Place To Raise Hell: Cheyenne Saloons.* Boulder, Colorado: Johnson Publishing Company, 1977.

Dodge, Grenville M. *How We Built the Union Pacific Railway.* Denver: Sage Books, 1965.

Dubois, William III, James L. Ehernberger, and Robert R. Larson. *Cheyenne Landmarks.* Laramie County Chapter, Wyoming State Historical Society, 1976.

Erdoes, Richard. *Saloons of the Old West.* New York: Alfred A. Knopf, 1979.

Fiedler, Mildred. *Wild Bill and Deadwood.* New York: Bonanza Books, 1965.

Field, Shawn Lass, ed. *History of Cheyenne, Wyoming.* Curtis Media Corporation, 1989.

Fleishman, Martha, and Carol Joy Justice. *Bugs to Blizzards, or An Army Wife at Fort D.A. Russell.* Cheyenne: Pioneer Printing Company and Stationery Co., 1974.

Flynn, Shirley E. *Let's Go! Let's Show! Let's Rodeo! The History of Cheyenne Frontier Days.* Cheyenne: Wigwam Publishing Company, LLC, 1996.

———. *Our Heritage: 100 Years at St. Mark's, Cheyenne, Wyoming, 1868–1968.* Cheyenne: St. Mark's Centennial Committee, 1968.

Flynn, Shirley E., and John Price. *Cheyenne's Historic Parks: From Untamed Prairie to a City of Trees.* Cheyenne: Historic Preservation Board, 2001.

Foy, Eddie, and Alvin F. Harlow. *Clowning Through Life.* New York: E.P. Dutton & Company, 1928.

Frink, Maurice. *Cow Country Cavalcade: Eighty Years of the Wyoming Stock Growers' Association.* Denver, Colorado: The Old West Publishing Co., 1954.

Frye, Elnora L. *Atlas of Wyoming Outlaws at the Territorial Penitentiary.* Cheyenne: Pioneer Printing and Stationery, 1990.

Gannett, Mrs. Lucy Ellen. *Lucy Ellen's ... Girlhood Days.* Denver: N.p., n.d.

Gorzalka, Ann. *Wyoming's Territorial Sheriffs.* Glendo, Wyoming: High Plains Press, 1998.

Gould, Lewis L. *Wyoming: A Political History, 1868–1896.* New Haven: Yale University Press, 1968.

Hanson, Margaret Brock, ed. *Powder River Country: The Papers of J. Elmer Brock.* Cheyenne: Frontier Printing, Inc., 1983.

Harper, Helen E. *A Priceless Heritage: A History of First Baptist Church, Cheyenne, Wyoming, 1877–1977.* N.p., n.d.

Hart, Herbert M. *Old Forts of the Northwest.* Seattle: Superior Publishing Company, 1963.

Heitman, Francis B., comp. *Historical Register and Dictionary of the United States Army.* 2 vols. Washington, D.C.: Government Printing Office, 1903.

Herlihy, David V. *Bicycle: The History.* New Haven: Yale University Press, 2005.

Homsher, Lola. *Guide to Wyoming Newspapers, 1867–1967.* Cheyenne: Wyoming State Library, 1971.

Homsher, Lola M., ed. *South Pass, 1868: James Chisholm's Journal of the Wyoming Gold Rush.* Lincoln: University of Nebraska Press, 1960.

Horan, James D. *The Pinkertons: The Detective Agency That Made History.* New York: Crown Publishers, Inc., 1967.

Horn, Tom. *Life of Tom Horn: A Vindication.* Norman: University of Oklahoma Press, 1964.

Hufsmith, George W. *The Wyoming Lynching of Cattle Kate, 1889.* Glendo, Wyoming: High Plains Press, 1993.

Jahns, Pat. *The Frontier World of Doc Holliday.* Lincoln: University of Nebraska Press, 1957.

Kays, Robert L., ed. *Cheyenne, Wyoming: The Magic City of the Plains.* Greater Cheyenne Chamber of Commerce, n.d.

King, Robert A. *Trails to Rails: A History of Wyoming's Railroads*. Casper, Wyoming: Endeavor Books, 2003.

Kluger, James R. *Turning on Water with a Shovel: The Career of Elwood Mead*. Albuquerque: University of New Mexico Press, 1992.

Krakel, Dean F. *The Saga of Tom Horn*. Lincoln: University of Nebraska Press, 1954.

Kuykendall, Judge W. L. *Frontier Days*. N.p.: J. M. and H. L. Kuykendall, 1917.

Lake, Stuart N. *Wyatt Earp: Frontier Marshal*. Boston: Houghton Mifflin Company, 1931.

Lakeview Cemetery Tour, The Legacy Continues. N.p., n.d.

Lamar, Howard R., ed. *The Reader's Encyclopedia of the American West*. New York: Thomas Y. Crowell Co., 1977.

Langellier, John P., ed. *Wyoming's Capitol*. Cheyenne: Wyoming State Press, 1987.

Langtry, Lillie. *The Days I Knew*. New York: George H. Doran Company, 1925.

Larson, T. A. *History of Wyoming*, 2nd ed. Lincoln: University of Nebraska Press, 1978.

———. *Wyoming: A Bicentennial History*. New York: W.W. Norton & Company, Inc., 1977.

Lefors, Joe. *Wyoming Peace Officer*. Laramie, Wyoming: Laramie Printing Company, 1953.

McMurtrie, Douglas C. *Pioneer Printing in Wyoming*. Cheyenne: Privately printed, 1933.

Masterson, Bat. *Famous Gunfighters of the Western Frontier*. Published in Human Life Magazine, 1907. Ruidoso, New Mexico: Frontier Book Company, 1959.

The Medal of Honor. Washington, D.C.: United States Government Printing Office, 1948.

Miller, Nyle H., and Joseph W. Snell. *Great Gunfighters of the Kansas Cowtowns, 1867–1886*. Lincoln: University of Nebraska Press, 1963.

Moody, Ralph. *Stagecoach West*. New York: Thomas Y. Cromwell Company, 1967.

Morton, Katherine A., and William R. Dubois. *A Century of Service: First Presbyterian Church, Cheyenne, Wyoming, 1869–1969*.

Mumey, Nollie. *Nathan Addison Baker*. Denver: The Old West Publishing Company, 1965.

Nunis, Doyce B., Jr. *The Life of Tom Horn Revisited*. San Marino, California: The Westerners Los Angeles Corral, 1992.

O'Neal, Bill. *Fighting Men of the Indian Wars*. Stillwater, OK: Barbed Wire Press, 1991.

———. *Historic Ranches of the Old West*. Austin: Eakin Press, 1997.

———. *The Johnson County War*. Austin: Eakin Press, 2004.

Parker, Watson. *Gold in the Black Hills*. Norman: University of Oklahoma Press, 1966.

Parsons, Chuck. *Clay Allison: Portrait of a Gunfighter*. Seagraves, Texas: Pioneer Book Publishers, 1983.

Penrose, Charles Bingham. *The Rustler Business*. Wyoming: Douglas Budget, 1959.

Porter, Willard H. *Who's Who in Rodeo*. Oklahoma City: Powder River Book Company, 1982.

Reiter, Joan Swallow. *The Women*. Alexandria, Virginia: Time-Life Books, Inc., 1978.

Reps, John W. *Cities of the American West: A History of Frontier Urban Planning*. Princeton, New Jersey: Princeton University Press, 1979.

———. *Cities on Stone, Nineteenth Century Lithograph Images of the Urban West*. Fort Worth: Amon Carter Museum, 1976.

Rosa, Joseph G. *They Called Him Wild Bill: The Life and Adventures of James Butler Hickok*. Norman: University of Oklahoma Press, 1964.

Russell, Don. *The Lives and Legends of Buffalo Bill*. Norman: University of Oklahoma Press, 1960.

Schoenberger, Dale T. *The Gunfighters*. Caldwell, Idaho: The Caxton Printers, Ltd., 1971.

Secrest, William B., ed. *I Buried Hickok: The Memoirs of White Eye Anderson*. College Station, Texas: The Early West Series, 1980.

Seymour, Silas. *A Reminiscence of the Union Pacific Railroad, Containing Some Account of the Discovery of the Eastern Base of the Rocky Mountains, and of the Great Indian Battle of July 11, 1867*. Quebec: Printed by A. Cotel, 1873.

Smith, Helena Huntington. *The War on Powder River*. Lincoln: University of Nebraska Press, 1966.

Spring, Agnes Wright. *The Cheyenne and Black Hills Stage and Express Routes*. Glendale, California: The Arthur H. Clark Company, 1949.

———. *Seventy Years: A Panoramic History of the Wyoming Stock Growers' Association*. Cheyenne: Wyoming Stock Growers' Association, 1942.

Simonin, Louis. Translated by Wilson O. Clough. "A French View of Cheyenne in 1867." *The Frontier*, N.d.

Tanner, Karen Holliday. *Doc Holliday: A Family Portrait*. Norman: University of Oklahoma Press, 1998.

Trenholm, Virginia Cole. *Wyoming Blue Book*. Vol. I. Cheyenne: Wyoming State Archives and Historical Department, 1974.

Utley, Robert M. *Frontier Regulars, The United States Army and the Indian, 1866–1891*. New York: Macmillan Publishing Co., Inc., 1973.

Vandiver, Frank E. *Black Jack: The Life and Times of John J. Pershing*. 2 vols. College Station: Texas A&M University Press, 1977.

Voorhies, Luke. *Personal Recollections of Pioneer Life*. Privately printed, n.d.

Walker, Dale L. *The Boys of '98*. New York: A Forge Book, 1998.

Westermeier, Clifford P. *Who Rush to Glory*. Caldwell, Idaho: The Caxton Printers, Ltd., 1958.

Wheeler, Keith. *The Townsmen*. New York: Time-Life Books, 1975.

Woods, Lawrence M. *British Gentlemen of the Wild West*. New York: The Free Press, 1989.

———. *John Clay, Jr.: Commissionman, Banker and Rancher*. Spokane, Washington: The Arthur H. Clark Company, 2001.

Writers' Program of the Works Progress Administration. *Wyoming: A Guide to Its History, Highways and People*. New York: Oxford University Press, 1941.

The Young Men's Literary Club of Cheyenne, Centennial Papers and History. Cheyenne: The Young Men's Literary Club, 2002.

Articles

Allen, Frederick E., interview with Donald L. Miller. "Where They Went to See the Future." *American Heritage* (February/March 2003).

Baldridge, Melissa. "When a Town Becomes a Team." *American Cowboy* (July/August 2003).

Bohl, Sarah R. "Wyoming's Estelle Reel: The First Woman Elected to a Statewide Office in America." *Annals of Wyoming*, vol. 75 (Winter 2003).

"Buildings in Cheyenne, Dakota Territory, 1867." *Annals of Wyoming*, vol.15 (April 1943).

"Cheyenne Bells of the Late 1880's." *Annals of Wyoming*, vol. 17 (July 1945).

Coutant, C.G. "Thomas Jefferson Carr, A Frontier Sheriff," *Annals of Wyoming*, vol. 20 (July 1948)

Dunn, Nora G. "Reminiscences of Fourscore Years and Eight." *Annals of Wyoming*, vol. 19 (July 1947).

Ewig, Rick, ed. "Behind the Capitol Scenes: The Letters of John A. Feick." *Annals of Wyoming*, vol. 59, no.1 (Spring 1987).

Flynn, Shirley E. "Cheyenne's Harry P. Hynds: Blacksmith, Saloon Keeper, Promoter, Philanthropist." *Annals of Wyoming*, vol. 73 (Summer 2001).

———. "Renesselaer Schyler Van Tassell." *Annals of Wyoming*, vol. 71 (Summer 1999).

Fuller, E.O. "Cheyenne Looking North." *Annals of Wyoming*, vol. 23 (January 1951).

Gould, Lewis. "New Light on the Johnson County War." Montana, the Magazine of Western History, vol. 17, no. 4 (October 1967).

Hansen, Anne Carolyn. "The Congressional Career of Senator Francis E. Warren from 1890 to 1902." *Annals of Wyoming*, vol. 20 (January 1948).

Haycox, Ernest, Jr. " 'A Very Exclusive Party', A Firsthand Account of Building the Union Pacific Railroad." *Montana, the Magazine of Western History*, vol. 51 (Spring 2001).

Holsinger, M. Paul. "Willis Van Devanter: Wyoming Leader, 1884-1897." *Annals of Wyoming*, vol. 37 (October 1965).

Jackson, Hugh. "The History of Volunteering in Wyoming." *Annals of Wyoming*, vol. 59, no. 1 (Spring 1987).

Jackson, Turrentine. "Governor Francis E. Warren, A Champion of Women's Suffrage." *Annals of Wyoming*, vol. 15 (April 1943).

Jenkins, J. F. "Camp Carlin or Cheyenne Depot." *Annals of Wyoming*, vol. 5 (1927).

Krakel, Dean. "Was Tom Horn Two Men?" *True West* (January-February 1970).

Laurius, Roger D., and Jessie L. Embry. "Cheyenne versus Denver, City Rivalry for Trans- continental Air Routes." *Annals of Wyoming*, vol. 68 (Summer 1996).

"The 'Magic City' Cheyenne, Dakota Territory—1867." *Annals of Wyoming*, vol. 15 (April 1943).

Ralph, Julian. "Wyoming—Another Pennsylvania." *Harper's New Monthly*, June 1893.

Riley, Glenda. "Tearing Asunder: Divorce in the Old West." *Roundup Magazine*, vol. 11, no. 6 (August 2004).

Silva, Lee, with Richard Proctor. "Guns of the West." *Wild West* (October 2000).

Stelter, Gilbert A. "The Birth of a Frontier Town: Cheyenne in 1867." *Annals of Wyoming*, vol. 39 (April 1967).

Newspapers

Cheyenne *Daily Leader*
Cheyenne *Daily Sun*
Cheyenne *Daily Tribune*
Cheyenne *Sun-Leader*
Dallas *Morning News*
Frank Leslie's Illustrated Weekly
Northwestern Livestock Journal
Sheridan *Post*
Wyoming Eagle
Wyoming Tribune

Biographical Files, Wyoming State Archives, Cheyenne

Bresnahan, L. R.
Bristol, Daze
Carey, Joseph W.
Carr, T. Jeff
Converse, A. R.
Corlett, W. W.
Crook, Dr. W. W.
Glafcke, Herman
Hay, Henry G.
Mead, Elwood P.
Nagle, Erasmus

Post, M. E.
Reel, A. H.
Slack, Edward A.
Swan, Alexander
Van Devanter, Willis
Van Tassell, R.G.S.
Voorhees, Luke
Warren, Francis E.
Warren, Helen Smith
Whipple, I. C.

Collections, American Heritage Center, Laramie, Wyoming

Joseph M. Carey Papers
Hay Family Papers
Francis E. Warren Papers
Owen Wister Collection
Wyoming Stock Growers' Association Papers

Miscellaneous

Census of Cheyenne City, October 1878. Wyoming State Archives, Cheyenne.

Cheyenne Club File. Wyoming State Archives, Cheyenne.

"Cheyenne Historic Downtown Walking Tour." Cheyenne: Downtown Development Authority, 1998. Pamphlet.

Dubois, William III. "A Social History of Cheyenne, Wyoming, 1875–1885." Master's thesis, University of Wyoming, 1963.

Dubois, William III, interviews by Bill O'Neal, July 15 and 21, 2004.

Flynn, Shirley E., interview by Bill O'Neal, July 21, 2004.

Haas, William G. "The Story of the Inter Ocean Hotel." Typescript, Wyoming State Archives, Cheyenne.

J. Jordan to Sister. Cheyenne City, D.T., November 24, 1867.

McCreery, Alice Richards, private secretary to Governor W.A. Richards. Typescript, Wyoming State Archives, Cheyenne.

Osterfoss, Jim, interview by Bill O'Neal, July 12, 2004.

Records of the Brush-Swan Electric Light Company of Cheyenne. Wyoming State Archives, Cheyenne.

Report of the Organization and Proceedings of the Union Pacific Railroad Co. New York: Wm. C. Bryant & Co., Printers, 1864.

Report of Persons and Articles Employed and Hired at Santiago, Cuba, during the Month of July, 1898, and September, 1898, War Department. National Archives.

Report of Persons and Articles Employed and Hired at Tampa, Florida during the Month of April, 1898, War Department. National Archives.

The Resources and Attractions of Wyoming for the Home Seeker, Capitalist and Tourist. Battle Creek, Michigan: Wm. C. Gage & Son, Printers, 1890.

The State of Wyoming vs. Tom Horn. On file at Wyoming State Historical Archives, Cheyenne.

Taylor, Ed P. "Early Day Reminiscences." Typescript, n.d.

Tucker, George R. Autobiographical manuscript. John Alley Collection, Western History Collections, University of Oklahoma, Norman.

Union Pacific Railroad, Report of the Chief Engineer for 1866. Washington, D.C.: Philip & Solomons, 1868.

Union Pacific Railroad, Report of Gen. G. M. Dodge, Chief Engineer on Lines Crossing the Rocky Mountains. New York: W.C. Bryant & Co., Printers, 1867.

The Union Pacific Railroad Company, Progress of their Road West from Omaha, Nebraska, Across the Continent, 500 Miles Completed, October 25th, 1867. New York: Brown & Hewitt, Printers, 1867.

Walker, George S., to Miss Lola Homsher, State Historian. April 13, 1952.

Warren, Francis E. "Early Days in Cheyenne." Warren File, Wyoming State Archives, Cheyenne.

Wister, Owen. 1885 Journal. Owen Wister Collection, Laramie, Wyoming, American Heritage Center.

Index

BILL O'NEAL is the author of more than twenty books on frontier history and western films. His most recent publication, *The Johnson County War*, was named the Book of the Year by the National Association for Outlaw and Lawman History. Bill has appeared on television documentaries for the History Channel, TBS, the Learning Channel, TNN, and the A&E Channel. Bill is a member of the Western Writers of America and of numerous historical organizations. His wife Karon, a college math teacher, assists with research and manuscript preparation for each of his books.